JONATHAN SWIFT A
EIGHTEENTH-CENTU

Jonathan Swift lived through a period of turbulence and innovation in the evolution of the book. His publications, perhaps more than those of any other single author, illustrate the range of developments that transformed print culture during the early Enlightenment. Swift was a prolific author and a frequent visitor at the printing house, and he wrote as critic and satirist about the nature of text. The shifting moods of irony, complicity and indignation that characterize his dealings with the book trade add a layer of complexity to the bibliographic record of his published works. The essays collected here offer the first comprehensive, integrated survey of that record. They shed new light on the politics of the eighteenth-century book trade, on Swift's innovations as a maker of books, on the habits and opinions revealed by his commentary on printed texts, and on the reshaping of the Swiftian book after his death.

PADDY BULLARD is Lecturer in Eighteenth-Century Studies at the University of Kent, Canterbury. He is the author of *Edmund Burke and the Art of Rhetoric* (Cambridge, 2011), and an advisory editor to the Cambridge Edition of the Works of Jonathan Swift.

JAMES MCLAVERTY is Emeritus Professor of Textual Criticism at Keele University. With David Womersley he was one of the principal investigators on the AHRC-funded 'Textual Edition and Archive of the Works of Jonathan Swift' (2005–10), and serves as textual advisor to the Cambridge Edition of the Works of Jonathan Swift. He is the author of *Pope, Print, and Meaning* (2001).

JONATHAN SWIFT AND THE EIGHTEENTH-CENTURY BOOK

EDITED BY

PADDY BULLARD

and

JAMES McLAVERTY

CAMBRIDGE
UNIVERSITY PRESS

CAMBRIDGE
UNIVERSITY PRESS

University Printing House, Cambridge CB2 8BS, United Kingdom

Cambridge University Press is part of the University of Cambridge.

It furthers the University's mission by disseminating knowledge in the pursuit of education, learning and research at the highest international levels of excellence.

www.cambridge.org
Information on this title: www.cambridge.org/9781316600955

© Cambridge University Press 2013

First published 2013
First paperback edition 2015

A catalogue record for this publication is available from the British Library

Library of Congress Cataloguing in Publication data
Jonathan Swift and the eighteenth-century book / edited by
Paddy Bullard and James McLaverty.
pages   cm
Includes bibliographical references and index.
ISBN 978-1-107-01626-2 (hardback)
I. Bullard, Paddy, editor of compilation.   II. McLaverty, J.,
editor of compilation.
PR3727.J637   2013
828'.509–dc23
2012051261

ISBN 978-1-107-01626-2 Hardback
ISBN 978-1-316-60095-5 Paperback

Contents

Illustrations

Notes on contributors

PADDY BULLARD is Lecturer in Eighteenth-Century Studies at the University of Kent, Canterbury. From January 2005 to December 2009 he was an AHRC Research Fellow attached to the Cambridge Edition of the Works of Jonathan Swift, and Rank Junior Research Fellow at St Catherine's College, Oxford. His monograph, *Edmund Burke and the Art of Rhetoric*, was published by Cambridge University Press in 2011. He is currently completing a new scholarly edition of Burke's *Philosophical Enquiry into the Sublime and Beautiful*.

DANIEL COOK teaches at the University of Dundee. He completed a PhD at Cambridge before taking up an AHRC Research Fellowship on the Cambridge Edition of the Works of Jonathan Swift and then a Leverhulme Early Career Research Fellowship at the University of Bristol. Daniel has edited such books as *The Lives of Jonathan Swift*, 3 vols. (2011) and (with Amy Culley) *Women's Life Writing: Gender, Genre, and Authorship, 1700–1850* (2012).

IAN GADD is a professor of English Literature at Bath Spa University. He is a general editor of the Cambridge Edition of the Works of Jonathan Swift and is co-editor of *English Political Writings 1711–14* (2008), *English Political Writings 1701–11* (in preparation) and *Writings on Religion and the Church to 1714* (in preparation). He is editor of Volume I of *A History of Oxford University Press, 1478–2004* (forthcoming).

IAN HIGGINS is a reader in English at the Australian National University. He is author of *Swift's Politics: A Study in Disaffection* (Cambridge University Press, 1994) and *Jonathan Swift* (2004), and of many essays on Swift and his contexts. He is an editor (with Claude Rawson) of the World's Classics edition of *Gulliver's Travels* (2005), and is one of the general editors of the Cambridge Edition of the Works of Jonathan Swift.

STEPHEN KARIAN is Associate Professor of English at the University of Missouri. His book *Jonathan Swift in Print and Manuscript* was published by Cambridge University Press, and his articles have appeared in *SEL Studies in English Literature 1500–1900*, *Studies in Bibliography*, *Huntington Library Quarterly* and elsewhere. With James Woolley, he is editing Swift's complete poems for the Cambridge Edition of the Works of Jonathan Swift.

JAMES MCLAVERTY is Emeritus Professor of Textual Criticism at Keele University. With David Womersley he was one of the principal investigators on the AHRC-funded 'Textual Edition and Archive of the Works of Jonathan Swift' (2005–10), and serves as textual advisor to the Cambridge Edition of the Works of Jonathan Swift from 2005 to 2009. He has published articles and essays on the theory of textual criticism, Swift, Pope and Johnson, revised for publication David Foxon's *Pope and the Early Eighteenth-Century Book Trade* and David Fleeman's *Bibliography of Samuel Johnson*, and is the author of *Pope, Print and Meaning* (2001).

CLAUDE RAWSON is Maynard Mack Professor of English at Yale University. He is a general editor of the *Cambridge History of Literary Criticism*, the Cambridge Edition of the Works of Jonathan Swift, the Blackwell Critical Biographies and the Unwin Critical Library. From 1989 to 2001 he served as General Editor and Chairman of the Yale Boswell Editions. His publications include *God, Gulliver and Genocide: Barbarism and the European Imagination 1492–1945* (2001) and, as editor, *Politics and Literature in the Age of Swift: English and Irish Perspectives* (Cambridge University Press, 2010) and the *Cambridge Companion to English Poets* (2011).

PAT ROGERS is Distinguished University Professor, Eminent Scholar and DeBartolo Chair of the Liberal Arts at the University of South Florida. Before coming to USF in 1986, he was Professor of English at the University of Bristol. He has also been a fellow of Sidney Sussex College, Cambridge, and a visiting fellow at Christ Church, Oxford, and the University of Otago. He is a fellow of the Royal Historical Society, Corresponding Fellow of the English Association and Corresponding Fellow of the British Academy. He has written or edited eleven books on Alexander Pope, five on Samuel Johnson and his circle, and six on Daniel Defoe. He prepared the first full scholarly edition of *Pride and Prejudice* for the Cambridge Edition of the Works of Jane Austen in

2006 and edited *Jonathan Swift: The Complete Poems* (1983). He is the author, with Paul Baines, of *Edmund Curll, Bookseller* (2007).

SHEF ROGERS teaches in the English Department and is co-director of the Centre for the Book at the University of Otago. He is the editor of *Script & Print: Bulletin of the Bibliographical Society of Australia and New Zealand* and is currently completing a bibliography of travel books published in English in the eighteenth century.

ADAM ROUNCE is a senior lecturer at Manchester Metropolitan University. He has written on Dryden, Johnson, Churchill, Cowper, Akenside, Warburton, Joseph Warton and Godwin. His main ongoing research is with the Cambridge Edition of the Works of Jonathan Swift, for which he is co-editing two volumes, as well as contributing a Chronology.

MARCUS WALSH is Kenneth Allott Professor of English Literature at the University of Liverpool. He has edited *A Tale of a Tub and Other Writings* (2010) for the Cambridge Edition of the Works of Jonathan Swift, and two volumes of the Oxford University Press edition of *Christopher Smart: The Poetical Works* (1983 and 1987). He is author of *Shakespeare, Milton and Eighteenth-Century Literary Editing: The Beginnings of Interpretative Scholarship* (Cambridge University Press, 1997) and of essays on editorial history and theory, biblical interpretation, book history, and poetry and poetics. His current research investigates the forms, rhetorics and uses of the eighteenth-century literary edition, with a particular interest in the relations of texts and paratexts.

ABIGAIL WILLIAMS is Lord White Fellow and tutor in English at St Peter's College, Oxford. She is editor of *The Journal to Stella: Letters to Esther Johnson and Rebecca Dingley, 1710–1713*, forthcoming for the Cambridge Edition of the Works of Jonathan Swift, and principal investigator of a Leverhulme Research Project Grant, which will enable the creation and completion of the *Digital Miscellanies Index*. Her monograph, *Poetry and the Creation of a Whig Literary Culture: 1680–1714*, was published in 2005.

Preface

This volume gathers together twelve new essays on the history of the book in the eighteenth century, focused on the satirist and churchman Jonathan Swift. The phrase 'history of the book', as it is usually understood today, is an umbrella term that covers a range of distinct disciplines and research practices. Some forms of book history have practical, material concerns, while others are more abstract. Some of them fall within the pale of literary history, where the 'single author' approach that we have adopted in this volume is common. Others involve the study of social, commercial and mechanical phenomena that are far removed from the world of the solitary writer, scribbling away in the isolation of his or her study. On the empirical side there is the work of descriptive and technical bibliographers; of social historians investigating the print shop, guild or publisher's firm; of legal historians concerned with censorship or the history of copyright; and of library historians interested in the ordering of books. Tending more towards the sphere of ideas there is the work of editors, textual critics and theorists of hermeneutics interested in the text as intentional form. In practice, however, many involved in the history of the book produce work from across this spectrum of scholarly enterprise. In this collection we have tried to integrate the broadest possible range of book history methods in the study of a single author and, in each essay, to let sparks of insight play between the disciplines.

A range of recent research has concentrated on late seventeenth- and early eighteenth-century print culture, and on parallel developments in the world of manuscript circulation. Jonathan Swift (1667–1745) witnessed the dawn of modern authorship, and his career as a writer coincided with a period of rapid change in the print trade. These years saw the advent of modern fixed-term copyright, the professionalization of authorship, the emergence of female professional writers, the rise of *Works* by living literary authors and the gradual passing of an earlier culture of manuscript publication, among other crucial developments in the history of

print. The importance of this period to book history had been emphasized in recent work by Paul Baines, Maureen Bell, Roger Chartier, Robert
Darnton, Margaret Ezell, John Feather, Adrian Johns, Harold Love, Paula
McDowell, Don McKenzie, Lisa Maruca, James Raven and Pat Rogers,
to name only a few of its most prominent commentators. The vibrancy of
this field of inquiry is represented most conspicuously by the recent publication of *The Cambridge History of the Book in Britain: Volume V, 1695–
1830*, edited by Michael F. Suarez SJ and Michael L. Turner (Cambridge
University Press, 2009). Until now, however, no comprehensive account
of Jonathan Swift's uniquely complicated involvement with this scene has
been attempted.

But why focus a study of eighteenth-century book history on a single author when so many crucial aspects of that history – the manufacturing and supply of paper, for example, or the warehousing of printed
books – were simply beyond the sphere of any writer's influence? The case
for using Jonathan Swift as the frame for book history is made at length in
the introduction below. To sum it up, Swift was not only an author who
operated with unusual knowledge and skill within the print trade. He also
left behind him a major body of writing in which textual complications
are deeply entangled with material expression. It is the intelligence with
which that entanglement has been contrived by the author himself that
makes his work a compelling subject for historians of the book. There
are circumstantial reasons for the Swiftian focus as well. The editors of
this volume were able to call upon a network of researchers working at
the moment on textual criticism and book history specifically related to
Swift. Much of this research is connected with the on-going *Cambridge
Edition of the Works of Jonathan Swift*, 18 vols. (Cambridge University
Press, 2008–, and with the range of publications (including the journal
Swift Studies) and the series of *Proceedings* of the Münster symposia on
Swift) produced by scholars associated with the Ehrenpreis Centre for
Swift Studies at the Westfälische Wilhelms-Universität, Münster. *Jonathan
Swift and the Eighteenth-Century Book* grows out of this rich field of col-
laboration and investigation.

During the writing and assembly of this volume the editors have accu-
mulated many particular debts of gratitude. We would like to thank the
staff of the Upper Reading Room and of Special Collections at the Bodleian
Library, Oxford, for their courteous and efficient assistance. We also wish
to thank Janine Barchas, Marie-Lise Spieckermann, Michael F. Suarez SJ
and James Woolley for their help with the planning of the project. Our
two anonymous readers at Cambridge University Press offered detailed

criticisms that were of great importance to the editing and writing of the volume. Paddy Bullard thanks the School of English Research Seminar at the University of Kent, the delegates of the Early Modern History Research Seminar at Trinity College, Dublin, and of the 'Libraries: New Research Directions' symposium at the University of Reading, for their comments on early versions of research presented here – he is particularly grateful in this respect to Jennie Batchelor, Donna Landry, Graeme Murdoch, Jason McElligott, Rebecca Bullard and Michelle O'Callaghan. He would also like to acknowledge the generous advice of Hermann Real and Ian Gadd and of Anthony Miller, who saved him from an embarrassing error. James McLaverty wishes to thank the staff of the Library of Keele University, Michael Griffin, Robert Mahony, Ashley Marshall, Claude Rawson and Richard Rouse, and is particularly grateful to Steve Karian for making the breadth of his knowledge available to him. Linda Bree, our editor at Cambridge University Press, has been a constant source of encouragement and advice, and we are likewise very grateful to Maartje Scheltens and Anna Bond for their indispensable help with matters practical.

Abbreviations

Baines and Rogers, *Curll*	Paul Baines and Pat Rogers, *Edmund Curll, Bookseller* (Oxford University Press, 2007)
Case	Arthur E. Case, *A Bibliography of English Poetical Miscellanies 1521–1750* (Oxford: The Bibliographical Society, 1935)
CWJS	*Cambridge Edition of the Works of Jonathan Swift* (2008–)
Davis, *PW*	*The Prose Writings of Jonathan Swift*, ed. Herbert Davis *et al.*, 16 vols., (Oxford: Basil Blackwell, 1939–74) (2008–)
ECCO	*Eighteenth Century Collections Online* (Thomson Gale, online subscription database)
Ehrenpreis, *Swift*	Irvin Ehrenpreis, *Swift: The Man, His Works, and the Age*, 3 vols. (London: Methuen, 1962–83)
Ellis, *Discourse*	Jonathan Swift, *A Discourse of the Contests and Dissentions between the Nobles and the Commons in Athens and Rome*, ed. Frank H. Ellis (Oxford: Clarendon Press, 1967)
Ellis, *Examiner*	*Swift vs. Mainwaring: 'The Examiner' and 'The Medley'*, ed. Frank H. Ellis (Oxford: Clarendon Press, 1985)
ESTC	*English Short Title Catalogue*
Griffin, *Swift and Pope*	Dustin, Griffin, *Swift and Pope: Satirists in Dialogue* (Cambridge University Press, 2010)
GS	Jonathan Swift, *A Tale of a Tub: To which is added The Battle of the Books and The Mechanical Operation of the Spirit*, ed. A. C. Guthkelch and D. Nichol Smith, 2nd edn (Oxford: Clarendon Press, 1958)

GT	Jonathan Swift, *Gulliver's Travels*
Johns, *Piracy*	Adrian Johns, *Piracy: The Intellectual Property Wars from Gutenberg to Gates* (University of Chicago Press, 2010)
JSt (1948)	Jonathan Swift, *Journal to Stella*, ed. Harold Williams, 2 vols. (Oxford: Clarendon Press, 1948)
Karian, *Print and Manuscript*	Stephen Karian, *Jonathan Swift in Print and Manuscript* (Cambridge University Press, 2010)
Library and Reading, Part 1	Dirk F. Passmann and Heinz J. Vienken, *The Library and Reading of Jonathan Swift: A Bio-Bibliographical Handbook, Part 1: Swift's Library in Four Volumes* (Frankfurt am Main: Peter Lang, 2003)
Münster (date)	Hermann J. Real and Heinz J. Vienken (eds.), *Proceedings of the First Münster Symposium on Jonathan Swift* (Munich: Wilhelm Fink, 1985); Hermann J. Real and Richard H. Rodino, with Helgard Stöver-Leidig (eds.), *Reading Swift: Papers from the Second Münster Symposium on Jonathan Swift* (Munich: Wilhelm Fink, 1993); Hermann J. Real and Helgard Stöver-Leidig (eds.), *Reading Swift: Papers from the Third Münster Symposium on Jonathan Swift* (Munich: Wilhelm Fink, 1998); Hermann J. Real and Helgard Stöver-Leidig (eds.), *Reading Swift: Papers from the Fourth Münster Symposium on Jonathan Swift* (Munich: Wilhelm Fink, 2003); Hermann J. Real (ed.), *Reading Swift: Papers from the Fifth Münster Symposium on Jonathan Swift* (Munich: Wilhelm Fink, 2008)
Pollard, *Dictionary*	*A Dictionary of Members of the Dublin Book Trade, 1550–1800* (London: Bibliographical Society, 2000)

Pope, *Correspondence*	*The Correspondence of Alexander Pope*, ed. George Sherburn, 5 vols. (Oxford: Clarendon Press, 1956)
Rogers, *Poems*	Jonathan Swift, *The Complete Poems*, ed. Pat Rogers (Harmondsworth: Penguin, 1983)
SStud	*Swift Studies*
Swift–Pope *Miscellanies*	*Miscellanies in Prose and Verse*, 4 vols. (1727-32)
TE	*The Twickenham Edition of the Poems of Alexander Pope*, ed. John Butt *et al.*, 11 vols. (London: Methuen, 1939–69)
TS	Laurence Sterne, *The Life and Opinions of Tristram Shandy, Gentleman*, ed. Melvyn and Joan New, 3 vols. (Gainesville: University of Florida Press, 1978–84)
TS	H. Teerink, *A Bibliography of the Writings of Jonathan Swift*, 2nd edn revised and corrected by the author, ed. Arthur H. Scouten (Philadelphia: University of Pennsylvania Press, 1963)
Williams, *Corr.*	*The Correspondence of Jonathan Swift*, ed. Harold Williams, 5 vols. (Oxford: Clarendon Press, 1963–5)
Williams, *Poems*	*The Poems of Jonathan Swift*, ed. Harold Williams, 2nd edn, 3 vols. (Oxford: Clarendon Press, 1958)
Woolley, *Corr.*	*The Correspondence of Jonathan Swift, D.D.*, ed. David Woolley, 5 vols. (Frankfurt am Main: Peter Lang, 1999–)
Woolley, *Intelligencer*	Jonathan Swift and Thomas Sheridan, *The Intelligencer*, ed. James Woolley (Oxford: Clarendon Press, 1992)

Introduction

Paddy Bullard and James McLaverty

Jonathan Swift (1667–1745) lived through a period of extraordinary change in the history of the book. His career illustrates, perhaps more fully than that of any contemporary writer, the range of developments by which authors, booksellers and their public transformed the business of print during the first half of the eighteenth century. Throughout his life Swift conceptualized the book in differing and sometimes conflicting ways. As a political fixer he cultivated the reputation of a dexterous manager and patron of the press, but he was careful to keep his dealings with printers and booksellers hidden from public view. As a satirist Swift often placed the writing and publishing of books somewhere near the edges of human experience, despite the trade being an increasingly mundane and well-organized business in the early eighteenth century. He described authors and booksellers as madmen in confederacy, as libertines fathering bastards on the press, as unquiet spirits hovering over sepulchral codices. Swift was a creator of books, a visitor at the printing house, and an observer of the hacks, publishers and book-buyers who peopled the world of commercial print. He also wrote critically and satirically about the nature of text. The shifting moods of irony, complicity and indignation that characterize his commentary on the world of print add a deep layer of complexity to the bibliographic record of his own published works. The essays collected in *Jonathan Swift and the Eighteenth-Century Book* offer the first comprehensive, integrated survey of that record, and a thorough analysis of the challenges that it poses for modern literary historians and critics.

[handwritten margin note: always on the verge of destruction]

Swift's pre-eminence as author

A letter that Swift received from the printer John Barber dated 24 August 1732 suggests something of the depth of his entanglement with the book trade. Barber had worked closely with Swift on his political publications during the four years before Queen Anne's death in 1714. In return Swift had secured for 'my Printer' some valuable trade patents, including the printing of *The Gazette* in 1711 and the reversion for the office of Queen's Printer in 1713.[1] At around the same time Barber was elected to the common council of the City of London, later proceeding alderman in 1722 and finally Lord Mayor in 1732. Anticipating the ceremony of his installation twenty years after the period of his closest collaborations with Swift, Barber acknowledges how deeply obliged he is to the Dean for his advancement:

> It would add very much to my felicity, if your health would permit you to come over in the spring, and see a pageant of your own making. Had you been here now, I am persuaded you would have put me to an additional expense, by having a raree-shew (or pageant) as of old, on the lord-mayor's day. Mr. Pope and I were thinking of having a large machine carried through the city, with a printing-press, author, publishers, hawkers, devils, &c., and a satirical poem printed and thrown from the press to the mob, in publick view, but not to give offence; but your absence spoils that design.[2]

It is a striking and rather menacing image, the press carried above the mob like a pillory or a gallows. It may owe something to *The Grub-street Journal*, whose correspondents were much given to allegories of the press: a recent number had suggested that the Lord Mayor's procession was itself 'a prophetical, *figurative*, and *typical*, representation of a Procession of Printers, Booksellers, Authors, &c. to be some time or other *wonderfully* exhibited to the view of the whole Town'.[3] From a book historian's perspective the actors and audience represent a self-contained 'circuit of communication', an almost complete cycle in the production and distribution of printed books.[4]

It is particularly significant that Barber has dreamt up the scene together with Alexander Pope, Swift's pupil in the study of Grub Street and, like him, a fitting patron of its pageantry. Pope joins Barber in pressing Swift to accept a generous dose of flattery: that *he* remains the supreme example of the poet as street-level statesman, despite his years of Irish exile. They imagine a sort of proto-Situationist performance, with Swift as the magus-like director of an instantly responsive publicity machine. This is in many ways what he had been two decades previously when 'His Works were hawk'd in ev'ry Street, | But seldom rose above a Sheet'.[5] And Pope may also be acknowledging a Swiftian hint at the source of his own recent satire of municipal pageantry.[6] The first book of the *Dunciad* (1728), of which Swift was dedicatee, is set on the night after a Lord Mayor's procession:

(Pomps without guilt, of bloodless swords and maces,
Glad chains, warm furs, broad banners, and broad faces)
Now night descending, the proud scene was o'er,
Yet liv'd in *Settle's* numbers, one day more.[7]

Pope mentions Elkanah Settle, still alive in 1728, who had held the office of 'City Poet' and devised and then memorialized eleven Lord Mayor's pageants between 1691 and 1708. He was also John Barber's godfather, helping him to an apprenticeship with the printer George Larkin in 1689.[8] In his reply to Barber's letter Swift appears to acknowledge old conversations on these interconnected topics and characters – 'for I never approved the omission of those shows' – and recalls having seen the procession when Sir Thomas Pilkington was elected Lord Mayor, a year or two before Settle took charge.[9] Swift had written to Barber in the first place because he wanted his protégé Matthew Pilkington, a kinsman of the Williamite Lord Mayor, to serve as his chaplain during the period of his office. By drawing attention to the continuity of these old and new connections between authors and tradesmen, Swift confirms and extends the patterns of patronage, obligation and allegiance that Barber had gratefully evoked. And the printing press – emblematized in Barber's tableau almost as a symbol for the city itself – is at the centre of it all.

Swift and the book trade: overview engagement and disengagement

Swift's relationships with the people who manufactured and distributed his books were complicated. Both the English and the Irish book trades at this time depended on close personal, often familial, relationships, and Swift was willing to engage with the trade on a personal level: he was happy to dine with his printer and his bookseller, to use them as bankers, to join in the planning of intricate books and collections, to hunt down revised copy and to intervene to save them from prosecution. He was notably loyal to these collaborators; these were relationships that he expected to last. Some of his contemporaries, however, were even more intimate with the trade. John Dryden, William Congreve, Matthew Prior and Alexander Pope all worked more closely with their booksellers on the design of their books, and benefited financially from innovations in subscription and distribution to which Swift affected indifference.[10] 'I never got a farthing by anything I writ', Swift complained in 1735, 'except one about eight year ago, and that was by Mr Pope's prudent management for me' – meaning the £200 he secured for the copy of *Gulliver's Travels*.[11] But it is precisely Swift's preference for being seen to keep his distance from the trade that makes his dealings with it uniquely interesting to historians of the book. The pageant imagined by Barber involves workers from many sectors of the book trade: authors, publishers, press-workers and street vendors are all gathered around the press. And yet Swift, the man who directs the scene, the writer who is something more than an author, is not there. Barber assures him that 'your absence spoils that design'.

With Swift off the scene, all the half-hidden workings of the trade are exposed to historical attention – from the dispensation of high-profile patronage to the labours of devils and hawkers. Often Swift relied upon friends and intermediaries such as Erasmus Lewis, John Gay, Charles Ford and Matthew Pilkington to negotiate with booksellers on his behalf. This allowed him to perform a favourite trick, discussed by Ian Gadd in his chapter (pp. 58–9): leaving his most important manuscripts with booksellers in London, and then disappearing to Ireland a few days before publication, as he did with *Discourse of the Contests and Dissensions* (1701), with the *Tale of a Tub* miscellany (1704) and with *Gulliver's Travels* (1726). Ultimately, as Ian Higgins reveals in his essay on censorship and self-censorship (pp. 181–3), Swift's printers and booksellers stood between the author and the sanction of the law.[12] John Harding, the Dublin printer who had produced the first five *Drapier's Letters* for Swift in 1724, was particularly resolute when prosecuted for publishing seditious libel: he swore that he was unable to identify the Drapier, and it is even possible he died in prison while awaiting prosecution.[13] As Swift put it to Motte on 4 November 1732:

> I have writ some things that would make people angry. I always sent them by unknown hands, the Printer might guess, but he could not accuse me, he ran the whole risk, and well deserved the property.[14]

If Motte needed a reminder about the precariousness of this arrangement, he got it a year later when he was himself arrested and questioned at Westminster over his part in the publication of Swift's poem *To a Lady*.[15] John Wilford, the poem's publisher and also the distributor of *The Grub-street Journal*, had named Lawton Gilliver, who had in turn named Motte ('he was resolved, if he came into trouble, I should have a share of it'), whose questioning led to Matthew Pilkington and Mary Barber, who had brought the manuscript from Dublin, also being detained.[16] In other words, the government was obliged to dig through four levels of intermediary before it could be sure of Swift's responsibility for the poem. Even then it was unable to gather sufficient evidence to pursue the author, or was reluctant to do so.

Inevitably this cautious, yet half-negligent style of business often resulted in Swift losing control over the publication of his writings. When such a loss occurred, as it did most famously in the case of *Gulliver's Travels*, Swift was loudly resentful, even when his best friends were involved. Having given Pope a free hand in the arrangement of their *Miscellanies* (1727–32), he became increasingly irritated by the clumsiness with which they were edited and printed.[17] But the steps that he took to reclaim authority over his texts tended to be indecisive, if not desultory. Often they were limited to the private manuscript-based traditions of correction transmitted among his Irish friends, as was the case at first with *Gulliver*. Although (as Shef Rogers shows in his essay) *Gulliver's Travels* was a carefully planned and conceived book, an unknown courier dropped the holograph for *Gulliver* at Motte's shop on 8 August 1726. Several dangerous passages in the text were censored before publication, probably (as Swift conjectured in 1733) by Andrew Tooke, a schoolmaster, FRS and sleeping partner in Motte's business.[18] Swift's intimate dealings with his bookseller brother are described below. Swift insisted almost at once that the passages 'mingled and mangled' by Tooke should be restored, but he did so indirectly. He got Charles Ford to write to Motte on 3 January 1726–7 with a list of 109 corrections.[19] Motte incorporated many minor revisions requested by Ford in the second edition of *Gulliver* in 1727, but left the censored passages as he had printed them originally, in prudent defiance of the author. When the Dublin printer George Faulkner offered the opportunity to restore the text of *Gulliver* in the four-volume Dublin *Works* of 1735, Swift had to rely on readings recorded by Ford in an interleaved copy now preserved in the Victoria and Albert Museum.[20] Harold Love and Robert D. Hume have recently adopted the term 'nebulous authorship' to describe how at the end of the seventeenth century different members of the Duke of Buckingham's circle took diffused responsibility for the writings they produced.[21] Swift's negligence seldom disperses authorial presence in quite the manner they describe, but it does lead sometimes to a certain blurring of personal assignation in his works, and for all sorts of ambiguity of detail in the texts themselves. The history of Swift's dealings with the world of print is a tale of collaboration and relinquishment.

Often Swift ceded control of his texts in a more deliberate way, drawing our attention as he did so to some hidden corner of the print trade. Throughout his career, as Ian Gadd describes in his chapter on the early phase of his dealings with the London press (pp. 51–64 below), Swift deputed 'my bookseller', Benjamin Tooke, or his printers John Barber and George Faulkner, to oversee the publication of commercially or politically sensitive material, often employing wholesale 'trade publishers' such as John Nutt, Abigail Baldwin and John Morphew. Their imprints offered extra layers of anonymity when it was necessary.[22] But just as often this same mechanism of publication worked against his interests. From 1714 the most prolific publisher to the trade, James Roberts of Warwick Lane, lent his imprint to further dangerous Swiftian titles first published in Ireland, including *Cadenus and Vanessa* (1726) and *The Lady's Dressing Room* (1732), while at the same time publishing the hostile 'gulliveriana' written by Swift's inveterate enemy Jonathan Smedley. These shadowy parts of the early eighteenth-century publishing world would still be obscure to us if Swift's dealings (and non-dealings) with them had not drawn the attention of book historians.

1691–1711 Dublin and London

As Pat Rogers shows in his chapter (pp. 87–100), Swift was until 1711 a miscellaneous writer with a satirical bent. He began with a desire to be a published poet, issuing two unsatisfactory Pindaric odes in the years 1691 and 1692. One, *An Ode to the King on His Irish Expedition*, was published in Dublin, while the other was published in London. At this time the Dublin and London trades were still very different. In theory the Dublin trade was entirely in the control of one man, the King's Printer, who could license other practitioners if he wished. However, between 1660 and 1732 (when the patent had its privileges much reduced), there was significant relaxation in practice. The King's Printers in that period were the Crooke family, but from 1669 to 1693 the patent was held by Benjamin Tooke, Sr (a London bookseller, the father of the man who was to work with Swift), first for his sister Mary, the widow of John Crooke, and then with or for her children. The patent passed to Andrew Crooke in 1693. Their monopoly was challenged first by William Bladen, who had his press closed down in 1673, and then, much more successfully, by Joseph Ray, who became printer to the city in 1681 and resisted a similar attempt in that year. His position was supported by the Guild of St Luke, founded for cutlers, painter-stainers and stationers in 1670. Tooke had joined the Guild, becoming joint first warden of the stationers' section, and this new organization probably helped foster a spirit of co-operation in the trade. Ray prospered, and Mary Pollard thinks that Samuel Fairbrother, King's

Stationer and Printer to the House of Commons, who has a part to play in Swift's story, was his apprentice and succeeded him.[23]

In spite of these developments, the Dublin trade remained small and undifferentiated in comparison with London's. Mary Pollard estimates that there were probably no more than ten printers active in Dublin in 1709, and those who were printers often sold books and did their own binding.[24] When the Copyright Act was passed in Westminster in 1710, its provisions did not apply to Ireland, though they did forbid the import of copyrighted books into Britain, penalties being placed on anyone who 'shall print, reprint, or import ... any such Book or Books'.[25] One consequence of the Act was that it was unlikely that an author would be paid copy money by an Irish bookseller, and that created an incentive for ambitious authors to publish in London. Another was that a lively reprint trade grew up in Dublin, where marginally lower labour costs and duties on paper permitted cheap reprints of English books for the Irish market. That these books were sometimes exported to Britain, where they infuriated the copyright holders, is undeniable, but Pollard doubts that the trade was extensive.[26]

In London, on the other hand, as Ian Gadd explains in his essay, there had long been regulation of the trade through the Stationers' Company, and the passing of the Copyright Act in 1710 helped strengthen the notion of literary property and the growth and differentiation of the trade. Although some booksellers simply kept a shop, 'Topping' booksellers, as contemporaries and James Raven call them, had the capital to finance the production of books, paying for copy, supplying paper and employing their chosen printers. They were able both to engage in the extensive exchange of books, building up the stock of their shops, and to distribute their titles widely through the specialist trade publishers, imprints showing success in engaging provincial retailers in large-scale projects as well.[27] The limited size of the Dublin market did not really permit such developments.[28] The first half of the century also saw the development of successful printing houses in London – John Watts (working closely with the Tonsons); the William Bowyers, father and son; Samuel Richardson; Samuel Buckley – whose proprietors were ready to undertake work for the government (their shops often busy with other routine work such as newspapers) and to use their profits to finance projects of their own. Some measure of the relative activity of the Dublin and London trades (with Edinburgh included for comparison) is provided by a simple comparison of the *ESTC* figures for imprints in the decades of Swift's activity:

	1691–1700	1701–10	1711–20	1721–30	1731–40	1741–50
Dublin	675	1,114	1,428	2,481	1,818	2,057
London	16,219	18,277	18,916	14,837	15,941	15,820
Edinburgh	1,593	2,249	1,972	1,895	1,664	2,502

Some general impressions arise from this table.[29] The Dublin trade, owing to the King's Printer restrictions, started well behind the Edinburgh one, but by the end of the period it had caught up. On this indicator (probably misleading) the London trade was static: at the start of the period it was twenty-four times the size of the Dublin one; at the end it was still over seven times as large. The very high rise in Dublin's productivity in the 1720s is unexplained, but it may relate to the controversy generated by Swift's *Drapier's Letters* (1724) and its stimulus to Dublin book culture.[30]

That first poem published by Swift, *Ode to the King* (1691), draws us immediately into those personal relations that are now so difficult to recapture. The printer and publisher was John Brent of Dublin, whose wife Jane was Swift's mother's landlady when she visited Dublin and later (perhaps in 1695) became Swift's housekeeper; when she died in 1735 she was succeeded by her daughter Ann Ridgeway.[31] Brent's was an impressive shop, 'Airy, Great and Noble (and the Top Printing-House in all Dublin)', John Dunton tells us (Pollard, *Dictionary*, p. 52), but Swift seems not to have used Brent to print anything else, perhaps because he retired in 1704 at the age of sixty-five. In another sign of a persisting connection, however, Swift remarks in the *Journal to Stella* that he had once arranged for a boy to be apprenticed to Brent (*JSt* (1948), vol. II, p. 559). Swift sent his second poem, 'The Ode to the Athenian Society' (1692), to John Dunton who was then publishing the *Athenian Gazette* in London. His interest in the Athenian Society seems to have come from his relationship with Sir William Temple, to whom he was acting as literary secretary, with Temple's speaking to him so much in their praise and probably contributing to the *Athenian Gazette* himself (Williams, *Poems*, vol. I, p. 14).

Temple provided Swift with an example of successful authorship, and it was while editing Temple's work posthumously that Swift came to establish his crucial relationship with Benjamin Tooke Jr and to publish his own first major work, *A Discourse of the Contests and Dissensions … in Athens and Rome* (1701).[32] From the time Swift joined Temple at Moor Park in 1689 until his death ten years later, Temple had published a significant volume of work through eminent members of the book trade such as Richard and Ralph Simpson, Richard Chiswell, Jacob Tonson, and Awnsham and John Churchill. When Swift assumed responsibility for publication with Temple's *Letters* in 1700, he simply followed precedent and published with Tonson and the Simpsons. But for *Miscellanea* III (1701), he went to Tooke; he later sold Tooke the copyright of *Letters to the King* (1703) for £50, though Tim Goodwin's name also appears in the imprint, and then employed him again for *Memoirs* III (1709), receiving copy money each time.[33] The publication of *Miscellanea* III on 28 July 1701 was just three months before Swift's *Discourse of the Contests and Dissensions*, around 21 October.[34] The *Discourse*, a defence of Lord Somers and the three other ministers who had been impeached by the House of Commons, in a style that echoed Temple's, appeared anonymously and with only the name of a trade publisher or distributor, John Nutt, in the imprint. But Ehrenpreis shrewdly suspects that Tooke, who was later to collect the work in *Miscellanies in Prose and Verse* (1711), was, in the modern sense, the publisher (Ehrenpreis, vol. II, p. 92). What drew Swift to Tooke is unclear. He would have been used to the very common imprint 'Benjamin Tooke, printer to the King and Queen's most excellent Majesties' during his time in Ireland. If his *Discourse* had begun early in the summer, Somers may have directed him to Tooke as the publisher of the second edition of his own *Discourse Concerning Generosity* (1695).[35]

It is clear from Swift's correspondence that Tooke was responsible for the fifth edition of *A Tale of a Tub* in 1710 and *Miscellanies in Prose and Verse* (1711), a significant event in Swift's career and one of the subjects of Pat Rogers's essay (pp. 93–4). In the absence of any reference to copyright holders, it is reasonable to conclude that Tooke published both the first edition of the *Tale* in 1704 and the prose pieces that went into the *Miscellanies*.[36] *A Tale of a Tub* in 1704 was not the layered work it became in 1710, but it was already a work of some length (331 pages) and indulged in the detailed mockery of aspects of the modern book (list of publications, dedications, prefaces, side notes and hiatuses) discussed by Marcus Walsh and Claude Rawson in their essays in this collection (pp. 101–18 and 231–67). For Tooke to undertake so complex and potentially controversial a book, he must have been impressed by the editor of Temple's *Letters* and by the reception of the *Discourse of the Contests and Dissensions*.[37] He was repaid by three editions of the *Tale* in the first year and a fourth in 1705. Although the evidence from imprints is lacking, it seems likely that the success of the *Tale* made it easy for Swift to publish with Tooke the squibs and ecclesiastical papers of the years 1707 to 1711: the various Bickerstaff papers, *Letter Concerning the Sacramental Test*, and *Project for the Advancement of Religion*. At least one of these, *A Famous Prediction of Merlin* (1709), shows impressive typographical sophistication, as Valerie Rumbold has demonstrated in a recent article in *The Library*. The poem, Merlin's prophecy, is printed in black letter, with notes in roman by T. N. Philomath, on a two-sided half-sheet. At the head is a woodblock portrait of 'Merlinus Verax'. That Swift should want to play with popular publication is itself noteworthy, but this production shows intimate knowledge of Partridge's politics of the 1690s and appears to involve the acquisition and reuse of his woodblock.[38] Rumbold suggests various members of the book trade who might have helped Swift with this exercise, including Tooke, Dryden Leach and Tonson's printer, John Watts. To these might be added Benjamin Motte Sr.

Letters between Swift and Tooke in June and July 1710 provide a unique insight into what appears to be a relaxed but businesslike relationship.[39] Tooke had sent Swift Curll's *Complete Key to the Tale of a Tub* (which had attributed the work jointly to Swift and his cousin, Thomas Swift), doubtless in an attempt to hurry him along with the Apology and notes to the fifth edition and with providing extra copy for the *Miscellanies*. Swift, complaining vigorously about Curll and Thomas Swift, also blames Tooke for not having printed the Apology even though he had clearly neglected to revise it: 'I had neither health nor humour to finish that business. But the blame rests with you, that if you thought it time, you did not print it when you had it.' At the close of the letter, he says he will now send it:

> But, I dare say, you have neither printed the rest, nor finished the cuts; only are glad to lay the fault on me … If you are in such haste, how came you to forget the Miscellanies? I would not have you think of Steele for a publisher [i.e. editor]; he is too busy. I will, one of these days, send you some hints, which I would have in a preface, and you may get some friend to dress them up. (Woolley, *Corr.*, vol. I, p. 282)

This has the air of good-natured teasing over shared plans to bring out an enhanced *Tale of a Tub* and a volume of miscellanies. Swift clearly does not feel obliged to combine his zeal for action on the miscellanies with instant cooperation ('one of these days'), and in reply Tooke tacitly rebukes him with contrasting efficiency. He sends the new notes, which he suggests would be better at the foot of the page rather than at the end; he says the cuts are with Sir Andrew Fountaine, who was going to alter them but warns 'unless they are very well done, it is better they were quite let alone'; and, for the rest, he is waiting for Swift's revisions. The problem with both plans is that if they do not go ahead 'some rascal or other will do it for us both' (Woolley, *Corr.*, vol. I, pp. 283–4).

It is worth inquiring who might have printed the fifth edition of *Tale of a Tub*, a difficult task, with the footnotes added to an already side-noted and complex text. The most likely candidate is Benjamin Motte Sr, a close associate of Swift's bookseller's father. *A Tale of a Tub* was published without ornaments, which makes it difficult to identify the printer (that may have been the intention), but there are damaged types that link the fifth edition of 1710 with other books printed by Motte around that time. The dropped head of the dedication to Lord Somers has an 'N' with a bend just under the right-hand serif in 'JOHN' that appears in the dropped head 'TERENTII' of page 1 of Nicolaus Camus's edition of Terence's *Comoediæ Sex* (1709). The same 'N' appears as the initial letter for the text of the 'Praefatio' of George Cheyne's *Rudimentorum Methodi Fluxionum Inversæ Specimina* (1705) and in a slightly more bent state in 'WEST-INDIES' on the title page of Thomas Gage's *A New Survey of the West-Indies* (1711). This 'N' might not, however, be regarded as very distinctive. Slightly more so is the final 'R' of 'THE BOOKSELLER TO THE READER' in the *Battel of the Books*, which has a small circular break just above its left foot. It also appears in 'SPIRIT' in the section title of the *Mechanical Operation of the Spirit*. The same 'R' appears as the first in 'TO THE READER' of Owen Feltham's *Resolves: Divine, Moral, Political* (1709). All these texts other than *A Tale of a Tub* have 'Printed by Benj. Motte' or the like in their imprint. In addition, Motte uses a distinctive, but not unique, type in which italic capitals have a lead-in stroke to the ascender just below the serif, and that type is used in all first five editions of *Tale of a Tub*.[40]

These types would not make a strong case for Motte's work in isolation, but Swift's squib against Godolphin, *The Virtues of Sid Hamet the Magician's Rod*, was entered in the Stationers' Register on 7 October 1710, by Motte Sr to himself. It is difficult to see why a printer would own such a copy unless it was some sort of gift or reward, and Motte's successful printing of the revised *Tale of a Tub* (possibly coupled with help over *A Famous Prediction of Merlin*) might make such a gesture appropriate. There are interesting consequences for understanding the publication of *Gulliver's Travels*. Benjamin Motte Jr, the successor to Tooke's bookselling business and the publisher of the *Travels*, would have been bound to his father in February 1708 or a little earlier (he was born in 1693 and freed on 7 February 1715), so it is not impossible that he had a hand in printing *A Tale of a Tub* (which he republished on 21 December 1724, shortly after he went into partnership with Samuel Tooke) as well as in publishing the *Travels*. Certainly that might go some way to explaining Swift's loyalty to him.

(handwritten margin notes: "Swift's delight with his coincidence and haphazard"; "horrible poem")

The *Journal to Stella* confirms this impression of good relations between Swift and Tooke, with Tooke buying stock for Swift (*JSt* (1948), vol. II, p. 463) and dealing with Rebecca Dingley's financial affairs (*JSt* (1948), vol. I, pp. 231, 284, 301–2; vol. II, pp. 387, 391, 449, 575, 667). But as Swift told his correspondents on 17 October 1710 that 'Tooke is going on with my *Miscellany* (*JSt* (1948), vol. I, p. 62), it is a little surprising to find him taking such a different stance on 28 February 1711:

> Some bookseller has raked up every thing I writ, and published it t'other day in one volume; but I know nothing of it, 'twas without my knowledge or consent: it makes a four shilling book, and is called *Miscellanies in Prose and Verse*. Took pretends he knows nothing of it, but I doubt he is at the bottom. One must have patience with these things; the best of it is, I shall be plagued no more. However, I'll bring a couple of them over with me for MD, perhaps you may desire to see them. I hear they sell mightily. (*JSt* (1948), vol. I, pp. 203)

Those who wrestle with Swift's disavowals of engagement in Faulkner's *Works* in 1735 would do well to bear this parallel case in mind. Tooke is not the only one pretending to know nothing, though he is at the bottom of it.

1711–1714 London

By the time the *Miscellanies* appeared in the shops, however, Swift had assumed the role of a political writer, working for Harley and the ministry, though with an ambiguous status, having neither place nor pay. In this period he wrote the *Examiner*s XIII (2 November 1710) to XLV (14 June 1711), and published *The Conduct of the Allies* (1711), *Some Remarks on the Barrier Treaty* (1712) and *The Publick Spirit of the Whigs* (1714), all in support of government policy, with other pro-government squibs, some of which he labelled Grub Street. Towards the end of the period Swift saw himself as the ministry's impartial adviser and even historian, rather than propagandist, and prepared *Some Free Thoughts upon the Present State of Affairs* and *History of the Four Last Years of the Queen*, though in these exceptional cases he could not achieve immediate publication, the first appearing in 1741 and the second in 1758.

During this time he worked exceptionally closely with one book-trade figure, the ministry's printer, John Barber. Compared with Tooke, Barber was an upstart, without a background in the trade. He had managed Mrs Clarke's printing house after her husband's death, but by the summer of 1710, when Godolphin fell, he had developed a successful business of his own, serving as printer to the City of London.[41] Harley and St John saw the advantages of promoting their policies through the press, and Barber was their choice of printer, just as Swift was their choice of writer. As a result, Swift had a press, and a very good one, at his disposal for most of the period of the Tory government.[42] Ian Gadd's essay in this collection deals in some of the detailed arrangements between the two men (pp. 51–61), but it is worth emphasizing the closeness of the relationship. Swift often dined with Barber (with over twenty references in his accounts), though in the *Journal to Stella* he is usually referred to impersonally as his printer, whereas Tooke is referred to as 'Ben Tooke', presumably because Tooke had been discussed often with Esther Johnson and Rebecca Dingley, rather than because they knew him.[43] The first reference to him and his mistress Delarivier Manley is particularly dismissive: 'I dined with people that you never heard of, nor is it worth your while to know; an author-ess and a printer' (*JSt* (1948), vol. I, p. 154). After the fall of the Harley's ministry there was more of an equivalence of affection when Swift wrote about Tooke and Barber: in 1714 he noticed that Esther Vanhomrigh was 'picqued about my dearness to Ben and John', and he asked Charles Ford in 1718 to 'remember me to John and Ben when you see them.'[44]

Some sense of how closely Swift and Barber could work over a publication comes from the account of *A New Journey to Paris*, a fictional journey for Prior, in the *Journal to Stella* of 11 September 1711:

> This morning the printer sent me an account of Prior's journey; it makes a two-penny pamphlet; I suppose you will see it, for I dare engage it will run; 'tis a formal grave lie, from the beginning to the end. I writ all but about the last page, that I dictated, and the printer writ. (*JSt* (1948), vol. I, p. 357)

The absence of a bookseller as intermediary not only facilitated such rapidity of publication, with the author dictating directly to the printer, but also meant that Barber, in the case of popular works, could keep type standing and print off impressions of 1,000 copies a time in response to demand, or revise the text if he, the ministry and Swift agreed (*Conduct of the Allies*), or even recall and doctor a whole issue (*Publick Spirit of the Whigs*).[45] Swift was also easily able to play with print, the most striking example being *A Hue and Cry after Dismal* (1712), an imitation of a wanted poster, with a dramatic black-letter headline. Even if Barber did not himself print this work, he would easily have arranged it. Swift responded by playing his part in securing preferment for Barber, along with Tooke, to whom he was still loyal.

Only with *Some Free Thoughts upon the Present State of Affairs*, Swift's critique of the behaviour of Harley and St John, written towards the end of the ministry's period in office, when he had retired to Upper Letcombe, does a breakdown in the relations of writer and printer appear. Swift's chosen intermediary was Charles Ford, who as writer of the *Gazette* would have known Barber well, but by this point Swift's sense of the political antagonisms he was engaging was so strong that complete anonymity had to be assured.

> Here it is, read it, and send it to B— by an unknown hand, have nothing to do with it, thô there be no Danger. Contrive he may not shew it Mʳ L— [Erasmus Lewis] yet how can You do that? for I would not have him know that you or I had any concern in it. Do not send it by the Penny post, nor your Man, but by a Porter when you are not at Your Lodgings. get some Friend to copy out the little Paper, and send it inclosed with the rest, & let the same Hand direct it, and seal it with any unknown Seal.[46]

This fierce protection of anonymity is far removed from the casual dissembling over the *Miscellanies*, but these precautions set the pattern Swift was to adopt over many serious works in future. Barber, who must have had his suspicions about authorship, was unconstrained by any obligations, and showed the manuscript to Bolingbroke. Bolingbroke, through Barber, required changes that were not agreed, and before the matter could be resolved Harley had left office. Swift's *Thoughts*, losing their pertinence, went unpublished.

1714–1725 Dublin

When Swift returned to Ireland in 1714, he showed some desire for a Tooke-like arrangement, but that proved difficult and he seems to have settled for downmarket Barber alternatives instead. Some of Swift's political writing had already been reprinted in Dublin. In particular, *Conduct of the Allies* and *Some Remarks on the Barrier Treaty* had been published in Dublin first by John Hyde and then by Edward Waters.[47] John Hyde had been Master of the Guild of St Luke in 1718 and Pollard cites the tribute to him on his death on 17 November 1728 as 'the most Eminent and noted Bookseller in this City, a Man of so upright and unblemish'd a Character … as to render him the greatest loss the Publick could sustain' (*Dictionary*, p. 306). It was Hyde whom Swift recommended to collect Irish subscriptions for Prior's poems in 1719, and he was the bookseller later chosen to reprint *Gulliver's Travels* in Dublin. However, when Swift began his interventions in Irish political economy with *A Proposal for the Universal Use of Irish Manufactures* in 1720, he employed not Hyde but a printer, Edward Waters, using the imprint 'Printed and Sold by E. Waters, in Essex-street, at the Corner of Sycamore-Alley'. For Ehrenpreis, Waters was simply a 'crude and careless workman' (Ehrenpreis, vol. III, p. 129), and it is true that he worked with the deplorable Cornelius Carter and that Ian Gadd in *CWJS*, vol. VIII, thought no better of him. But he was very well connected. His wife Sarah was the daughter of Matthew Gunne, Master of the Guild in 1709, and from 1718 onwards her brother or cousin Richard was Hyde's regular partner in publication. In 1715 Waters had been arrested for printing *Advice to the Freeholders* and told the Council Board that he had done it for Hyde. Waters's business was possibly in some way a subsidiary of Hyde's, and Swift's move to Waters looks like a cautious step down one rung, which protected Hyde. Waters was arrested for printing Swift's *Proposal*, and refused to name the author. In a prosecution that infuriated and excited Swift, he was brought before the King's Bench, where Lord Chief Justice Whitshed refused to accept the jury's unwillingness to convict and sent them back nine times before they invited him to give a special verdict. Waters's trial was delayed and Swift, using all his connections, got the Duke of Grafton, Lord Lieutenant, to issue a *nolle prosequi* (Ehrenpreis, vol. III, pp. 123–30).

The experience with the *Proposal* shaped the handling of the *Drapier's Letters* in 1724. Once again a printer's name appeared alone in the imprint, 'Printed by J. Harding in Molesworth's-Court', and once again Swift has stepped down a rung. Pollard says that from 1718 to March 1720, Harding had used the address on the corner of Sycamore Alley that Waters used both before and after those dates (1711–24), and for the *Proposal for the Universal Use of Irish Manufactures*; presumably he had been apprenticed to Waters or worked for him. It is clear from Pollard's *Dictionary* that Harding was very busy with anti-government work, and Swift used him to print half-sheets against the proposed Bank of Ireland in 1721 and *The Last Speech and Dying Words of Ebenezor Elliston* (1722). The first five *Drapier's Letters* were printed (2,000 copies of the first letter) between February and December 1724, and an account of the manner of their submission to the printer is given in the Advertisement to volume IV of Faulkner's *Works* (1735):

> We are informed, it never lay in the Power of the Printer to discover him; for the Copies were always sent to the Press by some obscure Messenger, who never knew the Deliverer, but gave them in at a Window, as the Author himself observes in a Letter to *Harding* the Printer. His amanuensis was the only Person trusted; to whom about two Years after he bestowed and Employment of *40 l.* A Year, as a Reward for his Fidelity. [italics reversed]

The procedures that had been followed with *Some Free Thoughts* now became regular with Swift. The government responded in much the same way as over the *Proposal for the Universal Use of Irish Manufactures*: Harding was to be prosecuted, and was taken into custody; a jury refused to present Swift's writing as a libel and was dismissed; £300 was offered for the discovery of the author. Harding died on 19 April 1725. That Harding and his wife were enthusiasts for the cause is clear from her christening their son 'John Draper' on 18 May 1725. Swift showed his usual loyalty by employing Sarah Harding to print, among other works, *A Modest Proposal* and *The Intelligencer*. She was not a good printer and, after she married Nicholas Hussey, he must have been relieved to switch to George Faulkner.[48]

1725–1735 Dublin and London

After the astonishing success of the Drapier campaign, Swift operated, as Adam Rounce shows (pp. 199–213), for around ten years (until Faulkner's *Works*) with a two-channel approach to publication. Some works were published in the old way in London. As we have seen, *Gulliver's Travels* (1726) was brought out by Benjamin Motte Jr, the successor to Benjamin Tooke, and Swift received a copyright payment for it of £200. The text was probably subjected to some censorship, but that was an aspect of its combination of anonymity and respectability.[49] A similar respectability was aimed at in Dublin, for the bookseller chosen to reprint the *Travels* was John Hyde. This appears to have been an authorized edition, incorporating some Swift corrections, and it may also have involved a formal agreement with Motte.[50] In a letter Swift wrote to Motte on 28 December 1727, he told him he need not write to him through Mr Hyde any more, as though Hyde had been Motte's contact with Swift. Even after Hyde's death, a letter could come to Swift through Mrs Hyde.[51] It seems a fair assumption that, at Swift's prompting, Hyde had come to a financial arrangement with Motte for the republication of *Gulliver's Travels* that opened up easy communications between them.[52] That would explain why *Gulliver's Travels*, which was Motte's property, was never mentioned when in 1735 Motte took action in Chancery against Faulkner's duodecimo *Works*. The case was based on the *Miscellanies* alone. Presumably Hyde's rights, or Swift's, were passed on to Faulkner. Faulkner offered Motte a deal over the *Works*, but Motte turned it down on the grounds that he was being asked a high price for his own property. Mrs Hyde, on the other hand, subscribed for twelve sets.

Four volumes of *Miscellanies* (1727–32) were also published by Motte. The first was a reprint of 1711 (with £50 copyright money, probably on the grounds that the original fourteen-year term had run out). The other three (probably with payment of £100 each) were supposed to be joint enterprises with Pope, but Swift ended up providing nearly all the new copy and having some of his best poetry disdained.[53] Later, in August 1733, Swift sent over to London with his friend, the poet Mary Barber, six poems to be given to Matthew Pilkington, who through Swift's influence had been made chaplain to his old printer, John Barber, now Lord Mayor of London. In this case there were two reasons for publishing in London. The first was copyright money: Swift wanted Pilkington to sell the copyrights and take the money, just as he wanted Mrs Barber to launch a successful subscription edition of her poems in London (she eventually made an arrangement with Charles Rivington). The second was politics: two of the poems, *On Poetry: A Rapsody* and *An Epistle to a Lady*, made swingeing attacks on Walpole's administration.[54] The subsequent arrest of Swift's intermediaries showed the government's resentment.

In Dublin some works had continued to be sent to Mrs Harding in the usual way but, as Stephen Karian has shown in his essay (pp. 31–50), from the late 1720s Swift's attention focused on his poetry, and his relations with the book trade in that respect were very much attenuated. His attempt to provide an easy outlet for his work through a periodical, *The Intelligencer* (1728–9), had proved unsuccessful, and from that point onwards he operated chiefly, it seems, within a coterie, exchanging manuscripts. Those manuscripts seem to have made their way to the printer's chiefly through the agency of Swift's friends, and towards the end of the period Matthew Pilkington set up a route of publication through George Faulkner in Dublin to William Bowyer in London. That arrangement ensured copyright payments to Pilkington, but it generated rivalry in London with Pope's projects involving his new bookseller, Lawton Gilliver, and Benjamin Motte. That rivalry led indirectly to Faulkner's Dublin *Works* in 1735.

1735–1744 Dublin

Because in Ireland there was no copyright (though, as Adam Rounce explains in his essay (p. 203), there was some system of claiming copy through posting title pages),[55] there was no incentive to enter into formal agreements with booksellers and, as we have seen, many advantages in preserving a thorough anonymity. For an author as celebrated as Swift, publication in Dublin could be achieved with minimal personal initiative. Hyde's official reprinting of *Gulliver's Travels* had been followed by the reprinting of the *Miscellanies* by Samuel Fairbrother, the King's Stationer (1728–35), but without any evidence of an agreement with London. By May 1736 Swift and his friend Thomas Sheridan were angry with Fairbrother ('Fowlbrother', as they called him), Swift accusing him of improperly printing their work (Woolley, *Corr.*, vol. IV, pp. 293–7), but John Irwin Fischer has revealed that Fairbrother incorporated Swift's own corrections to the *Miscellanies* (possibly transmitted by Sheridan), opening up the possibility that in these cases Faulkner's corrections in the 1735 *Works* derive from Fairbrother, rather than from Swift himself.[56]

In his essay James McLaverty seeks to show how the combination of George Faulkner's replacing Sarah Harding as Swift's printer, Matthew Pilkington's desire to profit from being Swift's literary agent, Faulkner's links with William Bowyer and Swift's discontent with the *Miscellanies* led to the production of Faulkner's *Works* in 1735 (pp. 156–9). Swift presented the *Works* as something he was powerless to prevent, rather than as something he encouraged, the same stance he had adopted in 1711, when he had helped produce the Tooke *Miscellanies*. He gave enough encouragement to the *Works* for them to prove decisive for the shape of his remaining career. For a while he maintained good relations with Motte, but when Motte made his complaint against Faulkner in Chancery in October 1735, Swift sided with Faulkner. His letter to Motte of 1 November 1735 begins with a near-allegorical encounter:

> I had not received Your Letter three minutes, nor opened it, for, I was going abroad when Mr Faulkner stopped the Coach he was in, (for he was coming to see me) So I called at his Neighbors a friend of mine, and he came in to me. In the mean time I read your Letter, and gave it to him to read; he had many things to say in his defence, with which I cannot charge my Memory, but have advised him to answer. I know he passes for a perfectly honest man here, and a fair Dealer; And I confess that the many Oppressions we suffer from England sowr my temper to the utmost. (Woolley, *Corr.*, vol. IV, pp. 210)

Motte cannot get an independent hearing because Faulkner is on the spot. And his social position (the coach and his reputation) makes charges of piracy against him implausible. It would be neat if the friend was Pilkington, because his support, and the support of others in Swift's circle, was vital to Faulkner. But the most important point in this story comes at the end, where the encouragement of the Irish book trade starts to become a patriotic imperative. In a letter to Motte six months later, feeling runs even higher:

> But, I am so incensed against the Oppressions from England, and have
> so little Regard to the Laws they make, that I do as a Clergyman encour-
> age the Merchants both to export Wool and Woollen Manufactures
> to any Country in Europe, or any where else; and conceal it from the
> Custom-house Officers, as I would hide my Purse from a Highwayman, if
> he came to rob in the Road ... And, so I would encourage Booksellers here
> to sell your Authors Books printed here, and send them to all the Towns
> in England, if I could do it with Safety, and Profit (25 May 1736, Woolley,
> *Corr.*, vol. IV, p. 304–5).

Faulkner needed no encouragement to behave in this way and continued
to exploit his opportunities.

Even at the close of his exasperated letter to Motte, Swift says he has
some remaining works to be published in London, but his own attempts
at publication through the agency of William King, Principal of St Mary's
Hall, Oxford, were unsuccessful. *The History of the Four Last Years of the
Queen* was blocked by the second Earl of Oxford and Erasmus Lewis,
while *Verses on the Death of Dr. Swift* was censored and corrupted by King
himself, assisted by Pope. The publication of his letters in London by Pope
in 1741, an episode detailed by Abigail Williams in her chapter (pp. 125–7),
did nothing to redeem the London trade's reputation, and in this final
period Swift became ever more dependent on Irish routes to publication.
Those late works that achieved success in London – *Polite Conversation*
and *Directions to Servants* – did so with parallel publication in Dublin
through Faulkner. After his death Swift continued to be published in both
Dublin and London, the parallel multi-volume editions of Faulkner and
Hawkesworth transforming what had for so long looked like a dilemma
into a posthumous triumph. In his essay Daniel Cook explores how this
tradition of editing was carried on, in contrasting styles, by John Nichols
and Deane Swift (pp. 214–30).

The ethics of authorship

Stephen Karian shows in his essay (pp. 31–50) that the immediate prospect of publication became even less important to Swift in his final years
in Dublin, and the question of his agency even more obscured. And yet
his conception of himself as an author remained strong. In *Verses on the
Death of Dr. Swift*, possibly written in 1731 but published in 1739, the
second half of the poem is preoccupied with public judgement of the
Dean (however uncertain in focus and ironically nuanced): his works
'design'd │ To cure the Vices of Mankind', his independence, and his

defence of 'LIBERTY'.[57] And this commitment to liberty is also famously the focus of Swift's epitaph, which emphasizes ethical dedication:
'Abi viator, et imitare, si poteris, strenum pro virili libertatis vindica-
torem' (Go, traveller, and imitate if you can one who strove with all his
might to champion liberty).[58] This peculiar mixture of passionate serious-
ness, policy and carelessness displayed in Swift's attitude to his writings
was not simply the consequence of changing circumstances; it reflected
deep-rooted opinions about the ethics of the writer's life. The peculiar
nature of Swift's dealings with the press was to a great extent defined
by these opinions. As Paddy Bullard and Claude Rawson argue in their
chapters, they also have a place in the story of Swift's dealings with the
eighteenth-century book trade.

As his later writings frequently indicate, Swift believed that all sorts
of writing, printed or otherwise, are ethically perspicuous – that literary
works, in other words, give sufficient evidence of the greatness or meanness
of their authors' souls. This is the lesson of the episode at Glubbdubdrib
when Gulliver introduces the ghosts of Homer and Aristotle ('those two
Heroes') to the spirits of their many commentators: 'I soon discovered,
that both of them were perfect Strangers to the rest of the Company.'[59]
Printed books containing texts by heroic poet and skulking commentator
might sit together in a library, but at an ethical level they come from different worlds. Swift also thought that some kinds of speech act could be
performances of truly generous deeds. Indeed, he considered his *Drapier's
Letters*, written to avert a national crisis, to be a case in point:

> The Dean did by his Pen defeat
> An infamous destructive Cheat …
> Envy hath own'd it was his doing,
> To save that helpless Land from Ruin.[60]

But he was adamant that the acts of writing and publishing are not virtuous as such. They lend no honour to the author, even though, as his
patron Sir William Temple wrote, 'all the Great and Noble Productions of
Wit and of Courage, have been inspired and exalted by [Honour] alone'.[61]
The idea that literary accomplishment might confer any sort of nobility
or distinction upon an ordinary person bred to be, say, a housewife or a
lawyer was absurd to Swift (himself the son of a lawyer). And since books
could only ever be the symptoms or tools of virtue, it was similarly absurd
to find human value in their material forms. This is the point of the joke
with which Swift ends the 'Epistle Dedicatory' to *A Tale of a Tub*. The
dedicatee, 'Prince Posterity', is promised:

upon the Word of a sincere Man, that there is now actually in being, a certain Poet called *John Dryden*, whose Translation of *Virgil* was lately printed
in large Folio, well bound, and if diligent search were made, for ought I
know, is yet to be seen. (*CWJS*, vol. I, p. 23)

Claude Rawson discusses this passage as part of his reflection on Dryden's
role in Swift's satire (pp. 238–9). From the perspective of Posterity John
Dryden's personal insignificance is such that his very existence is barely
credible. His book titled *The Works of Virgil* (1697) is a folio of 690 pages
with 101 leaves of prints, but in the world of the *Tale* it is as reassuringly
ignorable as its author, despite its colossal size. In fact there is a direct
proportion (by the logic of Swift's satire) between its material bulk and its
cultural ephemerality. Book historians looking for meaning in the physical form of Swift's writings must consider that Swift was a moral realist.
He believed, following conventional Stoic thinking, that magnanimous
actions and virtuous persons are real in a way that material things such
as books are not. His faithfulness to this idea shaped and sometimes dis-
torted his dealings with those who published and traded in his writings.

Swift was willing to measure the value of books against the characters
of the people who wrote them, but reluctant to reverse the comparison –
that is, to judge author by book. His tendency to undervalue books as
material objects is an extension of that opinion, and it lends a theme to
his sallies in the quarrel between the ancients and the moderns. The 'modern' William Wotton had attacked Sir William Temple's ethicized view
of authorship (that love of honour is the common source of wit and of
bravery) in his *Reflections upon Ancient and Modern Learning*, arguing
that Temple 'confounds two very different Things together; namely, *Who
were the greatest Men … and Who have carried their Enquiries farthest?*'[62]
The first is an appropriate topic for rhetorical declamation, says Wotton,
but not for 'Discourses, wherein Men are supposed to reason severely'.
Swift's response to this reasonable argument is to extend it by a series of
uninvited inferences, and then to distort and exaggerate the inferences in
turn. So if moderns like Wotton think that a well-sustained inquiry in
a book is more valuable than a well-sustained *ethos* in a person, it follows (according to the satirist's logic) that they must be investing printed
books with moral qualities properly reserved for human beings. Indeed,
when John Milton talks of books being 'the pretious life-blood of a master
spirit', or Gabriel Naudé describes the contents of a library as 'Images, not
of the Bodies, but of the Minds of so many gallant men, as have [trans-
mitted to us] whatsoever was most excellent', that is what they are doing,

at a figurative level.[63] Swift's 'Battel of the Books' is conceived as a wild elaboration of this anthropomorphic conception of the book:

> In [*Books of Controversie*], is wonderfully instilled and preserved, the Spirit of each Warrier, while he is alive; and after his Death, his Soul transmigrates there, to inform them. This, at least, is the more common Opinion; But, I believe, it is with Libraries, as with other Cœmeteries, where some Philosophers affirm, that a certain Spirit, which they call *Brutum hominis*, hovers over the Monument ... So, we may say, a restless Spirit haunts over every *Book*, till *Dust* and *Worms* have seized upon it ... (*CWJS*, vol. I, pp. 145–6)

In the dedication to *A Tale of a Tub* Swift affirms that the (living) poet John Dryden is alive – here the rather grim joke is that both author and book are correspondingly dead. One of the epigrams Swift published in 1727 as 'Thoughts on Various Subjects' reads: 'When I am reading a Book, whether wise or silly, it seemeth to me to be alive and talking to me.'[64] Volume in hand, Swift is content to indulge himself with the illusion of human presence. But the indulgence indicates the strength of his preference for the living voice, and that qualified 'seemeth' still hints at his haunted sense of the book as a sort of grave.

Just beyond the obscure and turbulent realm of print, and to some extent defining its boundaries, Swift located the relatively humane sphere of the speaking voice. Often he conceptualized writing and print in terms of their relation to oral discourse. In *A Letter to a Young Clergyman* (1721) he recommended the achievement of an absolutely plain style, pitched at the true level of ordinary speech, by 'a Method observed by the famous Lord *Falkland* ... when he doubted whether a word were intelligible or no, he used to consult one of his Lady's Chambermaids, (not the Waiting-woman, because it was possible she might be conversant in Romances,) and by her Judgment was guided'.[65] The stipulation that any print, including popular romances, will be enough to adulterate the judge's vocabulary indicates how severely non-literary were Swift's standards of plain usage. In 1763 George Faulkner claimed that Swift had used a similar method while preparing copy for his 1735 *Works*. The printer was obliged to attend Swift every morning with proofs

> to read to him, that the Sound might strike the Ear, as well as the Sense the Understanding, and [he] had always two Men Servants present for this Purpose; and when he had any Doubt, he would ask them the Meaning of what they heard? Which, if they could not comprehend, he would alter and amend, until they understood it perfectly well.[66]

Elocution (always a hobby-horse for Swift) is set up here as a normalizing measure in the process of literary composition.[67] The act of reading aloud brings the text immediately before the tribunal of comprehensibility. The implication is that print does not do this, and that one of its characteristic effects is to cajole readers into a too-ready acceptance of obscurity. The burnished flatness of Swift's prose style is designed to create an illusion of the ready understanding that uneducated people experience (as he supposed) when they hear clearly expressed speech. Related to these ideas is the famous 'bull' that begins the first of the Drapier pamphlets, *A Letter to the Shopkeepers of Ireland* (1723–4): 'I do most earnestly exhort you', writes the Drapier, '… to read this Paper with the utmost Attention, or get it read to you by others.'[68] At the risk of blunting Swift's preposterous joke, it is worth noting the real point he is making here about the medium of the pamphlet: that the serious attention that its contents demands might best be achieved by putting it into a communal, discursive, oral setting. These are some of the limits of print in Swift's moral imagination.

The structure of this collection

The first section of *Jonathan Swift and the Eighteenth-Century Book* sets the scene by considering three important environments for the Swiftian book: the writing table (scene of composition and the source of material circulating in manuscript and escaping into print); the printing house (Swift's relations with printers and booksellers were particularly close while he was writing his English political pamphlets); and the library (from the 'Battel of the Books' at St. James's Library to Swift's own book-collecting and habits of annotation). The second section examines some characteristic species of Swiftian book: the miscellany and the collected *Works*; the mock book; the epistle or collection of letters; and early-modern travel books in their relation to *Gulliver's Travels*. In the third section, the perspective of scholarly inquiry broadens to take in some of the larger contextual issues that engage Swift's books. First are the pressures of censorship, libel law and self-censorship; second the interrelations of Dublin and London in the production of Swift's books; and finally the paradoxical and adversarial continuities between Swift, Sterne and later writers in the phenomenon of the mock edition.

Notes

1 Charles A. Rivington, *'Tyrant': The Story of John Barber* (York: William
  Sessions, 1989), pp. 22–5, 28–30; see Swift to Charles Ford, 16 February 1718–
  19, Woolley, *Corr.*, vol. II, p. 291; see also Swift to Esther Johnson, 15 January
  1711–12, *JSt* (1948), vol. II, p. 465: 'My printer and bookseller … are resolved
  to ask several other employments of the same nature to other offices; and I
  will then grease fat sows, and see whether it be possible to satisfy them. Why
  am not I a stationer?'
2 John Barber to Swift, 24 August 1732, Woolley, *Corr.*, vol. III, p. 529.
3 4 November 1731, *The Grub-street Journal*, ed. Bertrand A. Goldgar, 4 vols.
  (London: Pickering & Chatto, 2002), vol. II, page 1 of Number 96, referring to the procession described in the previous number; see also 30 October
  1732, vol. III, Number 148, 'The ART and MYSTERY of *Printing* Emblematically
  Displayed'.
4 Robert Darnton, 'What is the History of Books?', *Daedalus*, 3 (1982), 65–83
  (67–9); and 'What is the History of Books: Revisited', *Journal of Modern
  Intellectual History*, 4 (2007), 495–508 (503); cf. Thomas R. Adams and Nicolas
  Barker, 'A New Model for the Study of the Book', in Nicolas Barker (ed.), *A
  Potencie of Life: Books in Society* (London: British Library, 1993), 5–43 (p. 15).
5 Swift, 'Horace, Epist. I. VIII', lines 41–2, in Williams, *Poems*, vol. I, p. 172.
6 Cf. *A Tale of a Tub*, in *CWJS*, vol. I, p. 133; for pageantry and the Stationers'
  Company see Adrian Johns, *The Nature of the Book: Print and Knowledge in
  the Making* (University of Chicago Press, 1998), pp. 209–12; see also Paula R.
  Backscheider, *Spectacular Politics: Theatrical Power and Mass Culture in Early
  Modern England* (Baltimore: Johns Hopkins University Press, 1993), pp. 37–8.
7 *The Poems of Alexander Pope, Volume III, The Dunciad (1728) & The Dunciad
  Variorum (1729)*, ed. Valerie Rumbold (Harlow: Longman, 2007), pp. 26–7
  (book I, lines 73–94); for Swift and the *Dunciad* see Griffin, *Swift and Pope*,
  107–17.
8 Rivington, *'Tyrant'*, pp. 5–8.
9 Swift to Barber, 11 September 1732, Woolley, *Corr.*, vol. III, p. 541.
10 D. F. McKenzie, 'Typography and Meaning: The Case of William Congreve',
  in *Making Meaning: Printers of the Mind*, ed. Peter D. McDonald and
  Michael F. Suarez SJ (Amherst: University of Massachusetts Press, 2002),
  pp. 198–236; John Barnard, 'Creating an English Literary Canon, 1679–1720:
  Jacob Tonson, Dryden and Congreve', in Simon Eliot, Andrew Nash and
  Ian Willison (eds.), *Literary Cultures and the Material Book* (London: British
  Library, 2007), pp. 307–21; Matthew Prior to Swift, 4 November 1732,
  Williams, *Corr.*, vol. IV, p. 82 ('I have been engaged in Comma's, Semicolons,
  Italic and Capital, to make Nonsense more pompous and [furbelow] bad
  Poetry, with good Printing'); James McLaverty, *Pope, Print and Meaning*
  (Oxford University Press, 2001).
11 Swift to William Pulteney, 12 May 1735, Woolley, *Corr.*, vol. IV, p. 108; see
  'Richard Sympson' to Motte, 8 August 1726, Woolley, *Corr.*, vol. III, p. 9.

12 Ehrenpreis, *Swift*, vol. II, p. 712, makes the useful contrast of Swift's habitual caution over the untraceability of *The Publick Spirit of the Whigs* (1714) with Richard Steele's reckless self-publicity in *The Crisis* (1713): Swift evaded prosecution for seditious libel; Steele was expelled from the House of Commons.

13 Pollard, *Dictionary*, pp. 274–5; the story of Harding's death in prison is supported only by an ambiguous allegory in the broadside *Poem to the Whole People of Ireland* (1726), printed by Elizabeth Sadlier, who may have been the mother of John's widow Sarah.

14 Woolley, *Corr.*, vol. IV, p. 556; cf. George Faulkner's advertisement to the fourth volume of Swift's *Works* (Davis, *PW*, vol. XIII, pp. 186–7); cf. Pope to Swift, 16 November 1726, Woolley, *Corr.*, vol. III, p. 52: 'Motte receiv'd the copy (he tells me) he knew not from whence, nor from whom, dropp'd at his house in the dark, from a Hackney-coach: by computing the time, I found it was after you left England, so for my part, I suspend my judgment.'

15 Motte's later account of the incident to Swift is dated 31 July 1735, Woolley, *Corr.*, vol. IV, pp. 151–2.

16 See Ehrenpreis, *Swift*, vol. III, pp. 776–8; George Mayhew, *Rage or Raillery* (San Marino: Huntington Library, 1967), pp. 109–12; John Irwin Fischer, 'The Government's Response to Swift's *An Epistle to a Lady*', *Philological Quarterly*, 65 (1986), 39–59.

17 Swift to Motte, 9 December 1732, Woolley, *Corr.*, vol. III, pp. 563–4.

18 Swift to Charles Ford, 9 October 1733, Woolley, *Corr.*, vol. III, pp. 692–3.

19 Woolley, *Corr.*, vol. III, pp. 67–8; only eighteen of the corrections refer to the first two parts of *GT*, while thirty-eight refer to part III, and fifty-four to part IV.

20 See Swift to Ford, 9 October 1733 and Ford to Swift, 6 November 1733, Woolley, *Corr.*, vol. III, pp. 692 and 698.

21 Robert D. Hume, 'Editing a Nebulous Author: The Case of the Duke of Buckingham', *The Library*, 7th ser., 4 (2003), 249–77.

22 Michael Treadwell, 'London Trade Publishers, 1675–1750', *The Library*, 6th ser., 4 (1982), 99–134 (114–18); the phrase was first used by D. F. McKenzie in his 1976 Sandars Lectures, 'The London Book Trade in the Later Seventeenth Century'.

23 For information about the Irish book trade we are deeply indebted to Mary Pollard's research and publications, which we have drawn on freely: *Dictionary* and *Dublin's Trade in Books, 1550–1800* (Oxford: Clarendon Press, 1989).

24 Pollard, *Dublin's Trade in Books*, p. 69 and, for the structure of the trade, pp. 181–7.

25 The Act is reprinted from *The Statutes at Large* (London, 1724), vol. LV, pp. 147–50, in R. M. Wiles, *Serial Publication in England before 1750* (Cambridge University Press, 1957), pp. 261–6 (262). Some confusion has arisen over this point as a result of Pollard's reflections in *Dublin's Trade in Books*, pp. 69–70, possibly influenced by Swift's beliefs (Woolley, *Corr.*, vol. IV, p. 210). The claim that importation was not illegal until 1739 in Raymond Gillespie and Andrew Hadfield (eds.), *The Irish Book in English, 1550–1800*, The Oxford History of

the Book in English, vol. III (Oxford University Press, 2006), p. 85, is incorrect. The Importation Act (1739) strengthened and simplified the Copyright Act by allowing for inspection and penalties, and by disallowing importation of *any* book printed and published in England in the previous twenty years.

26 *Dublin's Trade in Books*, pp. 67–87.

27 See James Raven's comprehensive survey, 'The Book Trades', in Isabel Rivers (ed.), *Books and their Readers in Eighteenth-Century England: New Essays* (London: Leicester University Press, 2001), pp. 1–36, and Michael Treadwell, 'London Trade Publishers, 1675–1750'.

28 For Henry Dodwell's comments about the impossibility of exchange of copies in Ireland, see Pollard, *Dublin's Trade in Books*, p. 56.

29 *ESTC*, consulted 22 June 2012. Some of the problems in using this resource in establishing a general picture, especially with regard to dating, are outlined by Stephen Karian in 'The Limitations and Possibilities of the *ESTC*', *Age of Johnson*, 21 (2011), 283–97 (291–3).

30 It therefore offers some support to Sean D. Moore's view of this episode in *Swift, the Book, and the Irish Financial Revolution* (Baltimore: The Johns Hopkins University Press, 2010), pp. 134–67, even if his general thesis is unpersuasive.

31 For the identification and reproduction of this poem, see James Woolley, 'Swift's First Published Poem: *Ode. To the King*', in *Münster* (2003), pp. 265–83. For a story about Mrs Swift staying with Mrs Brent, see Ehrenpreis, *Swift*, vol. I, p. 29.

32 For the account of Swift's early relations with the trade we are indebted to Michael Treadwell's pioneering 'Swift's Relations with the London Book Trade to 1714', in Robin Myers and Michael Harris (eds.), *Author/Publisher Relations During the Eighteenth and Nineteenth Centuries* (Oxford Polytechnic Press, 1983), pp. 1–36.

33 The receipts are printed in Woolley, *Corr.*, vol. I, pp. 145–6 and 250, and are for £30, £50 and £40 respectively.

34 The dates are from Davis, *PW*, vol. I, p. xx, and Ehrenpreis, *Swift*, vol. II, p. 47 n. 2.

35 Tooke Jr had been freed from his apprenticeship to William Rogers only on 4 March 1695, so, if it is him, rather than his father, it is a very early publication.

36 As Stephen Karian and Ian Gadd point out in their chapters, Tooke was very quick to claim both *Tale of a Tub* and the *Miscellanies* when the Stationers' Register reopened after the Copyright Act; they were the first two items entered (Karian, *Print and Manuscript*, p. 16).

37 Marcus Walsh thinks *Tale of a Tub* was probably written between 1695 and 1697, though it would have been subject to later revision (*CWJS*, vol. I, p. xxxvi). An unestablished writer might have found it difficult to publish this work.

38 See Valerie Rumbold, 'Merlinus Verax, T. N. Philomath, and the Merlin Tradition: Print Context for Swift's *A Famous Prediction of Merlin* (1709)', *The Library*, 7th ser., 12 (2011), 400–12.

39 The letters, published by Deane Swift, are dated 29 June and 10 July 1710, Woolley, *Corr.*, vol. I, pp. 282–5.

40 Since we wrote this account, James E. May has sent us an advance copy of his essay, 'Re-impressed Type in the First Four Octavo Editions of *A Tale of a Tub*, 1704–5' in which he brilliantly demonstrates Motte's printing of these editions.

41 Rivington: *'Tyrant'*, pp. 5–21.

42 See J. A. Downie's pioneering *Robert Harley and the Press: Propaganda and Public Opinion in the Age of Swift and Defoe* (Cambridge University Press, 1979).

43 *The Account Books of Jonathan Swift*, ed. Paul V. Thompson and Dorothy J. Thompson (Newark: University of Delaware Press, 1984); *JSt* (1948), vol. I, p. 323.

44 Swift to Esther Vanhomrigh, 1 August 1714, Woolley, *Corr.*, vol. II, p. 41; Swift to Ford, 20 December 1718, Woolley, *Corr.*, vol. II, p. 286.

45 For full information, see Ian Gadd's textual introductions in *CWJS*, vol. VIII.

46 Woolley, *Corr.*, vol. I, p. 627 [1 July 1714]. The whole correspondence is usefully excerpted and the story told in Rivington, *'Tyrant'*, pp. 62–8.

47 For accounts of the editions, see *CWJS*, vol. VIII, pp. 365–8 and 393–6.

48 James Woolley has given exemplary accounts of Sarah Harding in his edition of *The Intelligencer* (Oxford: Clarendon Press, 1992) and in 'Sarah Harding as Swift's Printer', in Christopher Fox and Brenda Tooley (eds.), *Walking Naboth's Vinyard: New Studies of Swift* (University of Notre Dame Press, 1995), pp. 164–77.

49 For a recent interpretation of the evidence, see James McLaverty, 'The Revision of the First Edition of *Gulliver's Travels*: Book-Trade Context, Interleaving, Two Cancels, and a Failure to Catch', *Papers of the Bibliographical Society of America*, 106 (2012), 5–35.

50 For the evidence for Swift's revisions, see David Woolley, 'Swift's Copy of *Gulliver's Travels*, the Armagh *Gulliver*, Hyde's Edition, and Swift's Earliest Corrections', in Clive T. Probyn (ed.), *The Art of Jonathan Swift* (London: Vision Press, 1978), pp. 131–78.

51 Woolley, *Corr.*, vol. III, p. 149. It is unclear whether the letter sent through Mrs Hyde on ?31 July 1735 (Woolley, *Corr.*, vol. IV, p. 151) was unusual or not.

52 Ian Gadd toys with the same hypothesis as to the arrangements for *Conduct of the Allies*, though the evidence is too complex to rehearse here (*CWJS*, vol. VIII, pp. 350–1).

53 See James McLaverty, 'The Failure of the Swift–Pope *Miscellanies* (1727–32) and *The Life and Genuine Character of Doctor Swift* (1733)', in *Münster* (2008), pp. 131–48.

54 This whole episode is very difficult to reconcile with Sean D. Moore's thesis in *Swift, the Book, and the Irish Financial Revolution* that Swift was seeking, both through action and through metaphorical writing, to promote the Irish book trade.

55 There were, exceptionally, copyright payments, as Pollard explains, *Dublin's Trade in Books*, pp. 177–9.

56 John Irwin Fischer, 'Swift's *Miscellanies, in Prose and Verse, Volume the Fifth*: Some Facts and Puzzles', *SStud*, 15 (2000), 76–87.

57 Williams, *Poems*, vol. II, pp. 551–72 (565–6), lines 314, 347. For an account of Swift's play with indeterminacy in this poem, see chapter 6 of Karian, *Jonathan Swift in Print and Manuscript*, pp. 166–204.

58 For a full discussion of the significance of the epitaph, see Claude Rawson, 'Savage Indignation Revisited: Swift, Yeats, and the "Cry" of Liberty', in Claude Rawson (ed.), *Politics and Literature in the Age of Swift: English and Irish Perspectives* (Cambridge University Press, 2010), pp. 185–220.

59 *Gulliver's Travels*, part III, ch. viii, Davis, *PW*, vol. XI, p. 197.

60 'Verses on the Death of Dr. Swift', lines 407–8, 411–12, Williams, *Poems*, vol. II, p. 569.

61 Sir William Temple, 'An Essay upon the Ancient and Modern Learning', *Works*, 2 vols. (1720), vol. I, p. 168.

62 William Wotton, *Reflections upon Ancient and Modern Learning … With a Dissertation upon the Epistles of Phalaris, by Dr. Bentley*, 2nd edn with large additions (1697), p. 8.

63 John Milton, *Areopagitica* (1644), in *Complete Prose Works, Volume II, 1643–1648*, ed. Ernest Sirluck (New Haven: Yale University Press, 1959), p. 493; Gabriel Naudé, *Instructions Concerning Erecting of a Library*, tr. John Evelyn (1661), p. 6; the source of Naudé's images is probably Bacon: see *CWJS*, vol. I, p. 469 n. 18.

64 'Thoughts on Various Subjects' (1727), Davis, *PW*, vol. IV, p. 253.

65 Davis, *PW*, vol. IX, p. 65.

66 'To the Reader', *The Works of the Reverend Dr. J. Swift, D.S.P.D.*, 11 vols (Dublin, 1763), vol. I. p. iv.

67 For Swift on elocution see no. 66 (10 September 1709) of *The Tatler*, ed. Donald F. Bond, 3 vols. (Oxford: Clarendon Press, 1987), vol. I, pp. 453–61, probably written by Steele from hints by Swift ('Lysander'); see also Paddy Bullard, 'Pride, Pulpit Eloquence, and the Rhetoric of Jonathan Swift', *Rhetorica*, 30 (2012), 232–55.

68 Davis, *PW*, vol. X, p. 3.

PART I

Swift's books and their environment

CHAPTER ONE

Swift as a manuscript poet

Stephen Karian

[handwritten: Essay structure all over the place]

In *Jonathan Swift in Print and Manuscript* I explore the interaction between print and manuscript throughout Swift's career, and suggest that studying his career requires considering how some of his works circulated in manuscript.[1] In this essay, I want to go one step further to argue that we should regard Swift primarily as a manuscript-based poet, that is, as a poet who typically writes not for print publication and its largely unknown readership, but for manuscript circulation among a small group of readers or for oral delivery to a select audience.[2] This perspective of Swift as a manuscript poet greatly affects how we understand particular poems, as well as Swift's identity as a poet more broadly. It also might help us better understand why and when Swift chose to publish his poems. In addition, I suggest we use this perspective to reconsider the major collections of Swift's verse that appeared in his lifetime – especially George Faulkner's 1735 collection – to show that they too reinforce our sense of him as a manuscript poet. What emerges from this discussion is a greater awareness of Swift's complex and sometimes conflicting attitudes towards his own poetry.

In the following pages, I mainly explore the printed history of Swift's poems rather than their manuscript existence, because when it comes to Swift's writings the study of print can in fact help us understand the roles that manuscript circulation played in his career. We can know only so much from examining those manuscripts that do survive, and we therefore have to go further to reconstruct the contexts from which many of

Much of this essay's evidence is based on the digital archive of the *Swift Poems Project*, edited by James Woolley, John Irwin Fischer and me, and on a *Swift Poems Project* database that greatly assisted me in compiling information. For programming that database, I am indebted to Paul Miller, Digital Production Manager, Skillman Library, Lafayette College. Future discoveries may alter some of the numerical evidence presented here, but I suspect that such changes will not affect my broader arguments. Portions of this essay draw upon ongoing annotational research conducted by James Woolley and me towards the Cambridge edition of Swift's complete poems.

[handwritten margin note: pointless]

31

Swift's poems emerged. We should ask questions such as: What occasions – if any – prompted these poems? Who were the poems' original readers or audiences? How did they respond to the poems? In order to formulate answers to these questions, we often need to be somewhat speculative – not irresponsibly speculative or unreasonably speculative, but using speculation grounded in the evidence that we have and in reasonable probability. (This essay therefore is at times more suggestive than definitive.) *not reassuring*

I begin by distinguishing between print-based and manuscript-based poets. I define a print-based poet as one who primarily writes for print publication and does so in a timely manner such that usually less than one year elapses between a work's completion and its authorized publication. Consequently, most poems by a manuscript-based poet are not published in an authorized publication within one year of their completion. This definition is useful for at least three reasons. First, the distinction between authorized and unauthorized publication emphasizes the agency of the poet rather than of a bookseller or someone else operating outside the poet's wishes. Second, the duration of a year allows for various circumstances that might have delayed publication, an issue especially important for Swift, who lived in Ireland for most of his life but published mainly in London. Third, this definition does not require concrete evidence confirming that poems circulated widely in manuscript. Owing to the often scant survival rates of contemporaneous manuscripts, it is usually easier to establish that a poem was printed than that it was copied and handed about (and it may be impossible to establish that a poem was shared but not copied). In the case of Swift's poems, we can reasonably assume that many more manuscripts once existed than survive today, and the content of some of his poems suggests manuscript circulation, however limited that might have been.

This definition of a manuscript-based poet fits Swift quite closely – not as closely as it fits Rochester, but far more closely than it fits Pope. The 366 poems that can be confidently attributed to Swift alone and in collaboration total 17,714 lines. These totals include his various 'trifles' and riddles as well as verse in his prose and correspondence. Many of these poems are quite short, which is why for the following figures I include numbers for both lines and poems. When we examine the publication histories of these poems, we find that exactly half of them (comprising about one-quarter of his total lines of verse) were not published during his lifetime.[3] That fact alone is an important reminder as to how often Swift wrote poems for purposes other than immediate print publication.

When we turn to poems printed during Swift's lifetime, we find that only 29 poems totalling 3,634 lines (about 8 per cent of his total poems and about 20 per cent of his total lines of verse) were printed in authorized editions within a year of their composition. Therefore it is far more concise to list those that fall into this category rather than those that do not. These 29 poems are listed below, with dates of composition and remarks about initial publication when not published separately:

'Ode. To the King on his Irish Expedition' (1690)[4]
'Ode to the Athenian Society' (1692, in the supplement to the fifth volume of the *Athenian Gazette*)
'An Elegy on Mr. Patrige' (1708)
'A Famous Prediction of Merlin' (1709)
'A Description of the Morning' (1709, in *The Tatler*)
'The Virtues of Sid Hamet the Magician's Rod' (1710)
'A Dialogue between Captain Tom and Sir Henry Dutton Colt' (1710)[5]
'A Description of a City Shower' (1710, in *The Tatler*)
'An Excellent New Song, being the Intended Speech of a Famous Orator against Peace' (1711)
'The Windsor Prophecy' (1711)
'The Fable of Midas' (1712)
'Toland's Invitation to Dismal' (1712)
'Peace and Dunkirk' (1712)
'Part of the Seventh Epistle of the First Book of Horace Imitated' (1713)
'The Bubble' (1720)
'An Epilogue to be Spoke at the Theatre-Royal … in the Behalf of the Distressed Weavers' (1721)
'Prometheus' (1724)
'Stella's Birthday. March 13 1726/7' (1727, in the Swift–Pope *Miscellanies*)
'Corinna' (1727, in the Swift–Pope *Miscellanies*)
'Mad Mullinix and Timothy' (1728, in *The Intelligencer*)
'Tim and the Fables' (in collaboration with Thomas Sheridan) (1728, in *The Intelligencer*)
'An Answer to the Ballyspellin Ballad' (in collaboration with others) (1728)
'The Journal of a Dublin Lady' (1729)
'A Libel on Dr. Delany' (1730)
'To Doctor Delany, on the Libels Writ Against Him' (1730)
'An Answer to Dr. Delany's Fable of the Pheasant and the Lark' (1730)
'Traulus. The First Part' (1730)
'Traulus. The Second Part' (1730)
'On Poetry: A Rapsody' (1733)

Of the 29 poems listed above, 2 might have been excluded on the grounds that though they were initially printed under Swift's authority, they were probably not widely published under it. That is, these poems seem to have been privately printed and initially shared within a very limited circle, a pattern of transmission usually associated with manuscript circulation. Both are political lampoons: 'An Excellent New Song, being the Intended Speech of a Famous Orator against Peace' and 'The Windsor Prophecy'. 'An Excellent New Song' was printed and read aloud for an evening with the society of Brothers.[6] Swift intended to publish 'The Windsor Prophecy', but on the advice of Lady Masham he withdrew it from publication. He informed Stella that the poem 'is not published here, only printed copies given to friends', offering an important distinction between publishing and printing. Nonetheless, the poem was widely distributed.[7]

A few other poems barely made the list because they were written many months before first being published. 'On Poetry: A Rapsody', perhaps the most important poem listed here, was begun early in 1733 and possibly finished that summer, but was not published until late December of that year.[8] 'Corinna' was probably written in the summer of 1727, but it was not published until March 1728 in the 'Last' volume of the Swift–Pope Miscellanies.[9] Similarly, the final Stella birthday poem was written a full year before being published in the same Miscellanies volume, perhaps (only) because Pope needed more material to fill the collection.[10]

This list tells us much about Swift's poetic career in print and what might have prompted him to offer his poems to a print audience in those relatively few instances that he chose to do so. In the 1690s, Swift published only two poems: 'Ode. To the King' and 'Ode to the Athenian Society'. The ode to King William III might have been a self-financed publication to ingratiate himself with the King or possibly the Fellows of Trinity College Dublin.[11] The Athenian ode is in part a form of flattery directed towards his then patron Sir William Temple, who contributed to John Dunton's Athenian Mercury and who is referenced in the prefatory epistle.[12] That poem's appearance also reveals Swift's novice effort to attach his work to a more substantial publication, in this instance the folio supplement to the fifth volume of the Athenian Gazette. Similarly, Swift had hoped that his poem 'To Mr. Congreve' (1693) would appear with one of Congreve's plays: 'I onely design they should be printed before it.'[13]

At this early stage, Swift seemed to possess 'an Ambition to be heard in a Crowd', as he put it in the 'Introduction' to A Tale of a Tub (CWJS, vol. I, p. 34). That ambition is also evident in his decision to include 'Baucis and Philemon' and 'On Mrs. Biddy Floyd' in Jacob Tonson's Poetical Miscellanies. The Sixth Part (1709), a volume that connected his work to an important literary tradition that extended from Dryden to Pope, who made his print debut with his Pastorals in the same volume.[14] In the years

1708 to 1710, Swift also published his writings on the Bickerstaff affair (including two poems) and two 'Description' poems in the fashionable periodical *The Tatler*. And he planned for a collected volume of prose and verse that he published in 1711.[15] All of this evidence reveals Swift's focus on publishing his writings, a practice that continued with his propaganda work for the Tories, which included seven political poems in 1710–12.

It is not surprising that, relative to other years, 1708–13 show such a concentration of poems that Swift quickly published. During those six years, Swift was almost always in London: he was associating with the important writers of the day, he was in close contact with the bookseller Benjamin Tooke Jr and the printer John Barber, and towards the latter part of this period he held a favoured position as the chief Tory propagandist. After Swift left London in 1714, his frequency of prompt poetic publication fell off dramatically. 'The Bubble' was to some extent a continuation of his earlier period, because it was first published separately in London, and it was Tooke's last publication for Swift (the bookseller died in 1723). Of the poems later than 'The Bubble' in the above list, 'On Poetry: A Rapsody' is the only poem to be first published separately in London.

This list barely hints at the remarkable transition that Swift made in the late 1720s from being primarily a prose author to being primarily a poet, a transition explored by Arthur H. Scouten.[16] Scouten suggests that 1729 was the pivotal year, but in light of James Woolley's recent findings that back-date some of the Market Hill poems, we should assign the shift to 1728, the first of Swift's three visits to the Achesons at Market Hill.[17] Notably, the four poems listed above from 1728 to 1729 were written during the first Market Hill visit. Shortly after the second visit, Swift separately published five poems in 1730, the most in any single year. In fact, their publication is all the more remarkable given that all five were likely published in a three-month period from February through April. That unique burst shows how deeply invested Swift was in the controversy that erupted over Patrick Delany's 'Epistle to Lord Carteret'. Swift probably saw the attacks on Delany not only as an opportunity to defend his close friend and to attack his enemies and various 'Dublin dunces', but also as a chance to explore quite fully the corrupting power of politics and how it could transform even someone like Carteret – whom Swift admired – into the pawn of a debased system. Swift thus found himself in an ideal situation to feature his poetic talents and to offer his first published expression of explicit animus towards Sir Robert Walpole and George II. Not surprisingly, Swift valued his poem 'A Libel on Dr. Delany' highly, calling it 'the best thing I writt as I think', and was disappointed when Pope chose to exclude it from the 'Third' volume of the Swift–Pope *Miscellanies*.[18]

Swift's overall reasons for publishing his poems were thus varied and overlapping: to seek patronage, to further a hoax, to disseminate political propaganda, to defend his friends and to attack his enemies. But so too were the many reasons (some of which cannot be easily determined) for choosing not to publish his poems soon after writing them. The vast majority of Swift's poems, including his best-known and important poems, are missing from the above list: 'Cadenus and Vanessa', the other Stella poems, 'Epistle to a Lady', the so-called scatological poems, 'Verses on the Death of Dr. Swift' and 'The Legion Club', among others. For most of these poems, there was a lengthy gap between composition and publication. For some, such as 'Cadenus and Vanessa' and 'The Lady's Dressing Room', the first publications were not authorized by Swift, at least as far as we know. Swift's reasons for not immediately publishing at times owed much to political caution. For example, Swift didn't intend to publish 'The Legion Club', and especially not in Dublin, where the printer might be hanged, as he half-facetiously suggested to Thomas Sheridan.[19]

In many instances, Swift wrote his poems solely or at least primarily for a very limited audience. Hence the many poems written for and often about specific households, circles of friends and various individuals: Sir William Temple; the Berkeleys; Pope, Arbuthnot and Gay; Delany, Sheridan, Charles Ford, and George and John Rochfort; Stella; Vanessa; Orrery; and the Achesons. The limited nature of this initial and primary readership suggests how many of Swift's poems were originally designed as entertainment pieces. The Berkeley poems, especially 'The Humble Petition of Frances Harris', 'A Ballad on the Game of Traffick' and its response poem, were written to entertain the members of the household, from the servants to the Earl of Berkeley. Many of the Market Hill poems read like entertainment pieces, as does a poem such as 'The Journal', which entertained in part by mocking those who stand outside the spirit of summer carousing, such as the pedantic Dean Percival and his wife.[20]

Other poems were not designed as entertainment, but nonetheless grew out of a social occasion, however difficult it is to reconstruct now with certainty. For example, the frequent allusions in Swift's 'Ode to Temple' to Sir William Temple's 'Essay upon the Ancient and Modern Learning' augment the spirit of flattery shown elsewhere in the poem.[21] We perhaps will never know exactly why Swift wrote this poem, but we may assume that Temple was pleased to find his ideas reflected back to him in verse by his secretary. 'The First of April' reads like a versified thank you note to the members of the Cope family for being his hosts. 'Apollo Outwitted', written in praise of Anne Finch, seems to be a self-congratulatory poem for having 'Prevail'd on' Finch to publish her poems – a significant depart- ure from her general reticence towards print publication. The end of the poem probably alludes to the three Finch poems that appeared in Tonson's *Poetical Miscellanies. The Sixth Part* immediately before two of Swift's poems.[22]

In this context, 'Epistle to a Lady' is interesting for the ways in which it modulates between personal concerns and political ones, as Swift justifies ridicule directed towards both his friends and his enemies. We need not accept at face value the poem's claims that his 'gentle' satire would only 'smart' and that he is not agitated at all by rampant political corruption ('Safe within my little Wherry, | All their Madness makes me merry').[23] The poem does suggest to us, I think, that Swift is beginning to see his private relationships in more broadly public terms, and thus his experi- ence at Market Hill must have been quite formative.

All of this might prompt us to wonder about other poems whose con- tents do not obviously suggest that they were originally written for a small audience of friends. How might 'On Poetry: A Rapsody' or 'Verses on the Death of Dr. Swift' be reconsidered from the perspective of an ini- tial group of readers close to Swift? We know that Delany was one of the earliest readers of 'On Poetry: A Rapsody', but we do not know the extent to which he may have influenced its composition.[24] Prior to publication, 'Verses on the Death of Dr. Swift' was shared with Laetitia Pilkington, whose 'Eyes fill'd with Tears' upon reading about Swift's impending demise.[25] To consider the original audiences of these poems and others, one needs to examine with care the known chronology of composition and the possible relevance of subtle allusions and resonances.

This kind of admittedly circumstantial evidence offers some basis to re-examine the origins of 'The Lady's Dressing Room'. Drawing upon a range of external and internal evidence, Peter Schakel suggests that this poem was written at Market Hill, and I want to offer additional reasons that support his suggestion.[26] Schakel notes George Faulkner's date of 1730, which could place it during Swift's third and final visit to Market Hill from June to September of that year. Although Faulkner's dates are sometimes unreliable, this particular date is plausible.

Schakel cites the publishing history of 'The Lady's Dressing Room' as another reason to assign its origin to Market Hill. The separate London publication of the poem was also the first publication of Swift's 'On Cutting Down the Old Thorn at Market Hill', which raises the possibility

that 'The Lady's Dressing Room' and this Market Hill poem had circulated together in manuscript. However, this particular publication (Foxon
S869) almost certainly did not derive from a circulating manuscript; it
was printed by William Bowyer, who often coordinated with Faulkner
to reprint Faulkner's Dublin publications – including works by Swift –
in London.[27] Faulkner probably arranged this publication of 'The Lady's
Dressing Room' with Bowyer. 'The Lady's Dressing Room' and 'On
Cutting Down the Old Thorn at Market Hill' did circulate in manuscript
at this time, but not necessarily together.[28]

   Nonetheless, evidence from 'The Lady's Dressing Room' itself hints at
its likely Market Hill origins. Schakel connects the scatology of this poem
to that of 'My Lady's Lamentation and Complaint against the Dean' and
'A Panegyrick on the Dean in the Person of a Lady in the North'. Indeed,
the scene of Strephon 'lifting up the Lid' to view 'Those Secrets of the
hoary deep' is far less graphic than the 'spiral Tops, and Copple-Crowns'
described in 'A Panegyrick on the Dean'.[29] Schakel also relates the manipulation of voice and readers in 'The Lady's Dressing Room' to techniques
that Swift refined at Market Hill, and demonstrates the poem's connections to 'The Journal of a Dublin Lady'. To these points, one could add
how some topics covered in various Market Hill poems resonate with
the contents of 'The Lady's Dressing Room', specifically female concerns
about youth, beauty and fashion.[30]

   The literary and classical allusions in 'The Lady's Dressing Room' are
suggestive as well. Schakel links the famous Miltonic allusion in 'Those
Secrets of the hoary deep' to Swift's role as Lady Acheson's tutor.[31] In
'My Lady's Lamentation and Complaint against the Dean', Swift has
Lady Acheson utter: 'But, while in an ill tone, | I murder poor Milton'
(lines 155–6, Williams, *Poems*, vol. III, p. 856). Another author alluded to
in the poem is Lucretius, who was also part of Swift's lessons for Lady
Acheson.[32]

   The allusions to Milton and Lucretius are made explicit in the notes
to Faulkner's edition of the poem, as is a third allusion, which even more
tellingly connects 'The Lady's Dressing Room' to Market Hill. That allusion is the word 'adown' in line 103, a word that appears nowhere else in
Swift's poems. This word was glossed by Faulkner as a reference to the
writings of Dean Richard Daniel and Ambrose Philips, and it probably
functioned as an inside joke at Market Hill. Daniel was attacked at the
end of the Market Hill poem 'My Lady's Lamentation and Complaint
against the Dean' for his litigation against Nathaniel Whaley, a member of
the Market Hill circle, and Daniel is also mentioned in 'A Panegyrick on

the Dean'.[33] In various letters, Swift denigrates Daniel as an 'abominable puppy', 'the greatest Puppy and vilest Poet alive' and 'a damnable poet, and consequently a public enemy to mankind'.[34] Swift and possibly others at Market Hill probably parodied Daniel's paraphrase of the seven penitential psalms, as James Woolley suggests in an unpublished paper.[35]

The notes to Milton, Lucretius and Daniel appear in the space of six lines, soon after the witty employment of Pandora's box, the story of which, like so many classical myths, is recounted in Pomey's *Pantheon*, a work that Lady Acheson resented reading under Swift's tutelage. He has her call it 'That nasty Pantheon' in 'My Lady's Lamentation and Complaint against the Dean'.[36] *This is a reference to Francis Bacon?* ||

I would not press these points too far. Swift had addressed some of the same topics much earlier in 'The Progress of Beauty' (1719), though without the later poem's voyeurism and multivalent ending. I would also note that a rich and complex poem such as 'The Lady's Dressing Room' cannot be reduced to its possible compositional origins. I do believe, however, that there's reason to think that 'The Lady's Dressing Room' originated at Market Hill and was initially shared among the Achesons and possibly their neighbours. The poem's classical and literary allusions would have held special significance for that audience, particularly considering its antipathy towards Dean Daniel as well as Swift's tutoring of Lady Acheson in some of the texts referenced in the poem.

Despite such resonances, 'The Lady's Dressing Room' seems to have been written with a broader audience in mind.[37] When and how Swift intended to make it available to that audience is difficult to determine. In a letter to Pope, Swift refers to its London publication as based on 'a stol'n Copy' (Woolley, *Corr.*, vol. III, p. 489, 12 June 1732), a term also used in reference to the publications of 'The Grand Question Debated' and 'The Place of the Damn'd'. Given what we know of Bowyer's edition of 'The Lady's Dressing Room', Swift is either distancing himself from that edition or referring to the unauthorized Dublin edition, or both. Swift's comments about unauthorized distribution of his writings appear elsewhere, and they collectively speak to a pattern of manuscript circulation clarified in a letter to the Reverend Henry Jenney. That letter was prompted by the publication of 'An Answer to Hamilton's Bawn; or a Short Character of Dr. Swift' (1732) that attacked Swift for his supposed ingratitude towards the Achesons as portrayed in 'The Grand Question Debated' (1728). Swift's letter to Jenney, who is also mentioned in 'The Grand Question Debated', begins by responding to the seeming controversy, but he strays from the main topic to broader concerns:

What other things fell from me (chiefly in verse) were onely amusements in hours of sickness or leisure, or in private familyes, to divert our selves and some Neighbors, but were never intended for publick view, which is plain from the Subjects; and the careless way of handling them. Neither indeed can it answer the true ends of vanity or desire of Praise to let the world see such little sallyes of fancy or humor, because if they be ill or indifferently performd (which must often be the case) the loss of reputation is certain, and however well executed, after a week's vogue they are utterly forgot.

Swift then stops short: 'I know not how I come to be led so far from the subject of your letter.' He continues, claiming that he knows Jenney was not responsible for the 'Answer' poem and describing how 'The Grand Question Debated' circulated:

I knew how well you were acquainted with the whole history and occasion of writing those Verses on the Barrack, how well pleased the Master and Lady of the Family were with it, that you had read it more than once, that it was no Secret to any neighbor, nor any reserve but that against giving a copy. You knew well by what incidents that reserve was broken, by granting a Copy to a great Person; and from thence how it fell into other hands and so came (as it is the constant case) to be published, and is now forgot. (Woolley, *Corr.*, vol. III, p. 484, 8 June 1732)

By 'reserve', Swift means 'restriction'. Though Swift's comments here are concerned only with 'The Grand Question Debated', they could have been written to describe the manner in which other poems circulated in manuscript and came to be published without his authorization or involvement. Swift's comments elsewhere suggest that his poems were often entrusted to friends with the explicit prohibition against copying them for others or allowing them to be copied. Thus Swift's desire to control the circulation of his poems is an important reason why manuscript was sometimes his preferred medium. Earlier in this letter to Jenney, Swift indicates a similar process that led to the publication of 'The Journal', a poem 'published many years ago by the indiscretion of a Friend, to whom they were sent in a letter' (Woolley, *Corr.*, vol. III, p. 483). Referring to the Market Hill poems in general in a letter to Pope, Swift writes that 'they never went further: and my Lady Acheson made me give her up all the foul copies, and never gave the fair ones out of her hands, or suffered them to be copied. They were sometimes shewn to intimate friends, to occasion mirth, and that was all' (Woolley, *Corr.*, vol. III, p. 212, 6 March 1729). The Earl of Orrery corroborates these remarks when he describes Lady Acheson unlocking a cabinet to remove and then read a manuscript of Swift's then unpublished poem 'Death and Daphne'.[38] Similarly, when

Swift allowed Laetitia Pilkington to read and borrow his unpublished 'Verses on the Death of Dr. Swift', he imposed 'certain Conditions, which were, that I should neither shew it to any body, nor copy it, and that I should send it to him by Eight o'Clock the next Morning, all which I punctually perform'd'.[39] Given this pattern, a poem published without Swift's knowledge or authorization might well be described as coming from 'a stol'n Copy'.[40]

Comments about restrictive manuscript circulation sometimes coincide with self-disparaging comments about the quality of these poems. The poems are 'onely amusements', 'to occasion mirth, and that was all'. Though these remarks concern the Market Hill poems, they extend to a broader pattern in which Swift sometimes denigrates his poetic accomplishments. Swift does reveal his pride about his poems in an early letter to his cousin Thomas and often in the *Journal to Stella*.[41] But elsewhere Swift refuses to make heightened claims. 'To Mr. Delany' 'might as well have been in Prose' for it contains only 'simple Topicks told in Rime' (lines 10 and 12, Williams, *Poems*, vol. I, p. 215). Writing to Charles Wogan, Swift confesses that 'I have been only a Man of Rhimes, and that upon Trifles, never having written serious Couplets in my Life'.[42] In 'Epistle to a Lady', he writes that 'I the lofty Stile decline' (line 218, Williams, *Poems*, vol. II, p. 637). These comments show that Swift avoided a grand poetic manner, though he also admired poets who succeeded in that idiom. In this context, one might consider his remarks in 'Verses on the Death of Dr. Swift':

> In POPE, I cannot read a Line,
> But with a Sigh, I wish it mine:
> When he can in one Couplet fix
> More Sense than I can do in Six:
> It gives me such a jealous Fit,
> I cry, Pox take him, and his Wit.
> (lines 47–52, Williams, *Poems*,
> vol. II, p. 555)

This passage can be read as raillery that also conveys a partial acceptance of Pope as a poetic ideal. Nonetheless, Swift's late poems rival many of Pope's and they may well have influenced Pope's subsequent poetic style. The personal and poetic relationship between the two writers has been insightfully explored in a number of recent studies that collectively reveal a mutually competitive and emulative exchange of poetic craft.[43] Swift's concern with poetic skill and values is evident from the fact that after 'Cadenus and Vanessa', his longest poem is 'On Poetry: A Rapsody', which distinguishes between good and bad poetry and explores the financial and political benefits of writing and publishing poems that fawn over monarchs and politicians.

Furthermore, once Swift becomes primarily a poet after 1728, he becomes more of a critic of poetry, offering critical comments about the poetry of others. Hence late in his career he expresses opinions about the poems of Dean Daniel, Ambrose Philips, Edward Young, Stephen Duck and John Hughes as well as the poetic translations of Charles Carthy.[44] He also helps other poets, such as Mary Barber, Constantia Grierson, Matthew and Laetitia Pilkington, and Thomas Beach, revise and sometimes publish their work.[45] For Faulkner's editions of Pope's satires, Swift fills in blanked names and adds annotations to make them more accessible to middling readers.[46] Swift clearly cared a great deal about his own poetry as well as the poetic standards of his era.

When we consider how active Swift was as a poet and when we consider how infrequently he published his poems in a prompt way, we are confronted with the likelihood that he was quite ambivalent about publishing his poetry. This ambivalence did not stop him from writing poetry, but it may have affected how and when he offered his poems to an unknown readership. Though he tended not to publish promptly, he either kept his poems or entrusted them to others, such that many were collected and later published, in some instances after his death. Swift's ambivalence towards publishing his poetry thus directly relates to the significance of the major collections of his verse, specifically the 1711 *Miscellanies in Prose and Verse*, the Swift–Pope *Miscellanies*, and the 1735 *Works* published by George Faulkner. To these we might add the manuscript collections assembled and kept by Esther Johnson and Lady Acheson.[47] The activity of others – whether Pope, Faulkner, Esther Johnson or Lady Acheson – offered Swift a helpful way to manage his ambivalence towards publishing his poems: he could continue to hold them back from publication or at least not initiate publication, while also knowing that they would in fact survive and, in some cases, appear in print during his lifetime.

One way to demonstrate this phenomenon is to look again at some numerical evidence, specifically how these collections not only accumulate poems that had previously been printed, but more significantly introduce many previously unprinted poems. Swift's 1711 *Miscellanies* contains 14 poems, 5 of them printed for the first time in that collection. The Swift–Pope *Miscellanies* of 1727–8 contains these 14 and 22 others, 16 of them printed for the first time in that collection.[48] The 'Third'

Miscellanies volume of 1732 adds 9 more poems reliably attributed to Swift, 3 of which were previously unprinted. When we turn to the edition published by Faulkner, we find him to be an assiduous collector of Swift's verse. Faulkner's 1735 collection contains 129 poems by Swift, including all 45 poems from the Swift–Pope *Miscellanies*, and 84 more, 62 of which Faulkner printed for the first time.[49]

Faulkner's role as a collector of Swift's poetry merits further attention. In *Jonathan Swift in Print and Manuscript*, I argue that Faulkner initiated the 1735 edition of Swift's *Works* and that in this effort he was helped by Swift's English and Irish friends and to a lesser extent by Swift himself.[50] A brief examination of Faulkner's second volume suggests that the bookseller did not begin printing the volume with the expectation that he would add a significant number of poems to what had already been published. For Faulkner began printing with more limited goals in mind: to include all available poems that were definitely by Swift – thus excluding poems of uncertain authorship published in the Swift–Pope *Miscellanies* and in Samuel Fairbrother's Dublin reprints of those *Miscellanies* – and to present them in chronological order, as best could be determined. For about 250 pages, Faulkner mostly accomplished these goals, but at some point he gained access to dozens of poems, most of them previously unpublished. As a result, the latter part of the volume becomes chronologically quite chaotic, possibly because Faulkner did not receive these poems all at once or from the same person. Faulkner was probably delighted to sacrifice this sense of order for the benefit of being able to boast that his volume was 'enlarged by above a third Part, which was never collected before' and that many poems 'were procured from the supposed Author's Friends, who at their earnest Request were permitted to take Copies'.[51]

Faulkner's efforts as a collector occurred at a crucial time in the history of Swift's writings. He had access to Swift himself shortly after his peak period as a poet. Swift perhaps offered as little assistance as the preface suggests – 'we could never get the least Satisfaction [regarding dates] or many other Circumstances from the supposed Author' – but he presumably exercised veto power over publishing works that he did not write or that he otherwise wished to exclude.[52] Faulkner also had access to some of Swift's friends, who seemed willing to offer their manuscripts of previously unpublished poems. Faulkner's actions almost certainly preserved many poems that otherwise might have been lost, and he published them in texts that are authoritative to some extent.[53]

As far as we can tell, the vast majority of the poems first printed in Faulkner's 1735 edition did not previously circulate in manuscript in an

extensive way. This is somewhat surprising since one might have expected
widespread dissemination of some of them, such as Swift's verse attacks on
William Wood. Therefore, Swift's presumed restrictions against allowing
these poems to circulate were probably obeyed – at least until Faulkner
acquired them. The Faulkner edition thus allows us a peek at some of the
poems preserved in manuscript within Swift's circle and demonstrates that
Swift's trust in his friends had been mostly well placed.

All of these points demonstrate the extent to which Swift's activities
as a poet were closely interwoven with the efforts of many people. Swift's
interactions with them were often the primary occasions for him having
written the poems in the first place. They were often the initial readers of
the poems, their caretakers, their copyists, their collectors, as well as their
printers and publishers. We should therefore consider Faulkner's role as an
extension of the activities that were integral to the manuscript existence of
Swift's poems.

I want to end with a pair of contrasting images. The first is a reader
sitting alone in a study reading Swift's poems in Faulkner's edition. This
reader could well be Swift himself, since we know that he sparsely annotated the poems in his copy of the second volume.[54] This reader would
have encountered the poems nicely collected and bound together, though
with few contextual references to explain why they were written. The
second image is offered by Laetitia Pilkington, who describes this encounter: 'The Dean running into the Parlour, threw a whole Packet of manuscript Poems into my Lap, and so he did for five or six times successively,
till I had an Apron full of Wit and Novelty, for they were all of his own
Writing, and such as had not then been made publick, and many of them,
I believe, never will.'[55] In this second image, we glimpse Swift's play-
ful exuberance and intimacy at sharing a presumably chaotic packet of
unpublished poems with a specific and receptive reader. Both images cap-
ture something important about Swift as a poet, though perhaps in our
minds the first one dominates over the second. As I hope I've indicated
here, keeping this second image constantly in mind is one of the challenges and pleasures of studying Swift's poems.

Notes

1 Karian, *Print and Manuscript*, which also develops some of the points noted in
passing here.
2 In this essay, I use the term 'manuscript circulation' to encompass a range
of activities, from widespread copying and recopying of manuscripts (a phenomenon Harold Love defines as 'scribal publication', *Scribal Publication in*

Seventeenth-Century England (Oxford: Clarendon Press, 1993), esp. pp. 35–89) to a restricted form of sharing that does not include recopying. When the context of my remarks does not qualify the term 'circulation', I refer to this wide range.

3 The total of poems not published during Swift's lifetime would be slightly higher were they to include the twenty poems of 461 lines that first appeared in the tenth volume of *Miscellanies* in May 1745, about five months before Swift's death. For the canonical status of Swift's poems, see James Woolley, 'The Canon of Swift's Poems: The Case of "An Apology to the Lady Carteret"', in *Münster* (1993), pp. 245–64.

4 For the first printing of this poem, see James Woolley, 'Swift's First Published Poem: *Ode. To the King*', in *Münster* (2003), pp. 265–83.

5 For the attribution of this poem to Swift, see C. F. Main, 'Defoe, Swift, and Captain Tom', *Harvard Library Bulletin*, 11 (1957), 71–9, and George P. Mayhew, 'Swift's Political "Conversion" and His "Lost" Ballad on the Westminster Election of 1710', *Bulletin of the John Rylands Library*, 53 (1971), 397–427.

6 *JSt* (1948), vol. II, pp. 430–1 (5 and 6 December 1711).

7 *JSt* (1948), vol. II, p. 454 (4 January 1712). See also vol. II, p. 446 (26 December 1711).

8 See James Woolley, *Swift's Later Poems: Studies in Circumstances and Texts* (New York: Garland, 1988), pp. 61–3.

9 The date of this poem is discussed in my essay 'Who Was Swift's "Corinna"?', in Hermann J. Real, Kirsten Juhas and Sandra Simon (eds.), *Reading Swift: Papers from The Sixth Münster Symposium on Jonathan Swift* (Munich: Wilhelm Fink, forthcoming).

10 The Stella birthday poem was the final poem of the 'Last' *Miscellanies* volume. On 1 July 1727, Swift wrote to Thomas Sheridan asking him to send 'To Stella, Who Collected and Transcribed his Poems' 'for we want some to make our Poetical Miscellany large enough'. He also stated that 'I do not want [it] … entire, but some Passages out it, if they deserve it, to lengthen the Volume' (Woolley, *Corr.*, vol. III, p. 104). Sheridan presumably sent the final Stella birthday poem as well.

11 The first printing of the 'Ode. To the King' survives in a single copy in a volume of pamphlets that 'appears to have been among the nucleus of the Raphoe Diocesan Library formed by the Trinity vice provost and librarian John Hall'; James Woolley, 'Swift's First Published Poem', p. 274. For the suggestion that Swift financed this poem's publication for the hope of obtaining advancement, see Andrew Carpenter, 'Poetry in English, 1690–1800: From the Williamite Wars to the Act of Union', in Margaret Kelleher and Philip O'Leary (eds.), *The Cambridge History of Irish Literature*, vol. I (Cambridge University Press, 2006), p. 282.

12 In his *Life and Errors* (1705), Dunton claims that 'The late Sir *William Temple*, a Man of a clear Judgment, and wonderful Penetration, was pleas'd to Honour me with *frequent Letters* and Questions, very Curious and uncommon; in Particular, that about the *Talismans* are his' (p. 261).

13 Woolley, *Corr.*, vol. I, p. 118, from Swift's 6 December 1693 letter to his cousin Thomas. Swift had also considered publishing his 'Ode to Dr. Sancroft', but as with the Congreve poem, it was first published long after Swift's death; see his 3 May 1692 letter to his cousin Thomas in Woolley, *Corr.*, vol. I, p. 110.

14 For Swift and Tonson, see my 'Edmund Curll and the Circulation of Swift's Writings', in *Münster* (2008), pp. 115–16. For Pope and Tonson, see David F. Foxon, *Pope and the Early Eighteenth-Century Book Trade* (Oxford: Clarendon Press, 1991), pp. 12–23. The importance of Tonson's contributions to late seventeenth- and early eighteenth-century literary taste is helpfully discussed in John Barnard, 'Creating an English Literary Canon, 1679–1720: Jacob Tonson, Dryden and Congreve', in Simon Eliot, Andrew Nash and Ian Willison (eds.), *Literary Cultures and the Material Book* (London: The British Library, 2007), pp. 307–21.

15 Those plans are evident from his 'Subjects for a Volume' list transcribed by John Lyon, printed in *A Supplement to Dr. Swift's Works ... Volume the Second* (London, 1779), p. 373 (TS 88, vol. XXV), and reprinted in Ehrenpreis, *Swift*, vol. II, pp. 768–9. This list was written on a letter dated October 1708, and therefore the list itself could have been recorded at a later time. But the list was probably written no later than April 1709, because it does not include 'A Description of the Morning', first published 30 April 1709.

16 Arthur H. Scouten, 'Jonathan Swift's Progress from Prose to Poetry', in *The Poetry of Jonathan Swift: Papers Read at a Clark Library Seminar 20 January 1979* (Los Angeles: William Andrews Clark Memorial Library, 1981), pp. 27–51. See also Pat Rogers's tables of Swift's poetic career on a decade-by-decade basis in *Poems*, pp. 38–9.

17 James Woolley, 'Swift's "Skinnibonia": A New Poem from Lady Acheson's Manuscript', in *Münster* (2008), pp. 309–42, esp. pp. 329–39.

18 Woolley, *Corr.*, vol. III, p. 556 (4 November 1732, Swift to Benjamin Motte). I omit 'Epistle Upon an Epistle' from these 1730 poems because the evidence for Swift's authorship is not convincing.

19 Swift's reference to 'The Legion Club' and the possible fate of its printer appears in the 24 April 1736 letter he co-wrote with Martha Whiteway (Woolley, *Corr.*, vol. IV, pp. 286–7).

20 For the Market Hill poems as entertainment, see Peter J. Schakel, 'Swift's Voices: Innovation and Complication in the Poems Written at Market Hill', in Howard D. Weinbrot, Peter J. Schakel and Stephen E. Karian (eds.), *Eighteenth-Century Contexts: Historical Inquiries in Honor of Phillip Harth* (Madison: University of Wisconsin Press, 2001), pp. 114–32, esp. pp. 115–17. A later version of this essay appeared in *Münster* (2003), pp. 311–26. See also James Woolley, 'Swift's "Skinnibonia"', p. 328.

21 For these allusions, see A. C. Elias Jr, *Swift at Moor Park: Problems in Biography and Criticism* (Philadelphia: University of Pennsylvania Press, 1982), pp. 81–3. In contrast to Elias, however, I do not find Swift's praise of Temple to be ironic.

22 Line 63, Williams, *Poems*, vol. I, p. 121. My comments about 'Apollo Outwitted' owe much to Barbara McGovern, *Anne Finch and Her Poetry: A Critical Biography* (Athens and London: University of Georgia Press, 1992), pp. 93–5. McGovern reasonably suggests that Swift was the intermediary between Finch and Tonson. In contrast with McGovern, however, I believe that Swift wrote the poem not to persuade Finch to publish, but to commemorate his successful persuasion. The argument that Swift refers to an actual rather than a proposed publication is strengthened by Swift's meeting with Tonson on 16 January 1709, four days after writing to Robert Hunter about his verses on Finch; see Paul V. Thompson and Dorothy J. Thompson (eds.), *The Account Books of Jonathan Swift* (Newark: University of Delaware Press, 1984), p. 64, and Woolley, *Corr.*, vol. I, p. 230.

23 Lines 163–4, 264–5, Williams, *Poems*, vol. II, pp. 635, 638.

24 See Mary Pendarves's letter to Ann Granville: 'The Dean of St. Patrick's is writing a poem on poetry. Dr. Delany has seen what is done of it, he says 'tis *like himself*, but he gives us no hopes of seeing it yet awhile' (*The Autobiography and Correspondence of Mary Granville, Mrs. Delany*, ed. Right Honourable Lady Llanover, 3 vols. (London: Bentley, 1861), vol. I, p. 404).

25 *Memoirs of Laetitia Pilkington*, ed. A. C. Elias Jr, 2 vols. (Athens: University of Georgia Press, 1997), vol. I, p. 54.

26 Schakel, 'Swift's Voices', pp. 127–9.

27 *The Bowyer Ledgers*, Keith Maslen and John Lancaster (eds.) (London: The Bibliographical Society; New York: The Bibliographical Society of America, 1991), p. 145. For further discussion of Bowyer co-ordinating London publications with Faulkner, see Maslen, 'George Faulkner and William Bowyer: the London Connection', *The Long Room*, 38 (1993), 20–30, reprinted in *An Early London Printing House at Work: Studies in the Bowyer Ledgers* (New York: Bibliographical Society of America, 1993), pp. 223–33. On 5 February 1732, only a few months before the publication of 'The Lady's Dressing Room' in London, Matthew Pilkington writes to Bowyer that 'I find Mr. Faulkner sent you a little pamphlet of my writing, called *An Infallible Scheme to pay the Debts of this Nation*' (Woolley, *Corr.*, vol. III, p. 453). Later that year, Matthew Pilkington sends Swift's works to Bowyer for a collected edition; see *Corr.*, vol. III, pp. 527, 530–1, 548–9. Foxon references are to D. F. Foxon, *English Verse, 1701–1750: A Catalogue of Separately Printed Poems with Notes on Contemporary Collected Editions*, 2 vols. (London: Cambridge University Press, 1975).

28 The first publication of 'The Lady's Dressing Room' was probably the unauthorized Dublin edition with no name in the imprint (Foxon S871). The title page of Faulkner's edition (Foxon S873) claims that its text derives from an 'Original COPY' of the poem, possibly supplied by Swift himself. The substantive variants between these two Dublin editions suggest that they derive from different manuscripts. Lord Bathurst's 9 April 1731 letter to Swift implies that he has read or at least heard about a manuscript of 'On Cutting Down the Old Thorn at Market Hill' (Woolley, *Corr.*, vol. III, pp. 380, 381

n. 5). Possibly Bowyer acquired this poem from Faulkner, but Faulkner did not publish it until 1735.

29 Lines 89 and 98, Williams, *Poems*, vol. II, p. 528, and line 304, *Poems*, vol. III, p. 896.

30 For Lady Acheson's concerns about youth, beauty and fashion, see 'My Lady's Lamentation and Complaint against the Dean', lines 122–34 (Williams, *Poems*, vol. III, p. 855), 'To Janus on New Year's Day', lines 27 and 30 (Williams, *Poems*, vol. III, p. 863), and 'Skinnibonia', line 59, referring to 'Laces and Brocadoes' (Woolley, 'Swift's "Skinnibonia"', p. 322), which all fine ladies wore, including Celia of 'The Lady's Dressing Room'.

31 Line 98 parodies *Paradise Lost*, book II, line 891, and line 143 parodies book III, lines 710–13.

32 In 'The Lady's Dressing Room', Lucretius is alluded to in the note to line 99, where 'Prime of Meat' is glossed as 'Prima Virorum' from *De Rerum Natura*, book I, line 86. The note in Faulkner's separate publication (Foxon S873) specifically identifies 'Luc.' here. Lucretius is alluded to in the Market Hill poem 'The Journal of a Dublin Lady', lines 184–5 (Williams, *Poems*, vol. II, p. 450), and probably also in line 144 of 'A Panegyrick on the Dean', which mentions 'Epicurius' (Williams, *Poems*, vol. III, p. 891). For further discussion of the study of Lucretius at Market Hill, see James Woolley, 'Swift's "Skinnibonia"', p. 328 n. 49.

33 Line 223, Williams, *Poems*, vol. III, p. 858, and line 48, *Poems*, vol. III, p. 888.

34 Woolley, *Corr.*, vol. III, p. 196 (20 September 1728, to Charles Ford), p. 198 (21 September 1728, to the Earl of Oxford) and p. 211 (6 March 1729, to Pope).

35 James Woolley, 'The Market Hill Parody of Richard Daniel's *The Royal Penitent*', paper read at the East-Central American Society for Eighteenth-Century Studies conference at Bethlehem, Pennsylvania on 10 October 2009.

36 Line 150, Williams, *Poems*, vol. III, p. 856. The story of Pandora's box appears in François Pomey, *The Pantheon, Representing the Fabulous Histories of the Heathen Gods*, 7th edn, trans. Andrew Tooke (1717), pp. 181–2. The story of Venus' origins, used in lines 131–2 of 'The Lady's Dressing Room', is recounted in Pomey's *Pantheon* on pp. 125–6.

37 Similarly, 'The Journal of a Dublin Lady' was originally written at Market Hill but intended for a broader audience.

38 John Boyle, fifth Earl of Cork and Orrery, *Remarks on the Life and Writings of Dr. Jonathan Swift*, ed. João Fróes (Newark: University of Delaware Press; London: Associated University Presses, 2000), p. 168.

39 *Memoirs of Laetitia Pilkington*, vol. I, p. 54.

40 The 'Preface' to the Swift–Pope *Miscellanies* addresses similar concerns when referring to 'loose Papers in Prose and Verse … as have already stolen into the World … having been obtained from us by the Importunity, and divulged by the Indiscretion of Friends, although restrain'd by Promises, which few of them are ever known to observe, and often think they make us a Compliment in breaking' (p. 4). Possibly these comments refer more to Swift's works than to Pope's.

41 'I find when I writt what pleases me I am Cowley to my self and can read it a hundred times over' (Woolley, *Corr.*, vol. I, p. 110, 3 May 1692, to Thomas Swift). Swift's comments to Esther Johnson and Rebecca Dingley about his poems often convey poetic pride. Regarding 'The Virtues of Sid Hamet the Magician's Rod', he states that it 'is cried up to the skies' (*JSt* (1948), vol. I, p. 59, 14 October 1710). Of his 'Description of a City Shower', he says ''tis the best thing I ever writ' (vol. I, p. 62, 17 October 1710) and 'there never was such a Shower since Danaë's' (vol. I, p. 74, 26 October 1710). Of 'The Windsor Prophecy', he boasts that 'I like it mightily' (vol. II, p. 444, 24 December 1711). Also, 'The Fable of Midas' 'passed wonderfully at our Society to night' (vol. II, p. 488, 14 February 1712).

42 Woolley, *Corr.*, vol. III, p. 515 (July–2 August 1732). For an extended discussion of the implications of this remark, see Claude Rawson, 'Swift', in Michael O'Neill (ed.), *The Cambridge History of English Poetry* (Cambridge University Press, 2010), pp. 318–32.

43 See the following discussions: Scouten, 'Jonathan Swift's Progress from Prose to Poetry', pp. 32–45; Ehrenpreis, *Swift*, vol. III, pp. 883–98; Peter J. Schakel, '"Friends Side by Side": Theme, Structure, and Influence in the Swift–Pope *Miscellanies* of 1727', in *Münster* (1993), pp. 103–12; Phillip Harth, 'Friendship and Politics: Swift's Relations with Pope in the Early 1730s', in *Münster* (1998), pp. 239–48; James McLaverty, 'The Failure of the Swift–Pope *Miscellanies* (1727–32) and *The Life and Genuine Character of Doctor Swift* (1733)', in *Münster* (2008), pp. 131–48; Rawson, 'Swift', in *The Cambridge History of English Poetry*; Griffin, *Swift and Pope;* and Seth Rudy, 'Pope, Swift, and the Poetics of Posterity', *Eighteenth-Century Life*, 35 (2011), 1–29.

44 The verse exchanges over Carthy's translations appear in Williams, *Poems*, vol. II, pp. 665–72. Swift's criticisms of John Hughes are summarized in O.T.D., 'Swift's Portrait', *Notes and Queries*, 3rd ser., 3 (1863), 260; Harold Williams, *Dean Swift's Library* (Cambridge University Press, 1932), p. 59; and *Library and Reading, Part 1*, vol. II, pp. 931–2.

45 Swift's detailed 12 April 1735 letter to Beach is in Woolley, *Corr.*, vol. IV, pp. 87–9. For the others, see this discussion of Swift's involvement with group revision: A. C. Elias Jr, '*Senatus Consultum*: Revising Verse in Swift's Dublin Circle, 1729–1735', in *Münster* (1998), pp. 249–67.

46 See A. C. Elias Jr, 'Swift and the Middling Reader: Additions to the Faulkner Reprints of Pope's Satires, 1733–1735', *SStud*, 15 (2000), 61–75.

47 For analysis of these manuscript collections, see two essays by James Woolley: 'Stella's Manuscript of Swift's Poems', in John Irwin Fischer, Hermann J. Real and James Woolley (eds.), *Swift and His Contexts* (New York: AMS Press, 1989), pp. 115–32 and 'Swift's "Skinnibonia"'.

48 For the most part, these figures refer to the 'Last' volume of the Swift–Pope *Miscellanies*, but 'A Famous Prediction of Merlin' (one of the fourteen that appeared in the 1711 *Miscellanies*) appears in the second volume with prose writings.

49 These figures include poems from both the cancelled and uncancelled states of Faulkner's second volume; see Margaret Weedon, 'An Uncancelled Copy of the First Collected Edition of Swift's Poems', *The Library*, 5th ser., 22 (1967), 44–56. Volume II contains all but three of these 129 poems; one appears in volume I ('A Famous Prediction of Merlin') and two appear in volume IV ('Verses written by Dr. Swift [upon Orrery's gift of a paper-book and Delany's gift of a standish]' and 'Prometheus'). For the sixty-two poems Faulkner printed for the first time, I include 'A Beautiful Young Nymph Going to Bed', 'Strephon and Chloe' and 'Cassinus and Peter', because their first (separate) publication was 'set from pre-publication sheets of *Volume the Fifth* which were in turn set from pre-publication sheets of the verse volume … of Faulkner's edition'; see John Irwin Fischer, 'Swift's *Miscellanies, in Prose and Verse, Volume the Fifth*: Some Facts and Puzzles', *SStud*, 15 (2000), 76–87, quoted from 79.

50 Karian, *Print and Manuscript*, pp. 30–43.

51 Preface to volume II, sig. A2ʳ. Faulkner improved the poems' chronological order for the 12mo edition of volume II published in 1735. Nonetheless, some poems continued to be out of order in that edition and all subsequent ones, including the carefully prepared 1762 18mo edition, volume II of which at times arranges poems by content rather than strictly by chronology.

52 Preface to volume II, sig. A2ᵛ. Swift's veto power is strongly suggested by repeated remarks in his letters. Before the edition is published, Swift offers the warning that Faulkner 'should take care not to charge me with what I never writ' (Woolley, *Corr.*, vol. III, p. 693, 9 October 1733, to Charles Ford). Swift's 25 May 1736 letter to Benjamin Motte implies that Faulkner accepted this veto power for a broad range of reasons: 'he would take the Advice of my Friends, and leave out what I pleased to order him' (*Corr.*, vol. IV, p. 304). After the edition is published, Swift writes to Motte on 1 November 1735 affirming that Faulkner 'hath always behaved him self so decently to me that I can not treat him otherwise than as [a] well-meaning Man' (*Corr.*, vol. IV, p. 210). Even the poems cancelled from the second volume are reliably attributed to Swift.

53 Ehrenpreis observes that Faulkner preserved writings that otherwise would have been lost (Ehrenpreis, *Swift*, vol. III, p. 787).

54 Swift's copy of the six volumes of the 1737–8 octavo Faulkner edition is listed in the sale catalogue of his library auctioned after his death; see *A Catalogue of Books, the Library of the late Rev. Dr. Swift* (Dublin: Faulkner, 1745), p. 13, item 486. A type facsimile of this catalogue appears in Williams, *Dean Swift's Library* and a photo facsimile (with sale prices) appears in *Library and Reading, Part 1*, vol. IV, pp. 347–64.

55 *Memoirs of Laetitia Pilkington*, vol. I, p. 36. This incident probably occurred in 1730; see vol. II, p. 413.

CHAPTER TWO

Leaving the printer to his liberty: Swift and the London book trade, 1701–1714

Ian Gadd

In 1983 Michael Treadwell published 'Swift's Relations with the London Book Trade to 1714', an essay which, in a characteristically unassuming way, offered a number of important new findings about Swift's early printers and publishers.[1] It is an essay that has stood the test of time remarkably well and its research provides a bedrock for what follows here. Treadwell's primary focus was the relationships, familial as well as convivial, between Swift and the trade – from his Dublin housekeeper Mrs Brent, wife and widow of a London-trained printer, to his cousin, the London printer Dryden Leach – and while Swift's individual publications obviously featured in his account, their printing histories were left mostly unexplored. In addition, his essay did not consider the wider context of the book trade during the period. It is these areas that the present essay will explore, paying particular attention to two key figures in Swift's life at this time: the bookseller Benjamin Tooke Jr (1671–1723) and the printer John Barber (bap. 1675, d. 1741), who between them were responsible for nearly all of what Swift published between 1701 and 1714.

Well over two dozen of Swift's works appeared as separate publications in London between 1701 and 1714, ranging from single-sheet 'penny papers' to substantial works: among them were *Discourse of the Contests and Dissensions Between the Nobles and the Commons in Athens and Rome* (1701), *A Tale of a Tub* (1704), *Predictions for the Year 1708* (1708), *A Letter … Concerning the Sacramental Test* (1709), *A Project for the Advancement of Religion* (1709), *Some Remarks upon a Pamphlet* (1711), *Miscellanies in Prose and Verse* (1711), *The Conduct of the Allies* (1711) and *The Publick Spirit of the Whigs* (1714).[2] All were issued without Swift's name on the title page. In addition, he edited several editions of Sir William Temple's works for the press and wrote over thirty issues for *The Examiner* (1710–11). (Swift had published two odes in 1691 and 1692 but otherwise his involvement with the book trade prior to 1701 was directly related to his work for Temple.)[3] Stephen Karian has described these years, from Swift's first book-length publication to the fall of the Tory ministry and the death of Queen Anne, as Swift's 'first phase' as a published author. It was, as Karian observes, emphatically 'London' in character, despite Swift's spending prolonged spells in both Dublin and London. With the possible and marginal exception of John Hyde's Dublin edition of *Conduct*, which seems to bear some authorial revisions, Swift's preference during these years was always to publish in London, which, given the sophisticated nature of London's book trade in comparison with Dublin, seems unsurprising.[4] His work for Temple had brought him into contact with booksellers and printers in London as a young man, and he must have quickly learned that, while books were more expensive in England than in Ireland, their physical quality was better, their likely distribution wider and their potential impact greater: a popular book in London was much more likely to be reprinted in Dublin than vice versa, as Swift was himself to discover.[5]

From 1701, his publisher of choice was Benjamin Tooke Jr; from 1710, it became John Barber. We do not know why Swift chose Tooke: Treadwell makes the very plausible suggestion that Tooke's Irish connections may have been a factor; in addition, he may have found Tooke's relative youth and good connections as the son of a prominent member of the London trade attractive.[6] The two men became intimate (Swift categorized Tooke among his 'grateful' friends), and Swift regularly visited Tooke at Middle Temple Gate in Fleet Street, corresponded with him when away from London and trusted him sufficiently to handle financial affairs on his behalf.[7] Thus, when Swift arrived in London from Dublin in September 1710, Tooke attended on him almost at once and their business relationship continued much as before. Preparations for the fifth edition of the *Tale* (published later that year) and *Miscellanies* (published the following February) were under way, and Tooke was most likely the publisher of *The Virtues of Sid Hamet the Magician's Rod* and of *A Dialogue between Captain Tom and Sir H—y D—n C—t*, both of which appeared in early October.[8] That same month, however, saw a decisive change in Swift's role as an author and in his relationship with the London book trade. Following a meeting with Robert Harley, the new Chancellor of the Exchequer, Swift was recruited as a writer on behalf of the Tory ministry, being appointed almost at once as the editor of *The Examiner*. Barber had been *The Examiner*'s printer and publisher since it had begun in August, and while this may not have been the first time the two men had met, it marked the start of a new and different professional association for Swift.[9] As with Tooke, Swift grew close to Barber: by the end of the year, Swift was confiding to Esther Johnson and Rebecca Dingley back in Dublin that there was 'an intimacy between us, built upon reasons that you shall know when I see you'.[10] Swift was a frequent visitor to Barber's printing house in Lambeth Hill, and not just on business.[11] It was, though, political circumstance rather than personal preference that had brought Swift to Barber, and Swift was circumspect not only in discussing their relationship with others but, on occasion, in his dealings with the printer. Unlike Tooke, Barber is never named in his letters to Dublin; moreover, at least twice Swift submitted manuscripts to Barber anonymously.[12]

In his correspondence, Swift describes Tooke as his 'bookseller' and Barber as his 'printer', and while it is true that Barber ran a printing house and Tooke did not, neither occupational epithet precluded them from taking on the same role as far as Swift was concerned.[13] Both men were, in the modern sense, publishers, shouldering the financial and legal risks associated with the production and distribution of printed works. Tooke's name appears, though, on the imprints of only two Swift works in this period, *Project for the Advancement of Religion* (1709) and *Proposal for Correcting, Improving, and Ascertaining the English Tongue* (1712), and Barber's not at all.[14] Instead, the most frequently named on imprints are John Nutt, for *Contests and Dissensions* (1701) and the various editions of *Tale* (1704–10), and John Morphew, who first appears on the title page of *Predictions for the Year 1708* (1708) and then regularly through to *Publick Spirit* (1714). Swift never mentions Nutt; Morphew is named a few times in his Dublin correspondence but it seems likely that they were rarely, if at all, in direct contact.[15] In December 1711, Swift describes Morphew as 'the publisher' of *Conduct*, which seems a straightforward statement given the bald imprint, 'Printed for John Morphew'.[16] However, Barber, not Morphew, printed and published *Conduct*, and the work was entered under Barber's name in the Register of the Stationers' Company.[17] Swift was instead using the term 'publisher' in its contemporary sense, to describe an individual whose role was to act as the primary distributor of the work on behalf of a 'bookseller' (or publisher in the modern sense).[18] This was particularly useful for topical and potentially contentious pamphlets whose commercial success depended on speedy and effective distribution, and it had the added advantage of deflecting unwanted attention from the authorities. Both Nutt and Morphew were 'trade publishers' (to use the term D. F. McKenzie coined), as was Anne Baldwin, whose name appears on *The Famous Prediction of Merlin* (1709); Treadwell suggests that on this occasion Swift, rather than Tooke, may have underwritten publication.[19]

Only a few other names appear on imprints of Swift's works in this period. Ann Dodd, named on the title pages of Swift's Horatian imitations

Curll

of 1713 and 1714, was a 'mercury' (a hawker of pamphlets) employed by Barber in much the same role as Morphew but, as Treadwell argues, was able to reach a different kind of market.[20] Edmund Curll makes an unexpected appearance on the title page of *A Meditation upon a Broom-Stick, and Somewhat Beside; of the Same Author's* (1710), an edition that, although not directly approved by Swift, has nonetheless a decent claim to authority.[21] A couple of names appear to be spurious: neither 'T. Cole' named on the title page of an edition of *Publick Spirit of the Whigs* (1714) nor 'William Coryton, Bookseller, at the Black-Swan on Ludgate Hill' from the imprints of *A Short Character of His Ex. T.E. of W.* (1711) appear in any of the records of the Stationers' Company or on the imprints of any other works from the period.[22] The 'Cole' edition reprinted the unexpurgated – and suppressed – first edition of *Publick Spirit* (hence the need for a false imprint) and was typographically very different from the several Barber editions that appeared that year. The identity of 'Coryton' has not been previously challenged, probably because of the imprint's beguiling detail; however, the name only appears on editions of *Short Character*, and while there were Black Swan bookshops in Paternoster Row (John Churchill) and without Temple Bar (Daniel Brown), none has been recorded on Ludgate Hill. Swift reported publication in December 1710 ('[i]t has been sent by dozens to several gentlemen's lodgings … but nobody knows the author or printer') and a few weeks later remarked that the work 'was first printed privately here; and then some bold cur ventured to do it publickly, and sold two thousand in two days'.[23] The pamphlet's libellous nature probably deterred both Barber and Morphew, but it is entirely possible that Swift knew the true identity of that 'bold cur'.[24] Finally, there were a handful or so of Swift's works that circulated with only the barest of imprints, if at all, a sign either of their ephemerality (as was the case with the so-called 'penny papers' of July 1712) or their likely offensiveness.

Tooke, Barber, Nutt, Morphew and the others were just a handful among the many hundreds that made up the London book trade in the first decade of the eighteenth century. During that decade 364 individuals became freemen (or, occasionally, freewomen) of the Stationers' Company, the primary livery company for the book trade, while 661 apprentices were bound to Company members, of whom 293 completed their terms.[25] Although book imprints identify dozens of booksellers and bookshops (191 individuals were listed on book imprints in 1709, of which 75 per cent were solely booksellers), there were doubtless many more whose modest means or type of trade meant that they were never visible on a title page.[26] In addition, there were hawkers and mercuries upon whom trade publishers evidently depended but whose relationship with the book trade was informal and changeable. There were almost 70 printing houses, some of which were sizeable businesses running multiple printing presses: such was the one owned by Barber, who was appointed printer to the city from 1709. Excluding jobbing printing and periodicals, these printing presses were producing probably between 1,000 and 1,500 printed titles per year to serve an estimated adult reading population of over 1.2 million, at least 10 per cent of whom were based in London.[27]

Swift's first encounters with printers and booksellers coincided with a period of significant change for the English book trade as a whole. For most of his early life, the regulation of the trade was based on the so-called 'Printing Act', first enacted in 1662, which, to a large extent, reapplied the terms of the 1637 Star Chamber decrees concerning printing. The number of printing houses (with a few exceptions, including that of the King's Printer) was not to exceed twenty; no one was to establish themselves as a printer without informing the Stationers' Company; the number of presses and apprentices any printer could have was strictly limited; all works were to be licensed by an authorized individual prior to publication; all new publications not covered by existing printing privileges were to be entered into the Stationers' Company's Register; all book imports were to come through London only; and only properly apprenticed booksellers were to sell books, in London and elsewhere. The post of Surveyor of the Presses was formally established shortly afterwards; its first (and, as it seems, only) appointee was Roger L'Estrange, who served in this capacity, with some breaks, until 1688. Despite the strict terms of the statute and L'Estrange's active prosecution of his role, the regulations were only haphazardly enforced. Plague and fire helped reduce the number of printing houses from almost sixty in the early 1660s to thirty-three by 1668 but the stipulated twenty remained hopelessly unattainable. Licensing, the primary mechanism for the state regulation of the printed word since the early sixteenth century, appears to have been more honoured in the breach than in the observance, although its evasion provided a useful premise for acting against objectionable publications. Finally, the proposed regulation of the provincial book trade was clearly unworkable. Nonetheless, the Act ensured that the Stationers' Company retained its long-time regulatory dominance over the English trade: printing was effectively restricted to London, York and the two universities; the Company's Register was granted legal status as a guarantor of publication rights; and the Company's officers retained the right to search for illicit books, even though L'Estrange felt that they achieved precious little in this role.[28]

The 1662 Act was intended as a temporary measure but, with no alternative statute proposed, it was simply renewed by successive Parliaments. It lapsed in 1679, an unintended victim of the politics surrounding the Popish Plot, but was reinstated in 1685; ten years later it lapsed again, for good. The most immediate effect of this second lapsing concerned the location, number or size of printing houses: with no statutory restrictions to deter them, printers quickly established themselves in provincial cities, while the number of printing houses in London began to increase. There was evidently some concern about the loss of a licensing system, and licensing was the centrepiece of an unsuccessful bill under discussion during 1695. But the lapsing hardly ushered in a new permissive era for print, as Ian Higgins reminds us in his chapter below.[29] Blasphemy, sedition, obscenity and libel remained crimes: only two years earlier a London printer had been executed for printing treasonable pamphlets, while in 1698 Parliament passed a Blasphemy Act to re-enforce the existing law.[30]

The lapsing of the Act, however, took place against a background of more profound economic and structural changes in the trade as a whole. These were in part a product of a general economic downturn as well as enduring political uncertainty in the aftermath of the Glorious Revolution, but they were also a consequence of a growing political and economic crisis within the Stationers' Company from the 1680s. In essence, the Company lost much of its authority as a lobbyist and as a regulator, and the status of the Company's Register became increasingly doubtful: the number of entries consequently plummeted in the late 1690s. Economic and political power was shifting away from the Company and its established, senior members to less formal groupings of younger, more financially astute booksellers.[31] This is not to say that the Company ceased to play a role in the trade: not only were there practical benefits associated with training and welfare but also membership provided the opportunity to become a shareholder of the lucrative 'English Stock' and thus profit from the Company's fiercely guarded right to print primers, psalters, psalmbooks, almanacs and schoolbooks.

The changing importance of the Company in these years is, to an extent, reflected in the careers of Tooke and Barber, both of whom became freemen of the Company in the mid 1690s. Tooke's father, Benjamin Sr, had served as Treasurer of the English Stock between 1687 and 1702, which probably explains the near-instantaneous elevation of Tooke Jr to the privileged ranks of the Company's livery within two months of his freedom.

Barber, in contrast, was not called to the livery until 1705, by which time he was establishing himself as a rising printer. Both took advantage of their membership of the Company, binding apprentices, securing shares in the English Stock and entering items in the Stationers' Register. Tooke had greater faith in the Register, entering several items during the 1690s and early 1700s, while Barber in contrast used it only after the passing of the Copyright Act in 1710. Tooke seems to have had a closer relationship with the Company than Barber: he was elected to the governing body of the Company in 1719, and although he did not serve as a senior officer, it may have been his relatively early death in 1723 that was the decisive factor. Barber was considered for a similar promotion just a month after Tooke, but was never appointed, and he does not seem to have actively sought office within the Company again.

For both men, their commercial success was dependent on key appointments outside the Company. Barber was appointed as city printer in 1709, a position he held until the 1720s. In 1711, both men secured the rights to print the *Gazette*; in 1712 they were appointed as Stationers to the Ordnance; and in the following year they were granted the reversion of the patent of the Queen's Printer. In each case, Swift's intercession seems to have been crucial, and it is striking that the two men, who do not otherwise seem to have shared business interests, were evidently brought together primarily and possibly solely by the relationship with Swift. After Swift's departure for Ireland and the fall of the government in 1714, both men carried on their careers, although Barber's Tory, if not Jacobite, sympathies forced him outside of the political mainstream and may, in part, have led to the Company's decision against him in 1719. Canny financial and political manoeuvrings during the 1720s, however, enabled him to embark on a highly successful political career, which eventually saw him serving as Lord Mayor in 1732–3. Barber's name appears on its last title-page imprint in 1725 and with it his career as an active printer and member of the Stationers' Company seems to have come to an end.[32]

The years 1701 to 1714 saw a number of attempts to develop new legislation concerning the book trade but the few laws that were enacted marked a decisive shift from the priorities of the regulatory regimes of the previous century. The first of these, the Copyright Act of April 1710, seems to have gone wholly unremarked upon by Swift, although its provisions had the potential to affect him directly. (He was, to be fair, in Dublin when it was passed.) The copyright of his works published prior to April 1710 was confirmed until 1731; the copyright of any subsequent publications was to last fourteen years, with an extension of a further fourteen years if he was still alive.[33] An entry in the Stationers' Register was required in order to claim copyright, and the legislation prompted a resurgence of registrations from across the trade. Some of the works involving Swift had already been entered in the Register – his editions of the second and third parts of Temple's *Miscellanea* had been entered to Ralph Simpson and Tooke in 1690 and 1701 respectively – but his works appear much more frequently after the Act, as both Tooke and Barber placed renewed faith in the Register's legal status. Tooke pointedly entered the fifth edition of *A Tale of a Tub* and *Miscellanies in Prose and Verse* on the very date that the Copyright Act was enacted, while Barber entered *The Examiner* in late 1710 and several of Swift's works subsequently.[34] In all cases, though, the works were entered in their publishers' names, and copyright resided with them rather than Swift: it is entirely possible that he was unaware that the works had been registered at all.[35]

Swift may have ignored, or been ignorant of, the Copyright Act and its implications, but he was alert to the other new development in the regulation of the printed word: taxation. In a letter to Johnson and Dingley in January 1711, he reported that the government was 'intending to tax all little printed penny papers a half-penny every half-sheet, which will utterly ruin Grub-street, and I am endeavouring to prevent it'.[36] That summer, almanacs became subject to a stamp duty; the following summer, this was also applied to newspapers and pamphlets.[37] Swift appears to have been unmoved by the taxation on almanacs but when the latter statute came into force on 1 August 1712 he lamented that 'Grubstreet is dead and gone … No more Ghosts or Murders now for Love or Money.' He claimed that he had 'plyed it pretty close the last Fortnight [that is, prior to 1 August], and publisht at least 7 penny Papers of my own, besides some of other Peoples'. David Woolley has identified these as *Peace and Dunkirk* and *Toland's Invitation to Dismal* (both poems), and five prose broadsides: *A Dialogue upon Dunkirk*; *It's Out at Last*; *A Hue and Cry after Dismal*; *Dunkirk Still in the Hands of the French*; and *A Letter from the Pretender*. Excepting *Dunkirk Still in the Hands of the French* (which does not survive), and *A Letter from the Pretender*, all were advertised in *The Examiner*, which suggests a possible association with Barber; however, none was entered in the Stationers' Register and several were very poorly printed. Either way, Swift clearly hastened them through the press in advance of the statute.[38]

We do not know when Swift first stepped into a London printing house. It may have been as early as the 1690s, to deliver a manuscript or read over proofs in connection with the Temple editions. However, prior to 1710 it was probably a relatively rare occurrence. Tooke had no presses and hired printers as necessary: whatever contracts he made left no trace in either imprints or Swift's correspondence.[39] Consequently, we are not sure who printed *Contests and Dissensions* (1701), or any of the first five editions of *Tale* (1704–10), although we can identify William Bowyer as the printer of *Miscellanies in Prose and Verse* (1711) and, at the other end of the spectrum (and wholly unconnected with Tooke or Barber), Swift's cousin, Dryden Leach, as the printer of the short-lived new *Tatler* to which Swift contributed an essay in early 1711.[40] Swift seems to have always dealt directly with Tooke and, as Ehrenpreis notes, developed a habit of coinciding publication with his own departure from London, which, if nothing else, meant he was unable to see any of those works through the final stages of printing.[41] *that's the story, anyway...*

This relation to the printing house dramatically changed once Swift began working with Barber, in part because a visit to his publisher was now also a visit to his printer, but also because the nature of his writing changed. Swift was not unused to composing works to be printed in short order, but he appears to have been the initiator in such cases. With *The Examiner* and the series of political works on behalf of the Tory ministry that followed, in contrast, Swift was regularly up against a deadline. *The Examiner* appeared every Thursday during Swift's editorship (November 1710 to June 1711) and the pressure to produce about two thousand words per week was, at times, considerable: 'O faith, if you knew what lies on my hands constantly, you would wonder to see how I could write such long letters', he wrote to Johnson and Dingley in December.[42] Variant readings in different copies of numbers 26 and 41 suggest that Swift was making corrections at press, or at least at very short notice.[43] Swift visited Barber's printing house on several occasions in the run-up to the publication of *Conduct* in November 1711; once the work was published, Swift's involvement only intensified. Barber visited him a few days after publication to say that demand was such that he 'must immediately print a second edition': Swift spent the following afternoon in the printing house 'adding something to the second edition' and incorporating suggestions from Harley. The next day, Barber returned to Swift to inform him that a third edition was now under way; again Swift had to make further changes, prompted by Harley. A fourth edition was in the press only a week after the first had appeared, and Swift was wearying: 'I have made some alterations in every edition, and it has cost me more trouble, for the time, since the printing than before.'[44] The demand for copies was such that Barber kept much of the text in standing type: corrections were made, lines reset and formes reimposed. Throughout, Swift was making amendments and additions, often in the printing house itself, while the pattern of errors across editions suggests that neither he nor any of the press-correctors had a chance to read proofs during these hectic days.[45]

No other work of Swift's from these years seems to have demanded so much of him in the printing house, although one other proved almost as challenging for Barber. *Conduct* had prompted some official concern – Morphew was called before Lord Chief Justice Parker in mid December – but nothing further happened.[46] In the case of *Publick Spirit* (1714), however, Morphew and Barber, and their servants, were arrested and interrogated about the publication. At the same time, and again over only a matter of days, significant changes were made to successive editions of *Publick Spirit*: a three-page passage touching on the Union was initially modified and then wholly excised. Swift was well aware of the arrests (he received £100 from Harley to cover the men's 'exigencys') and he may or may not have been consulted on these changes, but he seems to have stayed well clear of the printing house.[47] Despite Swift's later bravado about the apparently paltry sum offered to identify the author, the experience of seeing his printer interrogated for several days by the House of Lords and facing a formal trial must have shaken him: in a letter a few months later he wryly noted: 'So well protected are those who scribble for the Government.'[48]

Scholars have long learned to be sceptical of Swift's denials of authorship. For every work he acknowledged as his own in his correspondence (even if he rarely named them), there was another that he pretended was nothing to do with him. 'No-body knows who it is', he wrote to Johnson and Dingley about the identity of the editor of *The Examiner* in early 1711; 'It is not Prior; but perhaps it may be Atterbury.'[49] In January 1712, he was delighted when Barber brought to dinner a copy of *Some Advice Humbly Offer'd to the Members of the October Club*, 'which he said was sent him by an unknown hand; I commended it mightily; he never suspected me'.[50] Even when authorship was admitted, Swift might seek to distance himself from the act of publication: 'Some bookseller has raked up every thing I writ, and published it t'other day in one volume [*Miscellanies in Prose and Verse*]; but I know nothing of it, 'twas without my knowledge or consent …Took pretends he knows nothing of it, but I doubt he is at the bottom.'[51]

We should perhaps be similarly sceptical of how Swift characterized his relationship with Barber as his printer. In *Some Remarks on the Barrier Treaty* (1712), he described the experience of publishing *Conduct* in these terms: 'I stopt the Second Edition, and made all possible Enquiries among those who I thought could best inform me, in order to correct any Error I could hear of: I did the same to the Third and Fourth Editions, and then left the Printer to his liberty.'[52] Swift's claim that he, as author, had had sufficient power to halt printing on several occasions in order to ensure textual accuracy and that he only allowed Barber to resume control after the fourth edition is simply contrary to the facts: the press did not stop for Swift but rather Swift stopped, repeatedly, for the press. We should not, of course, overread a passage whose purpose was primarily to deny claims that Swift had falsified details in *Conduct*, but it is telling that the very next work that he sought to publish, *Some Advice*, was submitted to Barber anonymously – an assertion of authorial primacy that also distanced the author as far as possible from the printing house. Similarly, while Barber never betrayed him during the publishing of *Publick Spirit*, the very real dangers of being an author in the printing house may well explain why Swift adopted a similar subterfuge with Barber over the publication of *Some Free Thoughts upon the Present State of Affairs* in July 1714, although with much less success.[53] Swift's experiences with Barber between 1710 and 1714 were an object lesson in how little liberty an author might have in an early eighteenth-century London printing house.

Notes

1 Michael Treadwell, 'Swift's Relations with the London Book Trade to 1714', in Robin Myers and Michael Harris (eds.), *Author/Publisher Relations During the Eighteenth and Nineteenth Centuries* (Oxford Polytechnic Press, 1983), pp. 1–36.

2 TS, nos. 478–598 *passim*. David Woolley, 'The Canon of Swift's Prose Pamphleteering, 1710–1714, and *New Way of Selling Places at Court*', *SStud*, 3 (1988), 96–123 and endpaper, provides the fullest canon of Swift's writings between 1710 and 1714.

3 Treadwell, 'Swift', pp. 3–7; Karian, *Print and Manuscript*, p. 13.

4 Karian, *Print and Manuscript*, pp. 13–15; *CWJS*, vol. VIII, pp. 348–9.

5 Treadwell, 'Swift', pp. 4–6.

6 Treadwell, 'Swift', pp. 10–11.

7 Paul V. Thompson, and Dorothy Jay Thompson (eds.), *The Account Books of Jonathan Swift* (Newark: University of Delaware Press, 1984), pp. 64, 68–9, 116, 142, 146; Treadwell, 'Swift', p. 19; Karian, *Print and Manuscript*, p. 18.

8 *JSt* (1948), vol. I, p. 13; *CWJS*, vol. I, p. xxxiv; TS, nos. 2, 524; Treadwell, 'Swift', pp. 18–19.

9 Davis, *PW*, vol. VIII, pp. 123–4; Ellis, *Examiner*, pp. xxiii–xxiv; Ehrenpreis, *Swift*, vol. II, p. 406.

10 *JSt* (1948), vol. I, p. 141.

11 *Account Books*, pp. 121, 126, 130–1, 133, 153, 156; Treadwell, 'Swift', pp. 23–4; *CWJS*, vol. VIII, p. 328.

12 *JSt* (1948), vol. II, pp. 710 (s.v. 'Barber, John'), 759 (s.v. 'Morphew, John'); *CWJS*, vol. VIII, p. 329. Barber was later categorized as an 'ungrateful' friend: see Karian, *Print and Manuscript*, pp. 18–19.

13 See, for example, *JSt* (1948), vol. II, p. 464.

14 Tooke's name also appears on the editions of Temple prepared by Swift.

15 Karian, *Print and Manuscript*, p. 18.

16 *JSt* (1948), vol. II, pp. 391, 437.

17 *CWJS*, vol. VIII, p. 342.

18 Swift also used the term 'publisher' to refer to the preparation of a work for publication: 'I would not have you think of Steele for a publisher [of the *Miscellanies*]; he is too busy', Swift to Benjamin Tooke, 29 June 1710, Woolley, *Corr.*, vol. I, p. 282. He refers to himself consistently as 'Publisher' of Temple's posthumous works: see *CWJS*, vol. I, pp. 193, 199 and especially 203: 'I may hope to be allowed one Word in the Style of a *Publisher*, (an Office lyable to much Censure, without the least Pretension to Merit or to Praise').

19 D. F. McKenzie, 'The London Book Trade in the Later Seventeenth Century' (unpublished Sandars Lectures, Cambridge, 1976), 27–9; Michael Treadwell, 'London Trade Publishers 1675–1750', *The Library*, 6th ser., 4 (1982), 99–134; Treadwell, 'Swift', pp. 13, 15–16.

20 Treadwell, 'Swift', p. 21.

21 Stephen Karian, 'Edmund Curll and the Circulation of Swift's Writings', in *Münster* (2008), pp. 99–129.

22 Michael Treadwell, 'On False and Misleading Imprints in the London Book Trade, 1660–1750', in Robin Myers and Michael Harris (eds.), *Fakes and Frauds: Varieties of Deception in Print and Manuscript* (Winchester: St Paul's Bibliographies, 1989), pp. 29–46.

23 *JSt* (1948), vol. I, pp. 115, 148.

24 The work is not entered in the Stationers' Register.

25 Michael L. Turner, 'Personnel within the London Book Trades: Evidence from the Stationers' Company', in Michael F. Suarez SJ and Michael L. Turner (eds.), *The Cambridge History of the Book in Britain: Volume V 1695–1830* (Cambridge University Press, 2009), pp. 309–34, especially Tables 14.2–3, 14.7; Paula McDowell, *The Women of Grub Street: Press, Politics, and Gender in the London Literary Marketplace, 1678–1730* (Oxford: Clarendon Press, 1993), pp. 42–3.

26 Don-John Dugas, 'The London Book Trade in 1709 (Part One)', *Papers of the Bibliographical Society of America*, 95 (2001), 31–58 (p. 46). It is not exactly clear how Dugas distinguishes booksellers from printers or printer-booksellers.

27 Michael Treadwell, 'Lists of Master Printers: The Size of the London Printing Trade, 1637–1723', in Robin Myers and Michael Harris (eds.), *Aspects of Printing from 1600* (Oxford Polytechnic Press, 1987), pp. 141–70; Michael Treadwell, 'London Printers and Printing Houses in 1705', *Publishing History*,

7 (1980), 5–44; Michael F. Suarez SJ, 'Towards a Bibliometric Analysis of the Surviving Record', in *The Cambridge History of the Book in Britain: Volume V 1695–1830*, pp. 39–65, especially 40–3, 50–1; Michael F. Suarez SJ, 'Introduction', in *The Cambridge History of the Book in Britain: Volume V 1695–1830*, pp. 1–35, especially 5, 11. A basic search of *ESTC* for all items with a London imprint and dated between 1700 and 1709 inclusive yields over 17,500 titles, but this obviously includes duplicates and works of indeterminable date that are tentatively dated to '1700?'

28 Michael Treadwell, 'The Stationers and the Printing Acts at the End of the Seventeenth Century', in John Barnard, D. F. McKenzie and Maureen Bell (eds.), *The Cambridge History of the Book in Britain: Volume IV 1557–1695* (Cambridge University Press, 2002), pp. 755–76, especially 756–8, 765–7.

29 Treadwell, 'Printing Acts', pp. 770–3.

30 Paul Hopkins, 'Anderton, William (1663–1693)', *Oxford Dictionary of National Biography* (Oxford University Press), 2004, www.oxforddnb.com/view/article/68204 (accessed 16 July 2012); Mark Rose, 'Copyright, Authors and Censorship', in *The Cambridge History of the Book in Britain: Volume V 1695–1830*, pp. 118–31 (p. 127).

31 Treadwell, 'Printing Acts', pp. 773–5; Cyprian Blagden, *The Stationers' Company: A History 1403–1959* (London: George Allen & Unwin Ltd, 1960), pp. 172–7.

32 *JSt* (1948), vol. I, pp. 316, 320–1, 323; vol. II, p. 464; Treadwell, 'Swift', pp. 9–11, 22–3, 25–6; Michael Treadwell and Michael Turner, 'The Stationers' Company: Members of the Court, 1600–1830', unpublished printout, 1998; D. F. McKenzie (ed.), *Stationers' Company Apprentices 1701–1800* (Oxford Bibliographical Society, 1978), pp. 18, 352, 422–3; Michael Treadwell, 'John Barber' and 'Benjamin Tooke, Jr', unpublished notes; Nicholas Rogers, 'Barber, John (bap. 1675, d. 1741)', rev. *Oxford Dictionary of National Biography* (Oxford University Press, 2004), www.oxforddnb.com/view/article/37148 (accessed 16 July 2012). Under the custom of London, Barber had to be a member of one of the 'Great Twelve' Companies to serve as Lord Mayor, so he brought his formal relationship with the Stationers' Company to an end in 1732 by transferring to the Goldsmiths'.

33 8 Anne c. 21; John Feather, 'The Book Trade in Politics: The Making of the Copyright Act of 1710', *Publishing History*, 8 (1980), 19–44; John Feather, 'The English Book Trade and the Law, 1695–1799', *Publishing History*, 12 (1982), 51–75.

34 G. E. Briscoe Eyre (ed.), *A Transcript of the Registers of the Company of Stationers from 1640–1708 A.D.* 3 vols. (London, 1913–14), vol. III, pp. 375, 494; Treadwell, 'Swift', pp. 5–6, 11–12, 32–3; Stationers' Company, 'Register of Copies 1710 to 1746', p. 67, and *passim*. *CWJS*, vol. I, p. xxxiv n.7, gives the date of Tooke's entry as 16 April.

35 Swift clearly recognized the commercial value of one's right to a copy as his receipts to Tooke in 1701 and 1709 indicate; however, there is no evidence that he was aware of how Tooke registered his own rights within the trade:

see Woolley, *Corr.*, vol. I, pp. 145–6, 250–1. The copyright of Swift's works deserves further exploration, not least as the book trade, despite the 1710 Act, carried on believing that copyright was 'perpetual' until 1774.

36 *JSt* (1948), vol. I, pp. 177–8.

37 9 Anne c. 23; 10 Anne c. 19; Feather, 'Law', 53–5.

38 *JSt* (1948), vol. II, pp. 553–4; *CWJS*, vol. VIII, 19–23; David Woolley, '*A Dialogue Upon Dunkirk* (1712) and Swift's "7 Penny Papers"', in *Münster* (1993), pp. 215–23.

39 Treadwell, 'Swift', pp. 19–20.

40 Keith Maslen and John Lancaster (eds.), *The Bowyer Ledgers* (London: The Bibliographical Society; New York: The Bibliographical Society of America, 1991), no. 60; Treadwell, 'Swift', pp. 26–7; Treadwell, '1705', pp. 14–15, 26–7.

41 Treadwell, 'Swift', pp. 11–13, 19–20.

42 *JSt* (1948), vol. I, p. 136

43 Ellis, *Examiner*, p. lxiv. Ellis claims that, in each case, Swift visited the printing house the night before publication but it is not clear on what evidence he bases this.

44 *JSt* (1948), vol. II, pp. 386, 297, 423–4, 427–30; *CWJS*, vol. VIII, pp. 341–3.

45 *CWJS*, vol. VIII, pp. 344–6.

46 *CWJS*, vol. VIII, p. 343.

47 *CWJS*, vol. VIII, pp. 446–56. The authorities seem to have been oblivious to the potential value of the Register in identifying the publisher of a work: both *Conduct* and *Publick Spirit* were clearly entered to Barber.

48 Woolley, *Corr.*, vol. I, p. 602. Although a trial date for Barber was set, it never took place.

49 *JSt* (1948), vol. I, pp. 185, 209.

50 *JSt* (1948), vol. II, p. 468.

51 *JSt* (1948), vol. I, p. 203; cf. Swift to Tooke, 29 June 1710, and Tooke to Swift, 1 July 1720, in Woolley, *Corr.*, vol. I, 282–5. Ehrenpreis notes: 'Of course, not Tooke, but Swift was at the bottom of it' (*Swift*, vol. II, p. 423).

52 *CWJS*, vol. VIII, p. 134.

53 *CWJS*, vol. VIII, pp. 380, 480–2.

CHAPTER THREE

What Swift did in libraries

Paddy Bullard

Squeezing, sinking, forgetting

For Jonathan Swift, the moment of a printed text's creation is never very far from the period of its decay and destruction. 'Books, like Men their Authors,' says the narrator of *A Tale of a Tub*, 'have no more than one Way of coming in to the World, but there are ten Thousand to go out of it, and return no more.'[1] Of the many deaths that a book might die, the speediest are domestic. Printed pages are martyred daily as firelighters, toilet paper and linings for pie dishes. But Swift's concern with what he called the 'duration' of literary compositions makes him imagine more lingering ends than these. A book might pass away because the language in which it is written is itself an impermanent medium. Swift hoped his project to establish an academy for ascertaining the English tongue would help ensure that 'old Books will yet be always valuable according to their intrinsic Worth, and not thrown aside on Account of unintelligible Words and Phrases'.[2] Still worse than linguistic obsolescence, however, is the fate of modern books – similar, perhaps, to that of the Struldbruggs in *Gulliver's Travels* – that escape recycling only to be buried alive in libraries: '*The Duration of which, like that of other* Spiders *Webs*,' says one of the Ancients in 'The Battel of the Books', '*may be imputed to their being forgotten, or neglected, or hid in a Corner*.'[3] The volumes of the ancients ought to be tokens of the endurance of fame, monuments to their authors more lasting than brass. But in modern libraries the surviving copy of an unwanted book becomes a wretched advertisement of its having 'gone out of the world' – an obscene reminder of its loss of readership, and thus of life.

Swift's susceptibility to reflections like these is one reason, perhaps, for the peculiar care that he took to record and preserve his own 'little library' of about 600 works. His activities as a reader and collector of books are unusually well documented for so prominent a writer. A series of autograph catalogues and shelf-lists survive, along with 100 or so books from his library that are still locatable today. A relatively high proportion of these contain marginal annotations, abstracts and other readers' marks.[4] This chapter looks for correlations between the archival evidence on one the hand, and that of Swift's writings about libraries in his satirical works on the other. The most memorable of these writings appears in the second of three satires in the *Tale of a Tub* miscellany (1704), titled 'A Full and True Account of the Battel Fought last Friday, Between the Ancient and the Modern Books in St. James's Library'; and in part 2, chapter 7 of *Gulliver's Travels* (1726). In his writings Swift tends to treat libraries as sites of literary conflict and cultural allegiance, of display, neglect and decay. But the evidence of his own collection suggests that he also felt the value of books as commodities, keepsakes and gifts, and that his sense of their personal associations could outweigh more pressing literary concerns. His was the working library of a scholar and public man. And yet it served to control even Swift's bristling antagonisms within a sociable, domestic and conversational sphere.[5]

Modern libraries typically become objects of satire in Swift's writings when they grow too large. His general concern is that the proliferation of printed texts in the modern age has been attended by a corresponding decline in literary quality – an anxiety probably inherited from the writings of his patron Sir William Temple.[6] In Swift's hands, however, this problem is deepened by ethical and political considerations. From an ethical perspective, it is dishonourable to own more books than one can master, merely for the sake of display.[7] From a public perspective, overgrown libraries have invidious implications as well. 'If Books and Laws continue to increase as they have done for fifty Years past,' he worries in *Thoughts on Various Subjects* (1727), 'I am in some Concern for future Ages, how any Man will be learned, or any Man a Lawyer.'[8] This connection between the redundant proliferation of books and of laws is made again in *Gulliver's Travels*. In Brobdingnag 'no Law ... must exceed in Words the Number of Letters in their Alphabet' – and (in the following paragraph) 'their Libraries are not very large'.[9] What ensures the liberty of the Brobdingnagians is that all kinds of civil knowledge are adequately compassable by both magistrate and citizen. So their modest libraries and their laconic laws both signify contempt for confined, specialized information that Swift recognizes as an attitude symptomatic of virtue. One consequence of the modern proliferation of books is the fragmentation of knowledge about the state, which has a further impact upon the freedom of individuals to contribute actively to the commonwealth.

As one would expect when dealing with Swift, these ethical and polit-ical concerns about the multiplication of books also have an imaginative and obsessive dimension. Swift's aversion to overgrown libraries is linked with a claustrophobic repulsion at the thought of being smothered by the weight of redundant print, or of being 'squeezed' by crowds of books. In the closing pages of his voyage to the Houyhnhnms Gulliver bravely acknowledges that 'Writers of Travels, like *Dictionary*-Makers, are sunk into Oblivion by the Weight and Bulk of those who come last, and there-fore lie uppermost'.[10] It is only Gulliver's deluded conviction that he is writing for 'the PUBLICK GOOD' that spares him from mortification at this reflection. In a more personal vein, when Swift expresses doubts in his 'Character of Primate Marsh' about the Archbishop's reputation for pro-found learning ('neither can it easily be disproved'), he does so by using a characteristic metaphor of jammed-in compression. It seems likely that this metaphor evokes Marsh's huge library as much as it does his scholarly abilities:

> An old rusty iron-chest in a banker's shop, strongly lockt, and wonderful heavy, is full of gold; this is the general opinion, neither can it be disproved, provided the key be lost, and what is in it be wedged so close that it will not by any motion discover the metal by chinking.[11]

Swift requires spaciousness of mind in the learned. He prefers liberty of access and simplicity of presentation in both the physical arrangement of books and in the mental arrangement of thoughts. In this sense his opin-ions have a certain correspondence with the grandly proportioned librar-ies being built at this time by Thomas Burgh at Trinity College, Dublin (1705–32), by Christopher Wren at Trinity College, Cambridge (completed 1695), by Nicholas Hawksmoor at All Souls College, Oxford (1716–20), or by Dr George Clark at Christ Church, Oxford (1717–72).[12] At least they will prevent squeezing. 'I hate a crowd where I have not an easy place to see and be seen', Swift writes to Bolingbroke and Pope:

> A great Library always makes me melancholy, where the best Author is as much squeezed, and as obscure, as a Porter at a Coronation. In my own little library, I value the compilements of Grævius and Gronovius, which make thirty-one volumes in folio (and were given me by my Lord Bolingbroke) more than all my books besides; because whoever comes into my closet, casts his eyes immediately upon them, and will not vouchsafe to look upon Plato or Xenophon.[13]

Swift's irony is not easy to follow in this passage. He seems to imply grati-tude for Bolingbroke's bulky gifts because they make his little collection

feel like a part of a 'great Library'. But he also finds it absurd that they
eclipse his classic volumes. Perhaps he feels that by monopolizing the
attention of browsers these pompous folios somehow free the texts of
Plato and Xenophon from their obligations to potential readers, and from
the squeeze of the lower shelves.

Swift made these remarks to Pope and Bolingbroke in 1729, but he had
worked through some of their implications twenty-five years earlier in 'The
Battel of the Books'. This short satire is his most thorough exploration
of the symbolic potential of libraries. The battle between the partisans of
ancient and of modern literature referred to in its title is maintained on
one side by 'resolution' and 'courage', and on the other 'by the greatness
of their Number, upon all Defeats, affording continual Recruits' – that
is, once again, by the endless proliferation of copies of modern books.[14]
There has been a population explosion among modern authors, who
find themselves as squeezed as the proverbial court porter. The hostilities
described in the 'Battel' are traced back to a land grab at the top of Mount
Parnassus – although in the library at St James's Palace, where the actual
battle takes place, ancient authors suffer as sadly as the moderns from lack
of room:

> *Virgil* was hemm'd in with *Dryden* on one side, and *Withers* on the other
> … Here a solitary *Antient*, squeezed up among a whole Shelf of *Moderns*,
> offered fairly to dispute the Case … But these denied the premises.[15]

This passage corresponds with another in the 'Preface' to the *Tale of a Tub*,
in which the hack-narrator notices how clichéd protestations about the
volume of trash produced by modern presses are often made by the authors
of overlong books. He illustrates the observation with an anecdote about
a man of girth who complains of being squeezed by the crowd watching a
mountebank in Leicester Fields: '*At last, a* Weaver *that stood next him could
hold no longer: A Plague confound you* (said he) *for an over-grown Sloven;
and who (in the Devil's Name) I wonder, helps to make up the Crowd half
so much as your self?… Bring your own Guts to a reasonable Compass (and
be d—n'd) and then I'll engage we shall have room enough for us all.*'[16] The
point is a good one, for all the spittle with which Swift makes it. Polemical
books (or polemical people) who puff themselves up with grievances make
an imposition on the world that is out of all proportion to any imposition
made upon them. Like his Scriblerian friends, Swift was deeply concerned
with the instrumentality of writing. He joked repeatedly about the intention of satire to accuse and to reform, and about the infinite capacity of its
objects for self-indemnification. The library in 'The Battel of the Books'

represents in its physical form all of that aggression and all of that recalci-
trance. It is an allegory of outrage frozen in vellum and calfskin.

Images of squeezing and crowding are one dimension of a larger scheme
of spatial imagination that informs Swift's satire in 'The Battel of the
Books'. Modern writings are contrasted with ancient literature in terms
of how they negotiate a matrix of vertical cases and horizontal shelves.
The scheme is a little obscure, because Swift is representing cultural circulation using images of what is really static space. So typically the books
of the ancients are small and nimble – probably Swift is thinking of the
popular 'petits Elzeviers' editions of the classics – whereas the moderns
are bulky and slow – like Bolingbroke's Grævius and Gronovius.[17] In the
world of the 'Battel' bodily freedom stands in for certain virtues of *anci-
enneté* – for politeness and decorum, easiness and wit. Ancient discipline
contrasts with the disorderliness of the moderns: one cause of the battle, we are told, is 'a strange Confusion of Place among all the *Books* in
the Library'.[18] In real life the keeper of the library at St James's Palace,
the arch-modern Richard Bentley, was notorious for his failure to restore
good order to the royal collection during the period of his office. Here
Swift has a local object for his satire.[19] The disorder of the Moderns is
also connected with their illiberal urge to control the circulation of books
within the library, and with their own tendency to inertia. '*Æsop*' is one
of the ancient texts treated barbarously by Bentley, who has 'chained him
fast among a Shelf of *Moderns*'.[20] The moderns are themselves held down
by their weight: 'For, being light-headed, they have in Speculation, a wonderful Agility, and conceive nothing too high for them to mount; but in
reducing to Practice, discover a mighty Pressure about their Posteriors and
their Heels.'[21] When the violence of the battle finally begins, it seems to
come as a counter-effect of the disorderly constraint in which modern
libraries were allegedly kept. It is impossible to mistake the relish with
which Swift depicts the literary slaughter of the engagement itself. Homer
lifts Perrault out of his saddle and hurls him at Fontenelle, 'with the same
Blow dashing out both their Brains', and so on.[22] But it is important to
note that the excitements of the fighting are not the occasion of Swift's
satire – violence is not its point.[23] Indeed, after the dense inventiveness
with which Swift describes the escalation of hostilities, the battle itself is
a routine exercise in mock-heroic pastiche. Swift perhaps signals a lack of
authorial interest by inserting so many mock lacunae ('*His pauca desunt*',
etc.) into this final section. This is because the violence of the 'Battel of
the Books' refers back to a more powerful ideal of Ancient pre-eminence
and peaceful (though strenuous) liberty. This basic principle – of cultural

[margin note:] Aldus Manutius too, or Maittaire?

[margin note:] So boring

violence contained by a broader eirenicism – can also be detected in the remains of Swift's own library.

Collecting, judging, gifting

Swift's personal library of about 600 volumes was a low-key affair compared with the prodigious institutional book hoards that were springing up all around him at the beginning of the eighteenth century. He had first-hand experience of one particularly interesting new library: as Dean of St Patrick's Cathedral he sat *ex officio* on the board of the Episcopal collection founded for public use by Archbishop Marsh in 1701. Swift was present at the annual visitation of the library's 'Guardians and Govenors' for 1718, and attended ten further meetings up to 1736, the year of his last visitation.[24] As Swift must have seen, institutional libraries expanded quickly by absorbing personal collections – in the case of Marsh's library, the 10,000-volume accumulation of Bishop Edward Stillingfleet (for whom Richard Bentley had acted as librarian), along with those of Marsh's first librarian Élie Bouhéreau, that of Marsh himself, and later that of Bishop John Stearne.[25] These private collections were in turn swollen by what became at the end of the seventeenth century an increasingly efficient trade in used books.[26] Swift thought that his own library was just imposing enough 'to make a shew as a Dean of St Patricks should'.[27] In fact it contained roughly the same number of titles as the collections of his friends Alexander Pope (about 600 or 700 titles, 176 of which have survived) and William Congreve (659 titles).[28] Jacob Tonson judged Congreve's library to be 'genteel & well chosen', so there is every reason to consider Swift's collection similarly adequate.

A degree of modesty was prudent, however, since the Dean who preceded him at St Patrick's, his friend Stearne, had gathered one of the most important private collections of printed books in Ireland, numbering some 7,000 volumes – one that Swift could hardly hope to rival.[29] Archbishop William King, Swift's principal patron in the Church of Ireland, was another voracious bibliophile whose collection of 7,160 books (at his death) eventually went to the diocesan library at Cashel, Co. Tipperary.[30] Stearne was himself a close ally of King's, and lamented their shared fate as 'book-worms'. On one occasion he begged the Archbishop to diagnose 'the cause and remedies of that disease which inclines men to buy more books than they can have much use for'.[31] Swift was no help. He had a running joke while resident in London that the wealthy Stearne should give him fifty or a hundred pounds 'for books, which I will lay out for you, if you will give me directions'.[32] Stearne was understandably reluctant to give another man the pleasure of spending his money, but Swift was determined that he should see it frittered one way or another. 'If you will not use me as your book-buyer,' he insisted in 1708, 'make use of [the collector and diplomat] Sir Andrew Fountain, who sends you his humble service, and will carry over a cargo as big as you please toward the end of summer.'[33] Fountaine was already working in this capacity – through Swift's mediation – for Archbishop King in the purchase of a valuable Talmud.[34]

This urge for vicarious collecting had abated by the time of Swift's friendship with the most extravagant bibliophile of his day, Edward Harley, second Earl of Oxford. Harley employed James Gibbs for the 'building and furnishing [of] a Vatican at Wimpole' to accommodate a collection of printed books that numbered 12,000 in 1717 and about 50,000 volumes by the time of Oxford's death in 1741.[35] As the correspondence of Harley's librarian Humphrey Wanley indicates, this collection was more accessible to visiting scholars than the libraries of colleges (or of the monarch at St James's).[36] Once again Swift invoked Fountaine's expertise when Oxford asked him to look out for purchasable collections of early Irish coins.[37] But he was able to oblige personally when Oxford asked to borrow Prideaux's *Marmora Oxoniensis*. Swift's copy of this book contained scholarly MS emendations by an Oxford epigraphist, one 'Doctor Mills, who it seems was very famous in that kind of literature'.[38] Harley wanted the copy for his protégé Michael Maittaire, who was preparing a new edition of the work. Maittaire never returned it, however, and a copy of the Prideaux edition, possibly Swift's, appears in the posthumous auction catalogue of his library.[39] The other major private collection to which Swift contributed was that of his friend the physician Dr Richard Mead. A six-volume set of Swift's *Works* (1737–8), characteristically inscribed in 1739 to 'The Very Learned Richard Mead, M.D. by the supposed Author', is now in the Hunterian Library at Glasgow University.[40] So Swift was connected with several of the most important private libraries of his time. But he seems finally to have been more interested in asserting his independence as a book collector, on however ordinary a scale, than in using the libraries of others.

On 19 August 1715, soon after taking up residence at the Deanery of St Patrick's, Swift made a manuscript catalogue of his books.[41] It lists 474 titles, running to 659 volumes on his shelves. When the library was sold in February 1746 the printed catalogue itemized about the same number of books – 450 titles, 657 volumes.[42] But there had been considerable fluctuation in the library's contents over the last three decades of Swift's life.

From a variety of sources, including a second shelf-list made by John Lyon in 1742, we know of approximately 165 titles that passed through Swift's study, or through his hands, without ending up in the 1745 sale catalogue. There are therefore some 615 titles that we can associate more or less closely with Swift's library, although only half of that number belong to the core of the collection, present in 1715 and in 1742. For perhaps one sixth of the 615-item total there is some evidence of Swift having inscribed, corrected, summarized or otherwise marked the printed text.[43] This is a high proportion – we must go back to the antiquary John Dee (1527–1609) to find a writer of comparable standing who left so many traces upon his books. From the numbers alone it is clear that Swift was an unusually active reader.[44] This activity often involved a kind of conversation with the text written upon the printed page. The tone of that conversation was often indignant or otherwise aggressive – the anti-Scottish invective of his notes on Clarendon ('Cursed hellish Scots!' – 'Greedy Scotch rebellious dogs' – 'Diabolical Scots forever', etc.) is not untypically virulent. But this preliminary assessment requires much qualification.

The habit of writing on his reading was one that Swift seems only to have developed late in life, so we must be cautious about taking his most violently indignant annotations as evidence of lifelong habits. Nearly all of the surviving examples of Swift's annotations belong to a brief period in the late 1720s and 1730s. There is no extant evidence of Swift marking his own books (except to autograph them) before 1719.[45] We know from a list of reading that he made while still a member of Sir William Temple's household that he abstracted four weighty historical folios in 1697, and a fifth in 1698.[46] But these abstracts seem to have taken the form of scholarly notes and extracts on detached papers. They are distinct from the critical 'judgements' that Swift inscribed in a few of his books during the 1720s.[47]

The surviving examples of these *judicia* suggest that Swift had a rather formal solicitude for his books, an officious desire that they should do justice to their subjects, and that justice should be done to them in turn. By calling them *judicia* – a word associated by the Humanists with *exempla* and *sententiae*, collectable sayings by authoritative men – Swift indicates an expectation that his comments will be read and transcribed by future readers.[48] Two themes predominate in this class of manuscript note. The first is Swift's assumption of the role of ultimate censor: he is concerned above all with judging his authors' capacity for judgement. Reading Herodotus in 1720, Swift admires the historian for the absolute equity with which he treats both Greek and barbarian. He is especially appreciative of the discretion with which Herodotus leaves learned readers to draw out (*hau-rire*) latent wisdom from the narrative. Jean Bodin's *Six livres de la repub-lique* (1576) is commended in 1725 for 'setting the Arguments on both Sides of the Question in the strongest Light' – although the author almost always judges wrong, in Swift's opinion. Again, Peter Heylin's *History of the Presbyterians* (1670) is characterized by a vehemence that Swift decides is entirely pardonable: 'His partiality appears chiefly in setting the actions of the Calvinists in the strongest light, without equally dwelling on those of the other side.'[49] These remarks show Swift practising a form of reading that was investigative and ultimately forensic. A second, related theme is criticism of the perversion of his authors' judgements by pro-monarchical sentiment. Jean Bodin's idea of a 'Royall Monarchy' is dismissed by Swift as 'visionary, unless every Country were sure to have always a good King', while Peter Heylin, unable to rise above received opinion in the 1670s, 'had too high notions of regal power, led by the common mistake of the term *supreme magistrate*'.[50] Towards the end of the 1720s, however, this sort of measured assessment of pro-monarchical argument gave way to an extreme, sometimes monarchomachic rhetoric concerning the morality of princes. This kind of inscription tends to be located not on the flyleaves, but in the margins of Swift's books.

During the late 1720s and 1730s Swift reads several books that are concerned in one way or another with kings, and finds them a consist-ent provocation for written comment. In 1710 he acquired a copy of *A Collection of Several Statutes ... Relating to High Treason* (1709) and, as Ian Higgins has observed, 'it can be assumed that he knew what it meant to imagine the death of his sovereign, [to] call in question his sovereign's right to the throne' – as well as what it meant to stop just short of these actions.[51] In fact Swift's most characteristic technique as an annotator was to skip over such treasonous thoughts, and to execrate not his current sovereign but the whole species of monarchs. The most violent attacks on the memory of a British king were written in Swift's copy of Herbert's *Life of Henry VIII*, where this 'Brute of a King' (569) is accused above all of acting true to his kind: Henry is 'A Dog, a true Kin(g)'; 'An impudent perjured true King'; 'Dog, Villain, <u>King</u>, Viper Devil Monster'; he cor-rupts Parliament 'As all Rogues of Kings do'.[52] In Swift's annotations to Davila's *Civil Wars*, Henri III of France is 'a false perjur'd Rogue as most Kings are'.[53] Similarly, in his much reread copy of *History of the Rebellion*, Swift finds unendurable Clarendon's frequent references to the 'word' or the 'honour of a king': 'never to be relied upon', Swift comments; 'usually

interesting list ↗

good for nothing'; 'how long is that phrase to last?'[54] By generalizing his reflections on royal hypocrisy Swift makes a mitigating gesture that really intensifies – no individual king is to be blamed, since monarchs are categorically vicious. This is a rhetorical move that corresponds with his refusal elsewhere to condemn individuals who belong to a corrupt class: 'I am no more angry with [Walpole]', he tells Pope in 1725, 'th[a]n I was with the Kite that last week flew away with one of my Chickins and yet I was pleas'd when one of my Servants shot him two days after.'[55] In a letter to William Pulteney dated 12 May 1735, Swift argued with similar irony that the desire for arbitrary power is universal in monarchs: 'as proper an object to their appetites as a wench to an abandoned young fellow, or wine to a drunkard'.[56] In the marginalia of Swift's copy of Clarendon, Charles I is no exception to such rules: 'What king doth not love [arbitrary power], and endeavour at it?'[57] The generalization of royal vice also sets up a favourite joke of Swift's: the making of an ironic exception for the living monarch. Thus in the censored monarchomachic passage from *On Poetry: A Rapsody* (1733) Swift instructs his reader:

> ... now go search all Europe round
> Among y[e] savage Monsters crown'd
> With Vice polluting every Throne
> I mean all Kings except our own ...

Similarly, when Philippe de Commines decides that an unwise prince is God's greatest plague on a realm, Swift writes in the margin 'Where can the[y] find a wise one? except K George 2[d]'; and when Davila says that Henri III was by nature above vengefulness, Swift admires this 'good thoroughpac'd Lye, like K. George's mentioning his own mercifull Disposition'.[58] The regularity of Swift's anti-monarchical marginalia across several volumes gives it a ritual quality, as though he were leafing through his books looking for opportunities to perform it. Moreover, the consistency of their wording suggests that Swift's most indignant annotations were written at around the same time – probably at some point during the second half of the 1720s or the early 1730s. It seems that Swift found in the pages of his personal library a textual site just secure enough to bear anti-monarchical inscriptions that were too dangerous for him to make in any other kind of papers, either published or private.

So the first impression given by Swift's marginalia is that the Dean went to his library to do literary combat: that his books were for battles, sometimes as sites for conflict, sometimes as virtual participants in the fighting. But closer study of the catalogues and surviving volumes from the library indicates that literary aggression was seldom a rhetorical end in itself. Swift is sometimes doubtful about the practical effectiveness of satire, and sometimes he likes to think of his own writings as performing certain kinds of speech act: he often thinks of them as being designed to cut, to wound or otherwise to dissect their objects.[59] But in the case of Swift's private marginalia, any possibility of directly touching the object of indignation is removed. The inscription can only have the most local of effects, since only Swift, or those most close to him, would ever read it. The performance of cultural violence that is traceable in these sources only makes sense, in fact, within contexts of personal intimacy and coterie allegiance that effectively contain Swift's aggression. During the last two decades of his life, the years of Swift's greatest activity in his library, the purpose of that library was as much to confirm and commemorate friendships as it was to provide the Dean with reading (or fuming) matter. We have seen already that some 165 titles were removed from Swift's library at the Deanery between 1715 and 1742, almost a third of the collection. Twenty-seven titles in the 1715 catalogue are marked as gifts either made or intended, the great majority of them to named persons. There is evidence of around sixty-seven titles in Swift's library having been given or received as presents; thirty-five of these gift volumes bear some form of surviving inscription, and at least thirteen of them also contain Swift's notes or reading marks. This high correlation between gifted and annotated volumes suggests the containment of aggressive reading within more broadly sociable practices. One can only speculate on the number of similarly annotated examples that have been lost – there has been roughly a one-in-six survival rate of identifiable copies from Swift's library since its dispersal – although it is also true that an autographed association copy is more likely to survive than an unmarked volume from the collection of a celebrated author.

There is evidence that some copies were gifted and regifted within Swift's circle, and that the practice served to memorialize networks of friendship stretching across generations. This is the case with two especially interesting titles that were only briefly in Swift's possession. First is a copy of his friend Thomas Parnell's translation of *Homer's Battle of the Frogs and Mice* (1717) that is now in the Dyce Collection at the Victoria and Albert Museum, London.[60] An inscription on the flyleaf records that it was the gift of the author to Swift, but Swift seems to have passed it on promptly to Esther Johnson – her autograph appears in the top right corner of the title page. This pattern of regifting association copies extended through Swift's most intimate circle. After her death in 1728, books from Esther Johnson's library passed to her companion Rebecca

Dingley, and Hermann J. Real has argued that thirteen of these volumes
were inherited in turn by Swift's and Dingley's executor Dr John Lyon,
eventually appearing in his 1742 shelf-list of Swift's library (but not in the
1745 auction catalogue) as 'More Books added M^{rs} E:J'.[61] A second example of regifting is Johnson's copy (now in private hands) of Pope's *Rape
of the Lock*.[62] Underneath Johnson's undated name on the title page is a
second autograph of Swift's friend Lady Acheson of Market Hill, dated
1729.[63] Since Johnson left no specific instructions about this or any other
volume in her will, it is likely that it was Swift who passed the book,
with all its Scriblerian associations, onto an important female intimate
of his later years. These discreet inscriptions do suggest, however, some
mutual desire to downplay their significance. In other gifts of books
Swift insisted that 'my name and ex dono' should be marked clearly at
the front of the volume, and we know from John Lyon that when Esther
Johnson gave books to the Dean, he 'distinguish'd every Book she gave
him – '*Esther Johnson*'s Gift to *Jonath: Swift*'.[64] The inscriptions are simpler here. Formal cases of the double gifting of books in and out of the
Deanery library include a 1636 Elzevir Virgil given to Swift by the wit
Anthony Henley. It was reinscribed by Swift's cousin Martha Whiteway
on 26 February 1738/9 when she passed it on in turn to his young relation
William Swift.[65] Another ramified example of bibliographic exchange is
the copy of Roland Fréart's *Parallele de l'architecture antique et de la mod-
erne* (1702) given to Swift by Richard Boyle, third Earl of Burlington,
on 26 June 1726, and inscribed: 'I give this book to Dr. Jonathan Swift,
Dean of St. Patrick's, Dublin; in order to constitute him Director of
Architecture in Ireland, especially upon my own Estate in that Kingdom
… Witness: A. Pope.'[66] In January 1738 Swift passed the volume on to the
Irish architect, portraitist and bibliophile Francis Bindon, 'hereby del-
egating him Director of Architecture through all Europe'. In these and
several other cases it is the repetition of the act of giving that deepens the
significance of each presentation – the earlier exchanges gaining as much
from the process retrospectively as the latter do immediately.

A high proportion of the books that Swift either received or donated
as gifts bear significant inscriptions in the form of *judicia*, corrections or
marginalia. The numbers suggest once more that when Swift marked up
his books he tended to have friends in mind rather than enemies, however
aggressive those markings may appear. Of the twenty-nine titles in the
library that we know to have been presents to the Dean from friends or
associates, all but four can be traced today. Of these twenty-five surviving
gifts, nine carry significant inscriptions by Swift – more than a third of

the surviving total.[67] Thomas Carte's *Life of Ormonde* (1735–6) was one of four titles both given (in this case by the author) and inscribed in the year 1735–6. It is a particularly interesting copy because it contains Swift's usual anti-monarchical generalizations (such as his characteristic 'As all kings do' motif) in a gift from a prominent Jacobite – this was an association that Swift usually took pains to render untraceable. A similarly high proportion of books given by Swift to his friends contain some form of significant marking. Of forty-two titles that are known to have been presents from Swift, some twenty survive today. Eleven of those twenty copies contain significant marking, more than half of the total.[68] Swift demanded tolerance of his recipients. There is scurrilous marginalia in the copies of Burnet's *History*, of Davila's *Wars of France* and of Howell's *Ancient and Present England*, which was given to an unsuspecting Mary Harrison (who married his relative and editor Deane Swift) in 1736. All three contain references to, among other things, irregular sexual practices.

[margin handwritten note: censorious / (ad to / this / paragraph]

So there was a (high proportion) of inscribed copies associable with Swift's library that were gifts to or from friends. Some of them carry inscriptions of a politically hazardous or otherwise private character. There is a significant incidence of regifting to and from the collection. And we know that Swift sometimes wrote marginalia in books belonging to his friends – a practice consistent with these patterns of donation and exchange – although only a single example of such inscription actually survives: the copy of Bishop Burnet's *History of his Own Time* in the Lansdowne Library at Bowood. The book was given by its original owner, Swift's guardian John Lyon, to Lord Shelburne in 1768. In an accompanying letter Lyon recalls Swift warning him: 'I am spoiling your books … but I cannot help remarking this fellow. I write only with a pencil; so that you may rub it out, when you please.'[69] A picture emerges of Swift writing upon his reading in a milieu of coterie exchange and intimate familiarity.

This conclusion about the essentially sociable uses to which Swift put his library is also supported by what his circle is known to have done with their printed copies of Swift's own writings. A wide range of documents show how Swift's friends kept copies of his printed works that had been censored or otherwise altered for the press. Swift encouraged them to make manuscript emendations to those copies, using original readings that he provided himself. The proliferation of emended copies of the first edition of *Gulliver's Travels* is one well-known instance of para-textual transmission that involved the marking of books within this sort of coterie setting.[70] Stephen Karian has traced clear patterns of author-derived manuscript emendation in printed copies of three of Swift's major later

poems, and these provide further evidence of such sociable practices.[71]
When Swift and his friends marked up the books in their libraries they
were leaving half-hidden traces of literary practices that signalized their
intimacy and allegiance.

Reading, shelving

We have seen that Swift was friendly with some of the most acquisitive
bibliophiles of his day, but that he shared with them neither the inclination nor the resources to hoard large numbers of volumes. His practice as
a book collector is characterized by open-handedness, and by his library's
service to the business of friendship. These positive aspects of Swift's attitude to book collecting are involved, however, with other tendencies. His
willingness to part with his books suggests at once a sense of their value
and a spartan reluctance to be encumbered with such possessions. This
reluctance is connected in turn with a traditionally philosophical preference for spoken language over its material traces in written texts, and
with the polite preference of the *honnête homme* for spontaneous wit over
studied writing.[72] There are several currents of opinion detectable in and
around Swift's libraries, both fictional and real, and they flow in different
directions. Swift's thoughts about libraries were complicated, but that is
not to say that they were incoherent. Indeed, their imaginative integrity
is demonstrated, two and an half decades after 'The Battel of the Books',
in one brief episode of *Gulliver's Travels*, where Swift's scruples about the
ordering of books take on their most positive form.

Of the several libraries described in his works, it is the royal collection at Brobdingnag in book 2 of *Gulliver* that occupies most shelf space.
The King of Brobdingnag's books fill a gallery twelve hundred feet long
by Gulliver's report. And yet despite its gigantic scale this is almost as
modest a collection as Swift's own. Here at last is a library proportioned
to the capacities of its users. The number of books in the collection, we
are told, 'does not amount to above a thousand volumes', even though
the Brobdingnagians 'have had the art of printing, as well as the Chinese,
time out of mind'. As it happens Gulliver does not appreciate the elegance
and economy of Brobdingnagian librarianship. This failure is part of his
general incomprehension of the giants' generous simplicity, which he sees
as a symptom of 'confined education' and 'narrow principles and views'.
He is baffled by the King's refusal to be told the science of making gun-
powder, and by his response when told that 'there were several thousand
Books among us written upon the *Art of Government*; it gave him (directly

contrary to my Intention), a very mean Opinion of our Understandings'. Brobdingagian culture has resisted print's natural tendency towards redundant multiplication, and it has done so out of simple prudence rather than backwardness.

There is something typically compulsive about the way Swift imagines the vertical and horizontal shelving matrix in the library at Brobdingnag, as there was in his depiction of the library at St James's Palace. The peculiarity in *Gulliver's Travels* is that the physical awkwardness of negotiating high book cases and extensive shelves is transferred, by the logic of diminished scale that controls all of Gulliver's experiences in Brobdingnag, from the wall of the library to the page of the printed text:

> The Queen's Joyner had contrived in one of *Glumdalclitch*'s Rooms a Kind of wooden Machine five and twenty Foot high, formed like a standing Ladder; the Steps were each fifty Foot long: It was indeed a moveable Pair of Stairs, the lowest End placed at ten Foot Distance from the Wall of the Chamber. The Book I had a Mind to read was put up leaning against the Wall. I first mounted the upper Step of the Ladder, and turning my Face towards the Book, began at the Top of the Page, and so walking to the Right and Left about eight or ten Paces according to the length of the Lines, till I had gotten a little below the Level of mine Eyes; and then descending gradually till I came to the Bottom; After which I mounted again, and began the other Page in the same Manner ...[73]

It is striking how closely this episode connects the macrocosm of the library with the microcosm of the printed book – case and shelf with the column and line of a page. Contrivances for reaching elevated storage space are common enough in rooms full of books, but here a design appropriate for a useful piece of furniture, the library ladder, has been reimagined as a machine for reading. The change of purpose is consonant with the economies of scale that characterize Brobdingnagian librarianship. Where one might expect to mount a library ladder to browse across many titles on a shelf, in this collection the ladder is an aid to absorption within a single text. Somewhere at the back of Swift's mind there is perhaps a recollection of the elaborate reading machines designed by humanist scholars in previous centuries, their purpose being to help the reader switch rapidly between a number of open books.[74] Where earlier reading machines distracted and diffused the reader's attention among several texts, however, Gulliver's moveable stairs focus his upon the book at hand. The unconscious oscillation of the reader's eye back and forth across the printed page becomes for Gulliver a deliberate action. Gulliver the reader pours his whole body into an absurd, but somehow salutary, series of peregrinations across the face of the text. Swift thought of reading with indexes as being rather like approaching a building by the back entrance.[75] Contrastingly, the inconvenient formality of Gulliver's reading techniques in Brobdingnag are presented as (a pair of) steps in the right direction – towards a proper commitment of self to the business of reading. In the royal library at Brobdingnag, Swift imagines an archive for the books of an old and healthy culture. The reader walks along the printed traces of the text as though he were following footsteps in snow. The process is slow, un-digressive, involving. But notice that here there is no writing on the text – the bodily proportions of reader to book seem to preclude that, and the ethical proportions are wrong as well. Writing marginalia is like beating the bounds around a page. It is a gesture that rehearses proprietorship, or that implies at least a presumption of mastery. Swift wrote: 'When I am reading a Book, whether wise or silly, it seemeth to me to be alive and talking to me.'[76] When he writes upon his reading Swift feels that he is affirming that life, and reciprocating that speech, even when the conversation is hectoring, as it usually is. But in Brobdingnag Gulliver must follow the text that he reads, rather than meeting it and hailing it. This is an innocent, even enviable action.

Notes

1 *CWJS*, vol. I, p. 23.
2 *CWJS*, vol. I, pp. 66, 150; Davis, *PW,* vol. IV, p. 15.
3 *CWJS*, vol. I, p. 152.
4 For facsimiles and accounts of these documents see Harold Williams, *Dean Swift's Library* (Cambridge University Press, 1932), pp. 7–38; *Library and Reading, Part 1*, vol. IV, pp. 289–364.
5 For libraries as the focus of 'complex relationships formed between authors, booksellers, purchasers, and readers' see Justin Champion, *Republican Learning: John Toland and the Crisis of Christian Culture, 1696–1722* (Manchester University Press, 2003), pp. 25–44 (p. 34).
6 See William Temple, 'An Essay upon the Ancient and Modern Learning', in *Miscellanea in Four Essays ... The Second Part* (1790), p. 6.
7 For overgrown and underread libraries in Swift's satire see *Some Remarks upon a Pamphlet*, in Davis, *PW,* vol. III, p. 197; *Four Last Years*, in Davis, *PW,* VII, p. 9; *A Character of the Legion Club*, lines 189–218, in Williams, *Poems*, vol. III, pp. 837–9; these were commonplace reflections: cf. J. Adams, *A Sermon Preached in St. Paul's Cathedral* (1702), p. 16: '... that unprofitable Vanity, which obtains so much now a-days, of collecting Great Libraries, which serve for nothing but to dress, or entertain in, while the well-bound Volumes enjoy as perfect rest, as their Authors do in their Graves'.

8 Davis, *PW,* vol. IV, p. 246.

9 Davis, *PW,* vol. XI, p. 136.

10 Davis, *PW,* vol. XI, p. 292.

11 Davis, *PW,* vol. V, pp. 211–12.

12 For Wren at Trinity see Adrian Tinniswood, *His Invention So Fertile: A Life of Christopher Wren* (London: Jonathan Cape, 2001), pp. 234–51; for Hawksmoor at All Souls see H. M. Colvin, *A Catalogue of Architectural Drawings at Worcester College, Oxford* (Oxford: Clarendon Press, 1964), items 61–81, pp. 11–15; for Clarke at Christ Church see James Weeks, 'The Architects of Christ Church Library', *Architectural History,* 48 (2005), 107–38 (pp. 116–30).

13 Swift to Bolingbroke and Pope, 5 April 1729, Woolley, *Corr.*, vol. III, p. 231.

14 *CWJS,* vol. I, p. 145.

15 *CWJS,* vol. I, pp. 147, 148.

16 *CWJS,* vol. I, p. 29.

17 *CWJS,* vol. I, p. 151; see D. W. Davies, *The World of the Elzeviers* (The Hague: Nijoff, 1960), pp. 145–52.

18 *CWJS,* vol. I, p. 147.

19 See Kristine Louise Haugen, *Richard Bentley: Poetry and Enlightenment* (Cambridge, MA: Harvard University Press, 2011), pp. 105–8; and Mark McDayter, 'The Haunting of St. James's Library: Librarians, Literature and "The Battle of the Books"', *HLQ,* 66 (2003), 1–26 (6–11).

20 *CWJS,* vol. I, p. 151; for chaining cf. *ibid.* p. 146, and 'The Legion Club', lines 208–9, in Williams, *Poems,* vol. III, p. 838.

21 *CWJS,* vol. I, p. 147.

22 *CWJS,* vol. I, p. 157.

23 For Swift as 'adversarial' reader see Brean Hammond, 'Swift's Reading', in *The Cambridge Companion to Jonathan Swift* (Cambridge University Press, 2003), pp. 73–86, at p. 76; and his 'Swift's Reading', in *Münster* (2003), pp. 133–64.

24 Visitations Book, s.d., Marsh's Library, Dublin; Swift attended the 10th visitation, 9 October 1718; 11th, 8 October 1719; 12th, 13 October 1720; 13th, 12 October 1721; 16th, 14 October 1725; 18th, 12 October 1727; 21st, 8 October 1730; 22nd, 14 October 1731; 23rd, 12 October 1732; 26th, 9 October 1735; and 27th, 14 October 1736.

25 See Muriel McCarthy, 'Introduction', in McCarthy and Ann Simmons (eds.), *The Making of Marsh's Library: Learning, Politics and Religion in Ireland, 1650–1750* (Dublin: Four Courts Press, 2004), pp. 11–31 (pp. 12–13); for Bentley in Stillingfleet's library see Haugen, *Richard Bentley,* pp. 62–5.

26 James Raven, *The Business of Books: Booksellers and the English Book Trade* (New Haven: Yale University Press, 2007), pp. 106–10.

27 Swift to Archdeacon Walls, 11 June 1714, Woolley, *Corr.*, vol. I, p. 612.

28 For Pope's library see Maynard Mack, *'Collected in Himself': Essays Critical, Biographical, and Bibliographical on Pope and Some of his Contemporaries* (Delaware University Press, 1982), pp. 307–21, and appendix A, nos. 1–176; for Congreve see John C. Hodges, *The Library of William Congreve* (New York Public Library, 1955).

what about the ones before? Bullard didn't look carefully enough. That catalogue refers to him as 'Dean of St. Patrick's', not by his name, until 1718.

29 'Catalogus librorum Quos, vir admodum Reverendus Joannes Stearne', 1745, Marsh's Library, Dublin; see Toby Barnard, 'Bishop Stearne's Collection of Books and Manuscripts', in McCarthy and Simmons (eds.), *Marsh's Library*, pp. 185–202 (p. 190).

30 Robert S. Matteson, *A Large Private Park: The Collection of Archbishop William King, 1650–1729*, 2 vols. (Cambridge: LP Publications, 2003), vol. I, pp. xxiii–xxiv.

31 King to Stearne, 12 November 1720, TCD, MS 750/6, p. 155, quoted by Barnard, 'Stearne's Collection', p. 201.

32 Swift to Stearne, 29 December 1711, Woolley, *Corr.*, vol. I, p. 408.

33 Swift to Stearne, 15 April 1708, Woolley, *Corr.*, vol. I, p. 185.

34 Swift to King, 15 April 1708, Woolley, *Corr.*, vol. I, p. 188.

35 John Newman, 'Library Buildings and Fittings', in Giles Mandelbrote and K. A. Manley (eds.), *The Cambridge History of Libraries in Britain and Ireland, Vol. 2: 1640–1850* (Cambridge University Press, 2006), pp. 190–211, at p. 209; *The Diary of Humfrey Wanley, 1715–1726*, C. E. Wright and Ruth C. Wright (eds.), 2 vols. (London: The Bibliographical Society, 1966), vol. I, pp. xi–lxxxiii (pp. vi, xxxi).

36 See Raymond Irwin, *The Origins of the English Library* (London: George Allen & Unwin, 1958), pp. 179–80.

37 Swift to Oxford, 26 October 1725, Woolley, *Corr.*, vol. II, p. 617.

38 Swift to Oxford, 17 November 1727, Woolley, *Corr.*, vol. III, p. 137.

39 *A Catalogue of the Large and Valuable Library of the late Learned and Ingenious Mr. Michael Maittaire*, 1749, item 199, p. 123.

40 Special Collections, Hunterian Library, Glasgow, Bo.3.5–10: 'To The Very Learned Richard Mead, M.D. by the supposed Author, who lyeth under many obligations to his Humanity and Friendship Jonath: Swift. Deanry House Dublin Novbr 7th 1739'; the formula 'supposed author' is also used by Faulkner in the preface to volume 1 of the 1735 *Works*.

41 Now in the Le Fanu papers at King's College, Cambridge; facsimile, *Library and Reading, Part 1*, vol. IV, pp. 291–322.

42 *A Catalogue of Books, The Library of the Late Rev. Dr. Swift* (Dublin, 1745); a priced copy of the catalogue made by John Putland is in the Forster Collection, V&A, London; a transcript of it is reproduced in *Library and Reading, Part 1*, vol. IV, pp. 347–64.

43 The 1745 *Catalogue* has 450 titles and 73 asterisks; of the 165 titles not present in 1745 we know of 31 that have some sort of inscription – although a higher proportion of inscribed copies is likely to have survived.

44 For Dee's marginalia see W. H. Sherman, *John Dee: The Politics of Reading and Writing in the English Renaissance* (Amherst: University of Massachusetts Press, 1995), pp. 79–112; for 'active reading' in the Renaissance see Lisa Jardine and Anthony Grafton, '"Studied for Action": How Gabriel Harvey Read his Livy', *Past and Present*, 129 (1990), 30–78; for active readers before Swift see H. J. Jackson, *Marginalia: Readers Writing in Books* (New Haven: Yale University Press, 2001), p. 49.

45 Earliest example is Swift's *judicium* dated 7 November 1719 on Aulus Gelius (gift of Erasmus Lewis), *Library and Reading, Part 1*, vol. I, pp. 688–90.

46 Thomas Sheridan, *Life of Swift* (1784), p. 25; see GS, pp. lv–lvi on context for the list; five of the thirty-six titles (and all but one of the folios) listed are marked 'abstracted': Sarpi's *Council of Trent* with its continuation by Johannes Sleidanus, a Diodorus Siculus, a Cyprian and an Irenaus, and Hobbes's translation of Thucydides.

47 Hawkesworth describes 'copious extracts' of these volumes 'found among his papers'; see 'Account', in *The Works of Jonathan Swift, D.D.*, 12 vols. (1755), vol. I, p. 10; dated examples of Swift's *judicia* are found in: Aulus Gellius (1706), dated 1719; Herodotus (1618), dated 1720; Bodin (1579), dated 1725; Heylin (1670), dated 1727–8; Baronius (1612), dated 1729; and Laud (1639), dated 1735; *Library and Reading, Part 1*, vol. II, p. 940 does not note the inscription (spotted by Davis, *PW*, vol. V, p. 295) before the title page of Swift's Clarendon, now in Marsh's Library, Dublin: 'Judicium de Authore'. *in Marsh*

48 See Erasmus, *On Copia of Words and Ideas*, tr. Donald B. King and H. David Rix (Milwaukee: Marquette University Press, 1963), p. 80: '[*judicia*] are also, as we have said, classified as *exempla*. And they are the *sententiae* of famous writers, of peoples, of wise men or renowned citizens.'

49 Herodotus: *Library and Reading, Part 1*, vol. II, pp. 840–1; Bodin: *Library and Reading, Part 1*, vol. I, pp. 241–2; Heylin: transcribed by Davis, *PW*, vol. V, pp. 255–6.

50 *Library and Reading, Part 1*, vol. I, p. 241; vol. II, p. 854.

51 *Library and Reading, Part 1*, vol. I, pp. 437–9; Ian Higgins, *Swift's Politics: A Study in Disaffection* (Cambridge University Press, 1994), p. 13.

52 *Library and Reading, Part 1*, vol. II, pp. 824–30, on pages 175, 230, 468, 445 of original.

53 *Library and Reading, Part 1*, vol. I, p. 504, on page 445 of original.

54 *Library and Reading, Part 1*, vol. I, pp. 943–4, 955; cf. similar examples in Carte (*Library and Reading, Part 1*, vol. I, pp. 351–4, page 117 of original).

55 Swift to Pope, 26 November 1725, Woolley, *Corr.*, vol. II, p. 623; cf. *Gulliver's Travels*, Davis, *PW*, vol. XI, p. 296.

56 Woolley, *Corr.*, vol. IV, p. 106.

57 *Library and Reading, Part 1*, vol. II, p. 940.

58 Lines 435–8, Rogers, *Poems*, p. 533; *Library and Reading, Part 1*, vol. I, pp. 444, 504.

59 See the analogy between wits and razors, *CWJS*, vol. I, p. 30; see also 'Thoughts on Various Subjects' (1735 version), Davis, *PW*, vol. IV, p. 251; *Vindication of Carteret*, in Davis, *PW*, vol. XII, pp. 157–8.

60 *Library and Reading, Part 1*, vol. II, p. 1376.

61 Hermann J. Real, 'Stella's Books', *SStud*, 11 (1996), 70–83 (pp. 76–7); cf. Williams, *Dean Swift's Library*, pp. 22–3.

62 Swift had urged Johnson to read Pope's *Windsor Forest* in March 1712–13, *JSt* (1948), vol. II, p. 635.

63 Hermann J. Real and Heinz J. Vienken, 'Books from Stella's Library', *SStud*, 1 (1986), 68–72 (p. 71).

64 Swift to John Winder, 13 January 1698–9, Woolley, *Corr.*, vol. I, p. 137; Real and Vienken, 'Books', 72, referring to Lyon's annotation in a copy of Hawkesworth's *Life of Swift*.

65 *Library and Reading, Part 1*, vol. III, pp. 1915–6; Swift gave a second Elzevir Virgil [*Library and Reading, Part 1*, vol. II, p. 1916] to Orrery in July 1738.

66 *Library and Reading, Part 1*, vol. I, pp. 646–7.

67 Browne, 1729; Carte, 1736; Gelius, 1706; Hughes, 1735; Laud, 1639; Pope, 1735; Temple, 1696; Virgil, 1636; Vossius, 1679. Since writing this article Chris Penney has drawn my attention to a 1543 New Testament inscribed by Swift to Pope in 1714, now in Bishop Hurd's Library at Hartlebury Castle. I have not found a record of this copy in *Library and Reading, Part I*. On the title page Swift has written the motto (from Psalm 118) 'intellectum da mihi ut vivam' and (a characteristic gesture) he has blotted out the name of the editor of the edition, Erasmus of Rotterdam.

68 Appian, 1551; Arbuthnot, 1727; Caesar, 1636; Davila, 1647; Grotius, 1669; Howell, 1724; Pope, 1729; Temple, 1696; Virgil, 1500; Virgil, 163; I have also counted the copy of Burnet's *History* that bears Swift's marginalia, but which appears in none of the library catalogues, in this number.

69 John Lyon to Lord Shelburne, 17 September 1768, transcribed by Harold Williams, *Dean Swift's Library*, pp. 61–2; other surviving annotations to books that do not appear in Swift's library catalogues are those in Addison's *Freeholder* (see Davis, *PW*, vol. V, pp. 251–5) and Macky's *Memoirs of the Secret Services* (see Davis, *PW*, vol. V, pp. 257–62); see also A. C. Elias Jr, 'Richard Helsham, Jonathan Swift and Library of John Putland', in McCarthy and Simmons (eds.), *Marsh's Library*, pp. 251–78 (pp. 262–3).

70 See most recently Michael Treadwell, 'The Text of *GT*, Again', *SStud*, 10 (1995), 62–79.

71 Karian, *Print and Manuscript*, pp. 148–65, 196–204; see also John Irwin Fischer, 'Swift Writing Poetry: The Example of "The Grand Question Debated"', in Rudolf Freiburg *et al.* (eds.), *Swift, The Enigmatic Dean* (Tubingen: Stauffenburg, 1998), pp. 41–6.

72 For critiques of writing in historical context see Dennis Baron, *A Better Pencil: Readers, Writers and the Digital Revolution* (Oxford University Press, 2009), pp. 3–18; for *honnêteté* and wit see Georges van den Abbeele, 'The Moralists and the Legacy of Cartesianism', in Denis Hollier (ed.), *A New History of French Literature* (Cambridge, MA: Harvard University Press, 1989), pp. 327–34 (332–3).

73 *Gulliver's Travels*, in Davis, *PW*, vol. XI, p. 119.

74 For examples (including Ramelli's reading wheel) see Roger Chartier, *The Cultural Uses of Print in Early Modern France* (Princeton University Press, 1987), p. 222; cf. Jardine and Grafton, '"Studied for Action"', pp. 46, 48.

75 *CWJS*, vol. I, p. 96; cf. *ibid.* p. 184.

76 'Thoughts on Various Subjects' (1727), Davis, *PW*, vol. IV, p. 253.

PART II

Some species of Swiftian book

CHAPTER FOUR

The uses of the miscellany: Swift, Curll and piracy

Pat Rogers

Swift's career, especially as a poet, was founded in large part on his presence in miscellanies. The authorship of the prose miscellany *A Tale of a Tub* remained controversial for many years, even though most people believed him to be responsible for the book, and all his early works had been anonymous. Appropriately, his *Miscellanies* of 1711 stand at the head of the revised Teerink bibliography (TS 2), having displaced the first of the smaller collections, put out by Edmund Curll a year earlier (TS 1, 1A). They made up the first broad statement of his literary achievements to date – even though the editor slily repressed Swift's name, most of the contents were already known to be his, or could be confidently assigned to him. They included a serious political essay, the *Contests and Dissensions*, along with famous satires in prose and verse such as the Partridge papers. The volume also incorporated 'A Meditation upon a Broom-Stick' as well as four poems that Curll had somehow got hold of and published in his own mini-collections. This first acquired the grandiloquent label *Miscellanies by Dr. Jonathan Swift* when Curll issued it on 8 May 1711, attaching to the previous items his key to the *Tale*, which had appeared in June 1710.

All these facts are well known. What does not seem to have been fully appreciated is the extent to which Swift's literary identity was forged by the miscellany. For much of his life Swift was known to his contemporaries as a miscellany author. In particular, his oeuvre was determined in large measure by his participation in the kind of *sub rosa* production that Curll made his own, and by his response to these appearances in print – most commonly in miscellanies – when he had authentic texts published. Sometimes his participation was willing, and sometimes it was not. The question has been clouded by a lack of understanding of the miscellany as a literary genre, and by uncertainty over the status of piracy. To explore the second of these issues, we need to consult the important work of Adrian Johns and Stephen Karian.

Swift and the eighteenth-century miscellany

Readers today face a number of specific difficulties when they encounter literature of the past. One of these derives from the location in which texts often appeared, and this applies especially to the book history of the early modern period. Works that we regard as autonomous objects made their first appearance as part of a larger whole, frequently unknown to us. Such volumes were commonly made up of seemingly disparate parts, and even when they were not formally styled 'miscellanies' at the time (though many were) they tend to be allocated to such a category nowadays. The texts in question range from short items, usually verse, to longer items in either prose or verse. As for what we could term the 'container' volume, this might consist of works by several hands (the more common pattern) or contributions by a single author. The latter group here holds a particular interest, since it did a great deal to establish the practice of issuing the collected or selected 'works' of a given author – again, the book could be put together by the author or a third party during his or her lifetime, or issued posthumously by an editor or publisher. In either event, the volume might be reprinted in an identical form, or published in successive editions with its contents augmented, pruned or revised. Such collections sometimes had full authorization, while others were the product of surreptitious or even piratical booksellers.

The canon of Swift's works provides examples of most of these forms of 'miscellany' publication. All students of his work will be aware that 'A Tale of a Tub' did not come before the public in May 1704 as a self-standing monument: rather, it emerged into the light as one portion of a triptych, albeit much the largest element of the three. By that stage Swift had already edited Sir William Temple's *Miscellanea*, containing letters and memoirs. His poems would soon begin to appear in prominent anthologies, most obviously from 1709 onwards in the case of Jacob Tonson's famous *Poetical Miscellanies*. After this, Swift's verse became a staple of the miscellany industry, appearing as it did in a variety of productions on both sides of the Irish Sea. 1711 saw the first edition of the only fully authentic assemblage of his works, the *Miscellanies in Prose and Verse*. Subsequently, only the series of Scriblerian *Miscellanies* (1727–32) can be seen as entirely respectable, although some later editions of his *Works* – most notably George Faulkner's four-volume set (1735, with subsequent revisions and additions) discussed by James McLaverty in his chapter (pp. 154–75) – have some claim to authenticity.

Plainly in this setting texts entered the world with a lower degree of independence than we expect in the works of modern authors. It would surprise us if we learnt that *Animal Farm* came out as part of a three-part omnium gatherum. Admittedly, some works, poems and short stories especially, come out in little magazines, journals and periodicals, and there has even been some attempt by Alexander McCall Smith to revive serial publication of novels.[1] But that is a different kind of literary project. The magazine, as it evolved through the period with examples such as the *Gentleman's Magazine*, never pretended to be a book: it was a serial publication, issued at set intervals, with a prescribed format and repeated contents (much of it factual information with no relation to literature). Despite the inclusion of poetic segments, it bore no resemblance to the standard miscellany. Collections such as Tonson's appeared at irregular intervals without a fixed pattern, and they had no extraneous contents outside the verse.

Consequently, a reader who encountered *The Rape of the Locke* in Bernard Lintot's collection of *Miscellaneous Poems and translations, by Several Hands* in 1712 would undergo a totally different experience from anyone today. We come on the *Rape* as a single, often highly edited, text or else as an item in a well-defined group – perhaps among the poems of Pope, or in a college-type anthology with its own palpable designs on a captive student audience. The modern reader can scarcely meet the poem with an innocent eye. By contrast, his or her counterpart three hundred years ago would have been dealing almost with an *objet trouvé*. The work has its own full-page bastard title, as though it only half-belonged in the volume (moreover, the page count skips at this point, so that it runs from 320 to 355, providing bibliographical evidence of a publishing afterthought). It occupies the final twenty pages of a book that contains about 350, and it is preceded by over forty separate items, covering both original and translated writing. Some of these contributions are signed, and indeed the very first segment of the volume is attributed to the hand of Mr Pope – still a new name to most people. But the *Rape* is presented anonymously. Much of Swift's output in this period made its way into the world in similar ways.

The first compilation of Swift's selected works, the *Miscellanies in Prose and Verse* (1711), issued under the imprint of John Morphew a year before the Lintot miscellany, replicates some of the features just mentioned. The contents are diverse (both prose and verse), and the genres represented include serious historiography, theological statement, satire, occasional *pensées*, mock astrology, Ovidian imitation, light social verse and two ambitiously transgressive exercises in urban pastoral. The volume is formally anonymous, despite a coy hint from the 'publisher', or as we should say editor, concerning 'the Person who is generally known to be the author of some' of the items. Unlike the Lintot volume, Morphew's includes previously published material, thus enabling the editor, also unnamed, to justify the appearance of a more legitimate version. However, instead of the authorial diversity promised by the formula 'by divers hands', the 1711 *Miscellanies* plainly offers itself as the product of an individual writer. Undoubtedly the Lintot model had a longer history and it was more widely employed: indeed, the Morphew variant seems to have evolved partly in imitation of the alternative multi-author form.

Recent scholars have examined the prevalence of this form of publication: the most useful studies include Barbara Benedict's historical contextualization of the anthology and Paddy Bullard's analysis of its evolution in the hands of writers such as Shaftesbury.[2] The topic will be vastly illuminated by the completion of the Digital Miscellanies Index project led by Abigail Williams of Oxford University.[3] This will ultimately provide an online database analyzing more than a thousand collections published in the eighteenth century, and it will serve to put the ventures that involved Swift in a much richer context. Fuller judgement must hang fire until this database is available, but we can already see that Swift participated, willingly or unwillingly, in one of the most vigorous modes of literary publication in the period.

Swift as miscellany writer

What, though, would count as willing participation? We need to know the status of piracy during Swift's career. In his discussion of what he calls 'the piratical enlightenment', Adrian Johns sees the period between 1695, when press licensing ended, and 1710, when the Copyright Act came into force, as a window of opportunity for illegitimate publishers. He even claims that 'as piracy as a *legal* category ceased to exist, so piracy as a *cultural* category blossomed'. With no judicial sanctions in place, 'at the same time it became legal to print and publish without being a member of the [stationers'] company at all'. The lapse of the Licensing Act 'made "piracy" legitimate'. In an attempt to remedy this situation, 'a cadre of oligarchs within the trade' put pressure on the government to introduce new measures that would restore a degree of regulation. (In fact, no fewer than twelve unsuccessful efforts were made to bring back the full system of registering books on publication.) The ultimate result, just before Swift's first volume of *Miscellanies* appeared, was the new Copyright Act, which took effect on 10 April 1710. This would be 'a notoriously confused and unsettled piece of legislation', which did not entirely settle the problems that had arisen during 'these years of no property'.[4]

Most people would accept the main lines of this story, and indeed Johns has not departed very far from the orthodox account. Ian Gadd's chapter (pp. 51–64) shows that the situation was complex as it affected Swift, or others seeking to use the prevailing conditions of publishing to their advantage. Contemporaries recognized the existence of pirates both before 1695 and after 1710, although they did not always agree on who had been guilty of such an offence. And while it is true, as Johns remarks, that the monopoly grip of the Stationers had loosened, it is not the case that piracy and non-Company status were the same thing among printers or booksellers.[5] Finally, while 'oligarchs' such as Jacob Tonson held many useful political contacts, they did not have everything their own way in or out of Parliament. The group regarded as most favourable to their cause, the Whig Junto (among them patrons and members of the Kit Cat Club such as Somers and Halifax), gradually lost influence at the centre of government. This was the case even before the Tories won an election landslide in 1710, bringing Harley and St John to power and launching Swift into a conspicuous place inside their propaganda machine.

Edmund Curll provides a complicated exception to some of the generalizations about the development of the trade. He never became a member of the stationers' guild, although he was summoned to 'take cloathing' in 1710, and declined to do so. Instead, he had already been admitted to the livery of the small Cordwainers' Company, and it was in this capacity that he styled himself a 'citizen' of London and took part in numerous municipal elections. This put him outside the 'central core', made up of 'a powerful group in the book trade', comprising a 'small oligarchy' of no more than twenty or thirty at any one time. According to Johns, these men were ranged against the illegitimate operators: 'the alternative was the pirate realm represented by the likes of Hills, Curll, and Rayner'.[6] This description fits Henry Hills in the first decade of the century and William Rayner in the fourth, as they lived almost entirely off the proceeds of illegitimate publications – though Rayner, like Curll, also sold patent medicines. However, the great bulk of Curll's output consisted of works in other categories – items whose rights he owned or shared; some that went back before any form of proper copyright existed; some that had been published on the Continent, and so did not come under the scope of the new Act;

some that had been written by living authors, but had never been published
and whose rights had never been sold to a bookseller; and some whose
legal status was questionable under the terms of the 1710 legislation. This
last category includes works issued by Irish booksellers (on this, see Adam
Rounce's chapter, pp. 203–4), as well as translations and certain anomalous
productions such as volumes of composite authorship and reference books.
In these areas Curll could, and sometimes did, mount a plausible-looking
challenge in the courts regarding the scope of the Act.[7]

Moreover, even if he remained outside the charmed circle of the stationers, Curll was able to infiltrate its power base. He co-published a wide
range of books alongside well-established members of the Company: for
example, he collaborated with Arthur Bettesworth on at least a hundred
occasions, and with William Taylor (who became rich through *Robinson
Crusoe* in 1719) at least forty times. Curll worked more than once with
Tonson and Bernard Lintot, as well as printers such as William Bowyer,
John Nutt and John Watts. As for John Morphew, the trade publisher
whose name appears in the imprint of Swift's first *Miscellanies*, he was
involved with Curll in almost sixty titles or editions between 1707 and
1716. The most striking instance is provided by James Roberts, who ended
up as master of the Stationers. As the most important distributor of his
time, the prolific Roberts was associated with his 'illegitimate' colleague
in around 140 volumes (including fresh editions). These facts are enough
in themselves to show that Curll did not operate in some hidden enclave
remote from the respectable trade – physically, too, his premises lay among
those chosen by the booksellers, first in the Strand and Fleet Street, and
then in the increasingly favoured region bordering on Covent Garden.

What all this reveals is that Swift had three possible outlets in practice,
when he considered bringing out his first assemblage of miscellaneous
works around 1709. It seems possible that he was inspired by the example
of Defoe, with *A Collection of the Writings of the Author of The True-born
English-Man* (1703) and *A Second Volume of the Writings of the Author of
The True-born Englishman* (1705), which each contained a wide variety of
items, some of which had passed with little notice on first publication.
He could have turned to an outright pirate such as Hills, but that would
have made no sense on any level other than as an act of pure obfuscation.
Alternatively, he could have sought out the upper echelon of the trade, and
this provided a number of options – though Jacob Tonson, the man most
associated with the word 'miscellany' at this juncture, was too firmly connected to the Whig cause to suit Swift's changing political allegiance, and
little material flowed in that direction beyond two poems (first published

in a different version by Curll) that Swift seemingly allowed to go into the Tonson *Miscellanies* in May 1709. A third choice would have been Curll as one of the few operators with a foot in both camps.

In the event, as we know, the *Miscellanies in Prose and Verse* appeared in 1711 under the imprint of John Morphew, although the true agent of publication was Benjamin Tooke Jr.[8] We should not forget that Morphew was the leading trade publisher on the Tory side at this juncture: his name appears on the title page of most of Swift's pamphlets on behalf of the Harley administration, including all eight editions of *The Conduct of the Allies* between 1711 and 1713, as well as in the colophon of *The Examiner*. He also served as the distributor of several pro-Sacheverell items, including a *Vindication* of the highflying preacher written by William King (1663–1712), one of the Christ Church wits and a writer congenial to Swift by this date.[9] By contrast, only a single work by Swift from this period (*A Famous Prediction of Merlin*, 1709) carries the name of Morphew's Whig rival among trade publishers, Abigail Baldwin, or of her son-in-law James Roberts, who took over the business on her death in 1713. As for Tooke, his list clearly shows that his connections lay chiefly with the Tories, as emerges from the preponderance of authors such as Lord Lansdowne (Secretary of War under Harley when the *Miscellanies* came out), Lady Winchilsea (whose *Miscellaneous Poems* appeared in 1713), Jeremy Collier, Laurence Echard (a historian regarded in his own time as firmly within the Tory camp) and Elijah Fenton. As Ian Gadd demonstrates in his chapter (pp. 51–63), most of Swift's works at this time were printed by John Barber, involved like Tooke in the *Gazette*, and an unregenerate Jacobite in later years.

But the *Miscellanies* do not represent the first occasion on which some of Swift's writings had been presented together. That had happened in March 1709, when Curll produced the third edition of *The Works of the Right Honourable the Earls of Rochester, and Roscommon*. This was actually a new incarnation of the second edition from around September 1707 (itself an augmented version of Benjamin Bragge's first edition from earlier in the same year). In the contents list to volume II, both 'Baucis and Philemon' and 'Mrs. Harris's Petition' were attributed to 'the Author of The Tale of a Tub'; however, a third item present in the collection, the poem we know as 'On Mrs. Biddy Floyd', was not. What were these pieces doing in a set of volumes apparently devoted to Rochester and Roscommon? The answer is that vol. II is a pure miscellany, with a sprinkling of works by Roscommon augmented by selections from Katherine Philips, Thomas Otway, William Walsh, Nicholas Rowe, Samuel Garth,

Joseph Trapp and others. So Swift's career as an anthology poet began in this surprising place; little of his earlier verse (including the odes from the 1690s) had yet seen print, and nothing had been collected in a composite volume. In other words, Swift makes his entry here as the colleague of authors such as Walsh, Rowe and Garth, names that are ubiquitous in the anthologies of this period. In February 1714 Curll would reintegrate Swift into this *galère*, with *A Collection of Original Poems, Translations, and Imitations, by Mr. Prior, Mr. Rowe, Dr. Swift, and other Eminent Hands.* This was a typical Curllian production, sticking together previously published items with a new title page. The four Swift poems come near the end of the volume, preceded by the deathless effusions of writers such as George Sewell and Edward Holdsworth, and succeeded by a work from February 1713, *The Olympick Odes of Pindar, in English Meetre. As they were lately found in an Original Manuscript of those Sublime Lyrick Translators, Thomas Sternhold, John Hopkins, and others. Conferred with the Greek.* We may wonder if Swift was more dismayed by the infringement of his rights or by the company he was made to keep.

Curll and Swift

Stephen Karian has suggested that Swift was all too well aware of Curll's publication of his poems, and was willing to make use of them for publicity purposes. The strongest evidence lies in the fact that Swift used Curll's 1710 text as the basis of the version found in Tooke's volume in 1711, even though the preface alludes darkly to the 'very Imperfect and Uncorrect Copies' of his works that had slipped into print. This leads Karian to speculate that Swift 'was involved' in the 1710 edition – in fact that he connived in the whole process, and may have fed Curll with material. If so, the comment to Esther Johnson on 14 May 1711 goes beyond genteel equivocation: 'And that villain Curl has scraped up some trash, and calls it Dr. Swift's miscellanies, with the name at large, and I can get no satisfaction of him' (*JSt* (1948), vol. I, p. 269). This has entered the realm of self-deceiving *mauvaise foi*. It was one thing for the author to write in understandable irritation of the 'Prostitute Bookseller' who had published *A Complete Key to A Tale of a Tub*, as he did in the postscript to the Apology (*CWJS*, vol. VIII, p. 323). It would be quite another to lead his closest woman friend to believe that he had played no part in creating the 1710 miscellanies, if the truth were as Karian suggests.[10]

In order to understand the role Curll may have had in the formation of Swift's canon, as well as his literary reputation, Karian lists four issues to which we should pay attention. The first contains a warning that 'we should not allow Alexander Pope's notorious squabbles with Curll to determine how we view the bookseller'. This caveat is especially important, Karian adds, since much of his discussion 'examines Curll well before Pope's *Dunciad* (1728)'. The general point is certainly valid. But Curll's quarrels with his most famous adversary go back as far as 1714, and sometimes relate to even earlier events. Swift found himself drawn willy-nilly into some of these disputes, and his opinions on the bookseller (deriving in part from the episode surrounding the *Miscellanies* of 1711) contributed to the shared view of the Scriblerians regarding literary piracy. Karian supports his contention by instancing some of Curll's legitimate publications, specifically his editions of Edward Young. It is evident that Curll did own the copyright of some works by Young, published between 1714 and 1741. But no such record exists with most of the authors he published, either by way of a documented sale of rights or other evidence. More typical is the case of Matthew Prior, who complained bitterly about the infringement of his rights in 1716, having endured what was probably illicit publication of his poems as early as 1707 – besides having spurious items such as 'The female Phaeton' repeatedly attributed to him. It is unlikely in the highest degree that Curll ever paid for many of the numerous works by authors such as Addison that legitimate publishers like Tonson and Lintot brought out in quasi-official versions, although he may perhaps have had title to some poems by Rowe.[11] Relatives or connections of deceased writers (for example, Robert Nelson or Thomas Burnet) took public exception to his methods. Most conspicuously, rival booksellers routinely objected to his breach of their ownership. This happened both in the columns of newspapers and in court: to cite just one case, in 1721 Robert Knaplock and Jacob Tonson Jr brought suit against him in Chancery over a book by Humphrey Prideaux. Further claims would follow in subsequent years, quite apart from the well-known lawsuits involving Pope.

The second point Karian makes runs as follows: 'in any discussion of Curll, we need to be precise in our use of the term "pirate"', a term that he says has been tossed around too lightly. Curll did not, he argues, pirate publications as Henry Hills did. The reason is that most of the so-called piratical items did not derive from previously printed material, 'but rather from manuscripts that had not yet appeared in print and that were not authorized to appear by their authors'. When he published such manuscripts, Curll annoyed writers, 'though they had little legal recourse, as current copyright law secured rights only for publications'. Again, the general point can stand: the Copyright Act had been chiefly designed to protect the interests of the trade, once their members had made deals with authors. Still, Curll's depredations went beyond merely lighting by chance on stray manuscripts. He actively sought them out, raiding the dustbins of literary men and women, and using the talents of a skilled picker-up of unconsidered trifles in the person of Richard Rawlinson, the antiquarian and nonjuring bishop.[12] He acquired supposititious title by dubious means, for example when he bought Pope's early letters to Henry Cromwell, the key item in his *Miscellanea* (1726), from Elizabeth Thomas, who was neither the writer nor the recipient of this correspondence.[13] Quite apart from grabbing manuscripts, he stretched the bounds of legitimate acquisition. Constantly he would extract some portions of a book to recycle, depending apparently on a concept of 'fair use' that the 1710 Act did not cover, and which did not yet really exist. He freely reprinted translations, thus potentially defrauding both publisher and translator.

The two other points by Karian call for less attention here. He remarks that Curll's name does not always appear in the imprint of works with which he can be associated from other evidence. If anything, Karian may underestimate the extent to which this happens – in part this is thanks to Curll's prolonged contact with trade publishers such as Morphew, Baldwin, Roberts and John Baker among others, as well as with mercuries such as Anne Dodd. The likelihood is that as many as two hundred books or editions fall into this category. Finally, Karian asserts that 'we should not assume that there is no textual relationship between Curll's publications of Swift's works and other versions of these works that Swift authorized'. As already indicated, Karian's essay convincingly shows that Swift did use Curll's miscellany of 1710 in assembling the text for his own collection in 1711. At the least, he concludes, it seems 'almost certain' that Curll 'thought such a connection existed'.[14]

In fact, Curll's connection with the items that went into the Swift miscellany lasted longer than has been realized. One route went via editions of Rochester and Roscommon. As Karian notes, *Poems on Several Occasions. By the Earls of Roscommon, and Dorset, &c.* (1714) (TS 519; Case 278), which retained 'Baucis', also formed the second volume in a reissue of the Rochester series published under Curll's imprint around May in that year as the fourth edition (not in TS or Case). Commonly both volumes are bound together in one, but the Roscommon half must have been separately available. Indeed the *Works* of Rochester, Roscommon and Dorset continued to appear through the succeeding decades in slightly altered guises. (Equally, Curll went on advertising the title in his lists for most of his life.) Some came out under the imprint of 'the booksellers of London and Westminster', generally a sign of cloudy origins. One version, simply 'printed in the Year' 1718, has the usual contents, with 'Baucis' among the 'miscellany poems by several hands' in volume II. This example (*ESTC* T94657) is not in Teerink or Case, and like other late printings is left out of Karian's list of Swift books with which Curll was concerned. However, the bookseller listed this title in a catalogue he issued in late 1718, as well as in a volume he published in November of that year. Since the price remains five shillings, it is uncertain whether he meant the newer version or was disposing of stock from 1714. Likewise he may or may not have been connected with a version from 1720–1 (not in TS; Case 323a; *ESTC* T152378); and another from 1731 (Case 323b; *ESTC* T96413). We are on firmer ground with *The Poetical Works of the Earls of Rochester, Roscomon, and Dorset; the Dukes of Devonshire, Buckinghamshire, &c.*, advertised by 'the booksellers' on 4 July 1739 (not in TS; Case 321d; *ESTC* T94654). Though the imprint carries no name, the list of new books (on p. [xvi]) in volume II can all be identified as some of his most characteristic miscellany productions. Such lists, especially if incorporated into the main sequence of pages (here a recto), generally figure among the most reliable signs of his hand. Moreover, the memoirs of Roscommon, previously simply addressed to a friend, are now inscribed to 'Mr. Pope' – exactly the kind of thing that Curll does so often.

These editions have a number of features in common. They all reprint 'Baucis'; after 1714, they all appear without a named publisher; they all carry the life of Roscommon, which was written by G[eorge] S[ewell], Curll's leading house author from about 1712, and which included a puff for each of two Curll publications. Since Teerink omits the later versions, we may have supposed that Swift's poetry had a little less currency than was the case. The reprints exemplify the continuing life of Swift's poem in a well-known set of miscellany verses, suggesting that such items had a life of their own that was probably beyond the control of the author.

Swift cannot have supposed that Curll would cease to hound him. He had already seen the tawdry *Complete Key to A Tale of a Tub* of 1710, with reprints in 1713, 1714 and 1724. As we have noted, he would find some of the miscellany items issued once more in *A Collection of Original Poems* (1714). Such publications attached Swift more firmly by name to his works, which he may not have desired in every case. Moreover, they obliged him to keep company with dubious stablemates, and fixed his standing as a miscellany author. In 1718 Curll purloined a little new material for his *Letters, Poems, and Tales: Amorous, Satirical and Gallant*, published on 11 January. This also contained work by another of Curll's authors, John Durant Breval.

The Swiftian items would be recycled in the Curllian edition of Swift's *Miscellanies* in 1720 and 1721, and then again as late as 1735 in *Mr. Pope's Literary Correspondence. Volume the Second*, both octavo and duodecimo editions (though the contents of these differ in other respects). So it went on: in 1719 and 1720, Curll was behind the attribution to Swift of some spurious or collective items. James Roberts is listed as the nominal publisher on the title page of some, but they appear in Curll's lists and they found a place in *A Second Collection of Miscellanies. Written by Jonathan Swift, D.D.*, which was advertised by Curll and others on 25 August 1720. Some of the contents reappeared in the so-called 'fourth' edition of *Miscellanies Written by Jonathan Swift, D.D. Dean of St Patrick's Dublin* in December 1721. In some states this volume contains at the start two extraneous items that are unlikely to be Swift's. Once more we find that the contents were reused, with additions and omissions, in the 'fifth' edition of the *Miscellanies*, dated 1736: they had already appeared in this form as part of the duodecimo edition of *Mr. Pope's Literary Correspondence. Volume the Third* around September or October 1735.

The major, but not the only, affront to the Scriblerian group in the following years came with the *Miscellanea. In two volumes. Never before published*, released by Curll on his birthday, 14 July 1726. This production has been seen as one of the chief motives inspiring Swift and Pope to begin their own series of *Miscellanies* a year later, and most attention has been devoted to Pope's response to the publication of his letters in the first volume. However, the collection contains several pieces attributed explicitly or implicitly to Swift. The bizarre company that his works, real or supposititious, are made to share includes *Laus Ululæ*, a mock encomium from the seventeenth century, translated by Thomas Foxton, one of Curll's regular hacks. Nor did the story end here, with the Swift–Pope *Miscellanies*, not to add *The Dunciad*, on the horizon. Curll persisted in filleting what works he could from Swift throughout the 1730s, and as just noted he slipped portions of Swiftiana into his volumes notionally devoted to Pope's correspondence. These culminated in *Dean Swift's Literary Correspondence*, published in May 1741, which was to provoke a famous Chancery suit brought by Pope that determined the copyright in personal letters for generations to come.[15] But by that time Swift was almost too far gone to care.

This abbreviated summary leaves out many episodes in the long struggle between author and bookseller. However, the narrative does show a number of things. First, for the remainder of his career Curll kept using the same methods he had first employed in 1709–10 to purloin unpublished material he could assign to Swift. The only question is whether

Swift connived on this occasion or subsequently. Second, Swift's smaller items first achieved wide general circulation in many Curll collections, even where they had first appeared in newspapers or shadowy Grub Street versions from London or Dublin. Third, some anonymous items were first claimed for Swift in these collections. Fourth, several pieces in prose and verse were *repeatedly* issued within the pages of a miscellany.

It goes without saying that Swift's works appeared in many other collections during his lifetime, often without his permission. Apart from Dublin reissues of the original *Miscellanies* by Samuel Fairbrother, individual items appeared in volumes put out by London publishers such as Charles Ackers, David Lewis and John Peele, not to mention the notorious incognito 'A. Moore'. But it makes sense to concentrate on Curll. His productions were the first to bring a number of Swift's writings together, and the first to attach a name to the author. They attained greater prominence because of his gift for self-publicity. At the same time, his noisy quarrel with Pope often drew Swift into the loop: it is noteworthy that poems by the latter regularly contain slighting references to figures with whom he cannot have had first-hand relations, and who came to his attention purely because Pope had identified them as Curll's hacks in *The Dunciad* and elsewhere. Finally, Curll filled the contested space surrounding piracy, around which so many miscellaneous publications thronged.

If Swift did indeed connive in Curll's earliest publications of his work, he was hoist by his own petard. Tooke could not have claimed the rights on items already in the public domain before an agreement was reached, and there was little that anyone could do to stop Curll from printing later manuscripts that he had acquired by one means or another. It seems likely that Swift wrote with absolute sincerity when he condemned his long-time tormentor as a pirate, no matter how we choose to narrow the scope of the term today. It may be that Swift took advantage of the visibility afforded to his work by Curll's collection to launch his own *Miscellanies* in 1711, but he found out to his cost that the bookseller would make this the basis of a lifelong strategy to exploit a reputation his collection had helped to create.

Notes

1 www.telegraph.co.uk/culture/books/corduroymansionsbyalexandermcca/ (accessed 25 July 2012).
2 See Barbara M. Benedict, *Making the Modern Reader: Cultural Mediation in Early Modern Literary Anthologies* (Princeton University Press, 1996); and Paddy Bullard, 'Digital Editing and the Eighteenth-Century Text: Works, Archives, and Miscellanies', *Eighteenth-Century Life*, 36.3 (2012), 57–80.

3 http://digitalmiscellaniesindex.org/ (accessed 25 July 2012). The editors of the Index kindly allowed the data in this chapter to be checked against a pre-publication version of their database. It is already clear that the Digital Miscellanies Index will show that Swift's poems were more widely reprinted than has previously been apparent.

4 Johns, *Piracy*, pp. 42–4, 111.

5 Cyprian Blagden, *The Stationers' Company: A History 1403–1959* (London: Allen & Unwin Ltd, 1960), pp. 153–77.

6 Johns, *Piracy*, p. 111.

7 See Baines and Rogers, *Curll*, pp. 7, 140, 289–90.

8 Swift to Tooke, 29 June 1710, and Tooke to Swift, 10 July 1710, Woolley, *Corr.*, vol. I, pp. 282–4.

9 Falconer Madan and W. A. Speck, *A Critical Bibliography of Dr. Henry Sacheverell* (Lawrence, KA: University of Kansas Libraries, 1978), item 992 (but see *ESTC* T50892). Some of Morphew's publications on the Sacheverell affair were actually really Curll's handiwork, and at least three were written by him; see *ibid.* items 107, 319–25, 339, 341–6, 350, 408–9, 606, 627, 645–6. As Marcus Walsh notes, by the date of the Apology to *A Tale of a Tub*, 'King's pro-Sacheverell, anti-Marlborough, high-Church Tory writings had made Swift think more favourably of him' (*CWJS*, vol. I, p. 323).

10 Karian, *Print and Manuscript*, pp. 65–6.

11 See Baines and Rogers, *Curll*, pp. 60–8.

12 Baines and Rogers, *Curll*, pp. 132–8.

13 See Pope's note to *Dunciad*, book II, line 66 (*TE*, vol. V, p. 106); Henry Cromwell to Pope, 6 July 1727, Pope, *Correspondence*, vol. II, pp. 439–40; Baines and Rogers, *Curll*, pp. 171–3.

14 See Stephen Karian, 'Edmund Curll and the Circulation of Swift's Writings', in *Münster* (2008), pp. 99–129. This is the most thorough investigation of the topic to date.

15 See Pat Rogers, 'The Case of Pope v. Curll', *The Library*, 5th ser., 27 (1972), 326–31.

CHAPTER FIVE

Swift's Tale of a Tub *and the mock book*

Marcus Walsh

Jonathan Swift had no general objection to books and texts. He believed in, and wrote that he believed in, the possibility of plain meanings, embodying 'the Author's Intentions', and worthy of 'candid Interpretation'. He approved of texts that, like the Father's Will that is the New Testament, consisted of 'certain plain, easy Directions'. His sermons in particular exemplify the clear text, embodying and communicating a plain meaning. He did not, however, value endless controversions of dangerous matters, and deeply resented a merely commercial proliferation of writing, agreeing with the humanist King of Brobdingnag, as Paddy Bullard has suggested in his chapter, that a library of a thousand volumes was sufficient to represent the curriculum of worthwhile knowledge. Swift abominated obscure writings, including allegories and hermetica, all texts so dark as to require and invite commentary, the *impedimenta literarum* of commentary itself, and the jargons of pedantry, law and scholasticism. He objected fiercely to the deliberate wresting of the words of Holy Scripture, and indeed to the forcing of any texts to 'Interpretations which never once entered into the Writer's Head'. These positions and values were wholly natural to an English or an Irish churchman and man of letters in the opening decades of the eighteenth century. They are positions and values shared too with many a literary humanist before Swift, before the new professionalizing philological humanism that he so abhorred was ushered in by Richard Bentley, and Bentley's continental forebears and contemporaries.[1]

Swift's *Tale of a Tub*, however, like so many of his published writings, is by no means a plain and straightforward text. If it presents, as Swift asserted in his Apology, 'the Author's Intentions', it does so in indirect and ironic ways. It is a commented text, and explicitly and repeatedly invites and requires commentary. It is full of dark matter. To many contemporaries of Swift, and to many modern critics, it has seemed a dangerously unstable, wrestable text. Swift desiderated in his Apology, however, knowledgeable and well-intentioned readers who would regard the *Tale* as rather less polysemous. Swift insisted the *Tale* was intended as a satire on 'the numerous and gross Corruptions in Religion and Learning', rather than on learning and religion themselves, and repudiated as unnecessary and 'ill-placed' the 'Cavils of the Sour, the Envious, the Stupid, and the Tastless'. As he is at pains to make clear in the Apology, among his main satiric devices in the *Tale* are 'Parodies, where the Author personates the Style and Manner of other Writers, whom he has a mind to expose'; this hint, Swift claimed, was sufficient 'to direct those who may have over-look'd the Authors Intention' (*CWJS*, vol. I, pp. 5, 6, 7).[2]

The *Tale of a Tub*, as published with the 'Battel of the Books' and 'Mechanical Operation of the Spirit', did not merely contain or speak through parodies, but presented itself in many different ways as a parodic book. Its formal as well as generic parodies take in title pages, prefaces, authors' dedications, the letter as learned report, the recipes of hermetic writings, digressions, accounts of Royal Society experiments, 'full and true accounts' of any number of historical events and lurid crimes, 'modern excuses' and much else.[3] In this essay I shall discuss some of those parodies in which Swift interrogates the ways in which modern books present evidence, and organize and make claims to knowledge. I shall be particularly concerned with Swift's experiments in and burlesques of learned referencing, in the forms of marginalia and footnotes; with his exploiting of two related and favourite resources of the new scientific and philological book, the catalogue and the list, especially catalogues and lists of books themselves; with his uses and representations of the blank, in which claims of knowledge are not met, and evidence evaporates; and with his applications of the conventional evidential tags and phrases of both old and new scholasticism.

The first edition of the *Tale of a Tub* has marginalia, providing references for, and occasional brief quotations from, passages alluded to in the text. The fifth edition is endowed, in addition to the existing marginalia, with footnotes. Some of the footnotes are written, no doubt by Swift himself, in a personated editorial voice, identifying references, correcting bibliographical information, translating foreign language quotations, clarifying the allegory, providing historical context. Many of the footnotes, in the narrative or allegorical sections of the *Tale*, are transcribed verbatim from William Wotton's *Observations upon The Tale of a Tub*, published in 1705 as part of his *Defense of the Reflections upon Ancient and Modern Learning*. These transcriptions turn Wotton into a leaden commentator, while profiting from his (mostly sensible and straightforward) explanations of the

Tale's allegory. Some of the notes, to more or less dubious passages in the *Tale*, provide more or less careful but for the most part ironizing learned references: Ctesias is cited as authorizing source for a suggestive passage about pigmies ('Vide excerpta ex eo apud *Photium*'), Pausanias for the dedication of temples to Sleep and the Muses by 'a very Polite Nation in *Greece*' ('Trezenii Pausan. 1. 2'). At the beginning of the 'Battel of the Books' the careful and circumspect reader is invited to consult the '*Annual Records of Time*', a reference to Wing's *Almanack*, then printed by Mary Clark; a marginal note quotes the *Almanack*'s sententious English motto, and provides in Latin the inappropriate and improbable bibliographical information 'Vid. Ephem. de *Mary Clarke*; opt. Edit.' Here the pedantic carefulness of Richard Bentley is the satiric mark.[4] These elements of the *Tale*'s apparatus are significant in its parodic refunctionings of scholarly method, and more especially of modern scholarly method.

The development of old and the appearance of new methods and forms of referencing were closely associated with the development of a professional historiography and philology at the beginning of the long eighteenth century. Marginalia and footnotes were important elements among a large set of newly prominent scholarly apparatuses: contents lists, catalogues, commentaries, bibliographies, glossaries, indexes, all of them list-like, divisible, more or less Ramist.[5] In discursive learned texts, the marginal note had made its historical appearance long before the footnote. Formally, spatially and functionally, the marginalium in the printed book had grown from an ancient tradition of the manuscript codex. Footnotes became truly practicable and consistent only with print. As a major formal outcome of this development, the footnote spread beyond the scholarly edition, where it had already found a home, into a whole new range of genres, including biblical criticism, literary scholarship and the encyclopaedia. The shift from marginalia to footnotes in discursive learned writing has been dated by a number of commentators with some precision to the turn of the eighteenth century: just the historical moment at which Swift was writing *A Tale of a Tub*.[6]

The rather abrupt transition from marginalia to footnotes in discursive scholarly books is exemplified and confirmed by a striking moment in the publishing career of Richard Simon, a French Oratorian priest and the leading biblical historian and textual critic of his time. Simon's learned and innovative *Histoire critique du vieux testament* (1682) and *Histoire critique du texte du nouveau testament* (Rotterdam, 1689) were both at once translated into English.[7] They were widely read, and became significant texts for the energetic 1680s English debate about the nature, reliability and interpretation of the Bible, a matter of some concern to Swift, and some centrality in the *Tale*.[8] In his earlier work Simon described his policy of documentation. His supporting quotations are provided 'in Abridgment onely and according to the sense'. References are given in the form of marginal notes, which identify quoted scriptural passages, as well as the authors and often the titles of his secondary sources. Bibliographical citations for his references are provided not at the point of quotation, but as a 'Catalogue' of quoted authors, placed 'at the end of the Book'.[9] In his later *Histoire critique du texte du nouveau testament*, however, Simon's page looks rather different, and his Preface gives an account of highly significant methodological changes. Though the 'numerous Quotations' from printed sources are again given in brief in Simon's text, now those quotations are given 'at large' in footnotes, providing the key words quoted in the text with their meaning-defining context.[10] As before there are marginal notes, providing references for citations (normally repeated in the footnotes), but now the references are fuller and more precise, identifying author, work, chapter or book number, and sometimes page number. The effect on the page, aesthetic and functional, is much in keeping with the evidential foundations and interlinking precision of his own scholarship. Simon's use of the footnote in his *New Testament* provided a model frequently followed, in England as well as in France, in discursive scholarly writing. It may be found, to cite an example known to Swift, in the published work of Joseph Bingham, in whose *Origines Ecclesiasticae: or, the Antiquities of the Christian Church* (2 volumes, 1708) footnotes provide references, occasional brief validating quotations and brief suggestions of supporting citations ('*Vid. Pearson Vindic. Ignat. Praef. Ad Lector*').[11]

In late seventeenth-century England, one of the more significant arguments about the methodology of scholarship took place between Dr Richard Bentley and the Christ Church mentors of the young aristocrat Charles Boyle. This argument of course figures large among the cultural and intellectual contexts of Swift's *Tale*. Christ Church claimed, and in some respects exemplified, a rather uneasy affiliation with an older gentlemanly humanism. Bentley uncompromisingly represented the new philology. Sir William Temple, in his 'Essay upon the Ancient and Modern Learning',[12] had praised the epistles of the sixth-century BC Sicilian tyrant Phalaris as a genuine example of the superiority of the ancients. Bentley, in his 'Dissertation upon the Epistles of Phalaris' appended to the second edition of William Wotton's *Reflections upon Ancient and Modern Learning* (London, 1697), demonstrated, with much detailed evidence from classical and more particularly Greek literature, history and philosophy, that the extant epistles were a much later production. Christ Church responded in the multiply-authored *Dr Bentley's Dissertation on the Epistles of Phalaris … Examin'd by the Honourable Charles Boyle, Esq.* (London, 1698), generally referred to as Boyle's 'Examination'; and Bentley replied in a much expanded version of the *Dissertation* (1699).

Bentley's *Dissertation* and Boyle's *Examination* both present themselves as heavily documented scholarly works. 'Boyle', however, is more squeamish about the methodologies of 'pedantry' and their apparatuses, in particular extensive and untranslated local quotation. 'Boyle' pronounces himself 'so far from valuing my self upon a multitude of quotations, that I wish there had been no occasion for those few I have produc'd'. He cites La Bruyère and St Evremond, for Bentley's instruction, as examples of 'Writers … who think well, and speak Justly, and quote little' (p. 228). He regularly breaks out of the drudgery of scholarly quotation to pursue an extended and elaborate discourse of anti-pedantic satire, during which there is little occasion for learned apparatus. We are here at some distance from the strengthening early Enlightenment concern for the substantiation of argument with primary evidence, and the explicit validation of the provenance of the evidence.

For Bentley, by contrast, scholarly documentation is a matter neither of routine nor of distaste. Despite its title, the *Dissertation upon the Epistles of Phalaris* is not so much a continuous thesis as a series of detailed interpretative interventions, addressing highly specific passages in a long work. His cases are made from learning, both familiar and first-hand, in metrics, chronology, geography, numismatics, biography, literature, history. Each point in the argument is supported by the analysis of apposite contextual evidence.[13] Notes, in the form of marginalia, certify and validate this apparatus, with references, demonstrations, parallels, original language quotations (in Latin and Greek) for translations provided within the text.[14] Bentley frequently excoriates 'Boyle' for his failures adequately to understand and identify his sources, joshing him in particular as one who knows his materials only at second hand, as an Oxford scholar unfamiliar with books even 'in the publick Library at *Oxon*', as a man who does not know how to use a catalogue, dependent on 'his Assistant … *that consulted Books for him*'.[15]

It is not the move in works of scholarship to footnotes as such that is consequential for Swift. Commentary both brief and extended had already appeared in printed marginalia in edited texts of all kind. The discursive writings of Bentley and Wotton, to whom Swift was most directly responding in the *Tale*, used marginal notes rather than footnotes. There is no reason to think that Swift invested with any special significance the positioning of notes at the foot of the page in *A Tale of a Tub*; it was his bookseller Tooke, not Swift himself, who argued for the new materials of the 1710 *Tale* appearing at the foot of the page rather than at the end of the volume.[16] What matters, rather, was Swift's reaction to a new methodology, based on a scholarly (or, to such observers as Swift, pedantic) emphasis on particular evidence, and to the forms and methods of detailed and local adduction, and complete and accurate reference, which that new emphasis made necessary. The marginalium and the footnote are both characterizing elements of the new methodology. The parodic marginalia and footnotes of the fifth edition of the *Tale*, cluttering the page and the narrative with the heavy footfall of referencing and quotation, restating the obvious or problematizing the plain, take Bentley and Wotton as their immediate cause, but they are, more broadly, part of an old humanism's anxious response to a new one.

If Swift's marginalia and footnotes respond to Bentley and to English and European developments in scholarly method, they are by no means the only formal features of the *Tale* that do so. It is one of the chief satiric jokes of the *Tale* that the moderns have laboured, to their own satisfaction, in the categorizing of every kind of knowledge, in many different organizing forms. To Swift, unimpressed by number, proliferation and taxonomies, such lists are delusive or abusive or both. The text and associated paratexts of the *Tale* feature a huge variety and number of parodic lists and catalogues. Modern systems and thinkers, and their characteristics and products, are preserved throughout in various forms of the catalogue or list, their proper rhetorical amber. Criticism is defined through her children, '*Noise* and *Impudence*, *Dullness* and *Vanity*, *Positiveness*, *Pedantry*, and *Ill-Manners*'; every true modern critic is defined by his genealogy, 'descending in a direct Line from … *Momus* and *Hybris*, who begat *Zoilus*, … who begat *Etcætera* the Elder, who begat *B*[en]*tly*, … and *W*[o]*tton* …' There are lists of fanatics and fanatic sciences, of modern madmen and of the schools of the modern academy: 'the *Spelling* School … The school of *Swearing*; the School of *Criticks* … with many others too tedious to recount' (*CWJS*, vol. I, pp. 82, 154, 61, 26).

Certainly late seventeenth-century England teemed with every kind of list, including catalogues, indexes, tables of contents, gazettes, glossaries, chronologies. Of the astonishing number and variety of 'catalogues', for instance, the great majority are of books (in libraries or for sale), followed at some distance by the nobility or the clergy. There are catalogues too, however, of saints and contented cuckolds, of doctors and of simples, of wits and of town beaus, of lawyers and of notorious and villainous lies, of Billingsgate and heads of Balliol.[17] Such catalogues are variously professional, informative, polemic, demotic and parodic. They indicate an overwhelming listing and categorizing tendency of the time, which is fully reflected in this major rhetorical mode of the *Tale*.

Swift responds to catalogue and list as pervasive and popular forms, but they are most important objects of his satire as manifestations both of the new science and of the new philology. If Wotton was particularly in Swift's mind, the many catalogues produced by members of the Royal Society represented a more general target. On the title pages of these new taxonomies the authors regularly 'shine' (as Pope would later put it) 'in the dignity of F.R.S.'[18] A *Catalogus plantarum Angliae et insularum adjacentium* (1670) is proudly described as the work of 'Joannis Raii ... Societatis Regiae Sodalis', and as the imprint of 'J. Martynj, Regalis Societatis Typographi'. Other works by John Ray FRS include *A Collection of English Words not generally used ... in two alphabetical catalogues ... With Catalogues of English Birds and Fishes* (1674). 'Nehemiah Grew, M.D. Fellow of the Royal Society, and of the Colledge of Physitians', wrote a *Catalogue and Description of the Natural and Artificial Rarities belonging to the Royal Society and preserved at Gresham Colledge* (1685), with a 'Prospect of the Whole Work' set out on two facing leaves, a complete classified landscape of its subject.

Above all, the *Tale* provides us with catalogues of the unBrobdingnagian proliferation of publications by modern authors, inventing, listing and caricaturing modern texts offensive because scholastic, or self-commenting, or allegorical, or dark, or foolish in other ways. The first element of the *Tale*'s elaborate paratextuality, after the title page, is a parodic version of the bookseller's standard in-book form of advertisement, a list of 'Treatises wrote by the same Author, most of them mentioned in the following Discourses; which will be speedily published':

> *A Dissertation upon the principal Productions of* Grub-street.
> *Lectures upon a Dissection of Human Nature.*
> ...
> *An Analytical Discourse upon Zeal,* Histori-theo-physi-logically *considered.*
> ...
> *A Critical Essay upon the Art of* Canting, *Philosophically, Physically, and Musically considered.*
>
> (*CWJS*, vol. I, p. [4])

Here the inclusiveness and the terminology of Wotton's *Reflections upon Ancient and Modern Learning*, the experimental dissections of the

Royal Society and the publications of dissent are all lampooned. In the Introduction to the *Tale*, a disparate selection of productions of Grub Street are subjected to a process of metamorphic enumerative bibliography, with both general and particular targets: a chapbook *Dr Faustus* as a work of alchemy, written by Artephius, the mythic and wondrously long-lived *Adeptus*; 'Whittington *and his Cat*', described as a work of Talmudic commentary (here the voice is recognizably Bentleian, turning the great classical philologist into a critic of chapbooks); the Catholic convert John Dryden's *The Hind and the Panther* as 'a compleat Abstract of sixteen thousand Schoolmen from *Scotus* to *Bellarmin*'; the chapbook tale of 'The *Wise Men of* Gotham, *cum Appendice*' as 'a just Defence of the Modern Learning and Wit', referring to the second edition of Wotton's *Reflections* (1697) with Bentley's *Dissertation* printed as an appendix, and applying the 'immense Erudition' of the Reverend William Wotton, FRS, to a fool's tale (*CWJS*, vol. I, p. 43).

Catalogues, like all forms of the list, are highly susceptible to parodic and imaginative reorderings, imitations and revaluations, and Swift had a few possible parodic predecessors. One, with which he was certainly familiar, was Rabelais's catalogue of the library of St Victor. All Rabelais's lists are powered (and supercharged in Sir Thomas Urquhart's translation) by an almost endless poetic fertility. Here five pages of inventive titles pillory (mostly) the ancient learned professions:

> The Codpiece of the Law.
> Cacatorium medicorum.
> The Chimney-sweeper of Astrology.
> The Kissbreech of Chirurgery.

'Of which library', we are told, 'some books are already printed, and the rest are now at the Presse'.[19] Thomas Browne's *Musaeum clausum or Bibliotheca Abscondita* (posthumously published in 1684), not demonstrably known to Swift, listed among other fictitious curiosities 'remarkable Books ... of several kinds, scarce or never seen by any man now living'.

At least two parodic bibliographies of the post-Restoration period are not only closer in time to Swift, but closer to Swift's methods, and certainly closer to his political and religious principles. The anonymous *Bibliotheca fanatica: or, The phanatique library being a catalogue of such books as have been lately made and by the authors presented to the colledge of Bedlam* (1660) invented dozens of book titles, and helpfully provided brief summaries of them, to mock or allege the doings of a wide cast of sectarians and parliamentarians:

Antiquity of the English Tongue

> *De antiquitate Typographia*, to shew, that Printing or Pressing was as antient as Grandfather *Adams*, learnedly put home by *Henry Hills* Printer, to the Taylors wife in Black-Friers.

At this date Henry Hills was a member of a Particular Baptist church, already printer to the council of state, and notoriously living with the wife of Thomas Hams, a Blackfriars tailor.[20] 'Pressing' and 'put[ting] home' have appropriate plural senses here.

> Animadversions and Corrections of St. *Paul's* Epistles, and specially of that sentence, *Godliness is great gain*; whereas it should be, *Gain is great godliness*; as is clearly proved by *William Kiffin*, Broaker of the Word.

Kiffin was a Particular Baptist minister, a hugely wealthy merchant in leather and cloth, and energetic sponsor of the parliamentary cause. He celebrated his material success as evidence of divine favour: 'it pleased God so to bless our endeavours, that, from scores of pounds, he brought it to many hundreds and thousands of pound: giving me more of this world than ever I could have thought to have enjoyed'.[21] The compact ironies of the characterizing phrase 'Broaker of the Word' anticipate Swift's exploitations of the links of 'trade' and dissent. A later mock bibliography attacked William Sherlock and other senior juring clergymen, with the form and title of *A Catalogue of books of the newest fashion to be sold by auction at the Whiggs Coffee-House … near the deanry of St. Paul's* (1691). Its items provide a framework for a series of satiric portraits:

> 6. *Non magna loquimur sed, &c.* By the pious Author and religious Practiser of the Letter to the dying Lord *Russ—l*, addressed chiefly to his Arch-Brother and *quondam* Pupil Dr. *Sh*[erlock], as an Antidote against Shame and Remorse.
>
> …
>
> 9. *Dux fœmina facti*: Conquest the best Title to Body and Conscience, by Dr. *Sh—k's* Wife, dedicated to her Humble Servant her Husband …

The 'pious Author' is John Tillotson, who had argued, in his letter to the condemned Lord Russell in 1683, 'the unlawfulness of taking arms against the king in any case'. Early in 1691 Tillotson was appointed to the see of Canterbury by King William, who had come to the throne through revolution. William Sherlock, one of the leading Anglican controversialists of the time, dramatically turned his coat from public and determined nonjuring to take the oath in August 1690, under the influence, many believed at the time, of his Xanthippean wife. Swift had, then, one or two forerunners in the satiric exploitation of the form of the bookseller's or library catalogue, not much less inventive than his own, and yet more contemporary and urgent.

Swift's satire draws too upon book conventions at the typographical level. The *Tale of a Tub* and its associated texts are frequently interrupted by blanks, characteristically and almost invariably marked by multiple lines of asterisks.[22] The Apology is followed by a Postscript, which claims that 'The Gentleman who gave the Copy to the Bookseller' was 'a Friend of the Author', and used 'no other Liberties besides that of expunging certain Passages where now the Chasms appear under the Name of *Desiderata*'. The existence and identity of that Gentleman, and indeed of the passages alleged to have been expunged, are of course uncertain; the Postscript's claim is more likely to be fiction than fact. The first block of asterisks frustrates our expectation that the adequacy of 'the *Ladder*' as 'an adequate Symbol of *Faction*' will be explained, the second supplants the Hack's promised explanation of the uniform effect of different vapours. A particularly substantial block of asterisks, in the 'Discourse Concerning the Mechanical Operation of the Spirit', stands for the intended deduction and explanation of 'the whole Scheme of spiritual Mechanism' – 'but it was thought neither safe nor convenient to print it'. Briefer sequences of asterisks politely avoid stipulating that ecclesiastical, as well as civil and military, offices might be appropriately staffed by recruits from the madhouse, and politely avoid saying that the spiritual ecstasies of the Quakers are frequently accompanied by a matching physical ecstasy:

> in the Height and *Orgasmus* of their Spiritual exercise it has been frequent with them *   *   *   *; immediately after which, they found the *Spirit* to relax and flag of a sudden with the Nerves, and they were forced to hasten to a Conclusion.

Blanks and asterisks enable in fact a multitude of prevarications, parodically enacting scholarly inadequacy, mendacity, prudishness and bad faith.[23] They are represented in the *Tale* as enabling devices for a variety of abuses of learning.

In the seventeenth-century book multiple asterisks were not infrequently used as Swift would use them in *A Tale of a Tub*, as graphic markers of gaps in the text, indicative often of professional scholarly scrupulosity. Lines or multiple lines of asterisks are used from time to time to indicate lacunae in transcriptions and editions and translations of classical texts, of Longinus and Manilius for instance.[24] In a very few such works asterisks are used with significantly greater frequency. In Philemon Holland's translation of Plutarch's *Moralia* (1603), for example, substantial blocks of asterisks in some places denote innocent lacunae in the copy:

* * * * * * * * * *

> In this place a great defect and breach there is in the Greeke originall, which can not be made up and supplied without the helpe of some ancient copie, not yet extant.[25]

In other places in this book asterisks are made to stand for obscuranda: 'And yet peradventure it were not amisse in this place to resound and pro-nounce aloud those verses of *Empedocles*, * * *. For under covert tearmes he doth allegorize ...'; in yet others, asterisks are a device to avoid the writer's duty of clarification: 'these Philosophers onely have perceived this duplicity, this composition and ambiguitie; whereby every one of us are two subjects, the one being substance, the other * *'.[26] Thus tacitly in this text, as in Swift's *Tale*, the knotty Point is unravelled, and the clear Solution reached.[27]

If the use of asterisks in classical texts and translations is limited, the parody-editorial use of asterisks is much rarer. It may be found, however, in one seventeenth-century book at least, an anonymously published piece of university wit, *Naps upon Parnassus* (London, 1658), attributed to the royalist painter and poet, and (from 1668) FRS, Thomas Flatman. Here the satirical poem titled 'The Common Fire', addressed to the poet's muse, is presented as a found and incomplete text. Editorial explanations, in a second voice, accompany the piece. The lines on certain poets who 'shake off their *Mam's* old clothes, as fetters | But *petticoat themselves with different Letters*', for example, are marginally glossed: '*I think he means [effeminated], a difficult place this!' The poem ends in asterisks and emp-tiness, the Ghost of Wit, delighting to walk after the Death of its Body:

> I may not bless Him, as I've blest the rest;
> For he holds nought in Common with the rest.
> * * * * * * * * * * * * *
> * * * Caetera desiderantur.
> * * *28

As in this instance from Flatman, the *Tale of a Tub*'s gaps, and their aster-isks, are regularly glossed by tags in learned Latin. The '*Ladder*', or gallows, is 'an adequate Symbol ... of *Faction* because' – and here the promised, and dangerous, explanation is silenced by five lines of asterisks and the marginalium '*Hiatus in MS.*' Jack's tatters are briefly described as offering 'to the first View a ridiculous Flanting', which serves only to make him resemble his enemy and opposite Peter, but the point, so far from being developed, evaporates into asterisks, and the marginal remark '*Desunt nonnulla*'. In the 'Battel', the fight among the books in the King's library is punctuated by lacunae: '*Hic pauca desunt*', '*Desunt non-nulla*', '*Ingens hiatus hic in MS.*', '*Alter hiatus in MS.*' The physical book of Cowley's *Mistress* is metamorphosed into a dove harnessed to Venus's chariot, but this modern myth breaks off into asterisks: '*Hiatus valdè deflendus in MS.*' The 'Battel' itself concludes, following the transformation of Bentley and Wotton into a brace of skewered woodcocks, with four lines of asterisks and a *Desunt cætera*.[29]

Nor are these various marks of absence the only learned verbal tags in the *Tale*. A plethora of such phrases, borrowed from medieval and modern scholastic, theological and legal uses, pepper the arguments of Peter, the brother 'that was the Scholar', or are used in connection with his text-wresting arguments, which are abuses of learning as well as of religion. Peter finds authority for adding shoulder knots to the brothers' coats by reading the Father's Will '*totidem verbis*', '*totidem syllabis*' and finally '*totidem literis*', phrases used in scholastic scriptural interpretation. The 'k' in 'Shoulder-knots' is found from the word '*Calendae*', which, we are told by Peter, 'hath in *Q.V.C.* been sometimes writ with a *K*'; the marginalium explains the three-letter acronym as '**Quibusdam Veteribus Codicibus*', and the footnote translates the marginalium: 'Some antient Manuscripts' (*CWJS*, vol. I, pp. 54–5, 56). Here Swift aims specifically at Richard Bentley's allegedly unprincipled methods of textual reference, though the phrase, and similar phrases, were in common scholarly use.[30] Martin and Jack liberate the Will from the strongbox that is the Vulgate, by making a '*Copia vera*', a legal phrase written (now as then) at the top of copies of legal instruments to certify a true copy or duplicate. 'Flame-colour'd Sattin', or the doctrine of purgatory, Peter justifies by the addition to the Father's Will of 'a Codicil annexed', a lawyer's phrase.[31]

The tags that mark the *Tale*'s lacunae were often used, as we might expect, as standard notations for missing or abrupted passages in classical editions, and in learned histories. A letter in *Disertissimi viri Rogeri Aschami* (1576) ends in a *Desunt cætera*; John Weever's *Ancient Funerall Monuments ... of Great Britaine* (1631) quotes, from 'a Manuscript in Sir *Robert Cottons* Libraire', a set of Latin rhyming hexameters against the Monks, which have to end in the same familiar phrase (p. 78); more than one section in two careful examinations of the politics and rights and wrongs of the civil war by 'P.D.' (that is, by Francis Nethersole) concludes with a *Desunt nonnulla*, or *Reliqua desiderantur*.[32]

Such phrases, however, had a far wider and more catholic currency. They were regularly used in printed editions of vernacular poetry, in Joseph Hall's *Virgidemiarum* (1602; p. 59) for example; at the end of the texts of 'To the Countesse of Bedford' and of 'Resurrection, Imperfect' in John Donne's *Poems* of 1633 (2nd edn, pp. 111, 162); and at the beginning of the text of Robert Herrick's 'The Apparition of his Mistresse' in the 1648 edition of *Hesperides* (p. 240).[33] Indeed, such phrases were so familiar as to be capable of being turned to various figurative applications. 'J.C.*M.D.*' exploits the doubleness of the Latin in a modesty topos, apologizing for pretensions to learning by one 'in a rural retirement, having no book but one of an imperfect edition, forc'd to read my self, *ubi multa desiderantur & à desunt nonnulla'*.[34] Henry Petowe justifies his writing a sequel to *Hero and Leander*, comparing Marlowe's unfinished poem to 'a heade seperated from the body, with this harsh sentence, *Desunt nonnulla'*.[35]

More significantly, certainly more significantly for Swift, the tags that he uses in the *Tale* are all, along with their other uses, part of the discourse of debate between Rome and the protestant churches concerning the reliability and sufficiency of the Holy Scriptures as a rule of belief. Central to the *Tale* is the conviction that the Father's Will – Scripture, or rather the New Testament – consists of 'certain plain easy directions' for the conduct of the Christian religion. The brothers go astray initially when Peter, 'he that was the Scholar' (*CWJS*, vol. I, p. 56), applies a variety of kinds of misreading in order to justify additions to the coats against the terms of the Father's Will: the devotional ornaments of shoulder knots, the materialism of gold lace, the false doctrine of purgatory represented by linings of flame-coloured satin, the pomps of silver fringe and the iconography of '*Indian Figures'*. An essential part of Peter's argument, applied in favour of gold lace, is the resort beyond the written ('scriptory') will, to Church tradition (the 'nuncupatory' will). It is just this demoting of the authority of the text of Scripture, and the strategic wresting of its meaning, that protestant divines imputed, in a thousand places, to the Church of Rome.[36] In many such places Anglican divines used phrases familiar to us from the *Tale* to accuse the Romanists of distortions and dismissals of written scripture. Thomas Beard, Oliver Cromwell's schoolmaster, found the Jesuit apologist Francis Coster, in his *Enchiridion* (1585), guilty of treating the scriptures like a pedant dismissing defective manuscripts:

> His words are these, *Omnia fidei mysteria, caeteraq; credita & scitu necessaria, ex corde Ecclesiae sunt clarissimè exarata, in membranis tamen tam noui quam veteris Testamenti multa desiderantur:* that is, *all the mysteries of faith, and other things necessary to bee beleeued and known, are most clearely engrauen*

in the heart of the Church, but in the leaues of the Olde and New Testament, many things are wanting. What can be more plaine?[37]

Thomas Bell, Romanist priest turned protestant controversialist, in the course of demonstrating in his *Catholique Triumph* (1610) that the Donation of Constantine was forged, quoted the words of a Romanist against the Roman position:

> *Quoniam absq; dubio, si non fuisset illud dictamen apocryphum, Gratianus in veteribus codicibus... inuenisset; et quia non inuenit, non posuit:...* For without doubt, if that report were not apocryphall, *Gratianus* would haue found it in the old Bookes ... but because he did not finde it, he did not set downe the same.[38]

Much later in the century, the royalist clergyman Francis Gregory, in his *Grand Presumption of the Roman Church in Equalling their own Traditions to the Written Word of God* (1675), repeated the regular accusation that the Romanists have falsified and forged the writings of the Church Fathers (second only in authority, in Anglican orthodoxy, to the holy scriptures themselves). Specifically, Gregory accuses Cardinal Bellarmine of censoring Chrysostom:

> St. *Chrysostom* left upon record an Expression which the *Roman* Church doth no way like, and that was this; *In times of Heresie there is no means to find out the Truth, save onely the reading of the Scriptures.* Bellarmine confesseth, *Totus hic locus è quibusdam codicibus nuper emendatis sublatus est;* This whole Passage is left out of some Editions newly set forth and corrected. But how comes St. *Chrysostom* thus to deserve the *Spunge?* (p. 115)

On such evidence it is possible to argue that Swift's use of such tags as *desunt nonnulla* and *quibusdam veteribus codicibus* are not merely parodies of neutral scholarly conventions, but are a part of his response to a century of argument between England and Rome about the reading of the text of scripture.

The *Tale of a Tub* is not a mock book in the same way or to the same degree as Pope's *Dunciad Variorum* of 1729. Swift's first great satire is by no means so predominantly based in form on a single, heroic, scholarly model, nor does it have a particular, identified mock hero. If Wotton and Bentley are the main scholarly targets of the 'Tale', as of the 'Battel of the Books', the formal and verbal methods of that notorious pair of moderns are personated in often fragmented and opportunistic ways. If worthy their parts in Swift's satiric play, they are nevertheless only the most prominent of a substantially larger cast of modern practitioners of dubious bookish typographies and paratexts. Even a partial examination

shows how conscious Swift was in the *Tale* of the manifold conventions
of the book, more especially of the learned book, and how alive he was
to the rich possibilities they offered to a satiric pen. His exploitations
of the possibilities of marginal and footnote reference and explication,
his numerous parodies of list and catalogue, his mocking echoes of the
scrupulous or deceitful *lacuna,* his scattering of the verbal or acronymic
jargon of the scholarly tag, are all weapons he brings to the battle of
the books. They are parts of his defence of an older literary humanism
against the modern, evidence-based, authenticating humanist scholarship
of Bentley, Wotton and such predecessors as Richard Simon, and against
the more disparate and demotic textual devices of a newly commercial
world of print.

Notes

1 *CWJS,* vol. I, pp. 6, 123, 10. All references to the *Tale of a Tub,* 'Battel of the
  Books' and 'Mechanical Operation of the Spirit' are to this edition. The dramatic widening in Swift and Bentley's time of the breach between two kinds of
  humanism – rhetorical, literary, evaluative on the one hand, forensic, scholarly,
  judicial on the other – is explored in John F. Tinkler's important essay, 'The
  Splitting of Humanism: Bentley, Swift, and the English Battle of the Books',
  Journal of the History of Ideas, 49 (1988), 453–72. I have argued at length for the
  basis in Anglican hermeneutics of Swift's preferences in texts and textual interpretation in 'Text, "Text", and Swift's *Tale of a Tub',* *Modern Language Review,*
  85 (1990), 290–303.
2 For the debate among modern commentators concerning the credibility and
  reliability of Swift's professions in the Apology, see *CWJS,* vol. I, pp. liii–liv and
  footnotes.
3 I have discussed these methods of parody in my Annotations to the 'Tale',
  'Battel' and 'Mechanical Operation of the Spirit' in *CWJS,* vol. I.
4 *CWJS,* vol. I, pp. 62, 97, 135, 143.
5 Cf. Anthony Grafton, *The Footnote: A Curious History* (London: Faber and
  Faber, 1997), pp. 23–4.
6 See Lawrence Lipking, 'The Marginal Gloss', *Critical Inquiry,* 3 (1976–7), 609–
  55 (pp. 621–2); Frank Palmeri, 'The Satiric Footnotes of Swift and Gibbon',
  The Eighteenth Century, 31 (1990), 245–62 (pp. 245, 252–3, 259, 260); Gerard
  Genette, *Paratexts: Thresholds of Interpretation,* tr. Jane E. Lewin (Cambridge
  University Press, 1997), p. 320.
7 Dirk F. Passmann and Heinz J. Vienken record Swift's ownership of Simon's
  Vieux testament (Rotterdam, 1685), but not of any copy of the *Nouveau testament,* in French or English (*Library and Reading, Part I,* vol. III, 1696–7).
8 See my 'Text, "Text", and Swift's *Tale of a Tub'.*
9 *A Critical History of the Old Testament* (London, 1682), Author's Preface, b4^{r-v}.

10 *A Critical History of the Text of the New Testament* (London, 1689), Preface, A4ᵛ.

11 Swift owned the second edition of volumes I and II (1710) and the first edition of volume III (1711).

12 Printed in Temple's *Miscellanea, the Second Part* (1690).

13 For example, in support of his insistence that Thericles was a potter, not a magistrate, Bentley lists and quotes 'no fewer than ten witnesses' (Richard Bentley, *A Dissertation upon the Epistles of Phalaris with an Answer to the Objections of the Honourable Charles Boyle* (London, 1699), pp. 109–10, 127).

14 In the 1697 edition, quotations in the Greek and Latin had been made within the text.

15 Bentley, *Dissertation*, pp. 408, 410, 378.

16 See *CWJS*, vol. I, pp. xxxiv–xxxv, 213–14, 279–80.

17 For instance: Henry Savage, *Balliofergus, or, A Commentary upon the Foundation, Founders and Affaires of Balliol Colledge … Whereunto is Added, an Exact Catalogue of all the Heads of the Same College* (Oxford, 1668); *The Catologue of Contented Cuckolds: or, A Loving Society of Confessing Brethren* (London, [1685?]); *A Catalogue of the Bowes, of the Town … to be Set by Auction* (London, 1691); Thomas Ouldman, *An Out-cry of Poets; or, a Catalogue of Wits to be Sold by Inch of Candle* (London, 1691); *A Catalogue of the Fellows and other Members of the Royal Colledge of Physicians, London* (London, 1694); *Explanatory Notes upon a Mendacious Libel called Concubinage and Poligamy Disproved … as being a Scurrilous Libel … As may Appear, by a Catalogue of Notorious and Villainous Lies, and Billingsgate Raileries … to be Shewed Therein. By J.B.B.D.* (London, 1698).

18 *Dunciad*, book IV, line 570, *TE*, vol. V, p. 398.

19 François Rabelais, *Gargantua and Pantagruel*, bk 2, ch. 7, tr. Sir Thomas Urquhart and Pierre Le Motteux (New York, London and Toronto: Everyman's Library, 1994), p. 193.

20 See *ODNB*, s.v. Henry Hills, senior (*c.* 1625–1688/9). Hills would later conform to the Church of England, and in 1685 convert to Catholicism, rising at last to become master of the Stationers' Company in 1687.

21 See *ODNB*, s.v. William Kiffin (1616–1701).

22 The asterisk, or *Asterism*, together with its uses, is discussed by John Smith, in his *Printer's Grammar* (London, 1755). In particular, 'Asterisms … denote an omission, or an hiatus; by loss of original Copy; in which case the number of Asterisms is multiplied according to the largeness of the chasm; and not only whole lines, but sometimes whole pages are left blank, and mark'd with some lines of Stars' (pp. 79–80). Swift's use of asterisks in *A Tale of a Tub* has been analyzed in Christopher Flint, *The Appearance of Print in Eighteenth-Century Fiction* (Cambridge University Press, 2011), pp. 113–26.

23 *CWJS*, vol. I, pp. 15, 40, 110, 113, 129, 156, 157, 158, 160, 164, 179, 186.

24 *[Peri Hypsous], or Dionysius Longinus of the Height of Eloquence, Rendered out of the Originall. By J. H. Esq;* (London, 1652), p. lxxx; Thomas Stanley, *The*

History of Philosophy in Eight Parts (London, 1656), p. 137; *Lucretius his Six Books of Epicurean Philosophy: and Manilius his Five Books*, tr. Thomas Creech (London, 1700) (*Manilius*, p. 82).

25 *The Philosophie, Commonlie Called, The Morals*, tr. Philemon Holland (London, 1603), p. 958; cf. pp. 1035, 1045, 1152, 1053, 1171. For further examples see Livy, *The Romane Historie*, tr. Philemon Holland (London, 1600), pp. 847, 1114, 1214; *Velleius Paterculus his Romane Historie*, tr. Robert Le Grys (London, 1632), pp. 19–20.

26 Plutarch, *Philosophie*, pp. 575, 1106; cf. pp. 713, 890. Asterisks used thus are not wholly confined to the learned classics: cf. Katherine Philips, *Poems. By the Incomparable, Mrs. K. P.* (London, 1664), p. 30.

27 See *CWJS*, vol. I, p. 110.

28 *Naps upon Parnassus. … Such Voluntary and Jovial Copies of Verses, as were lately receiv'd from some of the WITS of the Universities* (London, 1658), pp. 30, 31. The satiric use of the lacuna is more explicit and developed in Thomas D'Urfey's burlesque *An Essay towards the Theory of the Intelligible World … The Archetypally Second Edition* (London, [1705?]), a parody of John Norris, *An Essay towards the Theory of the Ideal or Intelligible World* (two parts, London, 1701, 1704). Here D'Urfey considers 'The Method of making a *Chasm*, or *Hiatus*, judiciously', in a short chapter in which a fragmented quotation from *Aeneid*, 4. 335, 549, itself broken up by dashes, is followed by a page made up wholly of dashes, with a marginal note: 'The Author very well understands that a good sizable *Hiatus* discovers a very great Genius, there being no wit in the World more Ideal, and consequently more refined, than what is display'd in those elaborate Pages, that have ne're a Syllable written on them' (pp. 162–3). In this D'Urfey no doubt learned from Swift's *Tub* as well as from Norris.

29 *CWJS*, vol. I, pp. 40, 129, 156–8, 160, 164.

30 See for example *CWJS*, vol. I, p. 66, and note 40, pp. 385–6.

31 See *CWJS*, vol. I, pp. 78, 396, 56, 375.

32 *Problemes Necessary to be Determined by All that Have, or Have Not Taken Part … in the Late Unnatural Warre* (1648), p. 22; and *A Strong Motive to a General Pardon* (1648), p. 8.

33 Cf. John Weever, *Epigrammes in the Oldest Cut and Newest Fashion* (1599), B8ᵛ (where *Desunt nunnulla* intervenes after only one line of the epigram 'In Titum'); Francis Hubert, *The Deplorable Life and Death of Edward the Second … Storied in an Excellent Poem* (1628), p. 91; Robert Heath, *Clarastella* (1650), p. 20.

34 [John Collop,] *Charity Commended, or, A Catholick Christian Soberly Instructed* (1667), B1ʳ. Cf. John Wilson, *A Good and Seasonable Caveat for Christians* (1646), A4ʳ.

35 'Epistle Dedicatorie', *The Second Part of Hero and Leander Conteyning Their Further Fortunes* (1598), Aiiiᵛ.

36 For fuller discussion, see my 'Text, "Text", and Swift's *Tale of a Tub*'.

37 Beard, *A Retractive from the Romish Religion* (1616), pp. 156–7.

38   *The Catholique Triumph: … Wherein is euidently prooued, that Poperie and the Doctrine now professed in the Romish Church, is the New Religion; And that the Fayth which the Church of England now mayntaineth, is the ancient romane Religion* (1610), p. 35. The tag is used in a more scholarly context by William Perkins, *Problema de Romanae Fidei Ementitio Catholicismo* (Cambridge, 1604), p. 54.

CHAPTER SIX

Epistolary forms: published correspondence, letter-journals and books

Abigail Williams

Jonathan Swift wrote thousands of familiar letters during his lifetime, but unlike his friend and correspondent Alexander Pope, he did not engineer the publishing of his correspondence.[1] A discussion of Swift's letters and the printed eighteenth-century book could, then, be a short one: Swift did not publish his letters himself, and the ways in which they were issued can tell us little about his concern for his works in printed form. But an examination of Swift's letters in print has a lot to tell us about Swift's textual afterlives, and about the role of public and private documents in a rapidly commercializing literary marketplace. In this essay I shall explore how some of the early printings of Swift's letters shaped his identity in the period immediately after his death. Different collections of letters presented competing versions of Swift: man of letters, jest-book joker or political loyalist. These publications not only reveal the relationship between the editing of Swift and the construction of his literary afterlife, but they also illuminate contemporary understanding of the nature of private and public material. The editors and booksellers who issued his letters knew that they did so without his sanction, and their editorial justifications found for publishing what was not intended to be published are both ingenious and revealing. In negotiating the competing demands of 'curiosity' and propriety, their prefatory defences provide antecedents to modern debates about the role of the press and the nature of public interest.

Swift and letters as works

No single collection of authorized correspondence appeared during Swift's lifetime. The one collection that Swift had any involvement in was the edition of letters between himself, Pope, Bolingbroke and Gay that appeared in 1741, *Letters Between Dr. Swift, Mr. Pope, &c. From the Year 1714 to 1738* (TS 60 and 62B), largely orchestrated by Pope.[2] This collection, which Pope had been planning since the early 1730s, began to take

119

shape in 1735, when Pope asked Swift to return his letters to him. Swift was reluctant, but after Pope had leaked to Edmund Curll two letters to Swift in 1736, and published three Pope–Swift letters in the *Letters of Mr. Alexander Pope, and Several of his Friends* in 1737, Swift seems to have consented. He may in part have been influenced by Pope's publication of the tribute to him in his *First Epistle of the Second Book of Horace Imitated* in May 1737.[3] Over the next two decades, a range of separate collections came out, all of which included different subsets of letters. In 1745 a group of letters and works relating to Swift's closest Irish friend, Thomas Sheridan, was published as '*Miscellanies. The Tenth Volume. By Dr. Swift*' (TS 66, vol. X). In 1765 the London editor John Hawkesworth published a volume of letters as a supplement to his on-going edition of Swift's *Works*, containing many letters derived from the hoard of manuscript material previously owned by Swift's cousin, Deane Swift, and acquired by him from Swift's friend and housekeeper, Martha Whiteway (TS 88, vol. XVI). In 1766 Hawkesworth published a further collection of letters sent to Swift and passed on from Swift's friend and one-time amanuensis John Lyon (TS 88, vols. XVIII, XIX, XX), with a second instalment in 1768, collected and edited by Deane Swift (TS 88, vols. XXI, XXII, XXIII).[4] The first time that all these groups of letters were brought together was in 1784, when they were included in Thomas Sheridan's seventeen-volume *The Works of the Rev. Dr. Jonathan Swift, Dean of St. Patrick's, Dublin* (TS 119). This was followed by John Nichols's 1801 edition, *The Works of the Rev. Jonathan Swift, D.D.* (TS 129) Thus in the decade before and the decade and a half after his death, Swift's letters came out in a series of discrete works. These collections had very different identities, shaped by the origins of the letters, and the nature of their contents. They did not acquire a uniform identity as 'Swift's correspondence' until the late eighteenth century.

There is no evidence to suggest that Swift planned to see any of his letters in print, with the exception of some of his later correspondence with Alexander Pope. He does not seem to have written any of his letters with a view to publication in print and did not regularly keep copies, telling Francis Atterbury 'I keep no copies of letters', and instructing Sir Andrew Fountaine to burn the uncorrected letter that he had sent him.[5] He writes to Pope in 1735: 'You need not fear any Consequence in the Commerce that hath so long passed between us, although I never destroy'd one of your Letters. But my Executors are Men of Honor and Virtue, who have strict orders in my Will to burn every Letter left behind me.'[6] But he was also aware of public interest in his letters, were they to be published. His good friend Lady Elizabeth Germain, writing in 1735, expresses her concern for the fate of her writings:

> I must recommend to you an affair which has given me some small palpitations of the heart which is, that you shoud not wrap up either old shoes or neglected sermons in my Letters but that what of them has been spared from going toward making Gin for the Ladies, may henceforth be commited instantly to the flames, for you being stigmatisd with the name of a Witt, Mr Curl will rake to the Dunghill for your Corespondance.[7]

Swift writes back deflecting the request with a compliment: 'as to the letters I receive from your Ladyship, I neither ever did or ever will burn any of them, take it as you please: for I never burn a letter that is entertaining'. He goes on to tell her why he keeps letters: 'It is true, I have kept some letters merely out of friendship, although they sometimes wanted true spelling and good sense, and some others whose writers are dead. For I live like a monk, and hate to forget my departed friends.' Then he adds: 'I confess also that I have read some passages in many of your letters, to a friend, but without naming you, only that the writer was a lady, which had such marks of good sense that often the hearers would not believe me. And yet I never had a letter of mine printed, nor of any others to me.'[8]

The exchange illustrates Swift and Germain's awareness of the likelihood of the letters being published, and their reluctance to see this happen. It also shows clear distinctions in contemporary understanding of the privacy of correspondence. Familiar letters were not private in the sense that they were exclusively for the eyes of the addressee – there are numerous references throughout Swift's correspondence to the wider readership of individual letters, or the use of letters as vehicles for news and as cover for enclosures for a wider circle of friends. So, for example, in his account books Swift notes receipt of a letter from Joseph Beaumont, which contains 'a bit from ppt', indicating that Esther Johnson was contributing to other correspondents' letters.[9] Johnson was also corresponding with Swift's other friends: in Letter 62, of 19 March 1713, Swift records that 'Dilly [Dillon Ashe] read me a Letter to day from ppt' (*JSt* (1948), vol. II, p. 641). This is a common feature of the early modern and eighteenth-century letter, and Clare Brant has argued that 'personal' is a more useful way of describing such letters, and for making the distinction between limited circulation and widespread publication.[10] But however open the personal letter was in this period, such a form of circulation was perceived as crucially different from print publication, much as the manuscript circulation of verse was different from print publication. Swift evidently kept some of his letters, and showed them to other people, but he saw both acts as testaments to friendships, rather than as forms of public self-representation.

Swift's position on the public and private is also complicated by the genres of his epistolary writing. The *Journal to Stella*, the set of sixty-five letters that Swift wrote to Esther Johnson and Rebecca Dingley during his time in London from 1710 to 1713, is a private record of public life. The letters are both correspondence and diary journal, offering an account of Swift's involvement with the Tory ministry on a diurnal basis. Given the nature and intimacy of the letters, it seems unlikely that Swift intended the letters to be published as they were. But he may have intended them to have some kind of afterlife. Swift wrote elsewhere of the role of letters as public history, writing to Pope in October 1735: 'I have observ'd that not only Voiture, but likewise Tully and Pliny writ their letters for the publick view, more than for the sake of their correspondents; and I am glad of it, on account of the Entertainment they have given me.'[11] For all his references elsewhere to the burning of letters, he seems to have expected Johnson and Dingley to keep his *Journal* letters, anticipating that he would be able to reread them in later years: 'I know 'tis neither wit nor diversion to tell you every day where I dine, neither do I write it to fill my letter; but I fancy I shall, some time or other, have the curiosity of seeing some particulars how I passed my life when I was absent from MD this time.'[12] It is significant that the *Journal to Stella* letters make up the only substantial set of correspondence between Swift and either of the two women that survives. We can tell that Swift reviewed the *Journal* letters at a later period, although it is hard to determine when or for what purpose. The cover of letter 1 bears an annotation in Swift's hand, in which he describes the content of the package of letters before him, writing 'Letters to Ireld from Septr. 1710 began soon after the change of Ministry', adding below 'nothing in this'.[13] This suggests that he had reviewed the contents of the letters once returned to him. The historiographical nature of this set of letters certainly seems to have given the correspondence more than a throwaway significance for Swift. He was to revisit the period covered by the *Journal* over and over again in his later prose and verse, and jokes and comments made in those letters resurface in later letters and works. At the end of a letter of December 1711, written in the midst of the final negotiations over the peace of Utrecht, he remarks to Johnson and Dingley: 'this is a long journal, and of a day that may produce great alterations, and hazard the ruin of England ... I shall know more soon, and my letters will at least be a good history to shew you the steps of this change'.[14] While he did not envisage the *Journal* letters as publishable history, some of their content had historiographical significance. The material was clearly reworked to form the basis of Swift's later prose writings on the politics of Queen Anne's reign, his *History of the Four Last Years of the Queen* (written 1713, published in 1758) and the *Enquiry into the Behaviour of the Queen's Last Ministry* (written June 1715).

Swift and works as letters

Swift might not have considered his correspondence to be part of his works, but there are numerous pamphlets and poems that demonstrate his use of epistolary form in the public domain. In total, Swift's bibliography lists fifty-eight works with the title letters or letter. In using the conceit of the letter in this way, Swift was not unusual: the letter as political pamphlet was well established by the end of the seventeenth century, and *ESTC* lists hundreds of religious and political works with titles containing the term 'letter' over the course of the eighteenth century.

The letter is used throughout Swift's career. Writing for the ministry from 1710 to 1714, he used the letter as way of making his voice heard in political debate: *Some Advice Humbly Offer'd to the Members of the October Club, in a Letter from a Person of Honour; A Letter from the Pretender to a Whig Lord; The Importance of The Guardian Considered, in a Second Letter to the Bailiff of Stockbridge.* In *The Examiner*, as later in *The Intelligencer*, letters provided ways of varying the series with differing forms of impersonation. When in 1724 he decided to make a major intervention in Irish politics, it was in the series of *Drapier's Letters*, with their carefully graduated addressees. In addition to this bookmaking with the letter or letters, we find Swift embedding letters in other writings (most famously the 'Letter from Capt. Gulliver to his Cousin Sympson' in *Gulliver's Travels*) and using the epistle form in his poetry, either to shape the whole poem ('An Epistle upon an Epistle') or satirically embedded ('Phillis, or, the Progress of Love'). Swift uses the relationship between addressee and text in a range of ways: 'A Letter to a Young Lady, on her Marriage' is a public letter to a real person, whereas *A Letter to a Young Gentleman Lately Entered into Holy Orders* is a public letter to a fictitious person. The *Drapier's Letters* are a series of pseudonymous public letters variously addressed to Irish individuals and classes. All of these letter-works are tracts of instruction or propaganda. The epistolary conceits are important framing devices: they position the works within a time and place, give dramatis personae, and provide a vehicle for comment and argument. Most have little of the epistolary beyond a salutation and complimentary ending. They are not letters in any very meaningful sense.

Of course, in distinguishing overmuch the difference between public fictional epistolarity and genuine correspondence we run the risk of downplaying the element of performance in the actual letter. Swift's correspondence is not necessarily much less deliberately crafted than the pamphlet letters, despite what Swift himself says about the naturalness of his letter-writing. He often tells his friends that his letters are unguarded and unstudied: 'Is it imagined that I must be always leaning upon one Hand while I am writing with the other, Alway upon the *qui vive* and the *Slip Slop* instead of an honest plain Letter … may I never think again if I think three Seconds whenever I write to the best or the worst of you.'[15] Nine years later he affirmed to Pope his belief that 'we neither of us ever leaned our head upon our left hand to study what we should write next'.[16] This was to become part of the myth and attraction of Swift as letter-writer. Over a decade later, Robert Boyle, Earl of Orrery, quotes a similar phrase with approval in his critical essays on Swift: 'I have often heard SWIFT say, "*When I sit down to write a letter, I never lean upon my elbow, till I have finished it.*"' Orrery then comments on the style of the letters: 'By which expression he meant, that he never studied for particular phrases, or polished paragraphs: his letters therefore are the truer representations of his mind. They are written in the warmth of his affections, and when they are considered in the light of kindness and sincerity, they illustrate his character to a very high degree.'[17] For Orrery, Swift's apparently unstudied letter-writing habits are an indication of their psychological and emotional transparency. However, as various critics have observed, this apparently unguarded sincerity belies the craft of Swift's letters. The actual correspondence shows altogether more studied forms of self-representation. Oliver Ferguson, Frederik N. Smith, Ashley Marshall and others have all emphasized the dramatic qualities of Swift's correspondence, and the ways in which he adopts different personae and voices to suit different readers, as in his letter pamphlets.[18]

Yet despite the fact that both correspondence and literary letter-writing share qualities of fictive self-representation, once again the crucial distinction between public and personal writing remains. Swift's writings about literary epistles and familiar letters suggest that he saw the two forms as offering very different kinds of utterance. So, for example, Swift seems to regard Pope's verse epistles in a fundamentally different way from his prose letters, and he pleads with Pope for a public memorial to their friendship in the form of a verse epistle addressed to him.[19] He writes to Pope in

September 1735 asking for a verse tribute that will enable their connection to assume more public form:

> Neither did our letters contain any turns of Wit or fancy, or Politicks or Satyr, but meer innocent friendship; yet I am loth that any Letters from you & a very few other friends should dye before me … I have the ambition, & it is very earnest as well as in hast to have one Epistle inscribed to me while I am alive, and you just in the time when Wit and Wisdom are in the height. I must once more repeat Cicero's desire to a friend, *Orna me*.[20]

We should probably take with some caution Swift's claim that his correspondence is unstudiedly natural, but for all this hidden craft, it seems clear that he did not view his letters as public monuments to his friendships.

The Swift–Pope letters and gentlemanly friendship

As we have seen above, in the final decade of his life, Swift assured his friends that the personal and informal nature of his correspondence would limit its public appeal. A month after the letter quoted above, he wrote again to Pope about the prospect of publication, observing: 'I believe my letters have escap'd being publish'd, because I writ nothing but Nature and Friendship, and particular incidents which could make no figure in writing.'[21] It was ironic, then, that the first sets of letters to appear in print, during Swift's lifetime, were marketed as documents of literary friendships. The first instalment in the afterlife of Swift in letters was the publication of his letters to and from Pope, Gay and Bolingbroke in 1741, in *Letters Between Dr. Swift, Mr. Pope, &c.*, and in the following year, the Dublin edition of *Letters To and From Dr. J. Swift, D.S.P.D.* The bibliographical history of the publication of Swift's letters to Pope is a complex one, and the story of the subterfuge in the soliciting and release of the letters has been told several times in greater detail than is possible here.[22] We now know that Pope solicited Swift's letters from 1733, and engineered the publishing of the letters, with some confused involvement on the part of Swift, as discussed earlier.[23]

The collection of letters that appeared after the protracted negotiations presented Swift the gentleman author in select company, and demonstrated precisely the familiar informal and conversational qualities that Swift had earlier claimed to Pope would guarantee their remaining private. The contents pages give an indication of the ways in which the collection effectively memorialized a series of close associations, as we can see from the descriptions provided of the letters:

Letter 3. Mr. Pope's Love and Memory of Dr. Swift.

Letter 15: Answer from Mr. Pope. The Regret of his [Swift's] departure. Remembrance of the Satisfaction past, Wishes for his Welfare.

Letter 24: From Dr Swift: His Remembrance of Mr. P's Friendship; with some considerations of his Circumstances.

Letter 36. Dr. Swift to Lord Bolingbroke … His Friendship for Mr. Pope.

Letter 42. From Lord B. That the Sense of Friendship Increases with the Increase of Years.

Letter 44 … Postscript by Lord Bol on the Pleasure we take in reading Letters.

Alongside 'friendship' the term 'raillery' also features prominently in the description of the contents of the letters, corroborating this sense of friends at ease with one another. When Orrery came to discuss the Pope–Swift letters in his *Remarks*, he observed that it was these free familiar letters that told the most about individual character, since 'no part of an author's writings give a greater insight into his natural disposition than his letters, (especially when written with freedom and sincerity)'.[24] Yet there is a tension here between the kinds of interest and revelation provided by familiar letters, and the intrusion of publication. At the same time as praising the letters, Orrery also laments

> that licence which of late has too much prevailed of publishing epistolary correspondences … At present, it satisfies the curiosity of the public; but for the future, it will tend to restrain that unsuspicious openness, which is the principal delight of writing to our friends.[25]

Orrery's sentiments are echoed by many writers of the period, who voice ambivalence about the publication of personal correspondence (while often encouraging it). There are several ironies in Orrery's contradictory statements: he fears that the more developed the culture of publishing private material becomes, the less those letters will sound as though they are private. Yet he himself had played a prominent role in coercing Swift's letters into print in the late 1730s. In addition, his own biography of Swift, the *Remarks*, had used the form of familiar epistolarity as a frame for his account of Swift's life and works.[26] But Orrery's pronouncements on the dangers of publishing personal correspondence and its potential consequences for the art of letter-writing also speak to wider debates about the relationship between letters and books. What he is saying is that we like private familiar letters precisely because they were not meant to be read by us. Part of the appeal of the familiar letter in this period was its performance of intimacy, the close access it seemed to promise. But the phenomenon of the familiar letter in print also raised ethical questions about editorial responsibility and the nature of authorial privacy.

Miscellanies and the curious reader

We might see the publication of the Pope–Swift letters in 1741 as ingenious self-fashioning on the part of Pope. Like the *Miscellanies in Prose and Verse*, it provided a material testament to writerly friendship and collaboration. The next series of Swift letters to appear in print was the result not of authorial intervention, but a combination of commercial and personal circumstances. In Robert Dodsley's 1745 printing of a selection of letters in *Miscellanies, the Tenth Volume* we find Swift in rather different company – these letters represent him alongside his closest Irish friend, the schoolmaster and wit Thomas Sheridan (1687–1738).[27] Most of the material in the *Miscellanies*, which includes sermons, prose, poetry and letters, came from the collection of manuscripts owned by his son, Thomas Sheridan the actor, elocutionist and biographer of Swift. Thomas Sheridan Senior had died in straitened circumstances in 1738, and shortly before his death he had had to sell his school and pawn his library to raise money.[28] The executors of his will sold his manuscripts for only £50 to his son, who issued proposals in 1743 in Dublin and in 1744 in London for publishing his father's works in four volumes, and in 1745 issued proposals in London for one volume, to be published by Dodsley.[29] No such edition of Sheridan's works ever appeared, but the Swift and Swift-related manuscripts Sheridan had left behind him were published as Swift's *Three Sermons* (1744) and as *Miscellanies X–XI* (1745–6). Dodsley's acquisition and publication of the material was part of a wider initiative by English booksellers to capitalize on Swift's popularity at this time. After Benjamin Motte's death in 1738, the principal owners of Swift's works in England were his partner and successor Charles Bathurst (with Gilliver), and Charles Davis (with Thomas Woodward). Mindful of the competition from Faulkner's editions of Swift, they resolved to co-operate to some degree for the reprint of Swift's works. Bathurst joined a group already consisting of Davis, Woodward, Bowyer and Faulkner. The outcome was the small octavo *Miscellanies* of 1742 onwards, of which volume X, containing the letters, was published by Dodsley in 1745. Before the *Miscellanies* appeared, Sheridan was little known to readers in London, but in Dublin, Sheridan was well known both as a teacher and as a writer – he was known for his mock-scholarly treatise, *Ars pun-ica* (1719), and he was associated with and ridiculed for merry writing: doggerel, cramboes, riddles and Anglo-Latin games.[30] He had spent several years gathering a collection of *bons mots* and apothegms, which were never published. It was this ludic mode that coloured the presentation of Swift in the *Miscellanies* correspondence. The letters to Sheridan resemble in some ways the manner of the *Journal to Stella* letters – Swift responds to inquiries, asks questions, invents rhymes and teases his correspondent. There are letters entirely composed of jokes about words ending in 'ling', letters in Anglo-Latin, and countless puns and riddles, and there are 'Thoughts on Various Subjects', collections of jests and short epigrammatic or joking narratives. One interesting feature is that the organization of the material moves from joking letters to joking poems and prose pieces: so we move from letter 36, a series of two-line riddles addressed to Sheridan, to 'The Blunders, Deficiencies, Distresses, and Misfortunes of Quilca', as if there is little distinction to be made between letters and prose works. In collecting letters and works in this way, the *Miscellanies* volume not only confused the distinction between private and public, but it created a version of Swift resembling the popular 'jest-book' Swift described by Anne Cline Kelly, the man of witty sayings and comic gambits rather than the patriot and gentleman author.[31]

The other striking feature of the collection is that it offered insights into Swift's relationship with Esther Johnson, and was the first step in the memorialization of that friendship. Sheridan knew many of Swift's Irish friends, but was most closely linked to Swift through Johnson – he reports on her last illness, and he wrote the tender verses signed by her friends.[32] The arrangement of the letters within the *Miscellanies* volume constructs a narrative of this three-way friendship, and the illness and loss of Johnson, offering readers a different form of intimate Swift to the one they saw in the Pope collection. The letters frequently involve or allude to 'the ladies', and the domestic detail of their lives, and we also have here Swift's most frank statements of his affection for the ailing Esther Johnson and his estimation of her significance to him: 'the Loss of that Person for whose sake Life was only worth preserving. I brought both those Friends over, that we might be happy together as long as God should please; the Knot is broken …'[33]

It is clear that the fashioning of Swift's epistolary afterlife in the *Miscellanies* was the product of various circumstances: Thomas Sheridan's poverty, his early death and his son's desire to make some money from the remaining manuscripts, the need to compete with Faulkner by issuing new manuscript material. *Miscellanies, the Tenth Volume* was not Sheridan's monument to Swift, or Swift's to him. But in publishing the letters, sermons and humorous material formerly owned by Sheridan, Dodsley effectively relocated Swift to Ireland, and replaced the high-minded and aspirational friendships of Bolingbroke and Pope with the tender and play-ful provinciality of Sheridan, Johnson and their mutual friends. The pref-ace to the collection acknowledges this shift in tone, implying that here we are getting Swift at play with his real friends. Facing the charge that Swift did not intend his letters 'for the Eye of the Publick', Dodsley argues that the letters have an interest 'to the Curious', showing how 'oddly' a great man can behave when in the company of those he is closest to:

> It may perhaps be objected against some of the Letters which will be found in this Volume, that they are too trifling, and were never intended, by the Author, for the Eye of the Publick. But as it was thought it would be an agreeable Entertainment to the Curious, to see how oddly a Man of his great Wit and Humour could now and then descend to amuse himself with his particular Friends, it is hoped this will apologize for the Publication of them.[34]

Swift had believed, or at least said, that the personal and familiar nature of his letters would secure them from public interest. Yet, as both the Pope edition and the 1745 *Miscellanies* revealed, part of the appeal of these early selections of letters was precisely the fact that they showed readers the pri-vate man behind the public figure of the prose and verse works.

Faulkner, Jacobitism and a posthumous imprimatur

As this preface to *Miscellanies, the Tenth Volume* suggests, public 'Curiosity' was central to the appeal of the familiar letter. Yet subsequent collections of Swift's personal letters are increasingly reluctant to advertise this aspect of readerly desire. A year after the *Miscellanies* appeared, George Faulkner issued most of the same material found in the *Miscellanies* volume as part of his eight-volume edition of Swift's works, *The Works of Jonathan Swift DD, DSPD* (Dublin, 1746). The letters were printed in the eighth vol-ume, in whose prefatory pages Faulkner printed Dodsley's advertisement, quoted above, from the *Miscellanies* volume. However, he followed this with his own preface. In it, he said that he had added some letters and historical notes,

> the Printer hereof having enquired for such Things among the Author's Friends, in Order to give Light into some Letters to Dr. S—n, which seem naturally to raise the Curiosity of impertinent People, or else being such Matters as are fit to vindicate, in some Sort, the Reputation of that excel-lent Man; whose Breast was as much inflamed with the sincerest Zeal for

the Protestant Settlement on the Throne of these Kingdoms ... as the Heart of any Man ever was.[35]

Faulkner's comments on contemporary responses to the publication of the letters illuminate a growing concern with the nature of public interest in Swift. In the context of his preface, 'Curiosity' is no longer a desirable readerly quality, but a form of impertinence. Faulkner suggests that 'Curiosity' means reading Swift's letters for evidence of his Jacobitism. He claims that his task as an editor is to 'vindicate' Swift's political reputation. In order to represent his author in a more respectable and less controversial light, Faulkner modifies the range of letters included. He takes out a letter of 2 August 1728, written by Swift from Market Hill, in which Swift had declared 'I hate Dublin, and love the Retirement here, and the Civility of my Hosts',[36] and also cuts two further more explicitly political letters in which Swift appeared openly hostile to the Hanoverian monarchy. One was a letter to Sheridan of 12 September 1735 in which he had joked about the 'sorrow' of royal birthdays, and another an Anglo-Latin letter of May 1735 in which he had written: 'Tomi ad visu toris torisque nota peni inani Hanno veri an interest. Arma gesti Caro lina has no credit. An das tomi Georgica notabit en dure' (Tom, I advise you Tories to risk not a penny in any Hanoverian interest. Her Majesty Carolina has no credit. And as to my George I cannot a bit endure).[37] To emphasize Swift's political loyalty to Ireland, and detract from any taint of Jacobitism created by the earlier inclusion of the anti-Hanoverian letters, Faulkner added in some of Swift's letters to Archbishop King. These new pieces demonstrated Swift's prominent role in negotiating on behalf of the Irish clergy with the Crown of England for the remission of the clerical levies known as the First Fruits. They also contained Swift's outright dismissal of all claims of his complicity with Bolingbroke and Jacobite plotting. In the newly included letter to King of 16 December 1716, Swift protested that he knew nothing of the Tory ministry's flirtation with the Pretender, and said: 'I beg your Grace to believe, that I am not mistaken in my self. I always professed to be *against the Pretender*, and *am so still.*' Again, the collecting and publishing of the letters was used to shape the Dean's identity: in the case of this Faulkner edition of 1746, it was used to confirm his political loyalty and orthodoxy.

For all his criticism of the 'impertinence' of other readers and editors, Faulkner himself was happy to draw on dubious sources for his publication. In defending his decision to publish personal papers, he recycles an earlier text by Pope and Swift:

We shall say no more concerning this Volume, than what the Author himself hath observed in Conjunction with Mr Pope, in the following Pages, about incorrect and private Papers published without an Author's Permission …[38]

What follows is Pope's preface to the 1727 *Miscellanies in Prose and Verse*, in which he had defended the decision to publish a collection of works:

Having both of us been extreamly ill treated by some Booksellers, (especially one *Edmund Curll*) it was our Opinion, that the best Method we could take for justifying ourselves, would be to publish whatever loose Papers in Prose and Verse, we have formerly written …[39]

The context for the preface is well known. In July 1726 Edmund Curll had published a collection entitled *Miscellanea* (discussed by Pat Rogers above, pp. 96–8), in two volumes, consisting of Pope's letters to Henry Cromwell and various other pieces, without the permission of any of the authors. Pope was offended not just by the unauthorized nature of the collection, but also because the pieces that did appear, and the company in which they appeared, did not adequately reflect his or Swift's status as a major writer. As various critics have established, by publishing the 1727 *Miscellanies*, Pope aimed to redefine the social and literary context of Swift's writings and his own, supplanting Curll's miscellaneous collection of major and minor authors with a more substantial monument to a great literary friendship.[40] Pope famously described the effect of the new publication: 'methinks we look like friends, side by side, serious and merry by turns, conversing interchangeably, and walking down hand in hand to posterity; not in the stiff forms of learned Authors … but in a free, un-important, natural, easy manner; diverting others just as we have diverted ourselves'.[41] Faulkner's use of the preface to the *Miscellanies in Verse and Prose* as a justification for his own publication of unauthorized letters in 1746 was, then, an ingenious piece of literary recycling. Faulkner borrowed Pope's words, out of context, to justify his own unauthorized publication of Pope and Swift's personal writings, granting his collection a kind of posthumous imprimatur.

Conclusion

The publishing of Swift's letters in the 1740s tells an interesting story about both the shaping of Swift's reputation through the letter collections, and the way in which the publication of private material was perceived. We can see very clearly the interplay of chance, commerce and personal ambition in the moulding of Swift's reputation in print. Swift had given no sanction for the wholesale publication of his letters, and so within the collections we see a debate unfolding around the value of publishing a great man's correspondence even when he did not intend to do so himself. One of the striking aspects of this investigation of the early letter collections is that it shows that even within a few years Swift's letters could appear in several different forms. This possibility of multiple identities was, of course, predicted by Swift himself in *The Life and Genuine Character of Dr. Swift* (1733):

> "'Tis own'd he was a *Man* of *Wit* ---,
> Yet many a *foolish thing* he writ ---;
> "And, sure he must be *deeply* learn'd ---!
> That's more than ever I discern'd ---;
> "I know his *nearest Friends* complain,
> "He was too *airy* for a *Dean* ---.
> "He was an *honest man* I'll swear ---:
> Why Sir, I differ from you there,
> For, I have heard another Story,
> He was a most *confounded Tory* ---!
> "Yet here we had a strong report,
> "That he was *well-receiv'd* at *Court* ---.
>   (Williams, *Poems*, vol. II,
>   p. 547, lines 74–85).

These few lines anticipate the competing versions of Swift that we have seen in these epistolary collections: the claim that 'many a *foolish thing* he writ' evokes the jest-book friend of Sheridan; the contested claim that he was a '*confounded Tory*' corresponds well with the uncertainty over his political views revealed by the letters. Swift would not have welcomed the publication of his correspondence, but he could also not have been surprised to find his letters used to create a variety of Swifts.

Notes

1 Only a minority of the letters that Swift sent and received survive. According to Ashley Marshall's recent survey of Swift's letters, David Woolley's edition of Swift's correspondence includes 1,516 letters, 809 of which are from Swift (or Swift and someone else), 633 letters to Swift (or him and someone else) and 74 in some way concerning Swift. For a survey of the range of the correspondence, see Ashley Marshall, 'Epistolary Swift', *Swift Studies*, 26 (2011), 61–107, pp. 62–3.
2 For a fuller discussion of the eighteenth-century editions of Swift's letters, see the introduction to Woolley, *Corr.*, vol. I, pp. 65–9.

3 For a full narrative of the negotiations over this collection, see Griffin, *Swift and Pope,* pp. 196–205. On the bibliographical detail of the editions of the collection, see Woolley, *Corr.*, vol. I, pp. 65–7.

4 The complex evolution of the Hawkesworth editions is discussed at length in TS, pp. 80–119.

5 Swift to Bishop Atterbury, 18 July 1717, Woolley, *Corr.*, vol. II, p. 253. A later letter from Martha Whiteway to Orrery asserts that Swift never kept copies of any of his letters. Martha Whiteway to Lord Orrery, [30 December 1740], Woolley, *Corr*, vol. IV, p. 648.

6 Swift to Pope, [3 September 1735], Woolley, *Corr.*, vol. IV, p.174.

7 Lady Elisabeth Germain to Swift, 27 May 1735, Woolley, *Corr.*, vol. IV, pp. 116–17.

8 Swift to Lady Elisabeth Germain, 8 June 1735, Woolley, *Corr.*, vol. IV, pp. 118–21.

9 *The Account Books of Jonathan Swift*, ed. Paul V. Thompson and Dorothy J. Thompson (Newark: University of Delaware Press, 1984), p. 137.

10 On the difficulty of distinguishing between public, private and personal in the eighteenth-century letter, and the relationship between print and manuscript, see Clare Brant, *Eighteenth-Century Letters and British Culture* (Basingstoke: Palgrave Macmillan, 2006), pp. 5–9.

11 Swift to Pope, 21 October 1735, Woolley, *Corr.*, vol. IV, p. 203.

12 *JSt* (1948), vol. I, p. 68.

13 British Library, Add MS 4804, fol. 35ᵛ.

14 *JSt*, vol. II, pp. 434–6.

15 Swift to Pope and Gay, [15 October 1726], Woolley, *Corr.*, vol. III, p. 35.

16 Swift to Pope, 3 September 1735, Woolley, *Corr.*, vol. IV, p. 177.

17 John Boyle, Fifth Earl of Cork and Orrery, *Remarks on the Life and Writings of Dr. Jonathan Swift*, ed. João Fróes (Newark: University of Delaware Press, 2000; London: Associated University Presses, 2000), p. 257. Hereafter cited as Orrery, *Remarks*.

18 Marshall, 'Epistolary Swift', pp. 61–107; Frederik N. Smith, 'Swift's Correspondence: The "Dramatic"Style and the Assumption of Roles', *Studies in English Literature*, 14 (1974), 357–71; Oliver W. Ferguson, '"Nature and Friendship": The Personal Letters of Jonathan Swift', in Howard Anderson, Philip B. Daghlian and Irvin Ehrenpreis (eds.), *The Familiar Letter in the Eighteenth Century* (Lawrence, KA: University of Kansas, 1966), pp. 14–33.

19 Lawrence Lee Davidow, 'Pope's Verse Epistles: Friendship and the Private Sphere of Life', *Huntington Library Quarterly*, 40 (1977), 151–70 (159, 160).

20 Swift to Pope, [3 September 1735], Woolley, *Corr.*, vol. IV, p. 174.

21 Swift to Pope, 21 October 1735, Woolley, *Corr.*, vol. V, p. 203.

22 Maynard Mack, 'The First Printing of the Letters of Pope and Swift', *The Library*, 4th ser., 19 (1939), 465–85; Vinton A. Dearing, 'New Light on the First Printing of the Letters of Pope and Swift,' *The Library*, 4th ser., 24 (1944), 74–80; A. C. Elias Jr, 'The Pope-Swift *Letters* (1740–41): Notes on the First

State of the First Impression,' *Papers of the Bibliographical Society of America*, 69 (1975), 323–43.

23 For a fuller account, see Griffin, *Swift and Pope*, pp. 196–205.

24 Orrery, *Remarks*, p. 242.

25 Orrery, *Remarks*, p. 242.

26 For a discussion of the epistolary form of the *Remarks*, see João Fróes, introduction to Orrery, *Remarks*, pp. 24–5.

27 On Swift's relationship with Sheridan, see James Woolley, 'Thomas Sheridan and Swift', *Studies in Eighteenth-Century Culture*, 9 (1979), 93–114, and also Jonathan Swift and Thomas Sheridan, *The Intelligencer*, ed. James Woolley (Oxford: Clarendon Press, 1992), pp. 20–6.

28 Woolley, 'Sheridan and Swift', p. 100.

29 *The Correspondence of Robert Dodsley*, ed. J. Tierney (Cambridge University Press, 1988), p. 80 n. 1.

30 *Ars pun-ica, sive flos linguarum: the art of punning: or, the flower of languages. In seventy-nine rules. For the farther improvement of conversation and help of memory. By the labour and industry of Tom Pun-Sibi* (Dublin, printed by and for James Carson, 1719). Sheridan's reputation in London had been marred by confusion over authorship. The London editions of *Ars pun-ica* identified 'Pun-Sibi' as Swift, and London reprints of *The Intelligencer*, both in other periodicals and in the collected edition, appeared with the implication that Swift was the author, so denying Sheridan the recognition that he deserved. Woolley, 'Sheridan and Swift', p. 100.

31 Ann Cline Kelly, *Jonathan Swift and Popular Culture: Myth, Media and the Man* (New York and Basingstoke: Palgrave, 2002), pp. 143–64.

32 Woolley, 'Sheridan and Swift', p. 107.

33 *Miscellanies, the Tenth Volume. By Dr. Swift* (London, 1745), pp. 118–19.

34 *Miscellanies, the Tenth Volume. By Dr. Swift*, p. iii; italics reversed.

35 *The Works of Jonathan Swift DD, DSPD, Volume VIII of the Author's Works, Containing Directions to Servants; and Other Pieces in Prose and Verse* (Dublin 1746), 'The Preface by the Dublin Bookseller', n.p.

36 *The Works of Jonathan Swift DD, DSPD*, p. 121.

37 Swift to Sheridan, 12 September 1735, Woolley, *Corr.*, vol. IV, pp. 181–2; Swift to Sheridan, May 1735, Woolley, *Corr.*, vol. IV, pp. 113–14.

38 'The Preface by the Dublin Bookseller', n.p.; italics reversed.

39 'The Preface by the Dublin Bookseller', n.p.

40 See Griffin, *Swift and Pope*, pp. 95–103; James McLaverty, 'The Failure of the Swift–Pope *Miscellanies* (1727–32) and *The Life and Genuine Character of Doctor Swift* (1733)', in *Münster* (2008), pp. 131–48.

41 Alexander Pope to Swift, 17 February 1727, Woolley, *Corr.*, vol. IV, p. 76.

CHAPTER SEVEN

Exploring the bibliographical
limits of Gulliver's Travels

Shef Rogers

On 28 October 1726 Benjamin Motte published in two octavo volumes *Travels into Several Remote Nations of the World. In Four Parts. By Lemuel Gulliver, First a Surgeon, and then a Captain of Several Ships* (T139451).[1] The work proved immediately popular, with two further London editions printed before the end of 1726.[2] The contents of the title page were somewhat restrained compared to the detailed descriptions of the contents found on the covers of other travel books, either factual or fictional, such as Aubrey de la Mottraye's *Travels through Europe, Asia, and into Part of Africa* (1723; T146753) or Daniel Defoe's *Life and Adventures of Robinson Crusoe* (1719; T72264). Motte's briefer title more closely resembled the title page of contemporary works, such as John Durant Breval's *Remarks on Several Parts of Europe* (1726; T89034), except that Motte's book retained a border of double rules typical of earlier works.[3] In addition to a somewhat modernized title page, Motte supplied a frontispiece engraving of Gulliver and a map preceding each of the four parts. For a reader strolling into Motte's shop, *Travels into Several Remote Nations of the World* would have looked very much like its numerous competitors in a book market that was very receptive to travel writing.

And yet no single reader can be specifically identified who ever thought that Swift's work described real voyages. Swift and his correspondents joked with each other about misreadings of the book, but both published and unpublished contemporary responses to the book consistently referred to the work as a satire.[4] In an insightful review essay on the 'The State of Swift Studies', Ashley Marshall notes that '[n]o other eighteenth-century text has yielded as little consensus on fundamental issues of interpretation as *Gulliver's Travels*'.[5] She argues that the central issue is the question of Swift's satiric intentions, a question that is complicated by uncertainty about the genre of *Gulliver's Travels*. I wish to explore this question of genre, locating Swift in a period before readers spoke or clearly conceived of the novel as a genre but when travel books were abundant and were taken seriously.[6] As we shall see, *Gulliver's Travels* has many features in common with travel books, though Swift is masterful at probing the boundaries of travel-book conventions, and expected his readers to negotiate their way successfully through his text, however vexing the journey might prove.

Motte and the context of publication

Although Benjamin Motte was known more as a retailer of Anglican theology than as a retailer of travel books, he was also known to Swift as the successor to Benjamin and Samuel Tooke.[7] As Ian Gadd describes in his chapter, Swift had been publishing works with the Tookes since his time as secretary to William Temple prior to the turn of the century, and appears to have been quite happy with their work. But by the end of 1724 both the Tooke brothers had died, leaving Benjamin Motte, a printer rather than publisher by trade, to manage the publishing business on his own, though in silent partnership with the Reverend Andrew Tooke, Benjamin and Samuel's eldest surviving brother.[8] Motte had taken on significant debt in entering into partnership with Tooke and had also married in 1725, so he was rightly hesitant about putting his professional reputation at risk. Yet he readily acceded to Swift's request for a copy payment of £200. Motte might well have known or suspected that Swift was the author of the book, but for the sake of plausible deniability or for the author's own security the manuscript was dropped off anonymously.[9] Thereafter Swift had nothing further to do with the book until the beginning of 1727, when Charles Ford wrote to Motte mentioning corrections (Woolley, *Corr.* vol. III, pp. 66–9). Swift probably saw Motte in person when he was back in England in mid 1727, but there is no surviving correspondence between the two men until the very end of 1727, when Swift wrote to Motte with amendments and suggestions for possible illustrations.[10] Thus the physical appearance and some of the textual omissions in the two volumes that appeared in October 1726 probably owe more to Motte than to Swift.

Swift was not happy about Motte's decision to delete certain passages from the *Travels*. Nonetheless, Swift remained loyal to Motte as his London printer until his death in 1738 because, despite his protestations, Swift fully understood Motte's dilemma. In the years before the publication of *Gulliver's Travels*, Swift had watched as John Harding, publisher of the fourth Drapier letter in Dublin, was arrested with his wife on 7 November 1724, refused to identify the author of the letter, and died on 19 April 1725, owing, some contemporaries thought, to his treatment in prison. Swift continued to publish his Dublin works with John's widow, Sarah Harding, until 1730.[11] Against such a backdrop of recent events, Swift was not jesting when he wrote to Alexander Pope that the 'Travells [would appear] when a Printer shall be found brave enough to venture his Eares' (Woolley, *Corr.* vol. II, p. 606, 29 September 1725).[12]

But in fact Swift might have been more precise in his letter: what he had to find was a publisher, not a printer, willing to take the risk. Once Motte agreed to publish the book by Christmas 1726 at the latest, he had to work reasonably quickly to complete the two volumes. To achieve faster production, he farmed out the job to multiple printers. From a careful examination of distinctive type ornaments, John C. Ross demonstrated that Motte employed five printers to print the first edition, all but one of them well established in the trade, while for the second edition he engaged one further printer, for a total of six.[13] The most common reason for such shared printing was speed. Not only could Motte produce the two volumes much more quickly, but in the event of a successful work he could reprint even more quickly.[14] Ross speculates that Motte may have also thought such a division of the text would diminish the possibility of advance copies leaking out and being pirated.[15] Michael Treadwell further suggests that Motte may have wished to limit any one printer's knowledge of the text in order to minimize the risk each printer faced, since none could perceive the full import of the work ('Observations', p. 176). As we have seen, Motte both valued Swift's publications and was conscious of the risk involved with this title, so any combination of these factors may have motivated his decision to employ multiple printers.

To diminish the risk, Motte arranged for Andrew Tooke to review the text and remove some of Swift's most dangerous satire, most notably five paragraphs from chapter three of part three. Even so, Tooke overlooked a reference to code that was subsequently deemed provocative enough (because of its association with Jacobite communications) to justify the trouble of removing a leaf (G6 of vol. II) and replacing it with a revised leaf deleting the worrisome text.[16] Surprisingly, some of the harshest satire (that directed at lawyers, statesmen and European colonial expansion in Book Four) was retained by Motte, because it was not considered 'particular' (i.e. aimed at specific individuals).[17] Motte tried as much as he possibly could to avoid altering Swift's text.

In many other ways, however, Motte did all in his power to enhance the resemblance of *Gulliver's Travels* to contemporary travel books. As Ross notes, English travel books of the first quarter of the eighteenth century exhibited 'a broad typographical semiotic, involving such features as the layout of the titlepage, the use of subsidiary titlepages where a volume includes more than one voyage, the style of the detailed list of contents, extended chapter heads, the style of running titles, the use and placing of sketch-maps, and modes of presentation of preliminary material'.[18] All these features are to be found in *Gulliver's Travels*. On the other hand, none of the books Ross examined uses the extra blank line between paragraphs or sets the first word of each paragraph in small capitals, two presentation conventions found in *Gulliver's Travels* that were more common in fiction.[19] Perhaps Motte and his printers knew exactly what sort of book *Gulliver's Travels* really was and offered subtle hints to attentive readers.

The single feature that caused Motte the most difficulty was the maps that preceded each Book. In a brilliant study of the details of these engravings, Frederick Bracher revealed that the maps were based on the most authoritative English map of the day, Herman Moll's 1719 world map.[20] Unfortunately, Swift's imaginary navigational details sometimes made placement challenging, as the countries Gulliver visits had to be set apart from already known countries. But Motte's mapmaker did his best, while the engraver struggled with the mapmaker's handwriting (or perhaps was in a hurry) and misspelled a number of place names.[21] Where Swift would have seen the misspelling of place names in the printed book as errors, he might have been more generous of spirit with regard to the map and instead appreciated the impressive effort and expense (for the separate production and printing of the engravings) on Motte's part to make the book as persuasive a travel book as possible.

Motte was also likely responsible for one of the most prominent and critically revealing features of the book, the frontispiece portrait of Gulliver.[22] The artist and the engraver of the frontispiece were English, based in London, and the three variant representations of Gulliver that adorn the early editions would seem to argue against a clear set of artistic instructions. The oval portrait frame resting on a plinth, the 'velvet-cloaked guise of a distinguished statesman or scholar', and the specifics of place and age all make the book seem authentic as well as authoritative (Barchas, *Graphic Design*, p. 28).

Finally, the payment to which Motte agreed for Swift's manuscript accords more with the sums expected for a travel book than those for a work of fiction. Although more than five hundred examples of bookseller payments to authors for their manuscripts survive from the eighteenth century, not all can be associated precisely with a single printed title. However, *Gulliver's Travels* is one of the approximately four hundred cases where we can identify the author, the publisher and the particular work with confidence, and thus are able to compare the relative publishing costs with those of other books from the period. We are doubly lucky in this instance, because we also have parallel data for a directly contemporary work, John Durant Breval's *Remarks on Several Parts of Europe* (1726; T89034).[23] Both titles were two-volume sets, but Swift's was an octavo with only a frontispiece and a few cuts, while Breval's work was a folio with about twenty-five plates. Swift's work sold for 8s 6d, while Breval's cost £2 10s bound (nearly six times as much), and was printed by Bowyer in 550 copies. Swift's work required 44 sheets of paper per copy, where Breval's required 169.5 sheets per copy (about four times as much paper). For his work, Swift was paid £200, or just over £4 10s per sheet, by Motte, where Breval received £462, or £2 14s per sheet, from Bernard Lintot. In the 1720s, for which I have located 48 payments, the average book brought its author a little over £97 and sold for just over 6s. Between 1710 and 1740 the only titles to have garnered more than £200 for their authors were Pope's translations of Homer (1715–20), John Urry's edition of Chaucer (1721) and James Thomson's *Liberty* [1735–6]. In 1760 Laurence Sterne received £250 for the first two volumes of *Tristram Shandy*, while Smollett was paid £210 in 1770 for the two volumes of *The Expedition of Humphry Clinker*, and Samuel Johnson earned £150 for his *Journey to the Western Islands of Scotland* (1775). Swift and Breval were paid well for their efforts. It is little wonder that Swift noted in a letter to William Pulteney of 12 May 1735 that 'I never got a farthing by anything I writ, except one about eight year ago, and that was by Mr Pope's prudent management for me'.[24] Ultimately, Motte made out much better on Swift's book than Lintot did on Breval's, because *Gulliver's Travels* went through five editions within twelve months. And if Swift was surprised by his own financial gain from the book, he thought Motte, who made good money off the book's first four editions, 'almost rich enough to be an Alderman' (Woolley, *Corr.* vol. III, p. 73, 14 February 1726/7).[25]

Swift's rhetoric of plausibility

Of course, Swift had also done his part in composing *Gulliver's Travels* to make the book read like a travel book. He introduced the famous parody of the storm description from Samuel Sturmy's 1669 *Mariners Magazine* at the opening of Book Two (vol. I, pp. ²3–4) to demonstrate to readers all the editorial work required to transform a journal of a sea voyage and the language of sailors into an engaging account. He also frequently reminded his readers of the faults to be found in those 'other' travel accounts.[26]

As Gulliver tells the King of Brobdingnag, 'I thought we were already over-stocked with Books of Travels: That nothing could now pass which was not extraordinary, wherein I doubted some Authors less consulted Truth than their own Vanity or Interest, or the Diversion of ignorant Readers' (vol. I, p. ²158). But Swift was also alert to more subtle indicators of tone through typography, as he comically revealed in this oft-cited passage from *On Poetry: A Rapsody*:

> Your Poem finish'd, next your Care
> Is needful, to transcribe it fair.
> In modern Wit all printed Trash, is
> Set off with num'rous *Breaks* —— and *Dashes* ——
>
> To Statesmen wou'd you give a Wipe,
> You print it in *Italick Type*.
> When Letters are in vulgar Shapes,
> 'Tis ten to one the Wit escapes;
> But when in C A P I T A L S exprest,
> The dullest Reader smoaks the Jest.
>
>   (lines 91–100)[27]

In *Gulliver's Travels*, by contrast, Swift prefers a restrained typography that limits italics to foreign words, translations of foreign terms and quotations, and place names, though he occasionally breaks out in satiric fits of italic type.[28] The consequence of this visually plain style is to endue Gulliver with a correspondingly direct manner that readers of the period associated with accuracy and sincerity. Gulliver's story is just as understated typographically as his title page.[29] Only when Abel Boyer reprints long extracts in *The Political State of Great Britain* does the text take on new emphases: 'through added italics and capitals, he draws attention to key sections of the work and to crucial aspects of Swift's irony'.[30] From the outset Swift had designed a book to both look and sound like a contemporary travel account, an aim that Motte both recognized and supported.

Swift and travel books

Swift's mimicry of travel books was not limited to their typographical features. He had long been interested in publications relating to travel. Several such accounts adorn his reading list at Moor Park in 1696.[31] He was familiar with Addison's *Tatler* 254 (23 November 1710), which celebrates the freedom of travel books, 'especially those that describe remote Countries, and give the Writer an Opportunity of showing his Parts without incurring any Danger of being examined or contradicted'.[32] In response to the visit of four Iroquois Indians to London in April 1710, Swift had considered writing an imaginary account of the visit. As he wrote to Esther Johnson about *Spectator* 50 (27 April 1711), 'Yesterday it was made of a noble hint I gave him long ago for his *Tatlers*, about an Indian supposed to write his travels into England. I repent he ever had it. I intended to have written a book on that subject. I believe he has spent it all in one paper, and all the under-hints there are mine too' (*JSt* (1948), letter XXI, vol. I, pp. 254–5). The next year both *Spectator* 271 (10 January 1712) and *Guardian* 92 (26 June 1713; written by Pope), referred to a husband–wife dwarf duo, and mentioned how the dwarfs were carried about in a box, inspiring at least some of the thoughts behind Book Two.[33] Dennis Todd, who documents Swift's extensive knowledge of human and animal curiosities, analyzes the way Swift 'dramatizes the shifts and scams we go through to avoid becoming conscious of the uncomfortable truths monsters have to tell us'.[34] Todd concludes that it is precisely the satirist's removal of wriggle room that makes Swift's *Travels* such a powerful narrative.

Over a decade earlier Swift had proposed in the manuscript of *Tale of a Tub* a 'project for the universal benefit of Mankind' – to publish in ninety-six folio volumes 'an exact Description of *Terra Australis incognita*' in a first edition of 100,000 copies, with a copy to be placed in 'every Parish Church in the three Kingdoms'.[35] That mock advertisement claimed that the benefit of the collection would derive not from new discoveries or better goods, governance or morals, the usual justifications for travel, but from the ability of intending criminals to identify that part of Terra Australis to which they wished to be transported. Even in his early imaginings, Swift did not regard travel as a source of social improvement, and it is probably wrong to look to his fully considered account in *Gulliver's Travels* for a redemptive alternative to contemporary Britain. Indeed, the King of Brobdingnag implies that one virtue of travelling is that it removes the traveller from the temptations to vice that appear to abound in England (vol. I, p. ²120), a clever reversal of the standard complaint that the Grand Tour corrupted the flower of England's nobility.

Though Swift himself never travelled outside the British Isles, his engagement with travel was nonetheless not all from second-hand reading. In an incident about which we know frustratingly little, Swift recorded his involvement with attempts to determine how to measure longitude at sea.[36] Swift's business manager in Ireland, Joseph Beaumont, pursued the topic to the point of madness, and Swift may have provided him some financial assistance in the project, for in a letter to a John Wheldon on 27 September 1727 he acknowledged that he had known and supported, to his cost, those who sought to determine longitude. He claimed the mathematicians Newton, Halley and Keill had all told him that calculating longitude was impossible, so he refused support and closed firmly, 'This is all I can say; but am confident you would deceive others, or are deceived yourself.'[37] Swift, having taken advice from the best minds of his day, acknowledged the limits of exploration and scientific advancement, and his personal experience only reinforced his doubts.

From Swift's invocation of the three scientists, we can also gain a sense of the serious role of travel writing in the period. Despite a degree of scepticism about travellers' veracity and the occasional fraudulent publication that challenged readers to distinguish fact from fiction, there was a strong interest in the new information to be found in these titles, and they were widely read and drawn upon by philosophers and natural historians.[38] Dirk Passmann's excellent study of *Gulliver's Travels* and travel books includes an appendix identifying the fifty most frequently owned travel books listed in library and sale catalogues of twelve major scholars and writers of the day, including Locke, Newton and Boyle. The natural philosophers tended to own more accounts than the humanistic scholars, and Locke, in particular, drew on his travel books for examples of human behaviour.[39] Swift similarly seems to have regarded travel narratives as case studies of human behaviour rather than as guides or repositories of new knowledge.

Swift's suggestive imagination

Not only did Swift read widely in the genre of travel, but he also possessed a powerful visual imagination that was adept at turning brief glances at images into larger insights about the world and human nature. Passmann has shown that a plate from the *Atlas Japannensis* (1670; R20211, p. 160) likely inspired the representations of the Yahoos.[40] From this same title, I believe the plate of the very large snail shell depicted in 'The Idol Canon' (p. 94) may similarly have spurred Swift to invent the shell that Gulliver 'broke my right Shin against ... as I was walking alone, and thinking on poor *England*' (p. 83), while a picture of a noble lady shaded by an attendant with a fan (p. 367) resembles Swift's description of a Laputan flapper. Passmann also points to Nicholas Gervaise's *Histoire Naturelle et Politique du Royaume de Siam* (1688) as inspiring Swift's representation of dust-licking approaches to the emperor in chapter nine of Book Three (*Improbable Lies*, p. 305).

Swift also knew, and disliked, Thomas Herbert's travels, originally published in 1634 and republished in four further editions within Herbert's lifetime.[41] Yet even a book Swift disdained afforded him suggestions towards *Gulliver's Travels*: only in the 1634 edition are the two plates depicting the islands of Grand Canaria and Teneriffa positioned one immediately above the other, their juxtaposition suggesting the idea of a flat floating island shading the island below, with the central peak of the lower island threatening to transfix the flat surface above. Swift's visual memory appears to have retained this striking image, transforming a chance placement into a powerful image of colonial exploitation (Figure 1).

Swift's imagination was not captured solely by visual features of travel books, however. His ability to recall and reshape narrative details from other travel accounts is equally evident in the excitements and hardships Gulliver undergoes. Rather than echo common circumstances from travel accounts, Swift has Gulliver forgo cultural comparisons and spiritual matters, elements that would have lent his work an air of truthfulness, in favour of a graphic physicality that initially sounds convincingly detailed but is ultimately intended to unsettle his readers. While Gulliver follows the admonitions to travellers set out by the Royal Society and John Locke to 'endeavour to see the Courts of Princes, to keep the best Company, and to converse with the most celebrated Men in all Arts and Sciences', he does not report so much on the nations he visits as on what he tells those nations about England.[42] Gulliver is frequently shipwrecked and meets with pirates, but is never imprisoned or threatened by hunger, exposure or torture by the Inquisition. Although acknowledgements of the role of Providence or divine order become less prominent in all travel books from the end of the seventeenth century, Swift's volumes are more reticent than usual on matters of religion, with no places of worship described, and only the burial rites of the Houyhnhnms mentioned.[43] The one significant religious scruple Gulliver expresses, his reluctance to trample on the cross in Japan, seems motivated primarily by Swift's desire to satirize Dutch commercialism and hypocrisy. In none of his shipwrecks or storms or abandonments does Gulliver pray for preservation or give thanks for reaching shore, or thank God for any of his rescues, instead attributing events to Fortune or his evil destiny. Swift may well have chosen to avoid difficulties with the church authorities by shunning such topics, but by doing so he also clearly distinguished Gulliver from Crusoe and other fictional mariners. The most original element in Gulliver's narrative is the scatology. As indicated by Gulliver's repeated apologies for raising such matters, Swift is well aware that his readers may be shocked by such material, indeed wishes them to be shocked into a closer critique of human weakness.

height I am fure it doth, and not it only, but any other Land in the
World, allowing its immediate afcent from the Ocean. The high peak
is by moft Geographers reputed the higheft in the World, by fome
faid to be fifteene miles high : though a third part may well fuffice to
beget credulity and wonder. It is feene by Sea-men, in a Serene Skie, a
hundred and twentie Englifh miles, and ferues as an apt Sea-mark vnto
Paffengers. The top of this Peake or Pyramide (exceeding thofe arti-
ficiall ones, built by the *Ægyptian Pharoas*, for their Sepulchres) by
reafon of their rare height and affinitie with the middle Aerie Region
are feldome without Snow.

   This Ile is diftant from the *Grand Canarie*, twentie leagues, or fixty
Englifh miles. *Hierro* or *Ferrum*, beares from the *Grand Canarie*
South, or South and by Weft.

A happie Tree.   This Ile is high, and by reafon of its extendure, towards the Tro-
picke of *Cancer*, fuch time as the Sunne is vernall, becomes exceeding
hot and fcalding; & is bleffed only in one Tree, which befides its fhade
(like the miraculous Rocke in the Defert) affords the Inhabitants
frefh and delightfull water, which by a heauenly moifture diftils it
felfe, to the peoples benefit, the Ile hauing water no where elfe, thats
potable.

   The great *Canarie* gaue its reprefentation to vs in this forme,

Figure 1 Thomas Herbert, *A Relation of Some Yeares Trauaile Begunne Anno 1626. Into*
Afrique and the Greater Asia ([1634], S119687), p. 4. Photograph reproduced with
permission from the copy held in Swift's Reading Collection,
University of Pennsylvania Libraries.

Swift and the reader

Ironically, despite all of the author's and publisher's efforts to present the account as a travel book, Swift's work seems to have fooled no one, and most contemporary readers immediately recognized the book as a partisan political satire. But everyone read it nonetheless, in appreciation of the creative imagination and clever control of tone that separated *Gulliver's Travels* from other travel books. It was this control of satiric tone that was ultimately Swift's most successful exploration. This broad success was no accident; we know that Swift worked very hard to ensure that his writing was accessible to even the meanest readers, which for him meant his servants. Faulkner tells us how Swift read the book aloud in the presence of two male servants as part of his revisions in preparation of the 1735 edition, noting that 'if they did not comprehend, he would alter and amend until they understood it perfectly well, and then would say, *This will do; for, I write to the Vulgar, more than to the Learned'*.[44]

Swift also had Gulliver write directly to the reader. A comparison of the two passages below highlights the difference in tone. I have chosen the preface to Charles Lockyer's *An Account of the Trade in India* (1711; T116400) as fairly typical; nearly all prefaces to travel books stress the problems of credibility and unpolished style, and most often in the rather deferential tone that Lockyer adopts.

I presume so far on [the Reader's] Candour, as to promise my self his favourable Construction of the Defects, he may meet with in the Stile and Expression. I confess I have been less solicitous about Words than Things; and if I have written so as to make my Meaning intelligible, the Truths I relate may be some Amends for the Oversights, I may have committed in delivering them.

(*An Account of the Trade in India*, p. [viii]; roman for italics)

THUS, Gentle Reader, I have given thee a faithful History of my Travels for Sixteen Years, and above Seven Months, wherein I have not been so studious of Ornament as Truth. I could perhaps like others have astonished thee with strange improbable Tales; but I rather chose to relate plain Matter of Fact in the simplest Manner and Style, because my principal Design was to inform, and not to amuse thee.

(*Gulliver's Travels*, vol. II, pp. [2]184–5)

Swift has Gulliver express the same sentiments as Lockyer, but in ele-
gantly balanced phrases, combined with specific details and a sense of
self-awareness in assuring us that he is not like those other travel writers.
His supposedly simple manner and style does not appear nearly so simple
when set alongside Lockyer's, but the ornaments of his prose, matching
'Matter of Fact' with 'Manner and Style', and evoking the Horatian ideal
only to reject the desire to amuse, help to establish a sense of Gulliver
as a thoughtful and skilled narrator. As Janet Aikins vividly demonstrates in her essay on reader response to Gulliver, the direct appeal to
the 'Gentle Reader' continues to evoke the complicity that assumes we
share in the education Gulliver undergoes, learning that immortality is
not desirable, that not all learning is valuable, that the human body is
not physically admirable.[45] And it is precisely our frequent unease and
resistance to being 'the reader' that makes *Gulliver's Travels* unlike the
many other books from which it borrows. Swift knows our limits and
intentionally pushes us beyond them, even as he invokes the platitudes of
travel prefaces.

One further example of parallel passages invites close examination
for two reasons. The first is that this is one of the most direct borrow-
ings in *Gulliver's Travels* from another travel book, and thus provides an
ideal test case to show how Swift transmuted his gleanings into gold. The
second reason is that this example provides a salutary warning against the
assumption that a book Swift owned is the most likely source of a Swiftian
conceit. The Penguin edition of *Gulliver's Travels* annotates a passage
on Lilliputian writing with a reference to *Purchas, his Pilgrimage* (1614),
Book VIII, chapter 13, which reads:

> And although they had not Letters, yet they had their wheele for com-
> putation of time, (as it is said before) in which their writings were not
> as ours from the left hand to the right, or as of the Easterne Nations,
> from the right hand to the left, or as the Chinois, from the top to the
> bottome: but beginning below did mount vpwards, as in that mentioned
> wheele, from the Sunne which was made in the Center, vpwards to the
> circumference.[46]

Yet as long ago as 1938 R. W. Frantz identified a more immediate source.[47]
A New Voyage to the East Indies, by a 'William Symson' (1715; T113736),
provided the basis for Swift's discussion of possible directions for
handwriting:

Their Way of Writing, is not like the *Europeans*, in a Line from the Left to the Right; nor like the *Hebrews*, from the Right to the Left; nor yet like the *Chinese*, from the Top of the Paper strait down to the Bottom; but from the Left Corner down to the Right, slanting downwards. (*A New Voyage to the East Indies*, pp. 35–6)	… their manner of writing is very peculiar, being neither from the left to the right, like the *Europeans*; nor from the right to the left, like the *Arabians*; nor from up to down, like the *Chinese*; nor from down to up, like the *Cascagians*; but aslant from one Corner of the Paper to the other, like Ladies in *England*. (*Gulliver's Travels*, vol. I, p. 94)

Purchas, a copy of which Swift owned, may have informed both 'Symson' and Swift, but Swift's immediate provocation was closer to hand, though not in his own library. Nonetheless, Swift surpasses both sources in turning a rather predictable list of the possible directions of writing into a delightful satiric flourish. Swift gradually moves from the familiar Europe to the known but less familiar Arabia, then to the exotic and less well-known China, and finally to the entirely unknown Cascagia. Swift then adds a step to ensure that he has covered all four cardinal directions and thus demonstrated a thorough knowledge of the topic, only to immediately reduce the whole grand review to bathos by his final satiric hit at fashionable female penmanship. All in a single plagiarized sentence.

Brean Hammond has recently argued that 'Swift did not read even-handedly, or to find "beauties" in what he read. Swift read adversarially.'[48] Not only did Swift do so, but he expected, and attempted to train, his readers to do so as well. It is helpful to understand the bibliographical context of Swift's works precisely because doing so enables us to see how he colonized earlier travel writers' techniques, discoveries and exaggerations to such brilliant effect, even as he fundamentally doubted the possibility of improvement from travel itself. Swift sought to convey to his readers the insights his view of the world brought, even if those insights were unwelcome. As Pat Rogers has argued in 'Gulliver's Glasses', the episodes that refer explicitly to the faculty of sight 'serve different rhetorical ends, but in each case seeing brings either pain or unwelcome news. It is as though looking too hard were an aggressive act for Swift.'[49] Reading, especially bibliographical reading, is an act of seeing, and the 'true' style that Swift sought to evoke in his travel book would, he hoped, help pierce his readers' resistance to truth, even if doing so meant destroying that '*per-petual Possession of being well Deceived*' that Swift had earlier identified as the basis of human happiness (*CWJS*, vol. I, p. III).

Notes

1 I have included *English Short-Title Catalogue* (*ESTC*) reference numbers both to make it easier for readers to locate the precise editions being discussed and to facilitate consultation of images of the relevant textual features via Gale's *Eighteenth-Century Collections Online* (*ECCO*) or via Hathi Trust digital surrogates freely available on the web. This first edition by Motte also appeared in a large-paper issue (T139454). All quotations from the *Travels* are from the regular-paper first edition as represented on *ECCO*. A superscript '2' before the page number indicates that the quotation is in the second part of that volume, because each of the four parts is separately paginated in the first edition.

2 TS, items 289–91, pp. 192–9. In addition to the authorized editions, the work appeared in two different serial versions begun at the end of November, in an abridged version and in at least one Dublin edition dated 1726. For full details of the serial issues, see TS, pp. 203–4 ff. The book was translated into Dutch, French and German in 1727.

3 Intriguingly, one 1726 printing dispensed with the title-page rules (T139450), but otherwise rules were retained in London through 1731, while the 1727 Dublin edition dispensed with them (T1862). Motte perhaps thought readers preferred the rules as a signal that *GT* was a travel book, or perhaps Motte's printers, most of whom were older than he, were simply conservative.

4 The most accessible compilation of comments from Swift's friends describing supposed readers confused by first readings of *GT* is in *Swift: The Critical Heritage*, ed. Kathleen Williams (London: Routledge & Kegan Paul, 1970), pp. 61–4. For a fuller consideration of *GT* and its satiric context, see Bertrand A. Goldgar, '*Gulliver's Travels* and the Opposition to Walpole', in Henry Knight Miller, Eric Rothstein and G. S. Rousseau (eds.), *The Augustan Milieu: Essays Presented to Louis A. Landa* (Oxford: Clarendon Press, 1970), pp. 155–73. Goldgar places *GT* in relation to the *Craftsman* and shows how within two months of its publication the work was universally discussed as a political satire. Abel Boyer, who had initially described *GT* as a romantic satire in the November issue of *The Political State of Great Britain* referred to it as a political satire in the December issue (p. 158). Just one month after publication of the first edition Anne Liddell, who claimed that her 'natural stupidity … could not penetrate the deep design of the author' described the book as 'fictitious voyages' designed 'to ridicule the deprived [*sic*] taste of mankind in general' (H. T. Dickinson, 'The Popularity of "Gulliver's Travels" and "Robinson Crusoe"', *Notes and Queries*, 212 (1967), 172). For other references to the work as satire, among many possible, see *Gulliver Decypher'd* (1727; T35926) and Abbé Desfontaines's 1727 comments extracted in *Critical Heritage*, p. 79.

5 Ashley Marshall, 'The State of Swift Studies 2010', *Eighteenth-Century Life*, 34 (2010), 83–105 (p. 91).

6 J. A. Downie argues convincingly that any history of the novel must reckon with *GT*. See 'Swift and the Making of the English Novel', *Münster* (1998), pp. 179–87.

7 That Benjamin Tooke's editions of Swift's *Tale* and the *Miscellanies* (1711) were the first two items registered in the Stationers' Company Register the day the new Copyright Act of 1710 came into effect indicates how highly Tooke valued Swift's work. Karian, *Print and Manuscript*, p. 16.

8 The essential facts of Motte's life may be found in J. J. Caudle, 'Motte, Benjamin (1693–1738)', *Oxford Dictionary of National Biography*, www.oxforddnb.com/view/article/19421 (accessed 20 Nov 2011). Michael Treadwell elaborates on the family and business ties between the Motte and Tooke families in his essay, 'Benjamin Motte, Andrew Tooke and *Gulliver's Travels*', in *Münster* (1985), pp. 287–304 and offers an excellent summary of Motte's life as printer and publisher in 'Benjamin Motte, Jr', in James K. Bracken and Joel Silver (eds.), *The British Literary Book Trade, 1700–1820, Dictionary of Literary Biography*, vol. CLIV (Detroit: Gale Research, 1995), pp. 198–202.

9 The precise date the manuscript was left with Motte is disputed, but it would make sense that Swift timed the events to afford himself deniability. See James McLaverty, 'The Revision of the First Edition of *Gulliver's Travels*: Book-Trade Context, Interleaving, Two Cancels, and a Failure to Catch', *PBSA*, 106 (2012), 5–35 (12–13).

10 See Karian, *Print and Manuscript*, for a discussion of the parallels to Swift's treatment of his *Four Last Years*, displaying his 'use of intermediaries to transmit texts to London, his limitation of a work – at least for a time – to a single copy, his reliance on a guardian to protect that copy, and [his fears about] the uncontrolled nature of manuscript circulation' (p. 98). On 28 December 1727, Swift wrote Motte to suggest possible scenes for illustration, a topic he had discussed with Pope and the artist John Wotton (Woolley, *Corr.*, vol. III, pp. 149–51).

11 For a full discussion of the publication and prosecution of the fourth letter, see Ehrenpreis, *Swift*, vol. III, pp. 264–308. Mary Pollard gives detailed information on the arrest and ultimately unsuccessful efforts to prosecute Harding. The claim that he died in prison rests on an interpretation of *A Poem to the Whole People of Ireland* (Dublin, 1726) and has not been substantiated (Pollard, *Dictionary*, p. 275).

12 J. C. Ross, 'The Framing and Printing of the Motte Editions of *Gulliver's Travels*', *BSANZ Bulletin*, 20 (1996), 5–19 (10 n. 13). Motte himself was later jailed briefly for his role in publishing Swift's *Epistle to a Lady* (1734).

13 John Ross and Michael Treadwell worked on this problem simultaneously, with Treadwell's slightly different results published in 'Observations on the Printing of Motte's Octavo Edition of *Gulliver's Travels*', in *Münster* (1998), pp. 157–77.

14 The standard discussion of shared printing is Keith Maslen's 'Shared Printing and the Bibliographer: New Evidence from the Bowyer Press', *An Early London Printing House at Work: Studies in the Bowyer Ledgers* (New York: Bibliographical Society of America, 1993), pp. 153–64.

15 Ross, 'Framing', p. 13. James McLaverty argues strongly for fear of piracy as a motivating factor in light of the substantial fee Motte had agreed to pay Swift for his work ('Revision', p. 15).

16 Ross, 'Framing', p. 12 and n. 19. Ross also explains that because Motte was producing both large-paper and regular issues of the book, he had to have two different versions of the revised text typeset in order to match the slightly variant running titles and page format of the two different issues.

17 The textual notes to Herbert Davis's edition remains the best for locating these changes at a glance: Davis, *PW*, vol. XI, pp. 301–22.

18 Ross, 'Framing', p. 7.

19 Ross, 'Framing', p. 8.

20 Frederick Bracher, 'The Maps in *Gulliver's Travels*', *Huntington Library Quarterly*, 8 (1944), 59–74.

21 Bracher, 'Maps', pp. 63–4. Bracher, p. 70, suggests that the absence of Lindalino from the maps implies the maps were an afterthought relying on the already printed text for the names. However, McLaverty, 'Revision', pp. 28–9, argues, I think correctly, that in fact neither Motte nor the anonymous mapmaker could have located the name Lindalino, because the passage was not included in the printer's manuscript.

22 Peter Wagner, 'Swift's Great Palimpsest: Intertextuality and Travel Literature in *Gulliver's Travels*', in *Crossing the Atlantic: Travel Literature and the Perception of the Other* (reprinted from a special number of *Disposition: American Journal of Comparative and Cultural Studies*, eds. Ottmar Ette and Andrea Pagni, vol. XVII, 42–3 (1992)) (Ann Arbor: University of Michigan Press, 1992), pp. 107–35 (pp. 112–20); Janine Barchas, *Graphic Design, Print Culture, and the Eighteenth-Century Novel* (Cambridge University Press, 2003), pp. 28–34. The Latin epigraph that is added to the frontispiece of the second edition was included in advertisements for the first edition from 28 October 1726.

23 Breval was best known to Swift and his contemporaries as the man behind the pseudonymous works of 'Joseph Gay' published by Edmund Curll, a number of which had engaged with works by Pope and other members of the Scriblerus Club. Yet Lintot paid Breval very well for his *Remarks*, and the book ultimately redeemed the author's reputation.

24 Woolley, *Corr.*, vol. IV, pp. 107–8. Woolley glosses this sentence as a reference to payment for Swift's part in the *Miscellanies*, for which Swift received £100, but I believe Pope advised Swift on the price of £200 that he set when initially negotiating with Motte, and Clive Probyn seems to support that view in his entry on Swift for the *Oxford Dictionary of National Biography*. Swift later made reasonable money on his sermons in 1744, but he did not know that would happen in 1735.

25 Swift is likely exaggerating here for comic effect, though Motte clearly prof-ited handsomely from the book.

26 Arthur Sherbo, 'Swift and Travel Literature', *Modern Language Studies*, 9 (1979), 114–27 (125).

27 Typography is that of the Dublin 1734 edition of the poem (T446).

28 Cf. vol. I, pp. ¹127–9 (describing English government to the King of Brobdingnag), vol. II, p. ¹92 (relating Laputans' skill in finding coded meanings, e.g. 'a *Sieve* to signify a *Court-Lady*') and pp. ²87–90 (explaining Houyhnhnm theories of health). Perhaps it is the unusual density of italics that alerted Andrew Tooke or Motte to the need to reduce the pointedness of Swift's satire in two of these passages. It is also possible that the density of italics reflects material composed at an earlier stage, when Swift was more focused on the satire and less on the narrative of the work.

29 Michael J. Conlon explains persuasively how this 'flatly empirical form of description' clashes with the wondrous events being described, and how the disjunction 'forces the reader to think divergently and to grasp the double perspectives Swift brings to Gulliver's experience' ('Performance as Response in Swift's *Gulliver's Travels*', in Christopher Fox (ed.), Gulliver's Travels, *Case Studies in Contemporary Criticism* (Boston, MA: Bedford St Martin, 1995), pp. 408–24 (pp. 411, 419)).

30 Phyllis J. Guskin, '"A very remarkable Book": Abel Boyer's View of *Gulliver's Travels*', *Studies in Philology*, 72 (1975), 439–53 (443).

31 *CWJS*, vol. I, pp. 273–4. In the index to *Library and Reading, Part 1*, Dirk Passmann and Heinz Vienken list 469 authors of travel accounts included in books held in Swift's library, a library of 657 titles that included works by 1,961 authors. All but fifteen of the travel works listed are to be found in the two major collections by Richard Hakluyt and Samuel Purchas.

32 Shef Rogers, 'An Extra Echo to Swift's Epigraph for *Gulliver's Travels*', *Notes and Queries*, 235 (2008), 326.

33 Aline Mackenzie Taylor, 'Sights and Monsters and Gulliver's *Voyage to Brobdingnag*', *Tulane Studies in English*, 7 (1957), 29–82.

34 Todd persuasively stresses the rhetoric of comparative normality that charac-terized advertisements for freak shows in the period; Dennis Todd, 'The Hairy Maid at the Harpsichord: Some Speculations on the Meaning of *Gulliver's Travels*', *Texas Studies in Literature and Language*, 34 (1992), 239–83 (260), also available as chapter five in his *Imagining Monsters: Miscreations of the Self in Eighteenth-Century England* (University of Chicago Press, 1995).

35 Not published until 1720 (T14972, pp. 264–6), this project is reproduced in *CWJS*, vol. I, pp. 268–70. In his introduction, pp. lxxxvii–xc, Walsh notes that there is no conclusive link to Swift for this material, but the quotation he cites describes a mode of manuscript access that Stephen Karian has shown Swift practised (see note 9 above).

36 From 1714 the British government had offered incentives to encourage the dis-covery of new methods for measuring longitude. For a brief and engaging his-tory of the matter, see Dava Sobel, *Longitude* (Harmondsworth: Penguin, 1996).

37 Woolley, *Corr.*, vol. III, p. 129. Cf. *GT*, Book III, ch. X; vol. II, p. 136, where longitude is one of the great expected inventions about which Swift is quite sceptical, linked as it is with 'perpetual motion' and 'universal medicine'.

38 The likelihood of being deceived by an early eighteenth-century travel title has been overstated. Of the nearly two hundred travel books published in English in the period 1700–26 (slightly more than seven per year), only nineteen are listed in Gove, and only seven of those, or under 4 per cent, were ever mistaken for factual. See Philip Babcock Gove, *The Imaginary Voyage in Prose Fiction: A History of Its Criticism and a Guide for Its Study, with an Annotated Check List of 215 Imaginary Voyages from 1700 to 1800* (London: The Holland Press, 1961). Thirty-seven titles listed by Gove were published between 1700 and 1726, of which nineteen (one of which was published in a serial rather than separately) were available in English in those years. Cf. J. Paul Hunter's claim that 'the highly circumstantial narrative [of *GT*] has the effect of raising questions about the authority of the genre – as well it might, since a high percentage of the books of exploration and discovery were written in London by authors who had never left home and whose facts were often wildly inaccurate' ('*Gulliver's Travels* and the Later Writings', in Christopher Fox (ed.), *The Cambridge Companion to Jonathan Swift* (Cambridge University Press, 2003), pp. 216–40 (p. 222)). Perhaps more confusing than those that set out to deceive were the authentic travellers who nonetheless managed to record highly implausible 'facts'.

39 Dirk Friedrich Passmann, Appendix E, '*Full of improbable lies*': Gulliver's Travels *und die Reiseliteratur vor 1726*, Aspekte der Englischen Geistes- und Kulturgeschichte 10 (Frankfurt am Main: P. Lang, 1987). David Pearson supports Passmann's point by demonstrating the converse, that readers in this period who were widely read but were not natural philosophers tended to own fewer travel titles, with no single travel title owned by all five of the collectors he surveys ('Patterns of Book Ownership in Late Seventeenth-Century England', *The Library*, 7th ser., 11 (2010), 139–67 (164)). On Locke, see David B. Paxman, '"Adam in a Strange Country": Locke's Language Theory and Travel Literature', *Modern Philology*, 92 (1995), 460–81, and, for a fuller discussion of the philosophical implications of Locke's use of travel writing, chapter 3 of Daniel Carey's *Locke, Shaftesbury, and Hutcheson: Contesting Diversity in the Enlightenment and Beyond* (Cambridge University Press, 2006).

40 Passmann, *Improbable Lies*, p. 207. Passmann's study remains the most thorough examination of Swift's engagement with travel books as sources for *Gulliver's Travels*. R. W. Frantz notes parallels to verbal descriptions of unpleasant monkeys urinating on those below from the travels of Lionel Wafer and William Dampier, both published in 1699 ('Swift and Voyagers', *Modern Philology*, 29 (1931), 49–57 (52)).

41 Swift's copy survives with his dismissive marginalia: 'If this Book were stript of its Impertinence, Conceitedness, and tedious Digressions, it would be almost worth reading, and would then be two thirds smaller than it is' (Davis, *PW*, vol. V, p. 243).

42 *A Collection of Voyages and Travels, Some Now First Printed from Original Manuscripts* (1704; T97848), p. lxxvi. John Locke wrote the introduction to this collection, drawing on 1666 *Philosophical Transactions* advice for sailors who go on long sea voyages. Such guidelines were frequently reprinted and were still considered relevant when Cook set out on his first voyage in 1768.

43 Gulliver's Lilliputian residence is a deconsecrated temple. It appears to have been chosen for its relatively immense size, not its religious associations, though the building's former function does increase the reader's shock at Gulliver's 'pollution' of it when he first arrives (vol. I, p. 26).

44 Cited in Janet E. Aikins, 'Reading "with Conviction": Trial by Satire', in Frederik N. Smith (ed.), *The Genres of* Gulliver's Travels (Newark: University of Delaware Press, 1990), pp. 203–29 (p. 206); Laetitia Pilkington recounts an even more condescending anecdote in which Swift questioned her about passages from his history of Queen Anne, *Memoirs of Laetitia Pilkington*, ed. A. C. Elias Jr, 2 vols. (Athens: University of Georgia Press, 1997), vol. I, p. 29.

45 Aikins, 'Reading', pp. 215, 221–5.

46 Jonathan Swift, *Gulliver's Travels*, ed. Peter Dixon and John Chalker (Harmondsworth: Penguin, 1967), p. 93 n. 45, citing p. 683 of the first edition (S121937).

47 Frantz, 'Gulliver's "Cousin Sympson"'. As Frantz notes, although no contemporary critics seem to have noticed 'Sympson's' plagiarism, the fact that Gulliver's imaginary cousin was in turn a deception is a delightful irony.

48 Brean S. Hammond, 'Swift's Reading', in *The Cambridge Companion to Jonathan Swift* (Cambridge University Press, 2003), pp. 73–86 (p. 76).

49 Pat Rogers, 'Gulliver's Glasses', in Clive T. Probyn (ed.), *The Art of Jonathan Swift* (New York: Barnes and Noble, 1978), pp. 179–88 (p. 187). Gulliver claims the Houyhnhnms 'have so far opened mine eyes and enlarged my understanding' (p. 305).

CHAPTER EIGHT

George Faulkner and Swift's collected works

James McLaverty

Of the monuments that George Faulkner planned to honour Swift, *The Works of J.S, D.D, D.S.P.D.* proved the most important.[1] A collection dependent on an identity its title cannot fully specify, a fusion of boldness and timidity, its volumes present Swift as celebrated author, rebellious Irish patriot and establishment Dean. The *Works* first appeared in four volumes in 1735 but Faulkner continued building up his tribute until the edition had expanded to twenty volumes by 1769. The *Works* were an extraordinary achievement for a bookseller based in Dublin, bringing together differing impulses in their undertaker – patriotic, entrepreneurial, scholarly – in spite of a difficult relationship with their living author. Swift, who knew what a posthumous works should be, was flattered, disappointed, encouraging, remote and interfering; the *Works* appeared in spite of as well as because of him. While Faulkner was later to claim that Swift 'corrected every Sheet of the first seven Volumes that were published in his Life Time' (Davis, *PW*, vol. XIII, p. 203), Swift often maintained that the volumes were printed utterly against his will and could claim 'I have never yet looked into them, nor I believe ever shall' (Woolley, *Corr.*, vol. IV, p. 67). This conflict, real or apparent, between bookseller and author points to other perplexing aspects of the edition. It discusses its 'supposed author' extensively and represents him visually, but it dare not name him; it seeks to meet the need for a 'compleat Edition' while knowing that, in the absence of *Tale of a Tub*, it is incomplete; and it boasts its Irish provenance while depending for its viability on English support, its chief subscriber turning out to be a bookseller from Preston in Lancashire. Faulkner's brilliance lay in the creative balancing of opportunities and restrictions, so that they worked to his advantage; the *Works* were an imaginative exercise in the art of the possible.

The proposals

Faulkner's proposals, dated 9 February 1733, were published in his *Dublin Journal* the following day, and, as they touch on all the contentious points, they are worth quoting in full:

The Writings of the Reverend Dr. J. S. D. S. P. D. were published six Years ago in London, in three Volumes, mingled with those of some other Gentlemen his Friends. Neither is it easy to distinguish the Authors of several Pieces contained in them.

But, besides those three Volumes, there are several Treatises relating to Ireland, that were first published in this Kingdom, many of which are not contained in the DRAPIER's LETTERS.

It hath been long wished, by several Persons of Quality and Distinction, that a new compleat Edition of this Author's Works, should be printed by it self.

But this can no where be done so conveniently as in IRELAND, where Booksellers cannot pretend to any Property in what they publish, either by Law or Custom.

This is therefore to give Notice, that the Undertaker, GEORGE FAULKNER, Printer in Essex-Street, proposeth to publish, by Subscription, all the Works that are generally allowed to have been written by the said Dr. S. in four Volumes; two of which shall be put to the Press at 4s. 4d. each; beautifully printed on a fine Paper in OCTAVO, neatly bound in Calves Leather, and lettered on the Back. The said two Volumes shall be deliver'd to the Subscribers by Michaelmas-Term at farthest: Eight Shillings and Eight Pence to be paid at the Time of subscribing, and the Remainder at the Delivery of the Book. And if the Subscriptions are not fill'd up by the first Day of MAY next, the Money shall be returned. Who ever subscribes for six Copies, shall have a Seventh gratis.

The first Volume shall contain the Author's Letters, written under the Name of M. B. DRAPIER, with two additional ones never printed before; and likewise, several Papers relating to IRELAND, acknowledged to be of the same Author.

The second Volume shall contain the Prose Part of the Author's Miscellanies, printed many Years ago in LONDON and DUBLIN; together with several other Treatises since published in small Papers, or in the three Volumes set out and signed JONATHAN SWIFT and ALEXANDER POPE.

The third Volume shall contain the Author's poetical Works, all joined together; with many original Poems, that have hitherto only gone about in Manuscript.

The last Volume shall contain the Travels of Captain LEMUEL GULLIVER, in four Parts, wherein many Alterations made by the LONDON Printers will be set right, and several Omissions inserted.

Which Alterations and Omissions were without the Author's Knowledge, and much to his Displeasure, as we have learned from an intimate Friend of the Author's, who, in his own Copy, transcribed in blank Paper the several Paragraphs omitted, and settled the Alterations and Changes according to the original Copy.

In this Edition, the gross Errors committed by the Printers, both here and in LONDON, shall be faithfully corrected; and the true Original, in the Author's own Hand having been communicated to us by a Friend in whom the Author much confided; and who had Leave to correct his own printed Copies from the Author's most finished Manuscript, where several Changes were made, not only in the Style, but in other material Circumstances.

N. B. A compleat Edition of the Author's Works can never be printed in ENGLAND; because some of them were published without his Knowledge or Liking, and consequently belong to different Proprietors; and likewise, because as they now stand, they are mingled with those of other Gentlemen h[i]s Friends.

The Author's Effigies, curiously engraven by Mr. VERTUE, shall be prefixed to each Volume. There will also be several other Cuts, proper to the Work. (The whole Work, is to be done on a beautiful Letter and a fine Paper.)[2]

It is noteworthy that from a book-trade point of view this was a solo effort; Faulkner was the undertaker, distributor and printer, as the imprints ('Printed by and for George Faulkner, Printer and Bookseller') would make clear.

The rival miscellanies

Faulkner's starting point in these proposals was the series of Swift–Pope *Miscellanies* launched in 1727. They were a problem, because they constituted a rival edition, but also a source of energy, because to Swift's mind they were inadequate.[3] The *Miscellanies* had followed the publication of *Gulliver's Travels* by Benjamin Motte in London in 1726. As a major work, *Gulliver* required the London trade's skills and market, and for its publication Swift turned to the successor to the business that had published *Tale of a Tub* in 1704 and *Miscellanies in Prose and Verse* in 1711, as Shef Rogers shows in his essay. The new *Miscellanies* planned with Pope were based on that 1711 collection, as Pat Rogers shows in his. The first volume was to reprint those materials with a payment of £50, and at least two further volumes were to follow at £100 each.[4] The collaboration was not a success. From Swift's point of view it was little short of a disaster: Motte was slow to pay for the copy; Pope was ultimately reluctant to provide material (he had planned to publish *The Dunciad* in the third volume but withdrew it); and Swift felt exploited. In a letter to Motte of 28 December 1727 he complained that five-sixths of the material in the third volume was his, and that while Pope and Gay had printed their works already elsewhere, he was including 'all the Poetry I ever writ [wor]th printing' (Woolley, *Corr.,* vol. III, p. 150).[5] When a fourth volume was proposed in 1732, Swift saw no justification for it at all, and, though he replied politely to Pope's requests for copy in a letter of 12 June 1732, there was a sting in the tail:

> As to other things of mine since I left you; there are in prose a View of the State of Ireland; a Project for eating Children; and a Defence of Lord Carteret; in Verse a Libel on Dr. D— and Lord Carteret; a Letter to Dr. D— on the Libels writ against him; the Bar[r]ack (a stol'n Copy) the Lady's Journal; the Lady's Dressing-room (a stol'n Copy) the P[lace] of the Damn'd (a stol'n Copy); all these have been printed in London. (Woolley, *Corr.,* vol. III, pp. 489–90)

They had been printed in London through a cooperative venture between Faulkner in Dublin and William Bowyer Jr, for whom he had once worked, in London.[6] The resulting conflict between them and Motte helped generate the 1735 *Works.*

Swift, George Faulkner and William Bowyer

In an important letter written to Motte on 4 November 1732, Swift explained that no printer or bookseller had any sort of property in Dublin, but if a Dublin printer ran the risk of publication he might claim the property in London.[7] For some years Swift had released material in Dublin through members of the trade such as Waters, Hyde, the Hardings and Fairbrother, but the difference now was that publication through Faulkner was leading to a copyright claim in London.[8] Because Faulkner had retained good relations with Bowyer and made repeated trips to London, he had access to the London market in ways his predecessors did not.

The course of the development of the association between Faulkner and Swift is unclear. In 1725 he had printed and published the collected edition of the *Drapier's Letters* as *Fraud Detected, or, The Hibernian Patriot* (the job was probably too big for Sarah Harding, their surviving printer). The reprinting of that collection in London by Bowyer (in association with the booksellers Charles Davis and Thomas Woodward) as the *Hibernian Patriot* five years later in 1730 marks a new development, and in the same year *A Vindication of His Excellency the Lord Carteret* was published by Faulkner and Bowyer in Dublin and London.[9] In early 1732 Faulkner became more closely bound to Swift by printing in his *Dublin Journal*, and as a half-sheet, a set of 'Queries' about the Sacramental Test, which led to his being prosecuted and perhaps imprisoned. According to Faulkner's own account, prefaced to the *Works* in 1763, he suffered 'severely in his private Property, as well as in his health', and he links this episode to the time when he was in the custody of the messengers for 'printing against the Reduction of the Gold Coin and some other Affairs', when he

> 'could never be prevailed on to discover the Authors, which endeared him so much to the Dean, that he gave him the Title of *his right trusty and faithful Friend*, and frequently offered to pay *Faulkner* the Expences he had been at on those Occasions, and to raise him Subscriptions, to reward him for his Fidelity and Sufferings, which *Faulkner* always refused.[10]

How better could Faulkner be rewarded than by further printing and publishing rights and opportunities? As Adam Rounce notes in his essay, we know that twenty-four Bowyer printings in this period with the imprint 'Dublin printed: London reprinted' came to him from Faulkner.[11]

A consequence of Swift's engagement with both Motte and Faulkner was that in 1732 there were two groups competing for the right to publish his work in London: Pope and Motte (not harmoniously) on the one hand, and Faulkner, Bowyer and Matthew Pilkington on the other. Pilkington, Swift's clerical protégé, was particularly active in promoting Bowyer's interests and even obtained a sort of assignment from Swift:

> Whereas severall scattered Papers in prose and verse for three or four years last past, were printed in dublin, by Mr George Faulkner, some of which were sent in Manuscript to Mr William Bowyer of London, Printer, which pieces are supposed to be written by me, and are now by the Means of the Reverend Mathew Pilkington who delivered or sent them to the s^d Faulkener and Bowyer, become the Property of the s^d Faulkener and Bowyer, I do here without specifying the s^d Papers, give up all manner of right I may be thought to have in the s^d Papers, to Mr Mathew Pilkington afores^d, who informs me that he intends to give up the s^d right to Mr Bowyer afores^d. (Witness my hand. Jul 22.1732. Jonath: Swift.)[12]

Although John Nichols tells us the copyright was transferred from Pilkington to Bowyer for 'a valuable consideration', the volume never appeared.[13] Both Pope and Motte objected, and Swift felt obliged to support his London bookseller's claim. The fourth volume of *Miscellanies* was entered in the Stationers' Register on 1 October to Motte and Lawton Gilliver, Pope's new bookseller, and Swift wrote to Motte expressing his dissatisfaction with it on 4 November 1732 (Woolley, *Corr.*, vol. III, pp. 556–7).

Faulkner was, however, by no means defeated. During the tussle over copy in the summer of 1732, Swift had written to Motte, showing that these disputes had made him think about a collection of his works:

> I am likewise desirous that some time or other, all that I acknoledge to be mine in prose and verse, which I shall approve of with any little things that shall be thought deserving should be published by themselves by you, during my life (if it contains any reasonable time) provided you are sure it will turn to your advantage. (Woolley, *Corr.*, vol. III, p. 503, 15 July 1732)

Although Swift contemplates this edition as something that might be published in his lifetime (he was later to imagine it happening after his death), the mode of selection of contents is left uncertain; the publication of a works was very much something that would have to be done to him. Authors, with the striking exception of Pope, did not publish their works.[14] But Motte showed no sign of instigating such a collection, and his recent volume of miscellanies was in Swift's view a failure. Here lay Faulkner's opportunity: one volume in London might prove impossible but four in Dublin would not, and the London market could be exploited in a different way, by subscription. When Swift wrote to Motte on 9 December 1732, only two months after the publication of the fourth *Miscellany*, he made it clear that plans for the *Works* were under way.

The subscription

The subscription for the *Works* was a great success, and it needed to be if a large enough market was to be tapped. In his 1763 account, Faulkner makes the subscription a feature of Swift's assent to the project. He, the editor:

> made Application to the Dean, who did not seem willing to consent, as the Publisher might be a Loser by printing them; the Editor told him he would run all Hazards, being very positive, he should be a great Gainer by them; but the Dean still persisted; then the Editor said, he would print them by Subscription, and make a faithful Return of the Subscribers Names to him, when he could easily judge whether he would gain or lose by the Undertaking. Accordingly Proposals were published, and Subscriptions came in very fast, which were shewn to the Author, who consented to the Printing. (Davis, *PW*, vol. XIII, p. 202)

Faulkner emphasizes Swift's concern for his business, but the subscription also met the demand for dignity and for access to the English market. Faulkner could not legitimately export his books to England, but he could accept subscriptions there. The *Dublin Journal* for 9 February 1734

announced that Faulkner was going to London for a month to collect subscriptions, and evidently Swift helped him, providing the letter to the Earl
of Oxford dated 16 February 1734 that begins, 'The Bearer Mr Faulkner,
the Prince of Dublin Printers, will have the Honor to deliver You this'
and goes on 'although for his own Profit he is engaged in a Work that very
much discontents me, Yet I would rather have it fall into his hands, than
any other on this Side.'[15] It was important, of course, while encouraging
Faulkner, to make it clear that the subscription was for him and not for
the author. Nevertheless, I suspect the subscription was strongly promoted
by Oxford and by Pilkington and Swift's other friends.

There were 888 subscribers for 1,152 sets, with 54 multiple subscribers
accounting for 318 sets. That compares well with 575 for 654 sets of Pope's
Iliad, though, of course, that represented an investment of six guineas rather
than 17s. 4d. The list is led, literally at the beginning of each alphabet, by
the titled: counting knights and all Ladies but not honourables, there are
106 of them. The royal family is absent but the higher ranks of nobility are
well represented: dukes of Buckingham, Hamilton, Kent (six sets), Leeds,
Marlborough, Norfolk, Portland, Queensbury, Somerset; duchesses of
Buckingham, Hamilton, Marlborough (two sets), Ormand, Portland,
Queensbury; earls of Abingdon (two sets), Arran, Abercorn, Coventry,
Derby, Egmont, Fingall, Grandison, Inchiquin, Lichfield, Meath, Oxford
(five sets), Orrery (ten sets), Strafford, Scarsdale, Shaftesbury, Thomond,
Winchilsea and Nottingham; countesses of Abercorn, Aylesford, Donegall,
Fingall, Oxford, Strafford; viscounts Bolingbroke, Boyne, Harcourt,
Mountcashel, Mountjoy, Netterville, Vane, Windsor; and viscountesses
Lewisham, Harcourt, Mountjoy. Oxford probably served as a central fig-
ure in the English subscription, drawing in family members (Portland)
and old allies (Bolingbroke and Kent).

The subscription was generously supported by the Irish clergy, with
ninety-nine clerical subscribers identified. They are led by Theophilus
Bolton, Archbishop of Cashel, who had opposed the proclamation against
the Drapier. The list also includes three bishops (Cork, Elphin (six sets) and
Killala), six deans (Ardfert, Armagh, Kildare, Killmore, Lismore, Raphoe)
and five archdeacons (Ardmagh, Cloyne, Cork, Derry, Glandlough). Of the
sprinkling of office holders, the most significant is perhaps Henry Boyle,
the Speaker of the House of Commons and Chancellor of the Exchequer,
who took six sets. Marmaduke Coghill (Commissioner of the Revenue
and friend of Swift) seems to have drawn in his colleagues. Thomas
Gonne, Town Clerk of the City of Dublin, subscribed, as did Walter
Lavit, Sheriff of Cork. Alderman Bennet, who took in the subscriptions in

Cork, subscribed for sixteen sets himself. There is only one judge, James Reynolds, Lord Chief Justice of His Majesty's Common Pleas, but the Irish Attorney-General, Robert Jocelyn, subscribed. A potential dilemma for John Carteret, a friend but Lord Lieutenant for most of the Drapier crisis, was resolved by Lady Carteret's subscribing for six sets. The current Lord Lieutenant, the Duke of Dorset, did not subscribe either, but his secretary, Walter Carey, subscribed for two sets.

Although Faulkner took advantage of Swift's influential friends, the subscription was also a popular success and the subscribers a mixed bunch. Many, of course, were gentleman, but thirteen merchants are specified, including Mr Knox in Bordeaux, seven doctors of medicine and seven aldermen. Some shopkeepers are identified (Richard French, druggist; Thomas Mead, linen-draper; Thomas Smith, hatter), while others have occupations registered (John Esdall, face-painter; Henry Giffard, patentee of Drury Lane; John Wooton, principal painter of the Houyhnhnms). Among writers and friends subscribing were James Arbuckle, Mary Barber, Thomas Carte, Patrick Delany (ten sets), Charles Ford, Matthew and Laetitia Pilkington, Thomas Sheridan, Deane Swift and Laurence Whyte. Touchingly, Rebecca Dingley subscribed from her small income; Pope did not.

What is unclear from the published list is how many of the subscribers were booksellers and how far this edition supplied the Dublin and English trades. From Dublin, Samuel Dalton is identified as a bookseller in the list, and from Pollard's *Dictionary* it seems likely that Mrs Hyde (Sarah, the widow of John, twelve sets), Henry Osborn (ten sets) and Cornelius Wynne (seven sets) were subscribing for resale to customers. Close allies in the trade may have had private arrangements. Three prominent figures in the London trade subscribed – Nathaniel Cole, solicitor to the Stationers' Company, John Barber, Swift's printer when he worked for the ministry, and Samuel Buckley, printer of the *Gazette* – but they all had literary interests.

The subscriber for the most sets, twenty-five of them, 'Jo. Hopkins', also turns out, as Pollard suspected, to be a bookseller, but not a Dublin one, as the litigation finally provoked in England reveals. Motte, wishing to maintain good relations with Swift, allowed the original octavo edition of the *Works* to go unnoticed, but his patience ran out with the cheaper duodecimo published later in 1735 and he filed a complaint in Chancery on 18 October 1735. His complaint against Faulkner, Arthur Bettesworth and Charles Hitch, Charles Davis and John Hopkins, and their answers (though Faulkner seems not to have responded), say much about Faulkner's business methods. John Hopkins was a bookseller in Preston, Lancashire. In June 1733, he says, Faulkner sent him proposals for the octavo edition and 'he took in subscriptions and subscribed for and ordered twenty-five compleat setts of the said work'; later he ordered twenty-six sets of the duodecimo. (I assume that as part of the subscription deal he got four further sets free each time.)[16] This was one way booksellers could be tied into the edition, but the arrangement with Bettesworth, Hitch and Davis was simpler. The defendants admit to knowing Faulkner and say that when he was last in England 'the said Faulkner Deposited with each of these Def^ts. One hundred Setts of the said works of the said J. S – – – – – [overwrites erased Jonathan Swift] and no more Each sett containing four Volumes in twelves which were to be placed in the Debtor side of the Acc^t. of these Def^ts. with the said George Faulkner and these Defendants further say that they have heard and believe that M^r. Thomas Woodward of Fleetstreet Bookseller also took a parcel of the said books to sell for the said Faulkner'.[17] The involvement of Davis and Woodward with Faulkner is highly significant, for they were the bookselling team involved with Faulkner and Bowyer in publishing Swift material in London between 1730 and the *Works*. The *Works* were not an abandonment of the London project but a continuation of it by other means. It was Davis's name that appeared on the fifth volume of *Miscellanies*, published in London in 1735, that gathered up the pieces first printed in Faulkner's *Works*. The involvement of Bettesworth and Hitch (father and son-in-law) is less easy to understand. They were an important bookselling partnership, with many connections in the trade. Although their names appear frequently in the Bowyer ledgers as customers, I have not discovered any other link with Swift, and yet they were willing to accept 100 (possibly 200) copies of the *Works* to sell. In his complaint Motte said he thought that 'divers other persons unknown to Your Orator' were similarly engaged, and, though the claim was formulaic, I suspect he was right. It is difficult to imagine that Faulkner failed to visit all the booksellers with whom he was on good terms, supplementing the subscription with what looks suspiciously like a wide trade distribution.

The contents

The Works of J.S, D.D, D.S.P.D. was published around the time of Swift's sixty-seventh birthday, 30 November 1734: one volume was delayed until 6 January 1735 but the other three were published on 27 November 1734. If they were intended as a birthday present, which Faulkner's professions of friendship make plausible but the history of his delays makes doubtful, that was only one of their many functions.[18] Primarily, as we have seen, they united some of Swift's works in an easily available collection, but they did not emerge quite as Faulkner had originally advertised them, even though he fulfilled the programme he had set himself. The advantages proposed for the edition were four: disentanglement of Swift's writings from those of his friends; inclusion of new works (especially two new Drapier's letters and many original poems); amalgamation of pieces independently published and those collected in the *Miscellanies*; and restoration of the text of *Gulliver's Travels*. The original plan was for the Irish pieces to appear in the first volume, followed by the augmented *Miscellanies*, the poems and *Gulliver*, but the order was changed, with the Irish volume being moved from first to last. Faulkner says in the Preface to the first volume, '*We have been advised to observe the following order*' (Davis, *PW*, vol. XIII, p. 182), suggesting he had been told to change it to better represent Swift's career, but that suggestion raises the difficult question of Swift's engagement in the edition.

Two recent studies have developed our understanding of the *Works* while stressing the difficulty of achieving any clarity about the nature of Swift's involvement. Stephen Karian's research clearly shows that Faulkner's own claims must be judged against a context of trade rivalries, while Ashley Marshall, in a thorough review of the contents of the four volumes, finds a messiness incompatible with Swift's own construction of a monument to his genius.[19] Although I am conscious that even monument-building Pope's second volume of *Works*, also published in 1735, is a bibliographical muddle, and that books are very difficult to keep in order, I would endorse this general picture. My impression is that Swift was engaged in the editing of his works in a patchy, truculent, interfering way; that much of the material was provided by friends but that some of it was supplied by Swift directly; that he helped prepare some texts and drafted some notes; that he looked over the completed volumes but did not read proof in any conscientious way. Swift's version, expressed frequently in his correspondence, is more negative. His letter to Poultney 8 March 1735 may stand for many:

> You will hear, perhaps, that one Faulkener hath printed four volumes, which are called my works; he hath only prefixed the first letters of my name; it was done utterly against my will; for there is no property in printers or booksellers here, and I was not able to hinder it. I did imagine, that, after my death, the several London booksellers would agree among themselves to print what each of them had by common consent; but the man

here hath prevented it, much to my vexation, for I would as willingly have it done even in Scotland. All this has vexed me not a little, as done in so obscure a place. I have never yet looked into them, nor I believe ever shall. (Woolley, *Corr.*, vol. IV, p. 67)

The undesirability of 'obscure' publication was one reason for being guarded; Motte's payments of around £550 for these texts were another. Even if Swift himself had not received any money, it was difficult for him to countenance this rival edition openly.

In the Preface to the first volume, Faulkner had already hinted at Swift's participation: 'the supposed Author was prevailed on to suffer some Friends to review and correct the Sheets after they were printed; and sometimes he condescended, as we have heard, to give them his own Opinion'. But the account he eventually gave in 1763, when he was in rivalry with Hawkesworth, Millar and the Ewings, removes the intermediaries. Information about subscription was

> shewn to the Author, who consented to the Printing, on the following Conditions; That no Jobb should be made, but full Value given for the Money; That the Editor should attend him early every Morning, or when most convenient, to read to him, that the Sounds might strike the Ear, as well as the Sense the Understanding, and had always two Men Servants present for this Purpose; and when he had any Doubt, he would ask them the Meaning of what they heard; which, if they did not comprehend, he would alter and amend until they understood it perfectly well, and then would say, *This will do; for, I write to the Vulgar, more than to the Learned*. Not satisfied with this Preparation for the Press, he corrected every Sheet of the first seven Volumes that were published in his Life Time, desiring the Editor to write Notes ... The Author being very communicative to the Editor ... (Davis, *PW*, vol. XIII, pp. 202–3)

Laetitia Pilkington seems to lend credibility to the story of the servant-test when she says that Swift told her insultingly that he would have his writing 'intelligent to the meanest Capacity, and if you comprehend it, 'tis possible every Body may', though it is possible that her account influenced Faulkner's. More persuasive, as A. C. Elias notes in his edition of Pilkington's *Memoirs*, is the evidence from the text.[20] Herbert Davis's collations of the prose works show consistent tinkering and some major excisions that complement the evidence of cancellation in the poems volume to suggest authorial engagement. Little suggestions of exasperation on Faulkner's part also bear witness to a working relationship. In the first volume he complains, '*This is all we have been allowed to prefix as a general Preface*' (Davis, *PW*, vol. XIII, p. 183), and who could have disallowed an expansion but Swift? In the Advertisement to the second volume, he concludes, '*Our Intentions were to print the Poems according to the Time they were writ in; but we could not do it so exactly as we desired, because we could never get the least Satisfaction in that or many other Circumstances from the supposed Author*' (Davis, *PW*, vol. XIII, p. 185). I suspect Swift gave some help with dating and annotation, but significantly less than Faulkner would have wished.

The first volume in the set was uncontroversial. At its heart was the work that had been collected in the 1711 miscellany and reprinted in the first of the Swift–Pope volumes. Some adjustments were made. *A Letter from a Member of the House of Commons in Ireland … on the Sacramental Test* was moved to volume IV, probably in order to insist on its topicality. Minor items were restored from the second volume of *Miscellanies* or taken from their fourth volume. The texts were subject to careful, though not systematic, revision. The *Proposal for Correcting and Improving the English Tongue*, for example, has a headnote beginning, '*It is well known, that if the Queen had lived a Year or two longer, the following Proposal would in all Probability have taken Effect. For the Lord Treasurer had already nominated several Persons without Distinction of Quality or Party, who were to compose a Society for the Purposes mentioned by the Author*' and goes on to speak of providing a large room for meetings (Davis, *PW*, vol. IV, p. 285). This voice is surely Swift's, as is that frequently pointing to the author's superiority to party during his period of power. Of smaller changes that are particularly likely to be authorial, the *Vindication of Isaac Bickerstaff* has added footnotes and the *Argument to Prove that the Abolishing of Christianity in England May … Be Attended with Some Inconveniences* has significant additions of italic for emphasis. There are consistent changes in styling throughout the *Works*, ably summarized by Valerie Rumbold in her forthcoming Cambridge edition of Swift's *Parodies, Hoaxes, Mock Treatises*: 'heavier and more explicitly grammatical punctuation; more self-consciously correct spelling; filling out of short forms ("although" for "though", "until" for "till"; replacement of "'tis" by "it is"); and replacement of third person present indicative in "—s" by the older form in "—th"'. These practices are in line with Swift's recommendations in his *Proposal*, but I suspect Faulkner took on the responsibility of implementing them.

The second volume was to gather the poems that had been dispersed in the Swift–Pope *Miscellanies*, and to add substantially to them 'by above a third Part, which was never collected before'. The collection is very substantial indeed, running to 480 pages, and here I suspect Matthew Pilkington and others played the part they had promised Faulkner when he undertook the edition, by supplying copy. But in this volume also we have the firmest evidence of Swift's hand, restraining the exuberance of Faulkner and his assistants. In a letter to the Earl of Oxford on 30 August 1734, Swift explained why there had been some delay in publication (Faulkner has ceased to be 'the Prince of Dublin Printers'):

> I have put the Man under some Difficultyes by ordering certain Things to be struck out after they were printed, which some friends had given him. This hath delayed his work, and as I hear, given him much trouble and difficulty to adjust. Farther I know not; for the whole affair is a great vexation to me. (Woolley, *Corr.*, vol. III, p. 753)

The poems struck out have been revealed in Margaret Weedon's account of a copy of volume II in the English Faculty Library, Oxford, containing both cancellans and cancellandum leaves.[21] There were four poems omitted: 'To a Lady', which had already been published by Wilford in London; 'A Dialogue between Mad Mullinex and Timothy', which had already been printed in *The Intelligencer* and *Miscellanies. The Third Volume*; 'Epigram on Fasting', first published here; and 'Traulus' (parts 1 and 2), which had already been published in 1730. The need to cancel 'To a Lady' was obvious; the government had acted against it and Samuel Aris, John Wilford, Lawton Gilliver, Benjamin Motte, Matthew Pilkington and Mary Barber had all been arrested and questioned.[22] The line of inquiry had stopped short of Swift himself, but, when reviewing the volume before publication, Swift or Faulkner would have realized that the poem could not be included. I think Weedon is right in suggesting that Swift took advantage of the need for cancellation to remove 'Traulus' and 'Mad Mullinex and Timothy' because they indulged in personal satire that was inappropriate to an author's works.[23] The 'Epigram' may have been overlooked or removed for its religious content. Ten new poems were introduced as replacements, but the revision did not stop there. 'The author upon himself', 'An excellent new song on a seditious pamphlet' and 'To Mr. Gay' were subjected to a form of self-censorship. Attacks on the Duchess of Somerset and William Whitshed were moderated, while direct reflections on the monarch in 'To Mr. Gay' were removed and the number of blanks in attacks on Walpole increased.

Faulkner's problems with the third volume were of a different kind. In his proposals he said that the text of *Gulliver's Travels* would be corrected from an interleaved copy owned by one of the author's intimate friends. It is natural to assume that the intimate friend was Charles Ford, who did possess such a copy, now in the Forster collection at the Victoria and

Albert Museum.[24] But it seems more likely that Faulkner's informant was Matthew Pilkington, possibly hiding behind an ambiguity about owner-ship. When Faulkner and Swift started looking for the interleaved copy, Pilkington himself was in London, serving as John Barber's chaplain, so on 29 June 1733 Swift wrote to his wife: 'If I am not mistaken, Mr. Pilkington hath an Edition of *Gulliver*, where the true original Copy is interleaved in Manuscript; I desire I may also see that Book' (Woolley, *Corr.*, vol. III, p. 659). Mrs Pilkington said she did not have the book, and it was only later, 9 October 1733, that Swift tried Charles Ford, saying that he could not 'with patience endure that mingld and mangled manner, as it came from Motte's hands' (Woolley, *Corr.*, vol. III, p. 693). Ford replied that he did indeed have such a book, but 'the blank leaves were wrong placed, so that there are perpetual references backwards and forwards … but I will try to get one of the second edition, which is much more correct than the first, and transcribe all the alterations more clearly' (Woolley, *Corr.*, vol. III, p. 698, 6 November 1733). I have argued recently that Ford was prob-ably reluctant to give up his own copy because he had without permission transcribed the Lindalino episode along with the corrections to Motte's text, but Faulkner was given access to the corrections.[25] He sums up the story neatly in his Advertisement:

> *We are assured, that the Copy sent to the Bookseller in* London, *was a Transcript of the Original, which Original being in the Possession of a very worthy Gentleman in* London, *and a most intimate Friend of the Authors; after he had bought the Book in Sheets, and compared it with the Originals, bound it up with blank Leaves, and made those Corrections, which the Reader will find in our Edition. For, the same Gentleman did us the Favour to let us transcribe his Corrections.*[26]

The consequence of Faulkner's persistence in tracking down revised copy is that his edition of *Gulliver's Travels* differs significantly from Motte's, restoring original readings and possibly providing some new ones. In Faulkner's text, the satire is more particular and partisan. The ribbons awarded for leaping and creeping correspond to the orders of chivalry (Part I); the decipherers of political codes discover representations of the King and Walpole (Part III); the attack on first ministers begins without defensive preliminary; the attack on lawyers is broadened; and the dis-paragement of the aristocracy uninhibited (Part IV). Very many smaller changes are adopted. Evaluations of the editions differ, but Faulkner undoubtedly gives us a *Gulliver's Travels* in which the experience of tussling with the government in the *Drapier's Letters* has been partially absorbed.[27]

Although the corrected text of *Gulliver's Travels* featured strongly in Faulkner's initial proposals, the fourth volume had pride of place, for there Swift figured as an Irish patriot, with several pieces brought together for the first time. Faulkner had already collected the *Drapier's Letters* as *Fraud Detected* back in 1725, but another sign of the close alliance with William Bowyer, and his partners Charles Davis and Thomas Woodward, is the use of the London edition of the collection, *The Hibernian Patriot*, as copy for the *Works*, which is unsurprising, as Bowyer sent Faulkner the first fifty-two copies of the printing.[28] To the items collected there, Faulkner added two further letters, one to Lord Chancellor Middleton and one to both Houses of Parliament. The letter to Middleton particularly animated Faulkner because the manuscript concluded with Swift's signature. The identity of the 'supposed author' of the collection was an open secret, the substituted letters on the title page a deference to the authorities rather than a disguise, but Faulkner was excited enough by the signature to mention it in both the Preface to the first volume and a short detailed headnote to the piece: '*It is delivered with much Caution, because the Author confesseth himself to be D— of St. P—k's; and I could discover his Name subscribed at the End of the Original, although blotted out by some other Hand*' (Davis, *PW*, vol. x, p. 97). This volume repeats some of the pieces that had been fought over for the fourth volume of the Swift–Pope *Miscellanies* (*A Modest Proposal* and the *Vindication of Carteret*) but it collects for the first time *A Proposal for the Universal Use of Irish Manufacture, Some Arguments against Enlarging the Power of Bishops, A Short View of the State of Ireland, An answer to a Paper Called A Memorial, A Proposal for an Act of Parliament to Pay off the Debt of the Nation* ('The Reader will perceive the following Treatise to be altogether ironical', the headnote warns) and, among others, the *Last Speech and Dying Words of Ebenezor Elliston* ('this Speech had so good an Effect, that there have been very few Robberies of that Kind committed since', the headnote assures us).

A curiosity of the volume is the placing of *A Letter from a Member of the House of Commons in Ireland, to a Member of the House of Commons in England Concerning the Sacramental Test* in first place. This letter was first published in December 1708 and had been reprinted in the other collections. Faulkner's headnote reveals Swift's motivation, and explains some revisions. He says he has found the letter in the second volume of *Miscellanies*: 'I have, therefore, taken the Liberty to make an Extract out of that Discourse, omitting only some Passages, which relate to certain Persons, and are of no Consequence to the Argument. But the Author's Way of Reasoning seems at present to have more Weight, than it had in those Times, when the Discourse first appeared' (Davis, *PW*, vol. II, p. 110). It was doubtless in order to exert this contemporary force that the letter was included with these recent Irish pieces. The chief omission was of the tribute to William King, Archbishop of Dublin, whose praise was also truncated in *Some Arguments against Enlarging the Power of Bishops*. King had died in 1729 and Swift must have felt his prominence dated the piece; he had omitted the attack on three English bishops in 1711 as 'Purely personal', a self-censorship paralleled by the cancellation of poems in this collection and by the omission of footnotes on Lord Allen and Richard Tighe in the *Vindication of Carteret*. These omissions were, I believe, based on decorum rather than fear of prosecution.[29]

In spite of their subscription status, the *Works* were a decent rather than luxury publication. Those who had not subscribed found themselves paying a guinea for the set, rather than the original 17s 4d:

> These books are printed in Octavo, in a beautiful new Dutch Type, and a fine Genoa paper, containing upwards of 1700 Pages, with a most beautiful frontispiece prefix'd to each Volume engrav'd by the famous Mr. Virtue. Price bound a Guinea.
>
> N.B. A few are printed on a Royal Paper for the Curious. Price Forty shillings. (*London Evening Post*, 12–15 October 1734)

The books are not as extravagantly laid out as the antecedent *Miscellanies*, which, like Benjamin Tooke's 1711 volume, used only part of the measure for Swift's prose, leaving a wide outer margin. The full headline in the *Miscellanies* measures 83 mm, but a line of prose occupies only 70 mm, leaving room for the occasional sidenote or for the reader's annotation. Paragraphs are spaced and there are 29 lines of type to the page. Faulkner uses a sheet much the same size as *Miscellanies* (1711), but he uses the whole of the measure for prose (83 mm, the same as the 1711 headline). There are 34 lines of type to the page. Nevertheless Faulkner's text does not look cramped; it is rather that 1711 is extravagant with white space. Although Faulkner says he has new Dutch type, it looks much more likely to have come from Bowyer second-hand (the dates of shipping recorded in the Bowyer ledgers are right); either that or the inking was very poor.[30] The 1711 volume is much better inked but it is on inferior paper. Faulkner says his is Genoa, which is highly likely, as that was Bowyer's favoured paper; I detect traces of a swan's head and neck on some sheets.

Faulkner's advertisements draw attention to his frontispieces. The first volume has a conventional portrait of Swift (often absent) and the third a portrait of Gulliver; the interest lies in those in the second and fourth volumes. The second presents a glorification of Swift's poetry. Pictured in a central medallion, Swift is about to be crowned with a wreath by a female figure. Before him lie three unidentified volumes, while to his right sits a martial female figure with a stringed instrument; to his left are putti, while above a winged naked female figure stands in glory. By the books is an octagonal medal bearing a head with wild hair, a satyr, I suspect, because the motto below the picture is from Horace's 'Art of Poetry', lines 241–2, 'Quivis speret idem' from the section considering the writing of satire in drama.

> I'll aim at a new blend of familiar ingredients; and people
> Will think it's easy – but will waste a lot of sweat and effort
> If they try to copy it.[31]

The emphasis is on the social engagement of Swift's verse and his closeness to the people, an art that hides art. Volume IV has a more disturbing frontispiece, one that might have preceded the set as a whole. Swift is seated, with St Patrick's Cathedral in the background and putti about to crown him with a wreath. He is giving Hibernia one script, while pointing to two others (Drapier's letters) lying on a table. Around him are distressed figures representing the state of the nation: one bare-thighed lies at his feet, while a mother breastfeeds one child and another weeps. The motto is the first line of the concluding ode of Horace's Book III: 'Exegi Monumentum Ære perennius', 'I have finished a monument more lasting than bronze'. Of course, the writer has made the monument, but Faulkner must have reflected that he might equally be the speaker of this motto himself.

The success of Faulkner's collection was celebrated in verse. Robert Mahony quotes from '*To the Author of the Dublin Journal*' (Faulkner himself):

> Poor, honest George, SWIFT's Works to Print!
> Thy Fortune's made, or Nothing's in't.
> Subscribers, a vast Number shew
> There is no want of Money now.
> The DEAN's so great a Man of Taste,
> All covet to read him in haste;
> More from thy Press than any other ...[32]

Laurence Whyte recognized the same commercial success in his 'To the Rev. Dr. Jonathan Swift, Dean of St. Patrick's, Dublin, on the publishing of a new Edition of his Works in four Volumes', but focused on the celebration of the *Works* as the embodiment of their author's genius:

> Yet with the Nation let me raise my Voice,
> And in thy Works, with Millions more rejoice.
> These Sheets must raise the Printer's Wealth and Fame,
> Since they receive a Sanction from thy *Name*;
> Since every Volume, Page, and nervous Line
> Declare their Lineage from a Stock Divine:
> These are thy Off-spring, which the Wise admire,
> And shew the Beauties of a learned Sire,
> Whether diffus'd in Metre or in Prose,
> The Stile is easy, and the Reasons close;
> The Thoughts extensive, free, and unconfin'd,
> To entertain and cultivate the Mind.[33]

In *Verses on the Death of Dr. Swift*, Swift imagines a country squire going to a shop to ask for 'Swift in Verse and Prose' a year after the author's death, only to be told it had all been sent off to the pastry-cook's (lines 253–68, Williams, *Poems*, vol. II, pp. 562–3). Faulkner's edition was an assurance of a better fate.

The initial success of the *Works* was sustained. Motte won his action against the distribution of the duodecimos in England, but, as we have seen, Faulkner had his allies in London and continued to collaborate with them.[34] Later in 1735 Charles Davis brought out the fifth volume of *Miscellanies*, reproducing the new Faulkner *Works* material from pre-publication sheets Faulkner had sent over.[35] In 1738 Faulkner reprinted and added two volumes with the political material from 1711 to 1714. In 1746 two further volumes appeared; by 1763 there were eleven volumes; and by 1769 twenty. Among the important works added were *Polite Conversation* (Faulkner played a major revising role in preparing an edition in 1738, incorporated as *Works* VI in 1741), *Directions to Servants* (Faulkner seems to have had a vital role in shaping the text as we know it in 1745, incorporated as *Works* VIII in 1751) and *History of the Four Last Years* (though Millar's London edition appeared first). *Tale of a Tub*, which was first published independently by Faulkner in 1756, did not appear in the *Works* (the same printing as 1756, but with cancels) until 1762. The comfortable collaboration with the London booksellers seems to have broken down temporarily when Faulkner was attacked by Hawkesworth in the preface to the first volume of his polished if inaccurate edition in 1755 (as Marshall points out, Orrery, who had originally subscribed for ten sets, had been very dismissive of Faulkner's edition in his *Remarks on the Life and Writings of Dr. Jonathan Swift* (1752)), but when Deane Swift took command of the English side of things in 1765 good relations and the sharing of copy seem to have been restored. Modern scholarship

has tended to vindicate Faulkner's claims to a relationship with Swift,
diligence in collecting materials, and accuracy in reproducing texts. As
Harold Love argued in a brilliant lecture in 1967, Faulkner set the pattern
for editions of Swift by establishing him as a hero author whose every line
was worth preserving.[36] Herbert Davis's collations in his collected edition
of the prose promoted Faulkner further as a faithful editor, even if one
who perpetuated some omissions and showed a tendency to make Swift
a more formal writer. The findings of the new Cambridge edition so far
confirm that impression.

Notes

1 For this aspect of *Works* (1735), see Robert Mahony's well-illustrated chapter
in his *Jonathan Swift: The Irish Identity* (New Haven: Yale University Press,
1995), pp. 1–24. Ashley Marshall has recently argued in a valuable reassessment,
'The "1735" Faulkner Edition of Swift's *Works*: An Analysis of Its Contents and
Textual Authority' (an essay to be published in *The Library*, which she has generously made available to me), that the monument was not of Swift's design, a
conclusion from which I would not dissent.
2 The transcription in Davis, *PW*, vol. XIV, pp. 42–3, differs from this one in a
number of small details.
3 A complication comes from Samuel Fairbrother's 1932 *Miscellanies*, a reprinting
with some authorial variants, but I suspect that at this point Faulkner regarded
that as a convenience for copy rather than a problem. For John Irwin Fischer's
discovery of the variants, see 'Swift's *Miscellanies, in Prose and Verse, Volume
the Fifth*: Some Facts and Puzzles', *SStud*, 15 (2000), 76–87, and for Stephen
Karian's interpretation of the consequences, *Print and Manuscript*, pp. 37–41.
4 The contract is in the Pierpont Morgan Library and is reprinted in Williams,
Corr., vol. V, Appendix XIX, and Robert W. Rogers, *The Major Satires of
Alexander Pope* (Urbana: University of Illinois Press, 1955), pp. 115–16.
5 I have given a more detailed account of Swift's unhappiness and its consequences in 'The Failure of the Swift–Pope *Miscellanies* (1727–32) and *The Life
and Genuine Character of Doctor Swift* (1733)', in *Münster* (2008), pp. 131–48.
6 For complications concerning 'The Lady's Dressing Room', see Stephen Karian's
essay in this collection, p. 39.
7 Woolley, *Corr.*, vol. III, p. 556
8 Swift's idea that publication in London gave you copyright was an
oversimplification. Other booksellers might respect your copy, but strictly the
work had to be entered in the Register with a valid claim behind it; see David
Foxon, *Pope and the Early Eighteenth-Century Book Trade* (Oxford: Clarendon
Press, 1991), pp. 111–14.
9 *The Bowyer Ledgers*, Keith Maslen and John Lancaster (eds.)(London: The
Bibliographical Society; New York: The Bibliographical Society of America,
1991), items 1471 and 1545.

10 Davis, *PW*, vol. XIII, pp. 204–6. Pollard, *Dictionary*, p. 199, thinks he was not imprisoned for printing the 'Queries'. See also her 'George Faulkner', *SStud*, 7 (1992), 79–96.
11 There were also three in which they shared the costs. A full discussion is to be found in Keith Maslen's 'George Faulkner and William Bowyer: The London Connection', in his *An Early London Printing House at Work: Studies in the Bowyer Ledgers* (New York: Bibliographical Society of America, 1993), pp. 223–33, an essay reprinted from *The Long Room*, 38 (1993), 20–30.
12 The assignment is in Harvard University Library and printed in Woolley, *Corr.*, vol. III, p. 509.
13 John Nichols, *Literary Anecdotes of the Eighteenth Century; Comprising Biographical Memoirs of William Bowyer*, 9 vols. (London, 1812), vol. II, p. 10.
14 For the irregularity of Pope's decision to publish his works, though Ben Jonson had done the same, see my *Pope, Print, and Meaning* (Oxford University Press, 2001), pp. 46–8.
15 I am grateful to Professor Karian for drawing my attention to this advertisement, which also responded to requests from Britain and Ireland by extending the closing date for subscriptions to 1 March. For the letter see Woolley, *Corr.*, vol. III, pp. 721–2.
16 Hopkins may have had regular dealings with Dublin. The *Journals of the House of Commons* (London, 1803–52), vol. XXXII, p. 412, report a complaint of his importation of William Burden's *The Gentleman's Pocket-Farrier* (1733), of which some copies have the imprint 'Dublin: Printed by S. Powell, for J. Hopkins, in Preston'.
17 National Archives C11/2249/4; C11/2249/4; C11/2248/22. In this transcription I have integrated the interlineated material.
18 Irwin Ehrenpreis provides an excellent narrative of Faulkner's publication of the *Works* (Ehrenpreis, *Swift*, vol. III, pp. 779–90). Faulkner's *Dublin Journal* for 2 December 1732 drew attention to poems to celebrate Swift's birthday; see *Memoirs of Laetitia Pilkington*, ed. A. C. Elias Jr, 2 vols. (Athens: University of Georgia Press, 1997), vol. II, p. 421. I suspect publication dates are more often related to birthdays than is generally allowed; Pope's publications often coincided with a birthday, his own or the King's.
19 Stephen Karian's impressive review of all the evidence is to be found in *Print and Manuscript*, pp. 30–42; Ashley Marshall's still more sceptical assessment of Swift's role in 'The "1735" Faulkner Edition of Swift's *Works*: An Analysis of Its Contents and Textual Authority'.
20 *Memoirs of Laetitia Pilkington*, ed. A. C. Elias Jr, vol. I, p. 29, vol. II, p. 398. But the stop-press corrections adduced, some of which are subjected to interesting analysis by Fischer in 'Swift's *Miscellanies, in Prose and Verse, Volume the Fifth*', pp. 85–7, are unlikely to arise from Swift's visiting the printing house or reading proof promptly. They might, as Fischer suggests, be the work of friends, see Elias, '*Senatus Consultum*: Revising Verse in Swift's Dublin Circle, 1729–1735', in *Münster* (1998), pp. 249–67, but printing house intervention seems more likely, especially if foul copy was involved.

21 Margaret Weedon, 'An Uncancelled Copy of the First Collected Edition of Swift's Poems', *The Library*, 5th ser., 22 (1967), 44–56.

22 See John Irwin Fischer, 'The Government's Response to Swift's *An Epistle to a Lady*', *Philological Quarterly*, 65 (1986), 39–59.

23 I tried to develop this argument in 'Naming and Shaming in the Poetry of Pope and Swift, 1726–1745', in Nicholas Hudson and Aaron Santesso (eds.), *Swift's Travels: Eighteenth-Century Satire and its Legacy* (Cambridge University Press, 2008), pp. 160–75. Karian adds a revealing quotation from Faulkner's preface to the 1746 *Works* on the exclusion of poems of private resentment (*Print and Manuscript*, p. 42), while in 'The "1735" Faulkner Edition of Swift's *Works*: An Analysis of Its Contents and Textual Authority', Marshall points out that such revisions were not carried out uniformly.

24 National Art Library, Forster 48.D.54 and 55. There are two other interleaved copies, Pierpont Morgan, 22489–90, and Princeton University Library, RHT 18th-598 vol. II (only), but they seem to derive from Ford's.

25 'The Revision of the First Edition of *Gulliver's Travels*: Book-Trade Context, Interleaving, Two Cancels, and a Failure to Catch', *Papers of the Bibliographical Society of America*, 106 (2012), 5–35.

26 Davis, *PW*, vol. XXI, p. xxxi. I have wondered whether the Princeton interleaved copy of *Gulliver's Travels* was Faulkner's copy, but the evidence is at present unclear.

27 For an argued preference for the first edition, see F. P. Lock, *The Politics of Gulliver's Travels* (Oxford: Clarendon Press, 1980), pp. 66–88.

28 Maslen, 'George Faulkner and William Bowyer', p. 227.

29 For a full account of the volumes' omissions (including *Tale of a Tub*, the early political writings, *History of the Four Last Years*, *Verses on the Death of Dr. Swift*), see Marshall, 'The "1735" Faulkner Edition of Swift's *Works*: An Analysis of Its Contents and Textual Authority'.

30 *Bowyer Ledgers*, ed. Maslen and Lancaster, microfiche A340, shows Faulkner buying 704 pounds of pica and long primer for £25.07.08 on 2 November 1732, which would be timely for this project. In his transcription ('George Faulkner and William Bowyer', p. 230) Maslen brackets the year, but I think it is discernible in the entry. Faulkner bought another 773 pounds of long primer on 10 November 1735, and 92½ pounds of brevier in 1737.

31 *Horace: Satires and Epistles; Persius: Satires*, ed. and trans. Niall Rudd (London: Penguin, 1979), p. 197.

32 *Jonathan Swift: The Irish Identity*, pp. 6–7.

33 Laurence Whyte, *Poems on Various Subjects, Serious and Diverting* (Dublin, 1740), pp. 181–5 (182–3). This subscription edition was sold by six booksellers, including Faulkner. I am grateful to Dr Michael J. Griffin for drawing this poem to my attention.

34 Lord Talbot's decision to continue the injunction was cited in Miller vs. Taylor (1769); see Donald Cornu, 'Swift, Motte and the Copyright Struggle', *Modern Language Notes*, 54 (1939), 114–24. Cornu also reports Swift's 1737

draft clause to restrict the assignment of copyright to ten years, a step that would have obviated his problems.

35 For some of the complexities involved, see Fischer, 'Swift's *Miscellanies, in Prose and Verse, Volume the Fifth*'.

36 H. H. R. Love, *Swift and His Publishers* (Melbourne: Monash University, 1969).

PART III

Swift's books in their broader context

CHAPTER NINE

Censorship, libel and self-censorship

Ian Higgins

Jonathan Swift wrote under conditions of censorship. He was a proponent of censorship, of the regulation of public discourse by official power, but also a brilliant exponent of the practical and rhetorical means of evading legal prosecution. The irony and obliquity of this politico-religious writer owe much to the regulatory environment in which his satire and polemic were produced. As a censor Swift was an extremist. As an artful libeller he was scandalous. In the years when Swift was the premier propagandist for the Tory government, he instigated the arrest of Whig journalists and pamphleteers for libelling the ministers or himself, hoping 'to swinge' them, and complained when they got out on bail or evaded prosecution.[1] Swift's call in *The Examiner* of 17 May 1711 for action to be taken against the author of *The Medley* for libel prompted the intended victim, the Whig author Arthur Mainwaring, to point out that Swift 'mistakes the Reign we live in', that under Queen Anne there is liberty to write against 'so notorious a Libeller' as *The Examiner*.[2] A libel is a publication of what is blasphemous, obscene, seditious or treasonable. The intention of a libel is to defame its target. The literature of libel, the art of slander, could mobilize public opinion. As Robert Darnton observes, by 'destroying reputations, it helped delegitimize regimes and bring down governments in many times and places'.[3] For Whigs, Swift was 'the most *scandalous* and most *flagitious* of all *Libellers*'.[4] This chapter considers Swift as censor and libeller and will conclude with some witness of Swift negotiating the perils of the treason statutes as the publicist of the *Memoirs* of a Jacobite. In Swift's authorial career we witness the triumph of the imaginative libeller over the ideological censor.

Censorship and self-censorship

The key features of the censorship under which Swift operated, the array of measures by which the state authorities sought to constrain discourse in the public sphere, can be summarized briefly. In 1662 Charles II's government passed the Printing Act, which imposed pre-publication licensing of books and pamphlets. The Stuart kings Charles II and James II used pre-publication censorship in conjunction with libel laws and the treason statutes to regulate the press. As Mainwaring's remark about Swift thinking himself in an earlier Stuart reign implies, the Restoration Stuart state was notorious for persecution of dissent. The Printing Act, or Licensing Act as it is also known, was allowed to lapse in 1695, mainly for commercial reasons as there was opposition to the monopolistic privileges the system of licensing granted, but the system had also posed practical difficulties and was cumbersome in implementation. It was also not especially effective in proscribing unlicensed printing. Other measures, legal and extra-legal, remained to control expression and seemed, in 1695, to offer better prospects for prosecuting the press. Since libellous authors were invariably anonymous, governments targeted printers, publishers, booksellers and books. They engaged in physical violence: harassment, arrest and interrogation of press personnel, destruction of presses and public book burnings. The common law of libel (covering criminal libel, blasphemous libel and seditious libel), the 'Act for the more Effectual Suppressing of Blasphemy and Prophaneness' (9 Will. III, c. 35 (1698)), and the treason statutes (based ultimately on 25 Edward III) were the main legal instruments for censorship. The sedition and treason laws, and what constituted seditious and treasonable libel, tended to elide in constructive practice. By the Hanoverian period, Swift mordantly observed, it was being argued that 'all Reflection | On Ministers, is disaffection'.[5] Early in William III's reign the exemplary execution of the Jacobite printer William Anderton demonstrated that writing, printing or publishing treasonable libel could be construed as an overt act of treason punishable by death.

There was also an incremental extension of the treason law so that in Anne's reign treason applied to overt acts of compassing and imagining the king's death and levying war against the king, but also to hindering the succession by writing and printing, and private correspondence with known adherents of the Pretender.[6] After the Revolution of 1688–9, the principal targets for censorship were the real subversives in church and state, publications against the established Christian faith (Blasphemy) and against the established dynasty (Jacobitism).[7] Censorship was also effected through copyright and economic legislation. 'An Act for the Encouragement of Learning, by Vesting the Copies of Printed Books in the Authors or Purchasers of such Copies' (8 Anne, c. 19, the 'Copyright Act' of 1710) required the identification of textual property enabling greater surveillance of those responsible for publications. The 1712 Stamp Act (10 Anne, c. 19) required imprints with the names of printers and publishers and imposed a tax on newspapers and pamphlets. Thus by identifying publications and increasing the costs of their production, the Stamp Act sought to regulate the popular press and suppress Grubstreet libelling. On 7 August 1712, after the Stamp Act had come into effect, Swift announced 'that Grubstreet is dead and gone'. In his *History of the Four Last Years of the Queen*, Swift expresses wholehearted support of 'some Effectual law for putting a Stop' to false and scandalous, and blasphemous, libels, but he laments the inadequacies of the Stamp Act to effect it and the parliamentary failure to pass a press bill registering printers and publishers. It was sabotaged, Swift felt, by an amendment requiring identification of authors as well, which he opposed.[8] Swift was not just interested in such legislation on textual property as an instrument of press control, since he was concerned for the property rights of authors. He appears to have written the clause in the Copyright Bill of 1737 stating that copyright should revert to authors after a period of ten years.[9]

From the beginning to the end of his authorial career, whether writing for or against the government of the day, Swift's writings irritated, provoked and sometimes alarmed the authorities, prompting incidents of censorship. His greatest works of satire and polemic were noticed or prosecuted by official power. *A Tale of a Tub* (1704) was regarded by many as a blasphemous libel. Swift believed that it prevented his higher preferment in the church since Queen Anne refused to countenance the reputed author of the allegedly impious work. *A Tale of a Tub* would find itself placed on the Roman Catholic Church's 'Index Librorum Prohibitorum'.[10] *A Short Character of his Excellency Thomas Earl of Wharton, Lord Lieutenant of Ireland* (1710) was noticed by Wharton in the House of Lords. The 'late pamphlet (called a Character of me)', he said, was an odious instance of defamatory accusations against him, but as if in ironic confirmation of Swift's claim in the pamphlet that Wharton was insouciantly insensible to moral satire, the Earl told the House: 'but I matter 'em not, and doubt not but to clear myself from the wicked calumny's of my numerous enemies'.[11] *The Conduct of the Allies* (1711) was attacked in Parliament as containing a treasonable passage, and Lord Chief Justice Sir Thomas Parker found it open to treasonable interpretation.[12] The Tory trade publisher John Morphew, whose name appeared on the imprint, was taken up and interrogated, but he refused to identify the author. Morphew and the Tory printer John Barber were taken up for publishing *The Publick Spirit of the Whigs* (1714), which the House of Lords condemned as 'a false, malicious, and factious Libel'. There was a proclamation offering a reward of £300 to discover the author.[13] 'So well protected are those who scribble for the Government', Swift sardonically observed.[14] Swift was the suspected author but he was not formally identified.

The five years immediately after the Hanoverian succession, from 1715 to 1719, are Swift's lost years. No political works by him in print have been identified. Swift seems to have practised the genre of silence as far as print publication is concerned during the Hanoverian Whig government's concerted attempt to censor the public sphere and to eradicate Jacobite disaffection. In the *Verses on the Death of Dr. Swift, D.S.P.D.* Swift would let the world know that he feared prosecution and even assassination during these years.[15] Most Swift scholars suppose that Swift retired from politics and concerned himself with his decanal duties in Dublin. But we do know that Swift was writing in these years. He was writing treasonable libels. A holograph manuscript of a poem on affairs of state has survived entitled 'A Wicked Treasonable Libel' (1718), which satirizes the king and the Hanoverian dynasty. (Swift pretends that he has transcribed the libel in order to discover and inform on the author.) In the *Verses on the Death of Dr Swift, D.S.P.D.* Swift images himself in these lost years:

> BY Innocence and Resolution,
> He bore continual Persecution;[16]

'A Wicked Treasonable Libel' projects a less innocent image of the politico-religious Tory writer in this period, more in line with the image presented in 'On the foregoing Picture' (1718–19):

> I spend my Time in making Sermons,
> Or writing Libels on the G[erman]s.
> Or murmuring at Whigs Preferments.[17]

Swift's apparent silence in the public sphere probably really owes much to the fact that the Whig government in these turbulent years immediately after the Hanoverian accession was able to shut down or disrupt the presses of those Irish printers who favoured the Tory cause, such as Cornelius Carter, Edward Waters and John Harding, printers who published Swift's polemic in Ireland.[18] But it was not just Whig censorship under which Swift suffered. His *History of the Four Last Years*, which was initially composed in 1712–13 and intended for publication, and into which Swift put considerable personal investment, and upon which he continued to work until as late as 1737, remained as an unpublished manuscript, effectively censored by his Tory friends in his lifetime. His greatest satire, *Gulliver's*

Travels (1726), was also subjected to what might be called friendly censorship. The London printer Benjamin Motte and his business associate the Reverend Andrew Tooke censored the first edition, altering and adding to the text in politically sensitive areas, as Swift complained when he saw the printed book.[19]

Swift's return to political polemic in print after five years of silence saw his Irish printers being arrested for his major works in defence of Ireland, such as *A Proposal for the Universal Use of Irish Manufacture* (1720) and *A Letter to the Whole People of Ireland* (1724), the fourth of the *Drapier's Letters*. In 1728 Swift wrote of 'all the Warning I have in vain given the Publick, at my own Peril, for several Years past' and in the *Verses on the Death of Dr. Swift, D.S.P.D.* he writes that in defence of Liberty 'he boldly stood alone; | For her he oft expos'd his own'.[20] But it was the anonymous author's printers who were in peril and were taken up by the authorities and prosecuted. On reading the fourth *Drapier's Letter* Bishop William Nicolson recognized that it had the scandalous stylistic signature of the Dean of St Patrick's. Quoting the offending passage where Swift asserts that Ireland is not a depending Kingdom bound by laws enacted by the Parliament of England, the Whig Bishop reported to Archbishop William Wake, deploying a gallows trope: 'Thus My Lord, we are come to the highest Round in our Ladder; And, if no Mark be set on this insolent Writer, little Safety will be expected.'[21] A proclamation was issued against the pamphlet and a £300 reward offered for the identity of the author, but it was the printer who was prosecuted and imprisoned. Swift's escape from prosecution for the *Drapier's Letters* and other works, and the government's inability to prevent the circulation of his defiant polemic, do show the limitations in the apparatus of censorship and of the law of seditious libel as a means for governments to regulate the press in Ireland. James Kelly points out that from the late 1720s the focus of censorship shifted to press coverage of the proceedings of Parliament through the invocation of parliamentary privilege. True to scandalous form, Swift's late satiric libel 'The Legion Club' is a searing, virulent invective against the Irish House of Commons and its proceedings in defiance of the censorship.[22]

There may well be no such thing as free speech or uncensored human communication. There are externally imposed and internalized constraints on what we say, from the laws of the land and public speech codes to the self-censorship that takes place in social intercourse: the calculated falsehoods, the white lies, the half-truths, the omissions and silences. The moral satirist in Part IV of *Gulliver's Travels* presents lying – to have '*said the Thing which was not*' – as indeed endemic to the human species and the ontology of human communication. After learning the Houyhnhnm language, Gulliver's first request of his Houyhnhnm master is that he collude in the human habit of mendacity and conceal the fact that he wears clothing (which distinguishes Gulliver from the brutish Yahoos): 'that the Secret of my having a false Covering to my Body might be known to none but himself'.[23] Certainly in Swift's lifetime, which spanned from 1667, soon after the Stuart Restoration, to the attempt at a second Stuart restoration in 1745, there were things in church and state that could not be said, except perhaps in the special circumstances of one's scaffold speech. Swift's correspondence discloses his acute awareness of the presence of censoring official power and the ever-present possibility of perlustration, and demonstrates his own practice of self-censorship.[24] Swift's literary remains attest to his habitual caution and a lifelong practice of self-censorship. Much is missing from the extant record. He refers many times to burning pamphlets and letters that for various reasons, political, personal or aesthetic, he felt should not see the light of day. It is estimated that less than five per cent of the letters Swift must have written in his lifetime have survived.[25] His letters on political subjects are exercises in self-censorship and caution. As he told the Earl of Peterborough in 1714: 'If your Excellency were here, I would speak to you without any constraint; but the fear of accidents in the conveyance of the letter, makes me keep to generals.'[26] What is extant is probably what Swift felt it was safe to write or what he and his friends thought safe to preserve. Ten correspondents in the Woolley edition of Swift's extant correspondence received more than twenty letters from Swift. Seven of them were Jacobites, sometime Jacobites or Jacobite sympathizers. Yet the politics expressed in these preserved or copied letters largely avoids topics, such as the Hanoverian dynasty's right to rule, that come within the ambit of the treason statutes. The only 'State Whig' among these ten correspondents was Archbishop William King, Swift's immediate superior in the Church of Ireland, and he suspected that Swift had become a Jacobite.[27] Swift was a print author. But many of his outspoken political works, particularly poems on affairs of state, early and late, remained in manuscript, circulating, if at all, at first among coteries of friends, or were not printed in full.[28]

Censor

In published and unpublished work Swift repeatedly distinguished between a right to freedom of thought and liberty of conscience, and the right to publish one's thoughts. Publication of opinion 'ought to be kept under the strictest regulation'. Writing or discourse against the limited monarchy and established religion should 'be liable to the severest punishments the law can inflict'.[29] Matthew Tindal was a major contemporary advocate of the freedom to publish (and indeed is an important figure in the history of the development of press freedom) whose arguments against censorship, as Swift recognized, drew upon Milton, Locke and Spinoza.[30] Swift's response to Tindal, whom he thought should be punished for the ironically entitled *The Rights of the Christian Church Asserted* (1706), is a stark epitome of his consistent position on freedom of expression. Swift is hardly delighted by freedom of opinion, but it is the publication of opinion that concerns him: 'Men must be governed in Speculations, at least not suffered to vent them, because Opinions tend to Actions, which are most governed by Opinions.'[31] This is a view articulated by the King of Brobdingnag in *Gulliver's Travels* on 'Opinions prejudicial to the Publick': 'a Man may be allowed to keep Poisons in his Closet, but not to vend them about as Cordials'.[32] As an advocate of censorship Swift had three kinds of author and their print publications particularly in his sights: heterodox and heretical writers against revealed religion (blasphemous works), writers against episcopacy (Presbyterian and other Dissenting publications) and radical Whig republicanism.[33]

The regulatory regime projected in *A Project for the Advancement of Religion, and the Reformation of Manners* (1709) is a censor's paradise. Swift activates the different senses of 'censor' – Roman censor, press censorship and critical censure in imagining 'that something parallel to the Office of Censors antiently in *Rome*, would be of mighty Use among us' inspecting into 'Morals and Religion'.[34] In the irreligious polity of *An Argument Against Abolishing Christianity*, the Blasphemy Act is said to be some 'obsolete Law' and the Blasphemy and Sacramental Test Acts are depicted as 'an old dormant Statute or two'.[35] 'What I principally insist on', writes Swift in the *Project*, 'is the due Execution of the old ['Laws'].' Swift's *Project* imagines them fully revived and vastly extended by the legislature. Swift called for the 'Censor' to use 'an annual *Index Expurgatorius*' on language, and he breaks his habitual practice of anonymity in attaching his name to *A Proposal For Correcting, Improving and Ascertaining the English Tongue* (1712), another authoritarian censor's vision, which proposes an Academy on the French model for regulating language.[36]

Swift's historical and utopian models for a civil polity have strict censorship of dissent as part of their institution. Swift approves the personal rule of Charles I as the apogee of politeness and the period when the English language reached its greatest perfection.[37] The apologia for Charles I's regime in Swift's 30 January martyrdom sermon implicitly supports Laudian censorship as reasonable, for Swift points to the virulent hate speech in Puritan libels inciting violence against the King and Bishops as a cause of the civil wars.[38] Analysis of offending Puritan libels has prompted one legal historian to indeed characterize Laudian censorship, controversially, as an attempt to impose civility through speech codes.[39] Swift's utopia, Houyhnhnmland, in Part IV of the *Travels*, has no books or writing at all, and is predicated upon the eradication of dissent and regulation of public conduct. Houyhnhnmland preserves '*Decency* and *Civility* in the highest Degrees', and while there is some difference of opinion concerning Gulliver and the Yahoos there is outward public conformity to the legislative authority.[40] Houyhnhnmland has among its classical utopian models Plato's *Republic* and *Laws*, and the laws of Lycurgan Sparta. George Orwell noted what must strike many modern readers as the political paradox in *Gulliver's Travels*. Orwell opined that, 'especially in Part III', Swift satirizes 'what would now be called totalitarianism. He has an extraordinarily clear prevision of the spy-haunted "police State", with its endless heresy-hunts and treason trials.' But in the Houyhnhnms this 'Tory anarchist' presents, as an ideal polity, a society that has reached 'the highest stage of totalitarian organisation, the stage when conformity has become so general that there is no need for a police force'.[41] We turn now from Swift the censor to Swift the libeller.

Libeller

The aesthetic implications of censorship across English literary history have been extensively studied.[42] Swift's perfection of a satirical irony of menaces where he does not mean what he says but he doesn't not mean it either,[43] his exploitation of ambiguity, of 'any verbal nuance, however slight, which gives room for alternative reactions to the same piece of language',[44] and habitual anonymity and inventive pseudonymity reflect both his genius and the modus operandi of an author aware that a 'Libel' is 'to be writ with Caution and double Meaning, in order to prevent Prosecution'.[45] In the course of *The Importance of the Guardian Considered, in a Second Letter to the Bailiff of Stockbridge. By a Friend of Mr. ST – – – le*, a libel on Richard Steele as a libeller, Swift accurately explains how a contemporary libeller (and satirist) could evade the laws on written defamation (*libel*), spoken defamation (*slander*) and scandal (*Scandalum Magnatum*):

You must know, Sir, that we have several Ways here of abusing one another, without incurring the Danger of the Law. First, we are careful never to print a Man's Name out at length; but as I do that of Mr. *St—le* : So that although every Body alive knows whom I mean, the Plaintiff can have no Redress in any Court of Justice. Secondly, by putting Cases; Thirdly, by Insinuations; Fourthly, by celebrating the Actions of others, who acted directly contrary to the Persons we would reflect on; Fifthly, by Nicknames, either commonly known or stamp'd for the purpose, which every Body can tell how to apply.[46]

It was the artful generality of *Gulliver's Travels*, his friends recognized, that would frustrate any attempt at legal prosecution of the political satire, much to the exasperation of Swift's Whig critics calling for such action, one of whom observed: 'whatever the Doctor deserves, 'tis given out that he has been so much upon his Guard, that no Forms of Law can touch him'.[47] Seditious particularity is concealed within the fictional carapace. For example, Laputa in Part III of the *Travels* is a dysfunctional arbitrary court, where the obsession with music, for example, and the presence of 'Strangers' would have helped identify the Hanoverian Court of George I and Hanoverian England where music was regarded as 'the reigning Amusement'.[48] Adultery is also a feature of this distracted court.[49] Contemporaneous seditious Jacobite polemic focused on the alleged sexual infidelity of princesses in the House of Hanover, George I's mother (Princess Sophia) and his first wife (Sophia Dorothea), and claimed that George I and George II were bastards.[50] Jacobite scandalous libel of the Hanoverian dynasty as illegitimate is activated, but obliquely, in Swift's satire. In the island monarchy of Laputa there is a necessary legal precaution in place: 'BY a fundamental Law of this Realm, neither the King nor either of his two elder Sons, are permitted to leave the Island; nor the Queen till she is past Child-bearing.' Swift's libellous innuendos against George I and II and their mothers are more explicit in the unpublished 'A Wicked Treasonable Libel', 'Directions for a Birthday Song' (1729) and in his private marginalia.[51]

Swift also drew upon the resources of the printing house for libellous innuendo. Part of the offensiveness of Swift's allegedly seditious polemic may well have been the political emphases of the typography. In the *Drapier's Letters* the Drapier reiterates that he is a loyal critic of the government in the Halfpence controversy. Yet other aspects of the pamphlets seek to link William Wood and corrupt practices with the Hanoverian court (an attack on the dynasty would take the tracts within the ambit of seditious libel and the treason statutes). The hated copper coinage is stamped 'with His Majesty's *Image* and *Superscription*'.[52] '*Wood*'s Coin' comes with '*Caesar's*' face and a threatened '*Proclamation*', says the polem-ical Drapier who has the menacing initials of M.B. [innuendo Marcus Brutus]. On the title page of John Harding's first edition of the first of the *Drapier's Letters*, Wood's name oozes in gothic or black letter. Italic and black letter were being used with seditious verve by Jacobite pamphleteers as innuendo. George I's proclamations and other legal documents were typically printed in black letter. In *The Second and Last English Advice To the Freeholders of England*, a Jacobite pamphlet of 1722, black letter is used for words such as 'Corrupt', 'Hannover', Hanoverian legislation, and for phrases made by the King in his speeches, which are then heavily ironized. Black letter becomes a typographical sign of a German dynastic tyranny. Readers are informed that noblemen taken prisoner after the Jacobite defeat at Preston, who surrendered upon assurances of George I's 'mag-nificent promises of Mercy' and 'Character of Lenity', were 'Pinioned' as if they were slaves. 'Pinioned' is the only word printed in gothic letter on the page.[53] John Harding's title page may well be insinuating who is behind Wood's coin when he prints Wood's name in black letter. Similarly, Swift's italicizing of 'Lenity' in the satire of the despotic and barbaric Emperor of Lilliput's spurious 'Lenity' in Part I of *Gulliver's Travels* is using a font for anti-dynastic innuendo.[54]

Invective against Walpole or the ministry was not treasonous, but in Swift's printed poem of 1735, 'To Mr. Gay', for example, the seering sat-ire of Walpole's corrupt stewardship (Walpole is represented as having the Crown and Parliament in his pocket) is perhaps given extra provocation by emphatic italics which appear to be recalling one of the most notorious of all Jacobite indictments of parliamentary corruption under a foreign king. Swift writes:

> A DEXT'ROUS Steward, when his Tricks are found,
> *Hush-money* sends to all the Neighbours round: ...
> His Policy consists in *setting Traps*,
> In finding *Ways and Means*, and *stopping Gaps:* ...
>   IN ev'ry Court the Parallel will hold;
> And Kings, like private Folks, are bought and sold:
> The ruling Rogue, who dreads to be cashier'd;
> Contrives, as he is *hated*, to be *fear'd*:
> *Confounds Accounts, perplexes all Affairs*;
> For, *Vengeance* more *embroils*, than *Skill repairs*.
> So, Robbers (and their Ends are just the same)
> To 'scape Enquiries, *leave the House in Flame*.[55]

'*Hush-money*' was a term minted by the Jacobite propagandist and barrister Charlwood Lawton in *A Short State of our Condition, with Relation to the present Parliament* (1693), which became notorious as the 'Hush-money paper'. It was a country critique of court corruption and a pensionary Parliament. Lawton accused the court of bribing members of the House of Commons by which 'the King can baffle any *Bill*, quash all Grievances, stifle Accompts'. Parliamentary critics have 'their Mouths soon stopped with *Hush-money*' by Henry Guy, the secretary to the treasury, using funds for the '*secret Service*'. The Hush-money paper was published anonymously without a licence and with no identifying printer's name, place of publication or date. The printer and hawkers of the unlicensed work were arrested and the anonymous author was charged with being a Jacobite, which Lawton certainly was.[56] His printer was William Anderton, a Jacobite, who was executed for publishing two anonymous treasonable libels in 1693 (his own *Remarks upon the Present Confederacy, and late Revolution in England* (1693) and Lawton's *A French Conquest Neither Desirable nor Practicable* (1693)).[57] Swift's italics perhaps invite readers to view the current Hanoverian court and Walpole through the lens of a famous libel. But in the 1730s, as the ghost-writer of a Jacobite's *Memoirs*, Swift produced an artful libel on William III and on prominent Scots Presbyterians.

Memoirs of Capt. John Creichton. Written by Himself, a small octavo book of 170 pages, was first published in 1731 without a printer's name or place of publication (the printer was George Faulkner, who had been in service as Swift's printer in Ireland since 1728,[58] and it was printed privately in Dublin). A modern formula for celebrity autobiographies is perhaps more appropriate than the 'Written by Himself' given on the title page, for these *Memoirs* are 'by John Creichton with Jonathan Swift'. It is an autobiographical account of an Irish soldier serving in Scotland, fighting in defence of the episcopal Church establishment during the 'killing times' in Restoration Scotland, and then for James VII against William III during the Jacobite counter-revolution led by John Graham of Claverhouse, Viscount Dundee. Over a third of the book is devoted to Creichton's Jacobite activism though the word 'Jacobite' is never used. Creichton was arrested in 1689 for treason and imprisoned for three years. The book is sympathetic to Creichton; indeed, it relishes and valorizes the activities of a man who appears in Scots Presbyterian martyrologies as a persecutor of the Saints and a man who murdered in cold blood.[59] Swift's involvement with this work was not revealed in his lifetime. The *Memoirs* first appeared in a posthumous edition of Swift's *Works* published by

Faulkner in 1762 with a 'Note' from Faulkner claiming that Swift prepared the *Memoirs* for the press from Creichton's memoranda and published it by subscription.[60] This Irish Jacobite's *Memoirs* was one of perhaps several literary projects, now obscure, with which Swift was involved while staying with the Irish Tory MP Arthur Acheson in Armagh in 1728 and 1729, a period when he was also visiting and keeping convivial company with Henry and Robert Leslie, former Irish Jacobite exiles like their famous father, Charles Leslie.

The few modern scholars who have addressed this neglected work in detail have seen it as edited and partly ghost-written by Swift in preparing it for the press, as a kind of fiction, as a fabrication, and as a foundational text in the history of the historical novel.[61] Certainly, Captain Creichton does seem to have stepped out of the pages of Swiftian fiction, and especially out of Part III, chapter 8, of *Gulliver's Travels*, 'A further Account of Glubbdubdrib. Antient and Modern History corrected.' In that necromantic place Gulliver compares past and present and has summoned before him 'some *English* Yeomen of the old Stamp', admirable exempla of simplicity, justice, spirit of liberty, valour and patriotism. Such 'pure native Virtues were prostituted for a Piece of Money by their Grand-children; who in selling their Votes, and managing at Elections have acquired every Vice and Corruption that can possibly be learned in a Court'.[62] In the 'Advertisement To The Reader' of the *Memoirs*, the Jacobite Captain is described as '*a very honest and worthy Man; but of the old Stamp: And it is probable, that some of his Principles will not relish very well, in the present Disposition of the World. His* Memoirs *are therefore to be received like a Posthumous Work*'. This 'remarkable Cavalier, in the Reigns of *Charles* II. *James* II. and *William* III', distinguished by his '*personal Courage and Conduct*', could have been one of the exemplary Dead of Glubbdubdrib.[63] He is a Spirit from a principled past summoned up by the ghost-writer Swift for contemporary polemical purposes. The work's emphases, selection of detail, and rhetorical strategies are characteristic of the literary pamphleteer as well as the writer of prose fiction. The work's wilful historical inaccuracy – the exaggeration, alteration of chronology, transposition and telescoping of events (Monmouth's rebellion, Argyle's uprising and the invasion of the Prince of Orange seem to take place in the same year, for instance) – are the strokes of the polemicist. The work's venomous anecdotes libelling Presbyterians, and the sensational salacious material concerning the sexual escapades of the sectarians, such as the anecdote about the Covenanter David Williamson who hid in bed with Lady Ker of Cherrytree's daughter in order to escape the King's troops but got the daughter pregnant while doing so, could have been taken from printed polemical works, rather than from Creichton. Swift is known to have possessed such episcopalian polemic as *The Scotch Presbyterian Eloquence* (1692), a source or corroboration for Creichton's anecdotes.[64] Creichton's story, published in 1731, is, among other things, a cautionary tale showing that the very survival of episcopacy requires the continued exclusion of Presbyterians from political power. It is a companion piece for Swift's Test Act tracts of the 1730s.

The work is also a masterpiece of artful libel on the memory of William III, contriving to defame the king while ostensibly defending him. In Creichton's *Memoirs* the rabbling of the episcopal clergy at the Revolution and afterwards is given extended circumstantial coverage. The Scots Whig bishop Gilbert Burnet, whose *History of His Own Times* these *Memoirs* are 'correcting', had reported 'that in the Western Counties of Scotland, the Presbyterians, who had suffered much in the course of many years ... generally broke in upon the Episcopal Clergy with great insolence and much cruelty'. Swift's marginal comment on this passage in a copy of Burnet's *History* is 'To reward them for which, King William abolished Episcopacy'.[65] However, in Creichton's published *Memoirs*, '*Justice*' is done 'to the *Memory* of *King William*'. Creichton opines: '*that Prince* ... would have acted much better than he did, with Regards to the *Civil and Ecclesiastical Constitution in Scotland*, if he had been permitted to govern by his own Opinions'.[66] This apologia presents William as a figurehead puppet of the Presbyterian Kirk. The *Memoirs* are a vehicle for Swift's rhetorical violence against Scots Presbyterians, with Creichton as his mouthpiece. It is reported that members of the Kirk advised William not to release the incarcerated Creichton, because if released the captain 'would *Murder all Scotland in One Night*'.[67] If he had done so Creichton would only have been enacting a Swiftian wish that 'the whole Nation to a Man' were hanged, beginning 'with Argyle and next with the Fanatick Dogs who teised' Swift's hero, Charles I's Scots military commander, the Duke of Montrose, at his execution, 'with their Kirk Scurrilityes'.[68] Swift loathed the Argyles. In annotation on Burnet's *History* Swift described the 8th Earl, who was captured and beheaded for supporting the Duke of Monmouth's rebellion, as 'the greatest Villain of his age'.[69] In Creichton's *Memoirs* it is reported that Argyle was captured while trying 'to get into a little Boat, and grappling with the Owner'. The deadpan observation is: 'It seems he wanted Presence of Mind, to engage the Man with a Piece of Money, to set him on the other Side.'[70] If Argyle had just thought to pay for his boat ticket rather than assault the boatman, he might have got away!

There is sustained and pervasive irony in the way that the conspiracy against James VII and II and the Williamite usurpation is narrated. Creichton's account activates charges against William III that were the stuff of Jacobite seditious libels such as Lawton's 'Hush-money paper' and the infamous *The Exorbitant Grants of William III* (1703). The euphemisms for William's arbitrary power and bribery are 'generosity' and '*Marks of his Bounty*'. The ironic use of qualifying clauses, innuendo and euphemism in a passage about the attempt to bribe the young Jacobite Lord Forbes into entering William's service against James recalls the account of the 'great Clemency' of the cruel and arbitrary king of Luggnagg, and his 'very honourable Offers' to Gulliver who pretends to be a Dutchman at his court.[71] In Creichton's apology for his Jacobitism, Swift is cautious, but nevertheless sympathetic to a Jacobite levying war against the Williamite settlement. Creichton admits he might have been wrong in continuing in his allegiance to James but he asks us to consider his conduct in the circumstances of the time and the oaths he had taken. Emphasis is placed on the circumstance that the episcopal religion, under which Creichton had been educated and 'for which I had always born the highest *Veneration*, was now utterly *destroyed*' and 'the *Presbyterian Kirk*, which had been my *greatest Aversion*, exalted in its Stead'. But 'supposing me in an Error', the candid reader must accept that Creichton followed his conscience in the crisis of allegiance at the Revolution and at great personal cost, having declined 'considerable Offers' to change his allegiance.[72] The irony and rhetorical strategy in the Captain's *Memoirs*, like that in the more famous Captain Gulliver's *Travels*, is the aesthetic outcome of a libeller's response to the censor.

At the start of his satiric career Swift mocked the ineffectiveness of general satire in modern times: ''Tis but a *Ball* bandied to and fro, and every Man carries a *Racket* about Him to strike it from himself among the rest of the Company', but should the satirist venture to be particular, to name and shame, then he 'must expect to be imprisoned for *Scandalum Magnatum*: to have *Challenges* sent him; to be sued for *Defamation;* and to be *brought before the Bar of the House*'.[73] The apologia for his satire in *Verses on the Death of Dr. Swift, D.S.P.D.* claims that Swift was no libeller, he 'lash'd the Vice but spar'd the Name', yet throughout this poem Swift's satiric victims are named.[74] In 'To Doctor D—L – – – Y, On The Libels Writ against him', written in 1730, around the time of the *Memoirs of Capt. John Creichton*, Swift condemns libels and counsels Patrick Delany that defamation is the price of fame, but the poem also witnesses the synonymity of libel and satire in the print culture.[75] At the end of his career Swift was writing outspoken poems on affairs of state in contempt of the censorship, such as his 'long Libel', 'The Legion Club'.[76] The rough justice of the satirist and the partisan project of the polemicist were to be attained, it seems, through that scandalous art that aims to defame and delegitimize.

Notes

1 *JSt* (1948), vol. I, p. 365; vol. II, pp. 381, 384–5, 568–9.
2 *The Examiner*, no. 42, 17 May 1711, Ellis, *Examiner*, pp. 427–33 (pp. 428–32); *The Medley*, no. 34, 21 May 1711, Ellis, *Examiner*, pp. 434–9 (pp. 437–8).
3 Robert Darnton, *The Devil in the Holy Water or the Art of Slander from Louis XIV to Napolean* (Philadelphia: University of Pennsylvania Press, 2010), p. 6. On the art of libel before Swift, see Alastair Bellamy, '"Raylinge Rymes and Vaunting Verse": Libellous Politics in Early Stuart England, 1603–1628', in Kevin Sharpe and Peter Lake (eds.), *Culture and Politics in Early Stuart England* (Basingstoke and London: Macmillan, 1994), pp. 285–310; M. Lindsay Kaplan, *The Culture of Slander in Early Modern England* (Cambridge University Press, 1997).
4 Abel Boyer, *The Political State of Great Britain*, 38 vols. (London, 1711–29), vol. VII, p. 236; *CWJS*, vol. VIII, p. 454.
5 See particularly: Philip Hamburger, 'The Development of the Law of Seditious Libel and the Control of the Press', *Stanford Law Review*, vol. 37, no. 3, Historical Perspectives on the Free Press (February 1985), 661–765; Murray Pittock, 'Treacherous Objects: Towards a Theory of Jacobite Material Culture' *Journal for Eighteenth-Century Studies*, 34, no. 1 (March 2011), 39–63 (40–4); *Verses on the Death of Dr. Swift, D.S.P.D.*, lines 275–6, Williams, *Poems*, vol. II, p. 563.
6 3&4 Anne, c. 14: 'An Act to Prevent all Traiterous Correspondence with Her Majesties Enemies'; 6 Anne, c. 7: 'An Act for the Security of Her Majesties Person and Government, and of the Succession to the Crown of Great Britain in the Protestant Line'. Swift possessed a copy of *A Collection of the Several Statutes, and Parts of Statutes, Now in Force, Relating to High Treason, and Misprision of High Treason* (London, 1709), see *Library and Reading, Part 1*, vol. I, pp. 437–9. See 'Treason' in Henry Boult, *A Supplement to the Abridgement of all the Statutes of King William and Queen Mary, and of King William III. and Queen Anne* (London, 1708), pp. 140–1; reprinted in Geoffrey Kemp and Jason McElligott (gen. eds.), *Censorship and the Press, 1580–1720*, 4 vols. (London: Pickering & Chatto, 2009), vol. IV, p. 284.
7 For a gathering of contemporary texts of censorship and for cases of writers and works censored, and for overviews of the extensive modern scholarship, see Geoffrey Kemp and Jason McElligott (gen. eds.), *Censorship and the Press, 1580–1720*. For an online database of some 2,600 works noticed or censored by the authorities, see Randy Robertson, 'The British Index, 1641–1700', http://susqu.academia.edu/RandyRobertson/Papers/1665622/The_British_Index (accessed 17 July 2012). And see Randy Robertson, *Censorship and Conflict in Seventeenth-Century England: The Subtle Art of Division* (University Park: The Pennsylvania State University Press, 2009). On cases of Blasphemy, see particularly David Stephen

Manning, 'Blasphemy in England, *c.* 1660–1730', unpub. PhD thesis (University of Cambridge, 2008). On government censorship of printers and publishers involved in Jacobite publications or works deemed disaffected, see R. J. Goulden, '*Vox Populi, Vox Dei*: Charles Delafaye's Paperchase', *The Book Collector*, 28 (1979), 368–90; Paul Monod, 'The Jacobite Press and English Censorship', in Eveline Cruickshanks and Edward Corp (eds.), *The Stuart Court in Exile and the Jacobites* (London and Rio Grande: The Hambledon Press, 1995), pp. 125–42; Pat Rogers, 'Nathaniel Mist, Daniel Defoe, and the Perils of Publishing', *The Library*, 7th series, 10 (2009), 298–313. And see generally Donald Thomas, *A Long Time Burning: The History of Literary Censorship in England* (London: Routledge & Kegan Paul, 1969), esp. pp. 38–73.

8 *JSt* (1948), vol. II, 553; Davis, *PW*, vol. VII, pp. 103–6.
9 'Dean Swift's Clause', Historical Manuscripts Commission, *Report on the Manuscripts of Earl Bathurst* (London, 1923), pp. 10–11.
10 Richard H. Thornton, 'English Authors, Placed on the Roman "Index" (1600 To 1750)', *Notes and Queries*, 11th ser., 12 (1915), 333.
11 *The Earl of Wharton's Speech to the House of Lords* [London, 1711]; Davis, *PW*, vol. III, pp. 175–84 (p. 178)
12 *CWJS*, vol. VIII, p. 69 and n. 36, p. 343.
13 A detailed account of the prosecution is in *CWJS*, vol. VIII, pp. 449–54.
14 Swift to the Earl of Peterborough, 18 May 1714, Woolley, *Corr.*, vol. I, p. 602.
15 *Verses on the Death of Dr. Swift, D.S.P.D.*, lines 379–98, and Swift's notes, see Williams, *Poems*, vol. II, p. 568.
16 *Verses on the Death of Dr. Swift, D.S.P.D.*, lines 399–400, Williams, *Poems*, vol. II, p. 569.
17 Williams, *Poems*, vol. III, p. 993; James Woolley, 'Writing Libels on the Germans: Swift's "Wicked Treasonable Libel"', in Rudolf Freiburg, Arno Löffler and Wolfgang Zach (eds.), *Swift: The Enigmatic Dean: Festschrift for Hermann Josef Real* (Tübingen: Stauffenburg Verlag, 1998), pp. 303–16 (holograph manuscript pp. 304–5).
18 See James Kelly, 'Regulating Print: The State and the Control of Print in Eighteenth-Century Ireland', *Eighteenth-Century Ireland*, 23 (2008), 142–74 (pp. 159–60); M. Pollard, 'Who's For Prison? Publishing Swift in Dublin', *SStud*, 14 (1999), 37–49.
19 James McLaverty, 'The Revision of the First Edition of *Gulliver's Travels*: Book-Trade Context, Interleaving, Two Cancels, and a Failure to Catch', *PBSA*, 106 (2012), 5–35. I am grateful to Professor McLaverty for allowing me to read this bibliographical study in advance of publication.
20 *An Answer to a Paper Called A Memorial* (1728), in Davis, *PW*, vol. XII, p. 22; *Verses on the Death of Dr. Swift, D.S.P.D.*, ll. 349–50, Williams, *Poems*, vol. II, pp. 349–50.
21 BL. Additional MS.6116, f. 137, Bishop William Nicolson to Archbishop William Wake, 30 October 1724; for the seditious passage Nicolson quotes, see Davis, *PW*, vol. X, p. 62. For the proclamation against the fourth *Drapier's Letter*, see Davis, *PW*, vol. X, p. 205.

22 Williams, *Poems*, vol. III, pp. 827–39.
23 *GT*, Part IV, Chapter iii; Davis, *PW*, vol. XI, p. 237.
24 On Swift's self-censorship in his correspondence, see Abigail Williams (ed.), *Journal to Stella: Letters to Esther Johnson and Rebecca Dingley, 1710–1713*, in *CWJS* (forthcoming); Abigail Williams, 'The Difficulties of Swift's *Journal to Stella*', *RES*, n.s., 62 (2011), 758–76; Ashley Marshall, 'Epistolary Swift', *SStud*, 26 (2011), 61–10/; Williams, *Corr.*, vol. V, Appendix XI, pp. 230–3; on the epistolary exchange between King and Swift on the charge of Jacobitism, see Ian Higgins, 'Jonathan Swift and the Jacobite Diaspora', *Münster* (2003), pp. 87–103 (p. 91 n. 27).
25 Marshall, 'Epistolary Swift', p. 63.
26 Woolley, *Corr.*, vol. I, p. 602.
27 Ashley Marshall, 'Epistolary Swift', 63–4; Archbishop King to Swift, 22 November 1716, Woolley *Corr.*, vol. II, pp. 189–94 (p. 193). His following letter implies that Swift was at the least complicit in the Pretenderism of the Tory leaders, see Archbishop King to Swift, 12 January 1716 [–17], Woolley, *Corr.*, vol. II, p. 215.
28 Works that are capable of a Jacobitical construction, such as, for example, the hagiographic pindaric 'Ode to Dr. William Sancroft', the Archbishop of Canterbury deprived in 1690 for refusing the oath of allegiance to William and Mary, a poem written at the request of another nonjuror, the Jacobite Francis Turner, Bishop of Ely (see Williams, *Poems*, vol. I, pp. 33–42), or the manuscript passage about the Lindalinian rebellion in Part III of *Gulliver's Travels* where the citizens project to kill the King and effect a Revolutionary change of government (i.e. treason and sedition), found in Charles Ford's interleaved copy, are suppressed by Swift (Davis, *PW*, vol. XI, pp. 309–10). Swift's most outspoken political poems circulated in manuscript or were not printed in full, see for a detailed study, Karian, *Print and Manuscript*.
29 'Some Thoughts on Free-Thinking', Davis, *PW*, vol. IV, p. 49.
30 'Remarks on Tindal', Davis, *PW*, vol. II, pp. 67, 91 (Milton); pp. 80, 97 (Locke); p. 72 (Spinoza). On Tindal and censorship, see Kemp and McElligott, *Censorship and the Press*, vol. IV, pp. 29–51 and Stephen Lalor, *Matthew Tindal, Freethinker* (London and New York: Continuum, 2006), esp. pp. 44–53.
31 'Remarks on Tindal', Davis, *PW*, vol. II, p. 99.
32 *GT*, Part II, chapter vi, Davis, *PW*, vol. XI, p. 131.
33 Swift's support for censorship can be followed across many of his works, see under 'censorship' and 'Press, censorship' in *Index to the Prose Writings*, Davis, *PW*, vol. XVI. Important statements of his position are at: Davis, *PW*, vol. II, pp. 10–11; pp. 60–61; vol. III, pp. 99–100; vol. VII, pp. 103–4.
34 Davis, *PW*, vol. II, p. 49.
35 Davis, *PW*, vol. II, pp. 28, 30.
36 Davis, *PW*, vol. II, p. 176; vol. IV, pp. 3–21.
37 Davis, *PW*, vol. IV, pp. 9–10, 94.
38 Davis, *PW*, vol. IX, pp. 221–2.

39 Debora Shuger, *Censorship and Cultural Sensibility: The Regulation of Language in Tudor-Stuart England* (Philadelphia: University of Pennsylvania Press, 2006), pp. 45–6; Robertson, *Censorship and Conflict*, p. 32.

40 *Gulliver's Travels*, Part IV, Chapters viii–x, Davis, *PW*, vol. XI, pp. 268, 271–3, 277–80.

41 George Orwell, 'Politics vs. Literature: An Examination of *Gulliver's Travels*' (first published in *Polemic* in 1946), in *The Essential Writings of Jonathan Swift*, ed. Claude Rawson and Ian Higgins, A Norton Critical Edition (New York: Norton, 2010), pp. 835–48 (pp. 840, 842, 843).

42 For early modern writing see especially Annabel Patterson, *Censorship and Interpretation: The Conditions of Writing and Reading in Early Modern England* (Madison: University of Wisconsin Press, 1984) and her *Reading Between the Lines* (London: Routledge, 1993); Christopher Hill, 'Censorship and English Literature', in *The Collected Essays of Christopher Hill*, 3 vols. (Brighton: Harvester Press, 1985), vol. I, pp. 32–71; Randy Robertson, *Censorship and Conflict in Seventeenth-Century England*, esp. pp. 19–20 on censorship as generative. On modern literature, emphasizing the productive aesthetic effects of the threat of government censorship on writers who had to negotiate it, especially in relation to indecency and obscenity, see Celia Marshik, *British Modernism and Censorship* (Cambridge University Press, 2006) and Stephen Burt, 'Empson and the Censor', *Modern Philology*, 107 (2010), 447–74.

43 A subject definitively explored by Claude Rawson in a number of studies, but see especially *God, Gulliver and Genocide* (Oxford University Press, 2001).

44 William Empson, *Seven Types of Ambiguity* (New York: New Directions, 1947), p. 1.

45 Swift, *The Examiner*, no. 42, 17 May 1711, Ellis, *Examiner*, p. 431.

46 *CWJS*, VIII, p. 229. See C. R. Kropf, 'Libel and Satire in the Eighteenth Century', *Eighteenth-Century Studies*, 8, no. 2 (Winter 1974–5), 153–68 (esp. 160–1).

47 John Gay and Alexander Pope to Swift, [7] November 1726, Woolley, *Corr.*, vol. III, p. 47; Alexander Pope to Swift, 16 November 1726, Woolley, *Corr.*, vol. III, p. 52; the Earl of Peterborough to Swift, [29 November 1726], Woolley, *Corr.*, vol. III, pp. 60–1; *A Letter from a Clergyman to his Friend, With an Account of the Travels of Capt. Lemuel Gulliver and a Character of the Author...* (London, 1726), reprinted in *Gulliveriana vi: Critiques of Gulliver's Travels and Allusions Thereto, Book One*. Intro. Jeanne K. Welcher and George E. Bush Jr (Delmar, New York, 1976), pp. 10–11.

48 John Gay to Swift, [3 February 1722–3], Woolley, *Corr.*, vol. II, p. 446; Williams, *Poems*, vol. II, p. 469.

49 Part III, ch. ii, Davis, *PW*, vol. XI, pp. 165–6.

50 For examples: [Matthias Earbery], *An Historical Account of the Advantages that have Accrued to England by the Succession in the Illustrious House of Hanover, Part II* (London, 1722), pp. 9–11, 16–17 and the Jacobite Duke of Wharton's 'Persian Letter' from *Mist's Weekly Journal* (24 August 1728), reprinted in Philip, Duke of Wharton, *Select and Authentick Pieces Written by the Late Duke of Wharton* (Boulogne, 1731), pp. 79–80.

51 Part III, ch. iv, Davis, *PW*, vol. XI, p. 172; 'A Wicked Treasonable Libel', in James Woolley, 'Writing Libels on the Germans', pp. 304–5; 'Directions for a Birthday Song', lines 15–20, Williams, *Poems*, vol. II, pp. 460–1; Davis, *PW*, vol. V, p. 265.

52 Davis, *PW*, vol. X, p. 21.

53 *The Second and Last English Advice, To the Freehoulders of Englan[d]* (London, 17??), p. 20.

54 Davis, *PW*, vol. XI, pp. 69–72. On Swift's use of italic, see especially James McLaverty, 'Italics in Swift's Poems', *SStud*, 26 (2011), 22–37, and on italic and title pages see his 'Swift and the Art of Political Publication: Hints and Title Pages, 1711–1714', in Claude Rawson (ed.), *Politics and Literature in the Age of Swift: English and Irish Perspectives* (Cambridge University Press, 2010), pp. 116–39. He shows that Swiftian use of black letter on title pages, as in the title page of the first *Drapier's Letter*, signifies the alien and strange (pp. 123, 138 n. 43). For Whig notice and parody of Swift's use of black letter, see *High Church Aphorisms, Written by those Twin-Brothers in Scandal, The Author of the Examiner and Modest Abel* (n.p., 1711), title page, p. 1 and *passim*.

55 'To Mr. Gay on his Being Steward to the Duke of Queenberry', lines 107–8, 121–2, 135–42, Williams, *Poems*, vol. II, pp. 535–6.

56 [Charlwood Lawton], *A Short State of our Condition, with Relation to the present Parliament* (n.p.: n.p., n.d.), 4pp. (pp. 2, 4). For Lawton's correspondence and work for the exiled Stuart court, see British Library, Add MSS 37661: Letter-Book of Lord Melfort 1692. On Lawton, see Mark Goldie and Clare Jackson, 'Williamite Tyranny and the Whig Jacobites', in Esther Mijers and David Onnekink (eds.), *Redefining William III: The Impact of the King-Stadholder in International Context* (Aldershot: Ashgate, 2007), pp. 177–99, which draws on the scholarship and bibliographical discoveries of Paul Hopkins (on the Hush-money paper see p. 193).

57 See Kemp and McElligott, *Censorship and the Press*, vol. III, pp. 391–412.

58 Swift to the Rev. John Worrall, 28 September 1728, Woolley, *Corr.*, vol. III, p. 200; Pollard, *Dictionary*, p. 204.

59 Robert Wodrow, *The History of the Sufferings of the Church of Scotland, From The Restauration To The Revolution: Collected From the Publick Records, Original Papers, and Manuscripts of that Time, and other well attested Narratives*, 2 vols. (Edinburgh, 1721–2), vol. II, pp. 589, 614; George Ridpath, *An Answer To The Scotch Presbyterian Eloquence: In Three Parts …* (London, 1693), p. 25.

60 Davis, *PW*, vol. V, pp. 120–81 (Faulkner's Note on p. 120).

61 Davis, *PW*, vol. V, pp. xvii–xxi; David Macaree, 'Truth and Fiction in *Memoirs of Captain John Creichton*', *Transactions of the Samuel Johnson Society of the Northwest*, 6 (1973), 11–26; Ralph Stewart, 'Swift and the Authorship of Creichton's *Memoirs*', *The Scottish Historical Review*, 72, no. 1 (1993), 80–9; Christopher Fox, 'Swift's Scotophobia', *Bullán*, 6 (2002), 43–65 (pp. 48–53); Brean S. Hammond and Nicholas Seager, 'Jonathan Swift's Historical Novel, *The Memoirs of Capt. John Creichton*', *SStud*, 24 (2009), 70–87.

62 Davis, *PW*, vol. XI, pp. 197, 201–2.

63 Davis, *PW*, vol. V, pp. 121, 120, 122.

64 Davis, *PW*, vol. V, p. 130; [Gilbert Crockat and John Monroe], *The Scotch Presbyterian Eloquence; Or, The Foolishness of Their Teaching Discovered From Their Books, Sermons, and Prayers; And Some Remarks on Mr. Rule's Late Vindication of the Kirk* (London, 1692), see p. 5 for the anecdote about David Williamson; *Library and Reading, Part 1*, vol. II, pp. 1072–3.

65 Gilbert Burnet, *History of His Own Times*, 2 vols. (London, 1724–34), pp. 804–5; Davis, *PW*, vol. V, p. 290.

66 Davis, *PW*, vol. V, p. 180.

67 Davis, *PW*, vol. V, p. 174.

68 Davis, *PW*, vol. V, p. 317.

69 Davis, *PW*, vol. V, p. 269.

70 Davis, *PW*, vol. V, p. 160.

71 Davis, *PW*, vol. V, pp. 165–6; *GT*, III, ix, Davis, *PW*, vol. XI, pp. 204–6. For the multiple innuendoes against William III in the account of the king of Luggnagg, see Anne Barbeau Gardiner, 'Licking the Dust in Luggnagg: Swift's Reflections on the Legacy of King William's Conquest of Ireland', *SStud*, 8 (1993), 35–44.

72 Davis, *PW*, vol. V, p. 168.

73 *CWJS*, vol. I, p. 32.

74 *Verses on the Death of Dr. Swift, D.S.P.D.*, line 460, Williams, *Poems*, vol. II, p. 571.

75 'To Doctor D—L – – – Y, On The Libels Writ against him', see especially lines 74–6, 169–70, Williams, *Poems*, vol. II, pp. 502, 505.

76 Swift and Mrs Whiteway to the Rev. Thomas Sheridan, [15–16 May 1736], Woolley, *Corr.*, vol. IV, p. 296; Williams, *Poems*, vol. III, pp. 827–39.

CHAPTER TEN

Swift's texts between Dublin and London

Adam Rounce

The publication by Swift of the same works in both Dublin and London follows the pattern of planning and apparent caprice that marks his career. Swift was at best ambivalent about publishing in Dublin or Ireland generally, yet concomitant with his discontent are strategies that exploit the differences between Irish publication and English, allowing Swift to use his London publishers to develop different versions of his texts, or to give them a cachet and authority that merely Irish publications lacked. This awareness of the utility of Dublin for his purposes, and equal need for the authority of London editions, leads to his apparent coolness, discussed by James McLaverty in his chapter, towards George Faulkner's 1735 *Works*, and subsequent competition between Irish and English publishers. This chapter offers a survey of the role of dual publication in Swift's career, and its significance in understanding the deliberately varied and often confusing publication history of his writings.

Early publications

The vagaries of Swift's publications in Ireland before his permanent (if sometimes unwilling) residence in Dublin in August 1714, make it fruitless to assume any particular authorial intent behind their appearing there. The most significant of his topical writings were published in Dublin shortly after their printing in London: in 1712 *The Conduct of the Allies* appeared in three separate Dublin editions, two of them printed by Edward Waters (who would play an important part in Swift's Irish writings); *Some Remarks on the Barrier Treaty* was published in three editions in Dublin in the same year; the minor related pamphlet *Some Advice to the October Club* was likewise reprinted there, a year after its London publication, in 1713. In 1714, *The Publick Spirit of the Whigs* was published in the same uncensored text as its London version.[1] Yet the case is very different with *A Tale of a Tub*, which did not appear in Ireland until its fourth edition of 1705 (only

a year after the appearance of the first edition in London); more pertin-
ent is the passing of time until its next Dublin appearance, in the seventh
edition of 1726. The most important changes of the fifth edition of 1710,
with the Apology, footnotes and illustrations, did not arrive in Ireland for
another sixteen years after its appearance in London.[2]

Looking at this mixture of alacrity and delay in Irish publication, a useful conclusion might be that Swift had no need to publish anything in
Dublin until or unless the work was of immediate polemic relevance, like
the English political pamphlets of the 1710s, and unlike the *Tub*. Irish
publication was thus an afterthought unless it was called for by the topicality of certain works. It is also clear that Swift's hostility towards Ireland
played a part in his dealings with print culture; until his final visit to
England in 1727, some works were designed explicitly for an English audience, and for the furthering of intellectual and literary ambitions divorced
from Ireland. Conversely (and somewhat ironically considering Swift's
uncertain loyalties) he also wrote works in the service of an ideal of Irish
patriotism or liberty, whose English publication and audience was of little
importance.

This was the case with the pamphlet with which Swift ended the apparent hiatus from publication that lasted from his return from England in
1714 until 1719. The *Proposal for the Use of Irish Manufacture* (published
in April or May 1720) appeared in Dublin, and would not be collected in
an English edition until 1735; its argument entirely concerned the effects
of the colonial British controls over the Irish economy and its imports.
In a point that Swift would make repeatedly in his Irish writings of the
next dozen years, the British constraints on the economy were disastrous
and could only be offset by demanding the patriotic (and in the immediate context of 1720 exclusive) use of Irish goods. It was not, of course,
a message that the government wanted to hear, and Edward Waters as
printer was summoned before the Grand Jury in Dublin on 30 May 1720,
to answer charges that the anonymous pamphlet was false, scandalous and
seditious. Waters would not own Swift as author, but was imprisoned and
tried at the King's Bench before Lord Justice Whitshed. Whitshed seems
to have forced the Jury to reconsider their verdict, until they brought in
what he wanted, whereupon Swift used his influence to help Waters, peti-
tioning the powerful with success.[3]

This was in some ways a skirmish before the larger battle, as the *Drapier's
Letters* episode would play out on a grander scale from 1724 to 1725:
polemic writings published in Dublin, the printer (John Harding, who
had worked for Waters previously) imprisoned (from 11 to 14 November

1724, after the publication of the fourth letter in October, and the offer of £300 reward for discovery of its author) and the absence of any apparent prosecution.[4] The difference was in the tangible result, in the scrapping of Woods's ill-omened coin, and the iconic status as folk-hero and patriot that it gave Swift. Yet for all that the fame of the episode was international, its publications remained local, for logical reasons: the *Drapier's Letters* had a lack of immediate relevance to London, and this, rather than quality of printing, was of importance. This is probably why the *Drapier's Letters* were not reprinted in London until 1730. Moreover, Swift was dependent upon reliable publishers and printers who were willing to take the risk of putting their names to such controversial writings. John Harding's original printings of the separate *Letters* were inferior in terms of typography and consistency to what Swift would require from more large-scale publishing houses, but this was relatively insignificant, given Harding's loyalty and quick means of distribution. Swift was not writing primarily for a polite audience, and Harding's printing was effective in presenting the sort of emphasis required, as can be seen in the first letter, 'To the *Shop-Keepers, Tradesmen, Farmers,* and *Common-People* of *IRELAND*', of October 1724:

> About three Years ago, a little Book was written, to advise all People to wear the *Manufactures of this our own Dear Country:* It had no other Design, said nothing against the *King* or *Parliament,* or *any Man,* yet the POOR PRINTER was prosecuted two Years, with the utmost Violence, and even some WEAVERS themselves, for whose Sake it was written, being upon the JURY, FOUND HIM GUILTY. This would be enough to discourage any Man from endeavouring to do you Good, when you will either neglect him or fly in his Face for his Pains, and when he must expect only *Danger to himself* and *Loss of Money,* perhaps to his Ruin.[5]

The message does not wrap itself in nuance, hence the extensive use of capitals and italics to lead the reader through the argument and to add to the robust clarity of its broadly drawn conclusions (which might also be intended with the oral dissemination of the pamphlet in mind).

This same emphasis would be retained when the letters were collected and reprinted as *Fraud Detected, or the Hibernian Patriot* in 1725, the first important publication of Swift by George Faulkner, the Dublin publisher who would have the greatest influence on his career. The celebrity of the *Drapier's Letters* necessitated a larger-scale edition than Harding's pamphlets had provided, and the more prominent Faulkner followed Harding's texts, for the most part, while giving the collection a durable printing that reflected their effect on contemporary Irish politics. There was still no rush to reprint in London, and the letters were not published there until 1730, as *The Hibernian Patriot*. This was *Fraud Detected* with small changes for house style by the printer, William Bowyer, that refine the text, without suggesting any authorial intention working behind it; its appearance in London is for posterity, rather than to make any new argument. It also reflected Faulkner's developing business relationship with Bowyer, as seen in the adoption by Faulkner of *The Hibernian Patriot* as the copy of the letters in his 1735 edition of Swift.

The title page of *The Hibernian Patriot* suggests how Swift was finding ways around the difficulties of publishing such works in London. The volume is 'Printed at *DUBLIN*. *LONDON*: Reprinted and sold by A. MOOR in St. *Paul's Church-yard*, and the Booksellers of *London* and *Westminster*'. James Woolley, noting how Swift used a similar procedure in reprinting *The Intelligencer* in London, records that 'A. Moor' is 'widely used as a fictitious imprint for dangerous or pirated books'.[6] That the subterfuge of using the pseudonymous Moor was necessary is shown by the holding back, in both the Dublin and London collections, of the sixth and seventh *Drapier's Letters*, to 'Lord Midleton' and 'Both Houses of Parliament', respectively. These would not be published until Faulkner added them to his edition of the *Works* of 1735. The 1730 edition hides behind the name Moor, and its claim to be a reprint from Dublin might have been intended to serve as possible camouflage against any legal proceedings. Moreover, there are records of this volume's production in the ledgers of William Bowyer's printing house, making it an example of the Faulkner–Bowyer/Dublin–London system of dual publication that Swift seems to have favoured in this period.[7]

Faulkner and Bowyer

Swift separated, perhaps necessarily, polemic works of immediate contemporary relevance from his more general writings. The example of *Gulliver's Travels* is germane to this distinction: its initial publication in London in 1726, under a veil of secrecy and with the frame of 'The Publisher to the Reader' encouraging the conceit of its verisimilitude, did not need or involve Dublin; it was (to simplify) a literary work, and this, along with its vastly greater length, divides its publication and transmission from Swift's contemporary pamphlets, which required a different kind of subterfuge.

It is also the case that Swift's perspective on his career was altering at this time. Stephen Karian's recent useful division of his writing defines his 'late period' as beginning around September 1727 (the end of Swift's final visit to England). It was a time, Karian argues, when therefore he 'was no longer seeking patronage that might alter his residence and ecclesiastical position in Ireland. That acceptance of his professional status seems to have liberated him towards being quite politically outspoken as a writer, even more outspoken than earlier'.[8] Although Karian relates this liberation to Swift's increased composition of poetry from this point, it is also relevant to his prose.

The apparent ambivalence of Swift towards his topical writings from this time onwards is marked, most explicitly when he told Pope in 1731: 'I write Pamphlets and follys meerly for amusement, and when they are finished, or I grow weary in the middle, I cast them into the fire, partly out of dislike, and chiefly because I know they will signify nothing.' A year later he described how 'As to Ireland … I remember to have published nothing but what is called the Drapier's letters, and some few other trifles relating to the affairs of this miserable and ruined Kingdom.'[9] He protests too much. For all his resignation, Swift still finished and published these writings, and still seems to have wanted them to appear in London (partly for the sake of his wider reputation), although he used the more relevant (but also more limited and parochial) Dublin in the first instance. The advantages and problems of publishing in Dublin are summarized by Máire Kennedy:

> Books cost less in Dublin than in London. Dublin printers were able to undercut their London rivals by reprinting in smaller formats, using cheaper paper, and not needing to purchase copyright. Advertisers were careful to point out the saving achieved by the purchase of an Irish edition, usually claiming that the production was as good, if not better, than the London edition.[10]

The factors that made Dublin so potentially profitable also encouraged piracy; the lack of copyright is another important motive behind Swift wanting a reliable method of publishing in London as well. The only (very flimsy) control over copyright offered by Dublin was related to reprints of books from London or elsewhere, and was signalled by a bookseller's intention to publish – this system of 'posting' was all that resembled literary property.[11] Given this, Swift needed to find a way to cover two bases, producing in London for intellectual posterity to give a printer or bookseller copyright, and to avoid Dublin's problems of censorship. Yet Dublin and London publishers needed each other – the absence of copyright in the former meant cheap reprintings were legion, and to obviate these, agreements were necessary.[12]

Before such an agreement was utilized between Dublin and London, Swift published two pamphlets concerning contemporary Irish economic problems in 1728: *A Short View of the State of Ireland* was published in March and swiftly followed by *An Answer to a Paper Called, A Memorial of the Poor … of Ireland*.[13] Both were angry works, showing contempt for official complacency in the ruination of Irish trade and agriculture. They were printed and sold not by Swift's previous Irish printer, Faulkner, but by John Harding's widow Sarah. The reasons for this, and for her subsequent publication of Swift and Sheridan's journal *The Intelligencer*, have been summarized by James Woolley. While her 'unimpressive printing might lead one to ask why she' was chosen, this is 'answered only in part by the fact that she succeeded her husband John as Swift's printer'. It was a question of loyalty: her husband had been imprisoned for publishing the fourth *Drapier's Letter* in 1724, and had died in April 1725, apparently a martyr to the Drapier's cause; Sarah Harding had been willing to continue the publication, if required. It is also, as Woolley says, a sign of Swift's likely need for discretion: 'Swift evidently valued deniability', particularly 'expecting that the bookseller would absorb the risks of prosecution or other legal harassment'.[14] As Swift wrote in 1732, 'no Printer or Bookseller hath any kind of property here. I have writ some things that would make people angry[.] I have always sent them by unknown hands, the Printer might guess, but he could not accuse me[,] he ran the whole risk, and well deserved the property, if he could carry it to London and print it there, but I am sure I could have no property at all.'[15] Sarah Harding, like her husband and other printers and booksellers, was willing to take the risk.

In the rather peculiar printings of *A Short View* and *An Answer to a Paper*, polemic intent overrode quality. As Woolley summarizes, 'Crude typography, cheap paper, shabby makeready, and at times careless proofreading were standard in the Harding shop.'[16] This is especially noticeable in *An Answer*, which uses italic for some stretches not for emphasis but to fill up missing roman type, as well as random switching of type sizes, uneven margins, and repeated errors and misprints. The result was the changes made in the 1735 Faulkner *Works*, which are necessary corrections, for the most part (Faulkner's emendations are in square brackets):

> the Duties will rather be lessen'd ~~then~~ [than] increased[.] But allowing no force in this Argument, yet so proeternatural [a] Sum as one hundred and Ten thousand pounds, raised all ~~one~~ [on] a sudden (for there is no dallying with Hunger[)] is just in proportion with raising a Million and [a] half in *England*, which, as things now Stand, would probably bring ~~even~~ that opulent Kingdom under some Difficulties.[17]

The plainness of text in Harding's printing meant that there was little room for the typographic emphasis so often used for heavy Swiftian irony. Yet her printings accomplished their end, and she continued to print Swift's next important work, the twenty numbers of the jointly written *Intelligencer*, from May to December 1728.

Harding's printing of the short numbers of *The Intelligencer* (few of which run to more than eight pages, and were in Woolley's words 'well within the normal range of ephemeral Dublin printing') shows what Swift wanted: he never used Harding for books, or anything extensive and lengthy (presumably as it was beyond her scope and means).[18] Secrecy was supposedly served by the papers being copied 'into an unknown hand' and then taken to the bookseller.[19] Swift did complain that readers were very much offended with the continual nonsense made by her printers' errors, while refusing (of course) to acknowledge authorship.[20] Yet aside from the vagaries of printing, highlighted by the many variants in issues of such small pieces, another quirk was rhetorical: the pointing of *The Intelligencer* was based around the spoken, rather than the written sentence.

These qualities specific to Harding's Dublin version were smoothed out in the editions collected in London in 1729 and 1730, the papers by Swift included in the third volume of the Pope–Swift *Miscellanies* (1732) and in Faulkner's 1735 Dublin *Works*. The first London collections were both entered into the ledgers of William Bowyer's print shop in May 1729 and June 1730, and were printed for Bowyer and Charles Davis. Bowyer distributed them via booksellers (the familiar 'A. Moor' in 1729, and Francis Cogan in 1730), and the second edition has the possibility of some authorial revisions, perhaps supplied from Dublin by George Faulkner, who had befriended Bowyer, worked in his shop in 1726, and was exactly placed to pass on such material.[21] Faulkner had imported the 1729 London *Intelligencer* edition to Dublin, and was by 1730 Swift's main Irish printer. The agreement between them was lasting: Keith Maslen describes how 'between 1729 and 1767 Bowyer printed some three score editions of Irish origin', many of them coming from Faulkner: 'Bowyer was certainly or probably indebted to his Dublin friend for a steady supply of mostly little pieces.' The evidence that Faulkner was, to a large degree, acting as a conduit for Swift in passing on works from 1730 onwards is compelling.[22]

Faulkner became the dominant printer and publisher in Swift's Irish career. Sarah Harding's last printing was one of Swift's most notorious works: *A Modest Proposal*. In contrast to subsequent Faulkner-printed writings, there are no significant differences between the Dublin and London editions. The first edition, by Harding, of October 1729 has the title 'A MODEST PROPOSAL For preventing the CHILDREN OF POOR PEOPLE From being a **Burthen to their Parents**, OR THE COUNTRY'. The first London printing of the same year even keeps the black-letter emphasis. The first London printing was published over the name of James Roberts, the biggest 'trade publisher' of the period; in Michael Treadwell's summary, 'It was simply one of the trade publisher's functions (and not the least important) to stand mute between the real proprietors and the authorities in time of any slight unpleasantness', and Roberts performed this role perfectly.[23] His edition's imprint, 'Dublin: Printed by S. Harding: | London, Re-printed; and sold by *J. Roberts*', might be a way of Swift's signalling authorship. Yet the three London printings of the pamphlet alone of 1729–30 do not in any way change or realign this notably Irish text for an English audience; it is only when it is collected in 1730 with two other pieces in *A LIBEL ON Dr. D — —NY, And a certain Great LORD* that the title is extended to *A MODEST PROPOSAL* For *Preventing the Children of poor People in Ireland*. Likewise the statement 'The number of Souls in this Kingdom' was not altered to 'in Ireland' until Faulkner's *Works* of 1735.[24] These anomalies apparently did not matter. The case is different with works where the Faulkner–Bowyer connection makes a more explicit link to revision of Irish versions.

There were advantages for all parties in the system that Faulkner and Bowyer developed: Bowyer received exclusive, non-pirated editions of Swift's work, Faulkner could profit from selling works in two places and Swift could publish in London: a method of preserving the copyright of his work. A good example of this is *A Vindication of His Excellency Lord Carteret*, first published in Dublin in 1730, and reprinted in London, despite the claims of its imprint 'London printed and Dublin re-printed'. It appeared in Dublin in April 1730 directly after the closing of Parliament, and was entered in the Bowyer ledgers for 30 April 1730. It was, as Maslen argues 'evidently first printed by Faulkner', and the claim of a Dublin reprint a feint in case of trouble.[25]

There is one curious feature of the London version that supports this interpretation. The *Vindication of Carteret, from the Charge of Favouring none but Tories, High-Churchmen and Jacobites* is a work that very much fulfils its title, justifying the Lord Lieutenant of Ireland's practice, and attacking the sneers and innuendo of his opponents. Prominent among these were Joshua Viscount Allen, who had recently denounced Swift's *Libel on Dr Delany* and the award of a diploma and gold box to its author. Allen in the pamphlet is 'that other miserable Creature *Traulus* who although of somewhat a different Species, yet seems very far to outdo even the Genius of *Pistorides*, in that miscarrying Talent of railing without Consistency or Discretion'. Pistorides is Richard Tighe, anti-Carteret Whig and a long-term enemy of Swift's.[26] In the 1730 London edition, these references were glossed by footnotes identifying Allen and Tighe, albeit through the standard practice of blanks: '*Pistorides *The Rt Hon. R—d T—gh, Esq; whose Grandfather was a Baker' (p. 5); '*Traulus *L—d V——t A——n, who spoke against the Libel in the Privy Council, and likewise in the House of Lords' (p. 8). The supposed Dublin 'reprint' does not gloss them at all, an absence suggesting a reticence to call further legal attention to the pamphlet. Herbert Davis mentions that even in the 1735 Dublin *Works* 'Faulkner did not dare to print the footnotes of the London editions, referring to Lord Allen and Richard Tighe'.[27] It would place a burden on Faulkner (or any printer) to run the risk of libel by identifying publicly figures already tacitly known to readers. The London edition could afford to be more detached. It is possible to see the London and Dublin versions of the *Vindication of Carteret* as discreetly different versions of the same text, and that features such as the footnotes are tailored to these different audiences.

The same is true of another work by Swift revised for its London publication, albeit in a curious manner that eludes complete explanation. This is a pamphlet originally printed in Dublin by Faulkner in 1732, and called *An Examination of Certain Abuses, Corruptions, and Enormities in the City of Dublin*. It was reprinted in London in the same year as *City Cries, Instrumental and Vocal, or An Examination of Certain Abuses, Corruptions, and Enormities in London and Dublin* ('*DUBLIN*, Printed; *LONDON*, Re-printed' and published by Roberts). Written from the persona of a credulous Whig, it is a mock catalogue of the supposed codes and treasonable secret messages conveyed by Tory and Jacobite supporters through absurd examples of street cries. It is noteworthy that the conclusion to the 1732 Dublin edition is more abbreviated; the London reprint has three further pages, adding yet another instance of the perniciousness of secret Jacobitism in the signposts bearing the mark of George the Second (meaning the second king, after the Pretender, the true monarch).[28] It might be asked why this conclusion was only included in London editions. Swift was able to publish in London things forbidden in Dublin, yet this conclusion could not offend or libel more than any other page of a work that is founded upon irreverent and ridiculous non-connections between everyday speech and subliminal messages of treason. Moreover, it seems to have been thought potentially libellous to the king in Dublin, but much safer when republished in London. It is possible to view the conclusion as an addition that shows Swift tailoring his message to his audience: it evinces an awareness of a different reading culture, just as the change in title of the pamphlet is altered from *An Examination of Certain Abuses ... in the City of Dublin*, to *An Examination of Certain Abuses ... in London and Dublin*. The satire of local Whiggery moves outwards, encompassing both cities; there is also the practical question of signs with 'Geo II' upon them being present in London, but not Dublin, making the pamphlet not specifically Irish (which did not prevent its being included in this form in Faulkner's canonical collection of Swift's Irish writings in the fourth volume of the 1735 *Works*).

It is not possible to say precisely how Faulkner managed the two texts, but it can be suggested that the longer London printing must have come afterwards, yet must also have been the text that was reduced (by Swift, Faulkner or some other agency) for the Dublin version before either was published (there are neither variants nor other differences to suggest two different sources). Copies of the Dublin original are scarce, suggesting that the onus on the pamphlet as satire was directed towards London. It remains a fine, somewhat enigmatic instance of the peculiarities of joint publication.

The legacy of dual publication

The legacy of publication in the two cities was a state of textual uncertainty, epitomized by the arguments over Faulkner's 1735 *Works*, and continued around posthumous publications. Swift's own deliberately ambiguous attitude towards Faulkner's edition (having failed in the attempt to get a London collection of his works in 1732) set the tone: 'There is no Propriety of Copyes here; they print what they please. The man behaved himself with all respect, and since it was an evil I could not avoyd, I should rather they had been printed correctly than otherwise.'[29] This has always seemed disingenuous, given the working relationship with Faulkner; the latter repeatedly stressed the degree of Swift's cooperation in the volumes, culminating in the 1762 declaration (part of a polemical defence of his practice) where Faulkner thinks 'he is most truly entitled to the Property of these Works; the Author having bestowed them to him, and corrected seven Volumes in his own Life-Time, as well as many small Tracts published at different Periods'.[30] The problem was that the extent of such correction was always disputed, through Swift's own smokescreen and the ambiguous degree of Faulkner's own corrections to the texts.

The 1735 *Works* has thus been bedevilled by counterclaims about its authority: when editing the *Drapier's Letters*, Herbert Davis summed this up in passing: 1735 'was produced with Swift's co-operation, and many of its variants must result from authorial intervention'. It thus 'provides us with a text in which the alterations indicate definitely that the revision was made by Swift himself', but he had of course to acknowledge that Swift 'refuses to accept full responsibility for the text', and it 'must not be taken to mean that Swift himself was in any way responsible for the constant changes in spelling, punctuation, and typography'. Mary Pollard touches on the problem in describing how Faulkner's 'tinkering' made the texts 'more and more conservative, and eventually leaving them more "Swiftian" than Swift himself'.[31] In Karian's helpful summary, 'the idea that Faulkner's edition is the ultimate authority for Swift's works presumes an attitude towards textual stability and fixity that Swift himself may not have held'.[32]

Faulkner's Dublin printing of works copyrighted in London had a lasting result in claims against Faulkner's copyright, as well as a wider textual uncertainty. John Hawkesworth challenged Faulkner's authority, citing passages from Swift's letters as evidence '*to prove that the Dean never revised any edition of his works for* Falkener [*sic*] *to print*'.[33] They proved no such thing, of course, but the competitive mood was reinforced by disputes over posthumous versions of works with different sources. When *The History of the Four Last Years of the Queen* appeared in 1758, Faulkner's Dublin printing was a riposte to Andrew Millar's London edition and the reprinting of this in Dublin by George and Alexander Ewing; Faulkner was angry at being anticipated (he had talked with Swift about publishing it as early as 1737). As Karian says, it challenged his attempt 'to maintain a Dublin monopoly of Swift publication'.[34] The result was Faulkner's *Appeal to the Public* of 1758, in which he asserted himself to be Swift's true publisher: 'no Edition can be so correct as that printed by him'.[35] The Ewings' immediate reply mocked Faulkner's obsession with denying legitimacy to any work of Swift appearing in Dublin without 'the essential stamp' of his imprint, and saw the point of Faulkner's appeal as 'whether he is to have half of the present Publisher's profit, or the whole'.[36]

It was inevitable that the comprehensiveness of Faulkner's growing edition, and his control of Swift's legacy, would be so challenged. The compromise of Deane Swift's revised 1765 London edition of Hawkesworth (the extra works from which were reprinted by Faulkner in Dublin from that date on) resulted in a consolidation that resolved many of the problems of dual publication. Faulkner had little choice but to come to some agreement for reprinting; as the editor of his correspondence points out, 'After 1765 Faulkner no longer had control of the remaining Swift material.' The editors (i.e. Deane Swift) opined that it might seem 'strange' that 'so many poetical, historical, and other miscellaneous productions' of Swift 'should have lain dormant', but Faulkner could not afford to miss them out from his updatings of previous editions.[37] Furthermore, Deane Swift had propinquity to both support and enable his publication of manuscript and unpublished material.

The disputes die down, and the knot of Swift editions is less tangled after 1765 in terms of authority, but anyone trying to chart the assorted appearances of pieces major and minor from the years 1735 to 1770 is partly dealing with the consequence of dual publication and Faulkner's attempt at a monopoly. But this is also the effect of Swift's own arbitrary stances, reflecting the inconsistencies of his attitude towards print – at times being minute and precise, at other points supposedly dismissive of both his works and their dissemination. As with so much of his writing, Swift's publishing in both Dublin and London left potential for misunderstanding and squabbles; such reactions were sometimes desired, almost always disowned and a natural consequence of his approach.

Notes

1 The 1712 *Conduct of the Allies* printings are TS 540 (John Hyde) and TS 541 (Edward Waters). The 1712 *Remarks on the Barrier Treaty* is TS 560 (Hyde) and TS 561 (Waters); the 1713 *Some Advice to the October Club* TS 557 (Cornelius Carter); the 1714 *Publick Spirit of the Whigs*, TS 599 (J. Henly), TS 600. For an account see *CWJS*, vol. VIII, pp. 348–9, 388, 381, 458.

2 *A Tale of a Tub*, 4th edn, reprinted in Dublin 'and are to be Sold only at *Dick's* and *Lloyd's* Coffee-Houses, and at the Printing-Press in *Fishamble-street*' (TS 221); 7th edn, Dublin, printed by A. Rhames for W. Smith (TS 232).

3 For the context of *A Proposal*, Waters's trial and Swift's appeal to Molesworth, Hanmer and others, see Ehrenpreis, *Swift*, vol. III, pp. 128–30, and Oliver W. Ferguson, *Jonathan Swift and Ireland* (Urbana: University of Illinois Press, 1962), pp. 49–59. It was published in London in *Miscellanies in Prose and Verse. Volume the Fifth* (1735), pp. 201–13 and incorportated in the Deane Swift *Works* of 1765, vol. VIII, pp. 170–6.

4 For John Harding (who had worked for Waters) and his imprisonment, see Pollard, *Dictionary*, pp. 274–5.

5 'To the *Shop-Keepers, Tradesmen, Farmers*, and *Common-People* of *IRELAND*' (Dublin: John Harding, 1724), pp. 2–3.

6 *Fraud Detected* (Dublin: George Faulkner, 1725); *The Hibernian Patriot* (London: A. Moor, 1730). For Moor, see Woolley, *Intelligencer*, p. 292, citing David Foxon: 'A. Moor near St Paul's ... Whether or not any such person

existed, the imprint was regularly used, fictitiously' (*English Verse, 1701–1750: A Catalogue of Separately Printed Poems with Notes on Contemporary Collected Editions*, 2 vols. (London: Cambridge University Press, 1975), vol. II, p. 172).

7 *The Bowyer Ledgers*, ed. Keith Maslen and John Lancaster (London: The Bibliographical Society; New York: The Bibliographical Society of America, 1991), no. 1471.

8 Karian, *Print and Manuscript*, p. 3.

9 Swift to Pope, 15 January 1730–1, Woolley, *Corr.*, vol. III, p. 355; Swift to Rev. Henry Jenney, 8 June 1732, Woolley, *Corr.*, vol. III, p. 484.

10 Máire Kennedy, 'Reading Print, 1700–1800', in Raymond Gillespie and Andrew Hadfield (eds.), *The Oxford History of the Irish Book: Volume III, The Irish Book in English 1550–1800* (Oxford University Press, 2006), pp. 146–66 (p. 151).

11 For this system of claiming copyright, see Mary Pollard, *Dublin's Trade in Books, 1500–1800* (Oxford: Clarendon Press, 1989), pp. 169–72, though she admits that 'How this posting-up worked in practice is not clear' (p. 170), and probably used a mixture of notices, posted at Stationers' Hall, and newspaper advertisements.

12 For Dublin and London's mutual need for each other, and deals to obviate cheaper Irish reprints, see Pollard, *Dublin's Trade in Books*, pp. 87–96.

13 Ferguson, *Jonathan Swift and Ireland*, dates the *Short View* (TS 663) as 19 March 1728, and the *Answer* (TS 665) a few days after (p. 144).

14 James Woolley, 'Sarah Harding as Swift's Printer', in Christopher Fox and Brenda Tooley (eds.), *Walking Naboth's Vineyard: New Studies of Swift* (University of Notre Dame Press, 1995), pp. 164–77 (pp. 164, 165). For her willingness to carry on publishing the letters after her husband's demise, see p. 167. Woolley also notes (p. 164) that Sarah had been arrested for printing *On Wisdom's Defeat in a Learned Debate* (1725), ascribed to Swift by Ehrenpreis (*Swift*, vol. III, pp. 314–16).

15 Swift to Motte, 4 November 1732, Woolley, *Corr.*, vol. III, p. 556.

16 Woolley, 'Sarah Harding', p. 168.

17 *An Answer to a Paper Called, 'A Memorial of the Poor ... of Ireland'* (Dublin: Harding, 1728), p. 10; *Works* (1735), vol. IV, p. 267.

18 See Woolley, 'Sarah Harding', p. 169. For Dublin edition sizes, see Pollard, *Dublin's Trade in Books*, pp. 116–20.

19 For the alleged transmission of the papers, see Woolley, 'Sarah Harding', p. 165; Swift to Motte, 4 November 1732, Woolley, *Corr.*, vol. III, p. 308.

20 Swift to Rev. John Worrall, 13 January 1728–9, Woolley, *Corr.*, vol. III, p. 206.

21 The original Dublin print of *The Intelligencer* (TS 666) was from May–December 1728. The London 1729 printings were by A. Moor (TS 34; Bowyer 1446) and 2nd edn, Francis Cogan (TS 35; Bowyer 1570); they were also reprinted in *Miscellanies*, vol. III, 1732 (TS 25) and *Works* 1735, I and IV (TS 3). Keith Maslen lists the Faulkner–Bowyer entries in the ledger in 'George Faulkner and William Bowyer: The London Connection', in his *An Early London Printing House at Work: Studies in the Bowyer Ledgers* (New York:

Bibliographical Society of America, 1993), pp. 223–33 (p. 231); the essay is reprinted from *The Long Room*, 38 (1993), 20–30. For the importing and possible revisions, see Woolley, *Intelligencer*, pp. 292, 293.

22 See Maslen, 'George Faulkner and William Bowyer', pp. 224 and 227: the Dublin editions by Faulkner 'are behind at least 24 of Bowyer's Dublin printed London reprinted editions', listed by *ESTC* numbers. See also Woolley, *Corr.*, vol. III, p. 464 n. 5 for the ordering of works of 1732 'implicating variously Swift as author, Faulkner as printer publisher and Irish go-between, Bowyer as London printer and proprietor'. There is also Swift's assigning copyright to Pilkington of works that 'were printed in dublin, by Mr George Faulkner, some of which were sent in Manuscript to Mr William Bowyer of London, Printer', 22 July 1732, Woolley, *Corr.*, vol. III, p. 509.

23 Michael Treadwell, 'London Trade Publishers, 1675–1750', *The Library*, 6th ser., 4 (1982), 99–134 (125, 110).

24 *A LIBEL ON Dr. D——NY* (TS 679; 'Reprinted for Capt. Gulliver'). *Works*, 1735, vol. IV, p. 227.

25 Maslen, 'George Faulkner and William Bowyer', p. 227. There is a reference in the pamphlet to writing on 13 April (Davis, *PW*, vol. XII, p. 168). Ehrenpreis posits that 'he might have added this sentence while the essay was in the press'. Carteret would be leaving for England soon after the end of Parliament, 'yet what Swift wished to write would have been risky to publish during Parliament time' (*Swift*, vol. III, p. 658). Parliament was prorogued on Wednesday 15 April 1730. The London printings are TS 697 (Bowyer, 1545, 24 April 1730) and 2nd edn, Bowyer 1576, 25 July 1730 (not in TS). See Maslen, 'George Faulkner and William Bowyer', p. 231.

26 For Allen and Tighe, see Ehrenpreis, *Swift*, vol. III, pp. 650–3, 362–5.

27 Davis, *PW*, vol. XII, p. 337. See *Works* (1735), vol. IV, pp. 289, 292, for the absence of notes.

28 The Dublin *Examination of Certain Abuses* is TS 718; the London *City Cries* (with Roberts's imprint) TS 719. The original ending of the pamphlet in the Dublin version is the bottom of p. 27 (Dublin) and p. 28 (London), which adds pp. 29–30. See Davis, *PW*, vol. XII, p. 232.

29 Swift to Ford, 9 October 1733, Woolley, *Corr.*, vol. III, p. 693. For the projected London edition with Bowyer, see the recent summary in Karian, *Print and Manuscript*, p. 25.

30 Faulkner, 'Preface' to *Works* (1762), vol. I, p. xiv; see also 1763 *Works* (Davis, *PW*, vol. XIII, pp. 202–3).

31 *The Drapier's Letters*, ed. Herbert Davis (Oxford: Clarendon Press, 1935), pp. 39, lxviii, lxxiv. Pollard, 'George Faulkner', *SStud*, 7 (1992), 79–96 (91).

32 Karian, *Print and Manuscript*, p. 43. See also his discussion of the context of Faulkner's disparate comments on the edition (pp. 30–43).

33 John Hawkesworth, 'Preface' to *The Works of Jonathan Swift* (London: C. Bathurst *et al.*, 1755), vol. I, pp. 14–15.

34 Karian, *Print and Manuscript*, p. 97. See pp. 92–8 for his account of the exceedingly tangled history of the manuscript, updating Harold Williams's 'Introduction', in Davis, *PW*, vol. VII, pp. xii–xxviii.

35 George Faulkner, *An Appeal to the Public* (Dublin, 1758), p. 8.
36 George and Alexander Ewing, *An Attempt to Answer Mr. Faulkner's Extraordinary Appeal to the Public* (Dublin, 1758), p. ii. Herbert Davis claimed it was published the same day as their edition. See 'Correspondence', *Library*, 4th ser., 16 (1935–6), 344.
37 Robert E. Ward, *Prince of Dublin Printers: The Letters of George Faulkner* (Lexington: University of Kentucky Press, 1972), p. 134 n. 110. 'The Editors to the Readers', in *The Works of Jonathan Swift* (Dublin: Faulkner, 1765), vol. XII, p. iii.

CHAPTER ELEVEN

Publishing posthumous Swift: Deane Swift to Walter Scott

Daniel Cook

Outwardly dismissive of George Faulkner's Dublin *Works* (1735), Jonathan Swift seemed hopeful that his London-based booksellers, Benjamin Motte and Lawton Gilliver, would raise a monument edition of his works in his name.[1] However, Motte died in 1738, and no plans appeared to be in place when Swift himself died seven years later. In 1755, John Hawkesworth, man of letters and member of Johnson's circle, finally superintended through the press the first of seven distinct stages of a significantly expanded edition.[2] It included an extended biography for the first time, along with a tranche of new materials, much of which he culled from revised printings by Faulkner and others over the next quarter of a century. Deane Swift, a junior cousin of the poet, damned the Hawkesworth collection as 'the vilest that ever was yet published'.[3] 'He must then have written either from conjecture or misinformation', he continues, 'and therefore what he wrote was many times false and sometimes ridiculous. In short, he published an edition of an Author whose writings he neither did, nor, for want of opportunities, could understand.' Thomas Sheridan the Younger, son of one of Swift's closest allies in Dublin, wrote to the bookseller William Strahan on 5 June 1784, seeking his aid in producing an improved edition: 'I have long beheld with indignation the shameful manner in which the Works of Dr. Swift have been published, which are now swelled to the enormous bulk of XXV volumes.'[4]

This chapter charts the different methodologies employed by those who sought to clean up Hawkesworth's edition. The printer and anecdotist John Nichols played an increasingly prominent role in the second half of the eighteenth century both as a tireless, if often misguided, collector of mislaid manuscripts and as a commentator on the texts.[5] Deane Swift had involvement with a number of the volumes and yet, in direct contrast with Nichols, sought to restrict rather than expand the body of printed works.[6] One of the most potent effects of Nichols's tireless research lay in the manner in which he shed stark light on the negligent editing practices of both Hawkesworth and Deane Swift. For all its bulk, the mid-century edition looked far from complete; the texts were often messy or heavily corrupted; and Hawkesworth included works that had long been identified as authored by Pope, Arbuthnot, Gay and others. A new edition was sorely needed; as a dedicated collector of, and expert on, Swift manuscripts, Nichols was among the most qualified for a role that he seemed keen to undertake. As the man directly responsible for rashly printed supplementary volumes to the Hawkesworth edition, perhaps he felt compelled to refine it on his own terms. Copyright problems intervened, however. As he later wrote, somewhat acerbically, in his *Illustrations of the Literary History of the Eighteenth Century*: 'A material obstacle in respect to the then existing state of Literary Property, as far as it related to Copyright (a right still held sacred by every respectable Bookseller), prevented *my* undertaking at that period a regular Edition of Swift.' 'Of the Twenty-five Volumes,' he goes on to say, '*Five* only were my exclusive property, and an *eighth* share of *Six* others, which had been purchased by Mr. Bowyer and myself; and … any proposal for an amalgamation was constantly opposed by some of the other proprietors, particularly Mr. Bathurst, who possessed an exclusive right to *Six* of the Volumes.'[7] Although not unheard of, particularly in an age of shifting copyright laws and rights to ownership, it would have been unusual for booksellers not to reach a compromise for a common gain.[8]

To Nichols's bemusement, the conglomeration of the twenty-five or so booksellers instead accepted the proposal of another member of Swift's extended circle, Thomas Sheridan the Younger, to produce a new edition in 1784. Like Nichols, Sheridan knew the canon existed in a state of disrepute, but he felt it needed pruning rather than augmenting: 'The first thing to be done in this edition, was, to disembroil these Works from the chaos in which they have hitherto appeared.'[9] He delivered a much tauter *Works* in seventeen volumes, much of which formed the basis of subsequent editions, including those overseen by Nichols and Walter Scott. In particular, Sheridan's biography of Swift – for which they paid him the princely sum of £300, an amount matched by the fee paid for his work as the editor of the other sixteen volumes – was widely treated as authoritative. However, Swift's twentieth-century editor Sir Harold Williams criticizes Sheridan's neglect of a large part of Nichols's research, particularly on textual matters in *Journal to Stella*: 'the larger omissions noted by Nichols are ignored'. 'No conscientious attempt is made to mend the text, which remains substantially that of Hawkesworth,' he adds. 'Indeed, the editor's carelessness is incredible.'[10] This is an exaggeration, if only a marginal one. Textual matters aside, Sheridan's edition proved influential in the way it reordered the works and in its introduction of a book-length biography as the first volume.

Sheridan died in 1788 but, nevertheless, some years had passed before Nichols was finally able to bring out his own authoritative edition in 1801. Ever diligent in his collecting, he expanded it further in 1803 and in 1808, before Walter Scott augmented it further still in 1814 and 1824. Scott's edition, it is worth pointing out, remained the base text of subsequent collections well into the middle of the twentieth century. Beyond their own limitations, Hawkesworth, Nichols, Sheridan and Deane Swift have always been indispensable to Swift studies, largely through their privileged access to papers now lost. As late as 1814, Scott was able to draw on the unique if often dubious insights of surviving members of Swift's extended circle. At issue here is the question of authority: who had the most right, and the most personal experience, to edit Swift's works? Who best understood the author's intentions? Which pieces did he wish to publish, and in what form? How complete might a complete edition be?

Burn all manuscripts

Deane Swift in particular positioned himself as a guardian of Swift's legacy as he sought to exclude, or to tamper with, those texts he considered inferior or otherwise unseemly, most notably the correspondence with Esther Johnson ('Stella'). For all of his bluster, though, Deane Swift failed to bring Swift's works into the reduced form he favoured. In November 1763, proposals were advertised under his name for a Clarendon Press edition to be published by subscription, 'as soon as possible', in two octavo volumes. Such a standalone edition did not appear. The notice also refers to 'another Edition printed in Three Volumes Twelves', issued 'in order to oblige those Gentlemen, who would be willing to complete Collections which they have made of the Doctor's Works in that Size'.[11] In 1765, the bookseller William Johnston sold *The Works of Dr Jonathan Swift … collected and revised by Deane Swift, esq; of Goodrich, in Herefordshire*; these three volumes (in small octavo rather than duodecimo) fitted in with the 1760 version of the by then standard Hawkesworth collection published in London. Perhaps Deane Swift intended to bring out his own, authoritative and pared-down selection of the works in due course, but at the time of his death in 1783 no further action had been taken.

Even though Deane Swift had ready access to Swift's papers, particularly through Mrs Whiteway, his mother-in-law who lived with Swift at the deanery at St Patrick's, the extant manuscripts seemed to trouble him. In the fifteenth volume of the *Works* (1765) he places great stock in his unique holdings and insists on their public value: 'we shall deposite [*sic*] them in the British Museum'.[12] And in a letter to Nichols he boasts of his role as a preserver of manuscripts, particularly letters: 'As for the Journal to Stella, not one line of it would ever have been printed, if it had not been for me: In short, I was the person, who about the year 1740 saved all that part of the Journal from the flames, which was published by Hawkesworth.'[13] However, Deane Swift also claimed in this letter that Swift never had 'the least intention that his Letters to Stella, which now go by the title of his Journal, or perhaps any other Letters in that collection, should ever be published'. He goes yet further and claims that 'if Hawkesworth had not published that part of the Journal, I never should have published the rest of it'. Evidently Deane Swift felt torn between his duties as a curator of Swift's surviving texts and as a familial guardian of his reputation. Another member of Swift's circle, Patrick Delany, for one, disagreed with Deane Swift's approach and, in a strident letter to him, insisted that 'there are few things [Jonathan Swift] ever wrote that he did not wish to be published one time or other'.[14]

The men quarrelled over the issue of whether all, or only a selection, of Swift's works merited publication. This was a question of taste, whether in terms of judging the quality of the writings or upholding the preferences of the author. After all, as Nora Crow Jaffe reminds us, Swift habitually downplayed the value of much of his verse.[15] But, more than that, Deane Swift held a common eighteenth-century assumption, as evidenced by the paucity of surviving printers' copies, that a manuscript, once published, lost any importance and therefore could be destroyed: 'I think it would be the best way to burn all manuscripts after a book is once printed, if it were for no other reason than because every edition of a book, after the first, (unless it be corrected by the author) is, generally speaking, worse than the former.'[16] To Deane Swift's mind, his cousin's materials were particularly worthless: 'the Original Papers which I gave myself the trouble to copy, are not worth the skin of a turnip'. Equally, though, he recognized that they had a vestigial importance: 'and yet I have still preserved them, and one day or other (if it please God that I shall live to publish an edition of Swift's Works, which I have long intended) I shall make a present of them, perhaps, with several other papers to the British Museum, if such trifles be deemed either valuable or curious'. His hesitant tone speaks volumes about his real thoughts on the matter: trifles are trifles, after all, and ought to be ignored.

Not only did Deane Swift discard manuscripts, he pointedly refused to read and thence to preserve texts not to his taste. In a letter dated 7 June 1778, he observed that 'five or six and forty years ago' Mrs Whiteway showed him Swift's 'Ode to King William', apparently in printed form, but that owing to its 'Pindarique way' he was unwilling to drudge through more than 'fifty or sixty lines of it'.[17] Deane Swift duly omitted it from the 1765 volume of the *Works*. At the reference supplied by Nichols to Samuel Johnson's *Works of the English Poets* a footnote flatly states that the piece 'cannot now be recovered'.[18] In 1780, however, Nichols printed an 'Ode to King William' in his own *Select Collection of Poems* – itself presented as a supplement to Johnson's anthology – with this joyful footnote: 'With much pleasure I here present to the publick an Ode which had been long sought after without success. That it is Swift's, I have not the least doubt ... He refers to it in the second stanza of his "Ode to the Athenian Society" ... See the "English Poets", vol. XXXIX, p. 10; and "The Gentleman's Journal", July, 1692, p. 13.'[19] The precision of the citations notwithstanding, the triumphalism of the collector is misjudged here: the poem does not match Deane Swift's description. After all, it is not in Pindarics, and it does not run to the fifty or sixty lines that turned the cousin's stomach so. Samuel Fairbrother, who had access to George Faulkner's unpublished manuscripts, seems to have found the right piece and printed an incomplete version in the fourth volume of his *Miscellanies* in 1735.[20] Hindered by the destroyer of manuscripts, Nichols had been led astray.

The contrasting attitudes Nichols and Deane Swift held towards their task is clear; and both have their flaws. Nichols reproduced in print the vast majority, if not all, of the manuscripts he could salvage, regardless of authority or quality. He worked diligently to augment the already bulky Hawkesworth edition, initially with one volume in 1775 (i.e. volume seventeen of the *Works*) as planned, though this quickly became three supplementary volumes in various formats by 1779. Nichols's 'Advertisement' to the 1775 volume traces the complicated publication history of this edition of Swift's *Works* up to this point. 'In this state was the collection', writes Nichols, 'when in the latter end of 1774, the present Editor, having occasion to peruse with attention the fifteenth and sixteenth volumes, was induced to read, in a regular series, the whole of Dr. *Swift's* Correspondence'. 'In this pursuit', he writes, 'he could not but be astonished to perceive that many pieces, which the Dean acknowledges as his

own, were not to be found in the most expensive editions of his Works.'
'To remedy that inconvenience', as he puts it, 'is the design of this volume; consisting of materials, which, if not entirely new to the world, are
such in the editions just mentioned.'²¹ Here Nichols proffered the creed of
an indiscriminate collector, as opposed to that of an editor: make materials widely available, regardless of their true value. Remarkably, Nichols
concedes that even though 'Many of [the pieces] are admirable; some of
them indifferent; and some, perhaps, rather below mediocrity.'

Soon enough Nichols would be far less coy about foisting his mass of
recovered materials onto readers but, for now, he buried his missive at the
back of the book. Under the second part of Nichols's index, as a footnote
situated below the entry entitled SWIFTIANA, signed 'N', the text *in toto*
reads: 'The Editor of the present volume hath endeavoured, as far as he
was able, to recover what he could trace out to be the Dean's; and he flat-
ters himself his search hath not been wholly unsuccessful.'²² Not unsuccessful, indeed, and not yet finished. In the 'Advertisement' to the first
volume of the 1779 *Supplement* to the *Works* – an expanded version of the
1776 *Supplement* – Nichols continued to seek the approval of the men of
taste who might object to the perils of unfiltered editing. Perhaps he had
Deane Swift in mind. 'It may perhaps be objected against some of the articles … that they are too trifling, and were never intended by the Author
for the eye of the publick.' 'But it was thought it would be an agreeable
entertainment to the Curious', he continues, 'to see how oddly a man of
his great wit and humour could now and then descend to amuse himself with his particular Friends.'²³ There was a strategic double play here:
Nichols seemed to be fully aware of the type of criticism Deane Swift
might level at his baggy collection – namely that some of the pieces were
insignificant, and that Jonathan Swift did not wish to see certain items
published – but, instead, he presented the contents as works of curious, if
not literary, value.

The small octavo *Supplement* reprinted in three volumes in 1779 was
an expanded version of the ad hoc volumes of 1775, 1776 and 1779. In the
section of the large octavo *Supplement* entitled 'Omissions and Principal
Corrections in Volume XVIII', Nichols had, by 1779, introduced a significant footnote: 'That part of the *Journal to Stella*, which was published
by Dr. *Hawkesworth*, appearing abundantly *more polished* than the other
given to the world by Mr. *Deane Swift*; it was natural to imagine that
some alteration had been made.' 'On examining', he adds, 'I find that in
the originals, now in *The British Museum*, besides a few corrections which
appear to have been by the Dean at the time of writing them, there are

some *obliterations*, and many whole sentences omitted.'[24] Here we have a stark illustration of the conflicting approaches to the materials. Nichols's hunch, which proved correct, took him back to the original manuscripts and thereby he discovered the extent to which Hawkesworth had taken liberties with the text. By Harold Williams's calculation we are dependent upon Deane Swift's edited version for nearly three-quarters of the *Journal*. By way of contrast, all but one of the originals of the letters published by Hawkesworth have survived. In the 1784 *Works*, incidentally, Sheridan relied on Hawkesworth's texts, and incorporated Deane Swift's footnotes, but made little improvement to either. Nichols's 1801 *Works* marked a real advance in the publication of this work. He revisited the corrections and additions he had printed in 1779 and clearly had returned to the extant materials. For the first time, Williams suggests, 'the letters appeared in a form which made some approximation to the manuscript', even if spelling and punctuation had been normalized.[25] Nichols even printed small excerpts on facing pages, thereby placing emphasis on the judgement of the readers rather than dictating to them. That said, Williams defends Deane Swift: 'whatever his shortcomings ... he gave to that part of the *Journal* which he edited a character and intonation more in keeping with that portion of the *Journal* which has been saved'.[26]

Many contemporary commentators, likewise, preferred Deane Swift's treatment of the work over that of Nichols.[27] In a notice of Nichols's *Supplement* in 1779, the *Monthly Review* observed: 'The *Journal to Stella*, in the state in which it was first written, deserved all that correction and alteration which the Editor complains of. It was not fit to appear before the public eye in its original form.'[28] Here Nichols's thoroughness is berated; it seemed a misguided principle for the editing of the *Journal*, a collection of letters that has long proved discomfiting for polite readers. Perhaps even his friend and fellow printer George Faulkner hinted at the potential dangers of the indiscriminate approach favoured by Nichols when he berated vulturine collectors: 'I know many people have laid themselves out to collect the most Grub-street trash that would disgrace the poorest and meanest of presses.'[29]

More last words

'What! more last words of Dean Swift!' exclaimed a commentator in *The Monthly Review* as early as December 1768. 'Aye', he continues, 'and more still may be expected, while there are relations or friends of the witty and ingenious Dean remaining, with hearts full of zeal for his fame, or impelled by a boundless admiration of his writings.'[30] Nichols's multi-volume

Supplement came under the sharpest attack. *The Monthly Review* in 1779 complained: 'Many things are admitted into this Supplement which add little to its value, and reflect no honour on Dean Swift.' 'Though we approve of the industry of the ingenious Editor, and heartily recommend this work to the curious reader', as the commentator puts it, 'yet, the impartiality of criticism obliges us, though reluctantly, to acknowledge, that Mr. Nichols employed his time to a purpose unworthy of his abilities, when he searched the *British Museum* for some originals to complete his useless list of omissions and corrections.'[31]

Without Nichols's efforts, though, a sizeable portion of materials would have been lost forever. For more than forty years Nichols raked over often heavily degraded Swiftiana in libraries, principally in the then relatively new British Museum Library, which opened its doors to the public in the late 1750s. In the Lambeth Palace Library he found authoritative copies of a number of new or previously corrupted items, including 'Horace, Book II, Ode I', 'Horace, Book I, Ep. V', 'The Present State of Wit' and 'Peace and Dunkirk', among others. He even found (and printed) annotations by Archbishop Tenison contained in the folio editions held at Lambeth.[32] By his own claim Nichols had sought out Swiftiana since 1762, when, aged seventeen, he worked as a 'humble Assistant' to William Bowyer on seeing the thirteenth and fourteenth volumes of John Hawkesworth's large edition of Swift's *Works* through the press. At this time Nichols (in his words) 'first acquired an inclination for becoming a Commentator, which I afterwards freely indulged, on the Works'.[33] While Nichols can be credited with recovering a not unsubstantial number of works for Swift's canon, he attributed an equal number of works to Swift that have been rejected over the years, such as 'Helter Skelter' and the epigram 'Behold! A Proof of Irish Sense!'[34]

During his long career in the London book trade Nichols benefited from friendships with Edmond Malone, Alexander Chalmers, John Duncombe and other leading scholars, and also with printers, especially his master, William Bowyer, owner of a cache of materials given to him by Swift's Dublin printer, George Faulkner.[35] Nichols also developed a strong working relationship with the librarian at Lambeth, the antiquary Andrew Coltée Ducarel. Thomas Astle supplied Nichols with further materials, as he warmly noted in the eighteenth volume of the 1801 *Works of Swift*.[36] Nichols frequently acknowledged his gratitude to the somewhat reclusive Isaac Reed, the owner of a volume of tracts that formerly belonged to Swift's friend Charles Ford. In a footnote to the 1803 *Works*, Nichols listed articles contained therein, 'which Mr. Ford attests to be "all writ by

Dr. Swift, now Dean of St. Patrick".[37] Here Nichols listed ten tracts, only four of which had appeared in the large Hawkesworth edition of the mid-century. *The Importance of the Guardian Consider'd*, in particular, was a text that long eluded Nichols. He had, in his words, 'in vain advertized for a copy of it, in most of the public papers, for many months'.[38] It eventually appeared in his 1779 *Supplement*. Perhaps, as his contemporaries did, it is fair to judge Nichols as a passable textual scholar at best, but as a truly excellent gatherer of texts, one to whom Swift scholars remain heavily indebted.[39]

Indeed, Nichols cannily exploited his position as the printer of the *Gentleman's Magazine*, the leading miscellany of the day. Under the pseudonym 'M. Green' (his second wife's maiden name) he printed a host of letters in which he sought out specific manuscripts. Many of the replies led him astray; but, as he perhaps realized, even erroneous responses would open up further possibilities. And he even treated his published volumes as deliberately incomplete. In the 1776 *Supplement*, Nichols went so far as to print a most wanted list of fourteen missing works by Swift. The list of desiderata yielded results remarkably quickly. Nichols sought out what seemed to him to be an elusive item, 'Peace and Dunkirk'; within months he gleefully announced the acquisition of it in the *Gentleman's Magazine* for June 1777.[40] By 1779, Nichols had recovered several pieces mentioned in his original 1776 list and had gathered 'Biographical Anecdotes' from John Lyon's annotations in a copy of Hawkesworth's 'Life of Swift'.[41] Yet Nichols was far from satisfied and, at his request, Malone sent Lord Charlemont an abbreviated list of desiderata in April 1779.[42] Nichols also sent a copy of the 1779 *Supplement* to Deane Swift, who died four years later, and in the meantime could not, or would not, offer any help. Nichols wrote as well to his heir, Theophilus Swift, asking for assistance, but the younger Swift replied that the edition was 'in a manner' finished by his father, and that it would be easy for him to 'complete any deficiencies under which it may at present labour'. Indeed, the younger Swift felt the canon was finally settled: 'I am *confident* that so *perfect* and *accurate* an Edition will never be given of Swift as it is now in my power to offer to the world.' Swift *fils* claimed to follow the model Bishop Hurd had established in his work on Warburton: a complete edition that is in fact a restricted selection. Such a selection would contain only pieces 'worthy [of] the pen of Swift; weeded and purged of such tracts, &c. as discredit him'.[43] For Theophilus Swift and his father, the collecting of Swift's works entailed the contraction rather than the expansion of volumes.

Commentators largely sided with the Swifts; they expressed immense dissatisfaction with the constant flurry of new material, much of which they considered not only discreditable, as Theophilus Swift would have it, but – perhaps worse still – trivial. 'Must we read every unimportant scrawl because it fell from the pen of Swift?' asked a reviewer of the *Miscellaneous Pieces, in Prose and Verse* (1789). He continued: 'must we witness every irritable and peevish expression of his splenetic and distempered hours? and be pestered with every quibbling conundrum of his gayer moments, when *vive la bagatelle* was all his conversation?'[44] Reviewers were wearied, particularly, by the appearance of new volumes of letters in the 1760s and well into the 1780s. In 1768, the *Critical Review* opined that 'these volumes are calculated more for the lovers than the admirers of the dean of St. Patrick's', largely because they revealed Swift off guard, not as the author of some of the greatest political and literary texts of his age but a man 'carelessly playing with his soil'.[45]

Turning lead to gold

By 1779, the collected works had swelled to twenty-five volumes (twenty-seven in small octavo, on ordinary crown paper, and octodecimo), though Sheridan had managed to reduce this down to seventeen healthily sized volumes. Ironically, Nichols based his 1801, 1803 and 1808 editions closely on Sheridan's 1784 collection, most notably in his reissue of the biography and in the ordering of the works. This is not to suggest that the new selections were derivative; on the contrary, Nichols introduced yet more co-textual scholarship and made numerous corrections, particularly in the eighteenth and nineteenth volumes of his 1801 edition. It might have become the standard edition Nichols had long hoped to produce. However, much to Nichols's chagrin, within barely half a decade of his final impression, 'the great Magician of the North', Walter Scott, produced a nineteen-volume edition based closely on his own. 'Laying his potent wand on my humble labours', as Nichols puts it, 'very soon, by a neat shuffling of the cards, and by abridging my tedious annotations, (turning lead to gold,) he presented to the Booksellers of Edinburgh an Edition somewhat similar to mine, and consisting of the same number of volumes.'[46]

The first edition appeared in 1814 in a run of 1,250 copies; the booksellers sought a reprint in 1824, to which Scott added some new pieces, corrected notes and careful revisions to the biography that appeared in the first volume, just as it had in Sheridan's 1784 edition. Nichols conjectured that Scott's profits from his edition were thirty times what he had received during his forty years of service.[47] For Scott, though, it was far from being what Nichols called 'a task of no great difficulty'. When, on 25 July 1808, Scott settled with Archibald Constable, the Edinburgh bookseller and publisher, to make a new edition of Swift's works, they assumed that the edition would be ready within two years. However, six years passed before it finally appeared. Not quite four months after he had undertaken the edition he complained to John Murray, 'I now heartily wish it had never commenced.'[48] In 1814, he wrote with evident relief to the Marchioness of Abercorn, 'Swift who rode me like Sinbad's old man of the sea for so many years is now sent to his fate ... It will be the last of my editorial labours.'[49] Meanwhile, Constable had become fretful over the delay with 'this most vexatious of all Books': 'Had the work been completed three years ago when [the] Trade were mad about everything where Mr. Scott's name appeared how very differently should we have stood in this business.'[50]

Scholars have recently endorsed Constable's concern about the textual-critical merits of the edition. John Sutherland, most notably, states that 'Scott's procedures in preparing his edition hovered between the lazy and the downright plagiaristic'.[51] Although commending Scott's edition on the whole, in 1825 *Blackwood's Magazine* resorted to the line held by the periodical press since the late 1760s, by censuring him for printing too many works of little merit.[52] Nevertheless, Scott received wide praise for the masterful way in which he marshalled Swift's materials into a more coherent whole. Even Harold Williams, although generally critical of Swift's early editors, claimed that Scott's edition, 'carried through with the extraordinary pace he commanded, is even now, in some respects, the most useful working set of the Dean's complete writings'.[53]

So, what did the great magician do exactly? Clearly his edition is not an entirely original piece of scholarship; nor is it simply a reprint of older Swift editions. Scott abridged Nichols's notes and anecdotes – putting them into a more readable and durable form – and added lengthy notes of his own; but he took the texts of Swift's works directly from Nichols and made only a cursory acknowledgement of his research. By comparing compositor's notes in Scott's ripped-and-pasted-up volumes with the final edition of 1814, Lee Potter has demonstrated that Scott used Nichols's 1801 and 1808 editions of Swift's *Works* as his copy text.[54] As a caveat, it must be stressed that it had been fairly common practice in the eighteenth century, and well into the nineteenth, to mark up print copies rather than to return to the manuscripts. Samuel Johnson, to take a famous example, used eighteenth-century editions as the base texts for his celebrated edition of Shakespeare in 1765; one of the period's most eminent medievalists, Thomas Tyrwhitt, relied on the 1687 reprint of Speght's Chaucer, despite its many flaws, when preparing his own collection of *The Canterbury Tales* (1775–8). And even if Scott was largely inattentive to textual criticism in Swift's case, he provided plenty of additional pieces: eighty-three letters, twenty-two poems and seventeen prose works – many of which both Harold Williams and Herbert Davis have judged as authentic. Indeed, Scott flagged up key textual issues that scholars still debate. A notable example concerns *On Poetry: A Rapsody*. In the 1824 edition, Scott reaches the conclusion shared by many today, namely that Swift himself had cancelled about fifty of the poem's most controversial lines in which he attacks the English bishops, George II and monarchy in general.[55]

Through his connection with Swift's extended circle, moreover, Scott was able to further our understanding, however tentatively, of the complex textual issues involved with *A Tale of a Tub* and other major works. In the 1755 edition of Swift's *Works*, Hawkesworth claimed that Swift himself had revised a copy of the 1710 edition of *A Tale* 'a short time before his understanding was impaired, and his corrections will be found in this impression'.[56] (Suffice it to say, such revisions, particularly ahead of Swift's mental decline, would have held strong authority.) In a letter to Nichols dated 25 April 1775, Deane Swift confirmed that such a copy did indeed exist.[57] A note in Scott's 1824 edition further adds that the copy bore an authoritative inscription: 'To Mrs. Martha Whiteway, a present on her birth-day, May 29, 1735, from her affectionate cousin, Jonath. Swift'.[58] The Whiteway copy seemingly passed to Theophilus Swift, who showed it to Scott. It is also possible, as Marcus Walsh suggests, that in the Dublin 'ninth edition' of the *Tale* published in 1756 Faulkner used the 'corrected Copy' of the 1710 edition.[59] No such claim is made in that edition; however, in a 1759 advertisement for the projected octodecimo edition the publisher promised it would include 'the Tale of a Tub, carefully printed from the last corrected Book, amended by the Author, which corrections were given to us by Deane Swift, Esq'. However, the Whiteway copy does not appear to have survived, and so our understanding of the extent to which editors were able to make use of it, or even the type of corrections Swift made, remains speculative. By comparing the various published versions, though, Walsh has conjectured that such corrections were confined to minor issues concerning shifting cultural context and linguistic usage. This would seem to confirm Scott's claim that '[t]he Dean had corrected, with his pen, all the abbreviations and elisions which were ordinary in the beginning of the century, by replacing *it is* for *'tis*, *the end* for *th'end*, and the like, but without any other alterations'. While this observation might disappoint those interested in the author's final intentions, to my mind it reveals a lot about the different attitudes towards the materials held by Swift's editors. Whereas Nichols would have been delighted to publish the text withheld from him, even with its unsubstantial changes, Deane Swift considered it to be insignificant. (Indeed, Nichols had been led astray by another copy of the *Tale*, which he purchased at the Chauncy auction in April 1790.)[60] Only by chance, and with the more forthcoming aid of Deane Swift's son, did Scott catch a glimpse of the Whiteway copy.

Aside from an intermittent contribution to textual scholarship, Scott's *Memoirs* of Swift – heavily but not exclusively reliant on Nichols's life of Swift, which is itself indebted to Hawkesworth, Delany, Sheridan and others, including a host of anonymous contributors to the *Gentleman's Magazine* – proved to be the most durable part of the 1814 *Works* well into the twentieth century. Although drawing extensively on freely available biographies, Scott also disperses a number of newly printed anecdotes throughout the *Memoirs*. On a smaller scale certainly, he followed Nichols's lead in hunting down lingering survivors of Swift's extended circle, particularly Theophilus Swift, who seemed to be far more liberal with his family papers than his father, and Thomas Steele, who inherited a cache of papers from his uncle, Dr Lyon, the man in charge of Swift's affairs in his final years. This is not to suggest that Scott's contribution to Swift studies relies solely on the success of his biography. On the whole, as we have seen, he was concerned with the provenance of the texts and other editorial concerns with which we continue to grapple.

The Scott edition, though derivative, particularly in its reliance on print texts, has a prominent place in the posthumous life of Swift's works. It built on – and extended further – the rigorous research undertaken in the second half of the century by Nichols in particular. It also benefited from the materials left by Deane Swift, a man largely sceptical of their material value, much to Nichols's frustration. Importantly, Scott reined in the increasing bagginess of the published corpus. Here Nichols stands at once as the hero and the villain. His textual scholarship looks inconsistent, to say the least, but throughout the 1770s and beyond he added substantial supplementary volumes to the corpus, which, though widely criticized, provided a veritable treasure trove of materials. The 1803 edition in particular had ballooned back to twenty-four volumes in duodecimo, signalling a return to the excesses of the mid-century collection. By condensing the volumes down, and recalibrating their contents, Scott established a sturdier canon of Swift's works. Filled with politically motivated niggles against the author of *Gulliver's Travels*, along with yet more extraneous detail, it was not the monument edition Swift desired. As a dense body of accreted scholarship, it nevertheless shaped Swift's canon well into the twentieth century.

Notes

1 On Swift's ambivalent dealings with publishers see Karian, *Print and Manuscript*, pp. 11–43.
2 For bibliographical details see TS, pp. 80–103. On Hawkesworth's editing of Swift see John Lawrence Abbott, *John Hawkesworth: Eighteenth-Century Man of Letters* (Madison: University of Wisconsin Press, 1982), pp. 47–64.
3 Deane Swift to John Nichols, 25 April 1778, in John Nichols, *Illustrations of the Literary History of the Eighteenth Century*, 8 vols. (London, 1817–58), vol. V, pp. 375–80 (p. 376).
4 Nichols, *Illustrations*, vol. V, p. 394.
5 See Daniel Cook, '*Labor ipse voluptas*: John Nichols's Swiftiana', in John Hinks and Matthew Day (eds.), *From Compositors to Collectors: Essays on Book-Trade History* (Delaware and London: Oak Knoll Press and The British Library, 2011), pp. 43–60 and Martin Maner, '"The Last of the Learned Printers": John Nichols and the Bowyer-Nichols Press', *English Studies*, 65 (1984), 11–22 and 'An Eighteenth-Century Editor at Work: John Nichols and Jonathan Swift', *Papers of the Bibliographical Society of America*, 70 (1976), 481–99. For detailed discussions of Nichols's editing of Swift see David Woolley, '*A Dialogue upon Dunkirk* (1712), and Swift's "7 Penny Papers"', John Irwin Fischer, 'Swift's Early Odes, Dan Jackson's Nose, and "The Character of Sir Robert Walpole": Some Documentary Problems', and James Woolley, 'The Canon of Swift's Poems: The Case of "An Apology to the Lady Carteret"', in *Münster* (1993), pp. 215–23, 225–43 and 245–64. For authoritative accounts of Nichols's dealings with the book trade see A. H. Smith, 'John Nichols, Printer and Publisher', *The Library*, 5th ser., 18 (1963), 169–90; Robin Myers, 'John Nichols (1745–1826), Chronicler of the Book Trade', in Robin Myers and Michael Harris (eds.), *Development of the English Book Trade, 1700–1899* (Oxford Polytechnic Press, 1981), pp. 1–35; Julian Pooley, 'The Papers of the Nichols Family and Business: New Discoveries and the Work of the Nichols Archive Project', *The Library*, 7th ser., 2 (2001), 10–52. Harold Williams has called Nichols 'an untiring worker' who 'was by no means a careful editor', one who 'brought genuine enthusiasm to his self-appointed task of presenting a complete collection of Swift's writings': see Williams, *Poems*, vol. III, p. xl.
6 On Deane Swift see Ehrenpreis, *Swift*, vol. III, pp. 904–8.
7 Nichols, *Illustrations*, vol. V, p. 394 (emphasis retained).
8 See Terry Belanger, 'Tonson, Wellington and the Shakespeare Copyrights', in R. W. Hunt, I. G. Philip and R. J. Roberts (eds.), *Studies in the Book Trade: In Honour of Graham Pollard* (Oxford Bibliographical Society, 1975), pp. 195–209. I am indebted to Ian Gadd for this reference.

228 Daniel Cook

9 *The Works of the Rev. Dr. Jonathan Swift*, 17 vols. (London, 1784), vol. II, A3ᵛ.

10 *JSt* (1948), vol. I, p. li.

11 'Advertisement', *Jackson's Oxford Journal* (12 November 1763), p. 3. See also Matthew Kilburn, 'History, Languages, Literature, and Music', in Ian Gadd (ed.), *The History of Oxford University Press: Volume 1, 1478–1780* (Oxford University Press, forthcoming).

12 *The Works of Dr. Jonathan Swift, Dean of St. Patrick's, Dublin* (London, 1765), vol. XV, pp. xxxi (in 8° ed., TS88).

13 Nichols, *Illustrations*, vol. V, p. 375. See also Harold Williams, 'Deane Swift, Hawkesworth, and *The Journal to Stella*', in *Essays on the Eighteenth Century: presented to David Nichol Smith in honour of his seventieth birthday* (Oxford: Clarendon Press, 1945), pp. 33–48.

14 Nichols, *Illustrations*, vol. V, p. 393.

15 Nora Crow Jaffe, *The Poet Swift* (Hanover, NH: The University Press of New England, 1977), p. 54.

16 Deane Swift to John Nichols (25 April 1778), Nichols, *Illustrations*, vol. V, p. 376.

17 Nichols, *Illustrations*, vol. V, p. 382.

18 Samuel Johnson, *The Works of the English Poets. With Prefaces, Biographical and Critical*, 68 vols. (London, 1779–81), vol. XXXIX, p. 10 n. See also *The Lives of the Most Eminent English Poets*, ed. Roger Lonsdale, 4 vols. (Oxford: Clarendon Press, 2006), vol. III, pp. 428–9.

19 *A Select Collection of Poems* ed. John Nichols, 8 vols. (London, 1780–2), vol. IV, p. 303.

20 *Vol. IV of the Miscellanies Begun by Jonathan Swift, D.D. and Alexander Pope, Esq.* (Dublin, 1735), new pagination, pp. 1–6. The ode was published in Dublin in late 1690 or 1691, according to James Woolley, 'Swift's First Published Poem: *Ode. To the King*', in *Münster* (2003), p. 265–83.

21 *The Works of Dr. Jonathan Swift, Dean of St. Patrick's, Dublin* (London, 1775), vol. XVII, p. v–vi.

22 *Works* (1775), vol. XVII, p. 677 n.

23 *A Supplement to Dr. Swift's Works*, 3 vols. (London, 1779), vol. I, p. xi. Unless otherwise stated I quote from this three-volume *Supplement* (small octavo).

24 *Supplement* (1779), large octavo, vol. II, p. 225 (emphasis retained). This also appears in the second volume of the small octavo *Supplement* as 'Omissions and Principal Corrections in Volume XIX' (p. 237 ff.).

25 *JSt* (1948), vol. I, p. lii.

26 *JSt* (1948), vol. I, p. lvii.

27 Later editors of the *Journal* did criticize Deane Swift: see *Journal*, ed. Ryland, p. xviii; *Journal*, ed. Aitken, p. vi. See also John Forster, *The Life of Jonathan Swift* (London, 1875), pp. 406–7.

28 *Monthly Review*, 61 (November 1779), 356–65 (p. 364).

29 Quoted in John Nichols, *Literary Anecdotes of the Eighteenth Century; Comprising Biographical Memoirs of William Bowyer*, 9 vols. (London, 1812–15), vol. III, pp. 207–8.

30 *Monthly Review*, 39 (December 1768), 453–61 (p. 453).

31 *Monthly Review*, 61 (November 1779), 356–65 (p. 364). See also *Edinburgh Magazine*, 47 (January 1780), 85–6.

32 See *The Works of the Rev. Jonathan Swift, D.D.*, 19 vols. (London, 1808), vol. I, p. cxlix.

33 Nichols, *Illustrations*, vol. V, p. 391.

34 See James Woolley, 'The Canon of Swift's Poems', pp. 247–8; Williams, *Poems*, vol. II, pp. 572–4; vol. III, pp. 843–4.

35 For Bowyer's relationship with Faulkner see Adam Rounce's chapter, pp. 201–10.

36 *The Works of the Rev. Jonathan Swift, D.D.*, 19 vols. (London, 1801), vol. XVIII, pp. 218–19 n.

37 *The Works of the Rev. Jonathan Swift, D.D.*, 24 vols. (London, 1803), vol. IV, p. 226.

38 *Supplement* (1779), vol. II, p. 69.

39 See 'Scrutator', *Gentleman's Magazine*, 47 (August 1777), 381.

40 *Gentleman's Magazine*, 47 (June 1777), 261.

41 Forster MS 579, The National Art Library at the V&A.

42 Maner, 'Eighteenth-Century Editor at Work', p. 492.

43 Theophilus Swift to John Nichols (9 June 1784), Nichols, *Illustrations*, vol. V, pp. 389–90.

44 *Monthly Review*, new series, 1 (January 1790), 1–9 (p. 1). *Vive la bagatelle* had been one of Swift's favourite mottoes. Pope in particular encouraged his friend to live his life by it: 'And Swift cry wisely, "Vive la Bagatelle"', *The Sixth Epistle of the First Book of Horace Imitated* (London, 1738), p. 15. However, Swift's early biographers, such as Lord Orrery, considered it one of his failings. See John Boyle, 5th earl of Orrery, *Remarks on the Life and Writings of Dr. Jonathan Swift, Dean of St Patrick's, Dublin*, 2nd edn (London, 1752), p. 181: 'I wish his thoughts had taken another turn.'

45 *Critical Review*, 25 (April 1768), 241–52 (242).

46 Nichols, *Illustrations*, vol. V, p. 396–7. Another Nichols edition in twenty-four volumes, duodecimo, was published in New York by William Durell and Co. in 1812–13.

47 For his labour, Scott received fifteen hundred pounds, a substantial increase on the nine hundred guineas he had received for his *Works of Dryden* (18 vols.) in 1808.

48 Scott to John Murray, 15 November 1808, quoted in *John Murray: A Publisher and His Friends*, ed. Samuel Smiles (Hopewell, NJ, 1891; The Echo Press, 2006), p. 39.

49 Scott to Lady Abercorn, 22 November 1814, *The Letters of Sir Walter Scott*, ed. H. J. C. Grierson, 12 vols. (London: Constable, 1932–7), vol. III, p. 521.

50 Constable to Cadel, 20 April 1814, *Letters of Sir Walter Scott*, vol. III, p. 344 n. 2.

51 John Sutherland, *The Life of Walter Scott: A Critical Biography* (Oxford and Cambridge, MA: Blackwell, 1995), p. 166.

52 *Blackwood's Magazine* (December 1825), 724ff.

53 Williams, *Poems*, vol. I, p. xliii.

54 Lee H. Potter, 'The Text of Scott's Edition of Swift', *Studies in Bibliography*, 22 (1969), 240–55. See also George Falle, 'Sir Walter Scott as Editor of Dryden and Swift', *University of Toronto Quarterly*, 36 (1966–7), 161–80.

55 *The Works of Jonathan Swift*, ed. Walter Scott, 2nd edn, 19 vols. (Edinburgh, 1824), vol. XIV, pp. 328ff. For a contrary view see Karian, *Print and Manuscript*, pp. 115–18.

56 In a footnote Hawkesworth asserts that 'the corrected Copy is now in the hands of Mr. Dean[e] Swift', *Works* (1755), vol. I, sig. A1ʳ.

57 Deane Swift writes, 'I have besides the Tale of a Tub, corrected by himself', Nichols, *Illustrations*, vol. V, p. 378.

58 *Works* (1824), vol. V, p. 378.

59 *CWJS*, vol. I, pp. 281–3. This paragraph is heavily indebted to Walsh's textual introduction to this edition.

60 See Cook, '*Labor ipse voluptas*: John Nichols's Swiftiana', pp. 51–2.

CHAPTER TWELVE

The mock edition revisited: Swift to Mailer

Claude Rawson

This paper revisits some paradoxical and adversarial continuities between Swift, Sterne and some post-romantic and modernist sensibilities, which have been a long-time preoccupation of mine, but in a context I had not previously understood: that of the mock-editorial phenomenon, in which works of fiction, whether satirical or not, take the form of editions of themselves, with footnotes and marginal scholia, pretended gaps in the manuscript and other features of learned communication. The role of the editorial pretence, as an authenticating device, often destabilized or undermined, has received acute attention, in relation to Swift and to eighteenth-century novelists, from both Alain Bony and Baudouin Millet.[1] The features I discuss typically have a strong visual presence, and involve a wide range of typographical and other non-textual features of bookmaking, whose playful or parodic functions become part of a primary mode of self-expression and are integral to meanings we used to think of as the province solely of textual content. That the angle of vision I am proposing no longer has the novelty it once had is largely due to the teaching of James McLaverty, Thomas Keymer, Christopher Flint and a few others.

The subject I hope to re-examine from this perspective was broached in an early book of mine called *Gulliver and the Gentle Reader*, which opened with the purely textual observation that the 'Preface' to Swift's *Tale of a Tub*, perhaps the most inventively and relentlessly satirical work in the language, carries the somewhat surprising declaration: ''Tis a great Ease to my Conscience that I have writ so elaborate and useful a Discourse without one grain of Satyr intermixt.'[2] There follows an extraordinary passage about the fertility of satire, by comparison with panegyric, to the effect that there are only a few things that can be said in the latter mode, while the subjects of satire are inexhaustible (a classic premise of Swift at all times), so that 'there is very little Satyr which has not something in it untouch'd before'.

> For, the Materials of Panegyrick being very few in Number, have been long
> since exhausted: For, as Health is but one Thing, and has been always the
> same, whereas Diseases are by thousands, besides new and daily Additions;
> So, all the Virtues that have been ever in Mankind, are to be counted upon
> a few Fingers, but his Follies and Vices are innumerable, and Time adds
> hourly to the Heap. ('Preface', *CWJS*, vol. I, pp. 30–1)

This inexhaustibility is at the heart of a peculiar conception of the unfinished text, which is simultaneously mimicked and enacted in the *Tale*'s
unending ending, in which the idiot author declares his determination,
having nothing more to say, to go on writing upon nothing.

The *Tale of a Tub*, with its two pendants, the 'Battel of the Books' and
the 'Discourse Concerning the Mechanical Operation of the Spirit', is an
edition of itself, mimicking the gestures of classical scholarship, with a
signposted apparatus of footnotes, marginal glosses and notably, in the
fifth edition's incorporation of Wotton's annotations, a modest but contentious whiff of the practices of the variorum commentary. It is also a
defective text, like many classical works, with gaps in the manuscript
liberally indicated by asterisks, and an uncompleted ending, which goes
with the territory, except that its incompleteness is programmed in. It
is a conclusion not only in which nothing is concluded, but in which
Nothing is the conclusion, since that is what the author, having nothing more to say, is determined to write about. Moreover, one of its two
appendices, the 'Battel of the Books', is a mock edition that breaks off in
mid-manuscript, with several lines of asterisks followed by *Desunt cætera*
(the rest is missing), while the other appendix, the 'Discourse Concerning
the Mechanical Operation of the Spirit', is subtitled 'A Fragment', as well
as being, like the other parts, a mock edition typographically advertising
incompleteness with asterisks and a marginal gloss drawing attention to
the fact ('Mechanical Operation', *CWJS*, vol. I, p. 179).

I shall return to some implications of these points, but would like to
dwell a little longer on Swift's speaker's affirmation that this most relent-
less satirical performance is 'without one grain of Satyr intermixt', a particular matter of pride when satire is so easy and panegyric so hard, and
when 'the Satyrical Itch' is so prevalent in England, though 'first brought
among us from beyond the *Tweed*':

> For it is well known among *Mythologists*, that *Weeds* have the Preeminence
> over all other Vegetables; and therefore the first *Monarch* of this Island [i.e.
> James VI and I], whose Taste and Judgment was so acute and refined, did very
> wisely root out the *Roses* from the Collar of the *Order*, and plant the *Thistles* in
> their stead as the nobler Flower of the two. ('Preface', *CWJS*, vol. I, p. 30)

For those aware of the approximate distribution of Swiftian sympathies between the two sides of the Tweed, these words amount to a somewhat ambiguous panegyric on the satirical itch:

> For which Reason it is conjectured by profounder Antiquaries, that the Satyrical Itch, so prevalent in this part of our Island, was first brought among us from beyond the *Tweed.* Here may it long flourish and abound; May it survive and neglect the Scorn of the World, with as much Ease and Contempt as the World is insensible to the Lashes of it. May their own Dullness, or that of their Party, be no Discouragement for the Authors to proceed; but let them remember, it is with *Wits* as with *Razors,* which are never so apt to *cut* those they are employ'd on, as when they have *lost their Edge.* Besides, those whose Teeth are too rotten to bite, are best of all others, qualified to revenge that Defect with their Breath. ('Preface', *CWJS*, vol. I, p. 30)

'This little Panegyrick' is a defence of satire that is an attack on satire all the more stinging for its crescendo of contempt for the toothlessness of the satirist, and its consequent falling back on the halitosis, which, in its universality, is Swift's idea of the fragrance of the common Yahoo. Part of the point is that the popularity of satire over panegyric is an index of human malice, and another is that its powerlessness is due to the human imperviousness to correction, since 'there is not through all Nature, another so callous and insensible a Member as the *World's Posteriors,* whether you apply to it the *Toe* or the *Birch*' ('Preface', *CWJS*, vol. I, pp. 29–30). This did not impair Swift's enduring commitment to the primordial satiric exercise of 'bum-stripping'.[3] There follow refinements of this argument that switch from the world's posteriors to its shoulders, 'which are broad enough' to bear all attacks upon them, so long as the attacks don't mention anyone, especially anyone powerful, by name, which tap into a debate about personal satire and restrictive laws of defamation ('Preface', *CWJS*, vol. I, pp. 31–2).

The latter are outside my subject, except that they are a special pre-occupation of the 'Fragment' on Mechanical Operation, which the author requests the recipient to '*burn ... as soon as it comes to your Hands*' (i.e. apparently before even reading it) ('Mechanical Operation', *CWJS*, vol. I, p. 187). The very last mock-editorial 'hiatus' in the whole book occurs in the 'Fragment,' with a marginal note saying '*it was thought neither safe nor Convenient to Print it*', which, not for the first time, blows the mock-editorial pretence, deflecting the parody to more 'substantive' or non-parodic purposes, a common feature of all Swift's writings:

```
*   *   *   *   *   *   *   *   *   *   *
*   *   *   *   *   *   *       Here the whole Scheme
*   *   *   *   *   *   *    of spiritual Mechanism
*   *   *   *   *   *   *    was deduced and ex-
*   *   *   *   *   *   *    plained, with an Appear-
*   *   *   *   *   *   *    ance of great reading and
*   *   *   *   *   *   *    observation; but it was
*   *   *   *   *   *   *    thought neither safe nor
*   *   *   *   *   *   *    Convenient to Print it.
*   *   *   *   *   *   *   *   *   *   *
```

(*Tale*, 5th edn (1710), p. 325)[4]

It is remarkable that, although this mimicry of incompletely surviving texts closely parodies the treatment of ancient texts in learned editions, Swift shows little interest in maintaining a fiction of mock antiquity, inserting instead more immediate causes for the textual lacunae: inadvertence, laziness, incompetence or anxious considerations of security. The fragmentation is all new, not old, and is due not to the erosions of time but to the scattered discontinuity of modern thought processes. Swift appears to differ from his satirical predecessors, Rabelais and Cervantes, who both profess the antiquity and incompleteness of their sources.[5] Both ascribe this incompleteness to traditional antiquarian hazards, to time, rats, moths or the indecipherability of Arabic or Gothic script.[6] Neither Rabelais nor Cervantes seems much given to the typographic reproduction of his defective originals, with minimal exceptions that bear no resemblance to the Swiftian display of asterisks.[7]

One of Rabelais's commonest signals of life's incompleteness (like some of Swift's) are his satirical catalogues, discussed by Marcus Walsh in Chapter 5, designed to show interminability or inexhaustibility (expansive in Rabelais, morally imprisoning in Swift), and thus necessarily implying an unfinished state. They are often, in Rabelais, typographically circumscribed, by being tabulated in columns, which set the material apart from the headlong flow of the prose and give a counteracting sense of monumental containment.[8] Swift's catalogues are more often than not embedded in the headlong copiousness of the narrative itself. His constrictions are those of an arresting incongruity, not those of a tabulated display, however overflowing with abundance. A typical list in the *Tale* or *Gulliver's Travels*, though shorter than Rabelais's, has its own way of signalling an inexhaustibility of folly or vice:

> I am not in the least provoked at the Sight of a Lawyer, a Pick-pocket,
> a Colonel, a Fool, a Lord, a Gamester, a Politician, a Whoremunger, a
> Physician, an Evidence, a Suborner, an Attorney, a Traytor, or the like.[9]

If that closing 'or the like' points to an unending series, the relative brev-
ity of the list, the opening sarcasm and the shock-collocations, 'a Lawyer,
a Pick-pocket, a Colonel, a Fool … a Politician, a Whoremunger', create
a freezing irony of alienation that gives substance to Coleridge's famous
description of Swift as the soul of Rabelais living in a dry place. Rabelais,
echoing a saying attributed to Augustine, said, in a copious riff on booz-
ing, that souls cannot live in a dry place.[10]

Swift's mock-editorial practice similarly differs from Rabelais's in
being more astringent and more sharply focused. The relative geniality
of Rabelais's recension of old moth-eaten records gives way to something
more modern, and also, in the modern way, more random: subject not
to time but to whim, affectation and vulnerability to censorship. The
mock-editorial pretence, near the end of the 'Mechanical Operation', the
last of the *Tale*'s asterisked lacunae, that the gaps are the result of acciden-
tal loss had already been dispelled in the *Tale*'s very first 'editorial' footnote
on a '*Hiatus in MS*' ('Introduction', *CWJS*, vol. I, p. 40 n.), as we shall see,
so that the parody is both enacted and, in a rather pointed manner, sub-
verted, in both the earliest and the final example of this typographically
most conspicuous parodic feature in the book.

The defence of satire that is an attack on satire, in what is in fact one
of the most satirical discourses ever written, is, and signposts itself as, a
gigantic ego-trip. The speaker will tell you simperingly that 'I am not like
other Men, to envy or undervalue the Talents I cannot reach' ('Preface',
CWJS, vol. I, p. 30), and that he has 'neither a Talent nor an Inclination
for Satyr', being 'so entirely satisfied with the whole present Procedure
of human Things, that I have been for some Years preparing Materials
towards *A Panegyrick upon the World*' ('Preface', *CWJS*, vol. I, p. 32). The
complacent inanity of the speaker comes through as a withering expression of authorial contempt, but the insistent disclaimers of satirical talent
or intent are a nudge and a wink, a mimicry of simpering confessional
ingenuousness that is also a primary exhibition of self. Arguably, the daz-
zling display of metaphoric argumentation in the 'Preface', and indeed
throughout the *Tale* as a whole, that 'copiousness of images', remarked on
even by the unsympathetic Samuel Johnson,[11] gives way at such points to
a look-no-hands knowingness, elbowing the reader into a complicit sense
that a satirical maestro is in on the act of denying the satire.

This is an unusual complicity in Swift. As Leavis and others perceived long ago, Swift's treatment of readers does not, like Pope's or Fielding's or Gibbon's, invite solidarity, but tends to generate a downbeat readerly discomfort. If there is an element of intimacy, it is that of a personal quarrel. The parade of satirical bravura turned some years later into the blend of earnestness, devilry and desperation with which Swift found himself affirming in the Apology of 1710 that '*there generally runs an Irony through the Thread of the whole Book*' ('Apology', *CWJS*, vol. I, p. 8). But the teller of the *Tale* itself is a fool with whose companionability and geniality Tristram Shandy was happy to declare himself willing to 'swim down the gutter of Time', and which we may be disposed to describe as proleptically Shandean, or mock-Shandean, a parody of something that did not yet exist.[12]

The truism, or so I have long considered it, that *A Tale of a Tub* is an advance parody of *Tristram Shandy*, has much to do with its character as a mock edition, and in turn with the mock edition's status as a precursor of, or model for, romantic, modern and postmodern forms of non-satiric expression, in fiction and poetry, from Sterne, Mackenzie and Byron, to Eliot's *Waste Land* or the writings of Nabokov, Vonnegut or Mailer. With the latter, Swift's tale-teller shares an interest in advertising as a mode of book production and confessional self-promotion. This often takes the form of parody, including visual and typographical parody, as an instrument of self-display. The close of the *Tale*'s 'Preface', almost as much as the ending of the whole *Tale*, expresses this.

> I have been for some Years preparing Materials towards *A Panegyrick upon the World*; to which I intended to add a Second Part, entituled, *A Modest Defence of the Proceedings of the Rabble in all Ages*. Both these I had Thoughts to publish by way of Appendix to the following Treatise; but finding my Common-Place-Book fill much slower than I had reason to expect, I have chosen to defer them to another Occasion. Besides, I have been unhappily prevented in that Design, by a certain Domestick Misfortune, in the Particulars whereof, tho' it would be very seasonable, and much in the *Modern* way, to inform the *gentle Reader*, and would also be of great Assistance towards extending this Preface into the Size now in Vogue, which by Rule ought to be *large* in proportion as the subsequent Volume is *small*; Yet I shall now dismiss our impatient Reader from any farther Attendance at the *Porch*; and having duly prepared his Mind by a preliminary Discourse, shall gladly introduce him to the sublime Mysteries that ensue. ('Preface', *CWJS*, vol. I, pp. 32–3)

The *Panegyrick upon the World* and the *Modest Defence of the Rabble* join the ranks of several other advertisements of works never to be completed

listed in the front matter as mock publisher's publicity, yearningly com-
plemented by the idea of two unenclosed Appendices to the present volume, additional to the two uncompleted 'appendices' actually included,
and which would have further contributed to an excess of front and back
matter as a proportion of the whole. (One of these non-writings uses a
titular formula Swift himself adopted, for example, in *A Modest Proposal*.)
The erection of advertising copy into the fabric of the substantive book
becomes, as we shall see, the expressed material of Norman Mailer's entire
volume, *Advertisements for Myself*, in which a possible awareness of predecessors, parody, self-parody and parody of self-parody, compete with
(or actually constitute) a primary self-display. The self-advertisements in
the *Tale* occur at the end of a 'Preface' which precedes the 'Introduction',
but which also follows the list of 'Treatises wrote by the same Author',
'An Apology *For the*, &c.' (including its indelicate innuendo, and possibly parodying Roger L'Estrange's *Brief History of the Times, &c.*, 1687),
a Dedication to Lord Somers, 'The Bookseller to the Reader' and the
'Epistle Dedicatory, to his Royal Highness Prince Posterity', the latter an
allusion to a Preface (actually two) addressed 'To Posterity' by L'Estrange,
of whom more later.[13]

This inflated copiousness of front matter is a parody of habits of
book publication, one of whose illustrious examples was Tonson's edition
of Dryden's Virgil, which appeared in 1697, while Swift was composing the
Tale.[14] It is in the *Tale* and the 'Battel of the Books' that Swift's hostility to
Dryden is made public, whether or not in reprisal to Dryden's saying, if he
did say, to his 'cousin Swift', that he would never be a poet. (How wrong,
if he said it.) Of more immediate interest is the connection established
in the 'Preface' between the failure to publish the two Appendices and 'a
certain Domestick Misfortune' that prevented that design. Dryden again
seems part of the sting, since there is a footnote in the 'Introduction' a few
pages later, annotating one of the teller's flights of whining autobiography,
that '*Here the Author seems to personate* L'estrange, Dryden, *and some others,
who after having past their Lives in Vices, Faction and Falshood, have the
Impudence to talk of Merit and Innocence and Sufferings*' ('Introduction',
CWJS, vol. I, p. 44 n.)

But in the 'Preface', when the teller mentions the domestic misfortune that curtailed his two texts, he declines (for once) to go into 'the
Particulars whereof, tho' it would be very seasonable, and much in the
Modern way, to inform the *gentle Reader*' (as well as being of great assistance for the aforementioned purpose of enlarging the volume's volume, a

self-validating feature of the book-production process). Dryden is doubt-less specifically included in 'the *Modern* way,' but Swift's mockery is more typically reserved for Dryden's confessional garrulity. I am not sure, in any case, that there are many examples of Dryden withholding an item of autobiographical information he has dangled before us, or flaunting his refusal to disclose it. This is Shandean territory, material Sterne handled in full knowledge of Swift's satire, but of which Swift can only have been aware partly and intuitively as he relentlessly ridiculed it in advance.[15]

Dryden's occasional complaints about his reduced circumstances, and his penchant for offering leisurely information about his state of mind and body at the time of writing, are an express theme of the *Tale*'s 'Preface'. It tells us 'that the shrewdest Pieces of this Treatise, were conceived in Bed, in a Garret: At other times (for a Reason best known to my self) I thought fit to sharpen my Invention with Hunger; and in general, the whole Work was begun, continued, and ended, under a long Course of Physick, and a great want of Money' ('Preface', *CWJS*, vol. I, p. 27). Readers will find in Dryden the want of money, though not the embellishments of that (in those days) low place of poets, the garret, and not, once again, the 'will tell/won't tell' tease of the 'Reason best known to my self', which is short-cut Shandean, a trick practised by Swift himself in the privacy of his correspondence with Esther Johnson and Rebecca Dingley, and an index, incidentally, of Swift's closeness to the things he derides.[16]

The reasons Swift does give for revealing this information are not Dryden's. The claim is that the information is necessary 'to assist the dili-gent Reader' in the 'delicate ... Affair' of reading his treatise, on grounds that don't seem to have had much prominence in Dryden's purposes:

> being extreamly sollicitous, that every accomplished Person who has got into the Taste of Wit, calculated for this present Month of *August*, 1697, should descend to the very *bottom* of all the *Sublime* throughout this Treatise; I hold fit to lay down this general Maxim. Whatever Reader desires to have a thorow Comprehension of an Author's Thoughts, cannot take a better Method, than by putting himself into the Circumstances and Postures of Life, that the Writer was in, upon every important Passage as it flow'd from his Pen; For this will introduce a Parity and strict Correspondence of Idea's between the Reader and the Author. ('Preface', *CWJS*, vol. I, p. 27)

This passage anticipates Sterne more than it accounts for Dryden. But it's obviously no coincidence that August 1697, while this was being written, is the month of publication of Dryden's Virgil, jeeringly described a few pages earlier, in the dedication to 'Prince Posterity', and with a precise focus on the format of book production, as 'lately printed in a large Folio, well bound', though it is the subject of a rumoured mystification as to whether 'a certain Poet called *John Dryden*' really exists ('Epistle Dedicatory', *CWJS*, vol. I, p. 23).[17] This may seem a ghoulish prefiguration, in its way, of the theme of the disappeared author, but the suspected non-existence of Dryden (as of other moderns, Tate, Durfey, Rymer, Dennis, Bentley, Wotton) plays on massive solidities of size ('large Folio ... Rheams ... near a thousand Pages of immense Erudition ... good sizeable Volume') combined both with nullity of content and the fact that these books can't be found because no one wants to read them ('Epistle Dedicatory', *CWJS*, vol. I, p. 23). Hence 'such a Secret' about their existence in the world, a tangible reprise of the themes of simultaneously excessive and absent matter implicit in the fragment format, and mirroring the parallel play of garrulity and evasion in the display of confessional mock mystification. The paragraph containing this joke begins with the affirmation 'that what I am going to say is literally true this Minute I am writing' ('Epistle Dedicatory', *CWJS*, vol. I, p. 23), which stakes out, in a declaratory or programmatic form, what Swift clearly regards as the intrusively inappropriate precision of '*this present Month* [my emphasis] of *August*, 1697' ('Preface', *CWJS*, vol. I, p. 27).

Dryden didn't quite talk like *that*, though it might be thought fair comment in a parody of his real garrulousness. But Swift is articulating a value later writers would consider a very high one, catching 'the Manners living as they rise', spoken by Swift's friend Pope, and capable of translation into a credo of the Romantic lyric.[18] To this was to be added what Richardson was to call writing 'to the *Moment*', an ambition with an extensive novelistic progeny, whose desired effects of immediacy or fictional illusion would be deeply unsympathetic to Swift outside the sphere of the parody or hoax, though within that sphere, witness his Partridge and Ebenezor Elliston pamphlets, he was a willing and accomplished performer. The self-congratulating excesses of trivial ephemerality Swift derides as being specifically 'in the *Modern* way' had yet to be transfigured into Romantic and modernist triumphs of epiphany, 'the very *bottom* of all the *Sublime*' ('Preface', *CWJS*, vol. I, p. 27), turning, in the Keatsian phrase that would have earned a not wholly uncomplicit Swiftian sneer, into 'the wordsworthian or egotistical sublime'.[19] By the same token, Swift's spider, with his dirt spun out of his own entrails, concluding at last in a cobweb, takes very little to convert into Keats's elated image of the 'beautiful circuiting' produced by the spider, spinning 'from his own inwards his own airy Citadel', not without passing once more through Pope's celebration of 'The spider's touch, how exquisitely fine!'[20]

Even in Swift's own satire, the image of the spider is capable of accesses of counterintuitive delight, in the manner of the *Dunciad*'s 'fragrant chaplets' blowing in 'cold December',[21] as when a Professor in the Academy of Lagado comes up with a scheme for manufacturing silk without silk worms:

> he proposed farther, that by employing Spiders, the Charge of dying Silks would be wholly saved; whereof I was fully convinced when he shewed me a vast Number of Flies most beautifully coloured, wherewith he fed his Spiders; assuring us, that the Webs would take a Tincture from them; and as he had them of all Hues, he hoped to fit every Body's Fancy, as soon as he could find proper Food for the Flies, of certain Gums, Oyls, and other glutinous Matter, to give a Strength and Consistence to the Threads. (*Gulliver's Travels*, III. v, Davis, *PW*, vol. XI, p. 181)

The signs are that these attractions will come to nothing, but their effect includes intimations not unassimilable to Keats's beautiful circuiting, not wholly swamped in the ugly solidities of 'glutinous Matter'. There was no work available to Swift that contains all the features the *Tale* identifies as types of modernity, but it seems clear that he apprehended, from the wordy excesses of 'L'estrange, Dryden, *and some others*', a future, in all its considerable strengths as well as weaknesses, which he was not going to like, but to whose appeal he was not altogether unresponsive. The *Tale* appropriated many of its forms in advance, and future writers, from Sterne to Beckett and Nabokov and Mailer, went on to appropriate the *Tale*, outfacing the parody, or harnessing it to their own more or less underisive purposes.

Here it seems appropriate to suggest an adjustment to Kenner's account of the *Tale*'s parody of bookmaking procedures as an attack on the impersonality of print: on the way type makes texts, and individual words, and their physical formatting through typographical means (size of font, capitals, italics, etc.), turn the work into a mechanical product, anonymous, divorced from the intimacies of a speaking voice presupposed in earlier forms of writing. The observations of Hugh Kenner and Denis Donoghue about the *Tale*'s character as a playful exploitation of print culture and 'a parody of the book as a book', are still of interest after half a century of print-culture babble, as well as bemused attempts at rebuttal from soi-disant historical scholarship.[22] A contrary emphasis recently proposed by Harold Love, in a study of a principal named target of Swift's *Tale*, Sir Roger L'Estrange, is that the resources of typography provided opportunities for an aggressive reaffirmation of vocality in print, 'a form of typographic shouting, a furious bid for attention'.[23] Love compellingly demonstrates that L'Estrange's practice, in his *Observator* (1681–7), exploits capitalization, italics, parentheses and black letter as an insistent declaration of personal, and indeed 'vocal', 'presence'.

Swift and Pope used black letter to deride antiquarian ('medieval') barbarism or legal pedantry. L'Estrange used it for emphasis, with black-letter capitals 'for maximum impact'.[24] The idiom is forthright, slangy and pushy, with uppishness mingling with street language. Far from being a denial of oral immediacy, it aspired to it; it used typography and 'font variation to suggest vocal emphasis' and as a 'repertoire of intonational cues', which 'might almost be seen as a primitive, graphic form of sound recording'.[25] Instead of reflecting the impersonality of print, an absence of personal voice, the impact is 'of an exhilarated but somehow also affronting' presence.[26] It is surely this sleeve-grabbing assertiveness that Swift is impersonating in the *Tale*, much as, in the 'Fragment' on the mechanical operation of the spirit, he exposed not a coldness or hypocrisy of Dissenters but the hideous sincerity of their spiritual and erotic excesses.

In Swift's *Tale* the resources of the mock edition (lacunae, footnotes, marginal scholia) combine with the more journalistic self-exhibition of L'Estrange's *Observator*. The 'Battel of the Books' is in a specific formal sense both an edition of an epic fragment and a newspaper account of a 'Battel Fought last Friday'. Parody of L'Estrange the typographical show-off, or Dryden the toadying and confessional multiplier of dedications and prefaces, also becomes for Swift a primary form of exuberant self-affirmation, in keeping with the declaration that there is not a grain of satire in the whole work, or the use of Wotton's hostile *Observations* as explanatory glosses for Swift's own text, and as the spotlit single source of what otherwise has the appearance of a variorum commentary. In jeering at self-affirmation, Swift gives it surplus value by trumping it, as Sterne was to trump Swift by unparodying or outparodying him.

The role played by typography, as well as by mock scholarship, as a mode of egocentric showing off is clear in Sterne, down to paraded awareness of Swift's prior mockery. If the *Tale*'s parody of L'Estrange's typographic ego trips becomes a second-time-round ego-trip, *Tristram Shandy* offers a third-time-round version, to end all ego-trips, or to begin an infinite series of new ones, of which the formally 'unfinished' character of the book, like that of Swift's *Tale*, is itself an integral sign. Sterne uses L'Estrange's typographical devices and more (wherever he gets them from):[27] all the routines of large-scale italicization, capitalization, interruption by parentheses, dashes and asterisks, blank (VI. xxxviii; vol. II, p. 567), black (I. xii; vol. I, p. 37–8), and marbled pages (III. xxxvi; vol. I, p. 269–70), boxed text (I. xii; vol. I, p. 35), pointing fingers (IV. xxvi; vol. I, p. 376), bold type and crossings out (VI. xi; vol. II, p. 516). Black letter, not used in the *Tale*, comes up not only as a mock-legal routine (as in Tristram's parents' marriage settlement, I. xv; vol. I, pp. 42–5),[28] but also (as in L'Estrange) for emphasis, especially in the heading for the two chapters of volume IX, which first appear in their own place as blank pages (vol. II, pp. 770–1), and are then relocated after chapter xxv, headed 'The Eighteenth Chapter' (vol. II, p. 786) and 'The Nineteenth Chapter' (vol. II, p. 789) prominently spelt out in black letter, unlike other chapters, which appear under roman numerals, thus adding further ostentation to their deliberate misplacing. (There is a smaller use of black letter for emphasis in two words in the Sermon in volume II, chapter xvii; vol. I, p. 151.)

The Shandean form of this appropriation is the most immediate and self-aware. The *Tale* is named as a model. The delay of 'The Author's Preface' until the twentieth chapter of volume III, and a commensurate postponement of the hero's birth, include a mimicry of the *Tale*'s surfeit of front matter, as well as a broader parody of narrative and discursive digressiveness and delaying tactics. The 'chapter upon chapters' in *Tristram Shandy* (IV. ix–x), and Tristram's eulogy of digression (I. xxii) look back to the *Tale*'s 'Digression in Praise of Digressions', as the latter looks back to L'Estrange's 'Preface … upon a Preface'. The first of two dedications 'To Posterity' in L'Estrange's *Brief History of the Times, &c.* (see note 13 above) opens by remarking how 'Fantastical' it is to have 'A Preface, *Methinks*, upon *a* Preface … '*tis such a kind of* Comment upon *a* Comment … ' (p. 1), the immediate allusion being to the *Brief History*'s subtitle, which is *A Preface to the Third Volume of Observators*. The liberal use throughout of black letter and other typographical horseplay combines with the self-conscious waggery, taken up and parodied by Swift, and then put through the Shandean process, with intervening coils of irony in all three authors contributing in themselves to the inward-looking jokerie that came to be called Romantic irony. Above all, the Shandean indulgence of typographical and bookmaking routines, the marbled and blank pages and the rest, largely unpurposeful in narrative terms, help us to see the mock-editorial and bookmaking parody of the *Tale* as a buttonholing excess even as it presents the routines it derides as buttonholing excesses. That Sterne went on to unparody the parody, offering in effect an additional layer of parody, would also have earned a Swiftian sneer, as another escalation of self-intoxicated complacency.

What Swift identified from the start as a pernicious feature equal to, and variously related to, the excesses of ephemerality and the dangers of the fictional hoax, was a species of readerly intimacy Swift would only admit in a mode of antagonism, but which Sterne embraced in the full literal sense Swift was emphatic about not intending. That 'Parity and strict Correspondence of Idea's between the Reader and the Author' at which the *Tale*'s 'Preface' jeers, and which is intermittently sustained all the way through to the idiot genialities of the teller's farewell in 'The Conclusion', is adopted by Tristram from the very beginning with puppyish, not to say dogged, fervour:

> As you proceed further with me, the slight acquaintance which is now beginning betwixt us, will grow into familiarity; and that, unless one of us is in fault, will terminate in friendship. – *O diem præclarum!* – then nothing which has touched me will be thought trifling in its nature, or tedious in its telling … let me go on, and tell my story my own way: – or if I should seem now and then to trifle upon the road, – or should sometimes put on a fool's cap with a bell to it, for a moment or two as we pass along, -- don't fly off, – … and as we jogg on, either laugh with me, or at me, or in short, do any thing, – only keep your temper. (*TS*, I. vi; vol. I, p. 9–10)

These genialities are unSwiftian, but even more unSwiftian is the unguardedness of direct address, 'don't fly off', 'keep your temper', the idea of the author (not just a derided mock author) wearing a fool's cap, and the invitation to be laughed with, let alone at.

Swift would allow his speaker to wear a fool's cap, but he would not share it, any more than we can imagine Pope doing so. It has been suggested that Pope placed one, in the form of a twisted birthday ode, at the top of Cibber's altar in the *Dunciad, in Four Books*. If so, he enlarged it to the size of a spire: 'A twisted Birth-day Ode completes the spire.'[29] Such aggrandizement resembles the treatment Swift gives to Dryden in the 'Battel of the Books', rattling in a helmet many times too large for his head and playing at being the Mr Virgil of his day ('Battel', *CWJS*, vol. I, p. 158). But this aggrandizement is programmed for simultaneous deflation, whereas Cibber's fool's cap has a grotesque monumentality, which is Pope's way of signalling enormities of inane stupor. This inverted grand style is what Swift shrank from, as he declined all lofty styles, inverted or other, and the reason he gave for declining it is the same reason for which he made sure, as did Pope in his different way, that the fool's cap worn by his narrator would not be seen on himself: the perennial anxiety about making 'a Figure scurvy'.[30]

I turn now to some mock-editorial routines in Swift, Fielding and Sterne, before moving to a few more modern examples. First a passage from the *Tale*'s 'Introduction':

THE *Ladder* is an adequate Symbol of
Faction and of *Poetry*, to both of which
so noble a Number of Authors are indebted for their Fame. * Of *Faction*, because   *   *   *   *   *   *   *
                  *   *   *   *   *   *   *
Hiatus in   *   *   *   *   *   *   *   *
MS.   *   *   *   *   *   *   *
     *   *   *   *

    * *Here is pretended a Defect in the Manuscript, and
this is very frequent with our Author, either
when he thinks he cannot say any thing worth
Reading, or when he has no mind to enter on the
Subject, or when it is a Matter of little Moment,
or perhaps to amuse his Reader (whereof he is frequently very fond) or lastly, with some Satyrical
Intention.*
(Tale, 5th edn (1710), p. 42)[31]

It is characteristic of Swift that, in the *Tale*'s very first '*Hiatus in MS.*', he
breaks the parodic illusion, giving us a note that sees through his author
even as the editorial pretence is ostensibly in complicity, an interesting
example of the difference between Swiftian parody and the genuine impersonation he would always be reluctant to indulge. This captures all the
overtones of derisive mimicry, including the fiction-breaking disclosure of
'*some Satyrical Intention*', in which the main narrator, his mock annotator
and the authorial satirist merge into one another in a hostile or alienating
prefiguration of Shandean 'intimacy'.

    Now consider this passage from the 'Digression on Madness':

* THERE is in Mankind a certain * *
     *   *   *   *   *   *   *   *   *   *
                  *   *   *   *   *   *   *   *
Hic multa   *   *   *   *   *   *   *   *
desiderantur   *   *   *   *   *   *   *
     *   *   *   *   *   *   *   *   *
     *   *   * And this I take to be a clear
Solution of the Matter.

    * *Here is another Defect in the Manuscript,
but I think the Author did wisely, and that the
Matter which thus strained his Faculties, was not
worth a Solution; and it were well if all Meta-
physical Cobweb Problems were no otherwise answered.*
(Tale, 5th edn (1710), p. 184)[32]

Consider Swift's 'parody' of the layout of an edition of a defective classical text, with asterisks and a sidenote signalling the gap, and a footnote glossing the '*Defect in the Manuscript*'. The gloss is not innocent, of course, but it is not even mock-innocent. Unlike the jokes in the 'Mechanical Operation', which suggest the political and legal dangers the lacunae are designed to avert, there is here a rudimentary display of fictional personality. The speaker's lazy-minded imperiousness, mingled with a sort of low cunning, are on display. This does not go very far, as a novelistic creation, but its very limitation as a novelistic effect is part of its specific satirical signature. Both notes suggest that the argument was not only not worth going into, but placed a strain on the faculties of the supposed author, so that the gap becomes a lazy halfwit's cop-out, a suggestion borne out by the bossy dismissiveness of 'And this I take to be a clear Solution of the Matter', coming after several lines of typographical void. Not far behind it is a passable mimicry of a satirist's own dismissive schoolmasterly hauteur.

Fielding turned this trick on its head in the dialogue between Jonathan Wild and the Ordinary of Newgate before Wild's execution:

> *Jonathan*
> AY, who indeed! I assure you, *Doctor*, I
> had much rather be happy than miserable.
> But† * * * * * * * * * * * * * * *
> * * * * * * * * * * * * * * * * *
> * * * *
>
> *Ordinary*
> N OT H I N G can be plainer.   St. * * *
> * * * * * * * * * * * * * * * * *
> * * * * * * * * * * * * * * * *
> * * * * * * * * * * * * * * * * *
> * * * * * * * * * * * * * * * * *
> * * * * * * * * * * * * * * * * *
> * * * * * * * * * * * * * * * * *
> * * * * * * * * * * * * * * * * *
> * * * * * * * * * * * * * * * * *
> * * * * * * * * * * * * * * * * *
> * * * * * * * * * * * * * * * * *
> * * * * * * * * * * * * * * * * *
> * * * * * * * * * * * * * * * * *
> * * * * * * * * * * * * * * * * *
> * * * * * * * * * * * * * * * * *
> * * * * * * * * * * * * * * * * *

* * * * * * * * * * * * * * * *
* * * *

† This Part was so blotted that it was illegible.[33]

The Ordinary (or chaplain) opens rather than closes a speech with the words 'Nothing can be plainer', invoking the authority of an undisclosed saint followed by an even longer stream of asterisks than Swift's. Preceding the Ordinary's cascade of asterisks is a shorter speech by Wild, also broken off, with a footnote explaining: 'This Part was so blotted that it was illegible.' The note appears at first sight to be pointing, as in the *Tale*, to a defective text, here, as it might be, of an old play. We know by now, however, that this vernacular counterpart to Swift's '*Hic multa desiderantur*' also resembles, with minor variations, the instantaneous or 'to the *Moment*' reporting of the *Tale*'s speaker. The material, as we are told at the end of the previous chapter, consists of Wild's own notes on the conversation, 'committed to Paper the Moment after it had past',[34] tempting us to suppose they may have been written in a drunken stupor, fraught with anxieties of damnation and perhaps a stream of abuse. The lacunae in this particular manuscript are the product of incoherence, doubtless compounded by liquor stains and the imperfect conditions of archival conservation at Newgate.

As in the *Tale*, the omitted material spares the reader some pretentious pedantry evidently spiced with the Ordinary's pious drivel and some streams of profanity from Wild himself. The mock-editorial gesturing lacks the compositional, as well as compositorial, finesse of Swift's *Tale*, offering crude sequences of broken words and syntax:

> *Ordinary*
> * are * Atheist. * * Deist * * * Ari
> * * * cinian * * * hanged * * burnt
> * roiled * oasted. * * * * * * * *
> Dev * * his An * * * * ell Fire * *
> ternal Da * * * tion.[35]

Against the elegant and telling economy of Swift's asterisks we are offered lurid snatches of the parson's hell-fire sensationalism and his addled theological bigotry. The resources of the mock edition, not for the first or last time, are exploited for rudimentary effects of fictional realism, whose more exalted versions include the rather less fragmented jottings of Clarissa five years later. The truncated phrases point in a crude way to a special form of free indirect style, found in perfection in Jane Austen, in which we are given the sense not of an extended thought process, but a zoning in and out of a clutch of salient or obsessive phrases. We see it in Mr Deasy's cliché-ridden letter to the paper in Joyce's *Ulysses*, something different from what we think of as the stream of consciousness.[36] It is satirically selected, but operates in an area where satire and the flow of a lived reality oscillate on the edge of each other, as in this passage from *Emma*:

> The best fruit in England – every body's favourite – always wholesome. – These the finest beds and finest sorts. – Delightful to gather for one's self – the only way of really enjoying them. – Morning decidedly the best time – never tired – every sort good – hautboy infinitely superior – no comparison – the others hardly eatable – hautboys very scarce – Chili pre-ferred – white wood finest flavour of all – price of strawberries in London – abundance about Bristol – Maple Grove – cultivation – beds when to be renewed – gardeners thinking exactly different – no general rule – garden-ers never to be put out of their way – delicious fruit – only too rich to be eaten much of – inferior to cherries – currants more refreshing – only objection to gathering strawberries the stooping – glaring sun – tired to death – could bear it no longer – must go and sit in the shade.[37]

The parson's scrappy utterances have none of the sharply observed vitality of Austen's account, just as Fielding's asterisks have little of the typograph-ical finesse of Swift's *Tale*.[38]

It was not by way of *Jonathan Wild* that Austen learned from Fielding her use of free indirect speech, but it is interesting to see Wild's broken phrases in the context of fictional practices that took their cue from the satiric conventions of the mock edition.[39] Without entering very search-ingly into the variously interesting question of *Jonathan Wild*'s place in the history of the novel, we may observe that Jonathan's conversation with the Ordinary moves quickly from its Swiftian mode of typographical parody to a manner more obviously characteristic of Fielding's other novels, in particular into a slightly less genial version of the (probably more or less contemporary) exchange between Joseph Andrews and Parson Barnabas, in which a lax bibulous clergyman is similarly warning the sinner of the perils of damnation, while being in a hurry to get back to his bowl of punch.[40] The Ordinary's sermon breaks off when the punch is brought in: 'But here, the Punch by entring put a Stop to his Reading at this time: Nor could we obtain of Mr. *Wild* any further Account of the Conversation which past at this Interview.'[41]

As the scene dissolves, with the arrival of the punch, Wild's state seems to pass from alcoholic befuddlement to complete coma, thereby curtailing the record we have been reading. The dialogue had given way, sometime earlier, to uninterrupted sermonizing, and an unguarded reading of the first edition might lead us to suppose that Wild had already fallen asleep, as people do in sermons, in a classic scenario of satire registered in *A Tale of a Tub*, section VI (*CWJS*, vol. I, p. 93). It was a behaviour that exercised Swift enough to provoke a sermon 'Upon Sleeping in Church' (Davis, *PW*, vol. IX, pp. 210–18). Since Wild's fragmentary notes are said to be the source of the report, quite how the text of the sermon had survived until that point is left unclear (a narrative slippage to which the pseudo-realistic fragment is predisposed, since it has to negotiate the survival of some of the pretended missing matter, while sustaining an awareness that the source is incomplete).

In the revised edition of 1754, however, an interesting adjustment is made. The text is changed to inform us expressly that Wild had indeed been asleep, but that he was now awakened rather than sedated by the arrival of the punch. In this version, the report that he had been asleep seems intended to highlight the presumably boisterous fact of his waking up. The focus thus switches, in the revised edition, from an atmosphere of comatose torpor and parsonical bibulousness to an animated and turbulent awakening. 'But here, the Punch by entring waked Mr. *Wild*, who was fast asleep, and put an End to the Sermon; Nor could we obtain any further Account of the Conversation which passed at this Interview.'[42] The closing phrases are almost identical in both editions except that after 'Nor could we obtain' the first edition's 'of Mr. *Wild*' (which seemed to suggest that he was now in the stupors of drunken sleep) is dropped, and the failure to 'obtain any further Account' becomes general, in the quite different confusion of a drunken commotion. It is now Wild's awakening that actually prevents the narrative from continuing, because the person writing it down (who in the new edition is no longer Wild) could not continue in the brouhaha.

This fact takes us back to an earlier change between the versions of 1743 and 1754, which may be thought of interest in that it perhaps pulls the text away from a non-realistic direction to which a knowing reader might have been attuned. At the end of the preceding chapter, the fragmented text, which in 1743 was said to have been 'committed to Paper [by Mr. *Wild*] the Moment after it had past' is said instead, in 1754, to have been 'taken down in Short-hand by one who overheard it'.[43] If Wild is now removed as the author of the notes, his state of waking or sleeping would not in itself be relevant to the completion of the report. If you consider these as alternative fictions accounting for gaps in the manuscript, there might seem little to choose between them. The only obvious reason for making the one change, in which the surrounding text is left undisturbed, is the other change, for which there is no obvious reason, except perhaps to correct an unimportant and barely noticeable slippage.

Or is there? 'The Moment after it had past' in the first version suggested an immediacy that Fielding, as a recent reader of *Pamela*, who had made his Shamela boast that she writes in the present tense, might have wished to deride sometime before 1743, and which Fielding might possibly have been disposed to celebrate as an admiring reader of *Clarissa* in the late 1740s. The initial jeering at writerly immediacy is too slight to have come fraught with pointed Richardsonian baggage, and I have no reason to think that it did. But why, then, make a business of changing the words in spring 1754 when the revised edition appeared? Not, evidently, because of any intervening admiration for *Clarissa*. Fielding had, by 1754, fallen out of love with that novel, whose author he accused, very likely at about the same time, of trying to reform 'a whole people, by making use of a vehicular story, to wheel in among them worse manners than their own'.[44] Could it be that the very recent publication of *Sir Charles Grandison*, which began to appear in London in November 1753, with its prefatory boast of a narrative written 'to the *Moment*', made the phrase stick in Fielding's throat as he was revising a text of his own that might be thought to risk a whiff of Richardsonian smugness, in a zone of fictional creation about which Fielding himself was not much more comfortable than Swift.[45] Could it be that in making this small change, Fielding was ensuring that he could not be seen to be making Richardsonian claims he had once mocked and later praised?

The unsurprising swerve away from Grandisonian contamination, if that is what it was, occurs in what is after all the frame narrative for the mock-editorial chapter of Book IV. I have suggested that the parallels with hiatus-filled pages of a *Tale of a Tub* are close enough to imply some degree of conscious allusion, down to the mock bossiness for which asterisks act as a kind of lazy or complacent cover: 'this I take to be a clear Solution', 'Nothing can be plainer.' Fielding is keen to give the mock-editorial horseplay plenty of visibility through a liberal display of asterisks. But they are splashed across the page in broad strokes, and Fielding's interest in the mock edition is perfunctory. He displays none of the *Tale*'s attention to typography, little annotation, no marginal scholia or other signs of witty interest in the bookmaking process. In this sense, the variously deplorable Penguin edition manages to be not entirely misleading when it misrepresents the original (in this case *1754*) by reducing the visual presence of gaps to approximately 10 per cent and replacing several hundred asterisks with a few dozen dots.[46]

This chapter of *Jonathan Wild* is of interest in the present context because it brings in the resources of the mock edition as a momentary flourish in what is essentially a quasi-novelistic patchwork. *Jonathan Wild* is only intermittently a mock edition, though it is a mock version of a criminal biography, which is itself a kind of belowstairs version of a mainstream genre. If the traditions of learned wit passed through Fielding on their way to Sterne, it was not mainly by way of *Jonathan Wild*, but the incidental presence of the mock edition as a set piece in that work is itself an index of the extent to which the genre had penetrated into the history of fictional forms even before *Tristram Shandy*.

Sterne's asterisks often resemble Swift's in page layout, and are consistent with his project to outparody, or unparody, Swift's *Tale*. In one sense, they are an affirmation or validation of the fragment as a mode of expression in its own right, rather than a negation of classical completeness, which reflected moral and cultural disorder. Madeleine Descargues-Grant sees Pope's *Dunciad*, and its treatment of the fragmented, the broken, the unfinished, the ugly, as the negative inverse of the Shandean celebration.[47] If this is true of Pope's containment of these forces in the virtuoso orchestration of his couplets, it applies a fortiori to the *Tale*, which enacts a stylistic surrender to tumbling chaotic prose and the visible typographical display of lacunae, while participating in the game in a negative way.

Fragments of incoherent text are often assimilated, in the *Dunciad* and elsewhere, to solidities of broken or misshapen objects, scraps of food, cloacal scraps of rejected print, embryos and ruins, in that realm of Nonsense 'Where things destroy'd are swept to things unborn' (book 1, line 242 (cf. book 4, line 230), pp. 130, 305). All are antitheses of the classically complete, though a physical ruin, as well as a textual one, may acquire grandeur from the monument it evokes. Johnson was reminded of this potential when, in his *Life of Edmund Smith*, he expressed admiration for Smith's unfinished poetical drafts, while, as Elizabeth Harries points out, deciding to omit them from his edition of the poet.[48] There is a sense of how imposing a fragment can be (mostly in the singular, and in the form of a natural object or ruin) throughout Pope's translations of Homer, an expression, perhaps, of the growing taste for ruins that seems to have developed *pari passu* with the increasing value accorded to uncompleted texts, which Pope and Swift did not endorse, and about which Johnson evidently had mixed feelings.

Johnson mostly despised Sterne, as Swift would have done. But the difference between Sterne's affectionate indulgence of asterisks and Swift's mockery of them is part of an evolution Swift angrily predicted. He would have regarded it as par for the course that Sterne's asterisks, unlike, for the most part, Swift's own, were usually deployed as a sexual tease. They share this with a whole range of effects, both verbal and pictorial, beginning with the long dashes surrounding Tristram's conception, and the advice to 'skip over' the rest of the chapter (I. iv; vol. I, p. 5), a trick used by Fielding in *Tom Jones* and *Amelia* in a more urbane register, the coyness as to the narrator's relationship with 'dear, dear *Jenny*' (I. xviii; vol. I, p. 56), and culminating most spectacularly with the blank page about the Widow Wadman's indescribable beauty, which is logically left undescribed in word or image (VI. xxxviii; vol. II, p. 567). Asterisks accompany several lubricious episodes involving Trim (VIII. xx, vol. II, p. 700; IX. xxviii, vol. II, p. 797), as well as the blushing widow herself (IX. xx, xxii; vol. II, pp. 772, 777), following the two entirely blank deferred chapters (IX. xviii–xix), themselves a mock-editorial or mock-bibliographical variant, or prototype, of a device applied to plot-structuring purposes in some fiction of the period, including Mackenzie's *Man of Feeling* (1771).

'Structuring' is not really what happens in *Tristram Shandy*, whose structure is to have no structure and whose narrative mode is to follow its own motions in absolute denial of plot. The structuring of *Tristram Shandy* is cumulative but local, privileging the momentary as a matter of principle in precisely the way the mock author of the *Tale* was castigated for doing. It follows that, unlike Mackenzie's missing chapters, the lacunae in *Tristram Shandy* make their point, as visual effects tend to do, through local impact. (Mackenzie's missing chapters are just noted as missing, with a modest scattering of asterisks, not reproduced as blank pages.)

The mock edition with gaps takes a non-humorous or straight-faced turn in sentimental fiction of the eighteenth century. There may seem little in common between *A Tale of a Tub* and Mackenzie's *Man of Feeling*, but Mackenzie's novel too purports to be an edited fragment, whose gaps are not due to the impersonal accidents of time to which ancient texts are subject but to the fact that a fictive curate used parts of the manuscript as wadding when he went 'a-shooting'.[49] The device of the fragment here, as in the *Tale*, is no mere imitation of random incompleteness, but comes with an element of whimsical affect, parallel to the sketchy joke about the *Tale*-teller's lazy lack of intellectual stamina, but acquiring, in the case of Mackenzie's novel, a certain charge of sentimental pathos. The novel accordingly begins at chapter xi, and proceeds in a fragmentary way, which permits the author to select his scenes and incidents for purposes of an artistic design belied by the pretended randomness. This includes the revelation of character, the heightening of scenes of pathos, and a whole range of structural considerations, over and above the use of the fragment form as a species of authenticating device.

The structuring possibilities of fragmentary narrative are not, of course, dependent on typographical signs, which can serve as indicators or which have their own satirical or affective force. But the novelistic manipulation or dislocation of narrative records, including the exploitation of pretended gaps, may exist independently of the typographical devices that Sterne and Mackenzie have in common. A minimally typographic modern variation on the selective fragment occurs in Eric Ambler's spy novel, *The Intercom Conspiracy* (1970), whose Foreword reports that the 'two-part manuscript' of a book by the mysteriously missing narrator has been classified by the security services, but that his secretary possesses a 'very rough first draft' with 'letters, transcribed tape recordings, interviews and statements', including material 'extensively blue-pencilled' by the original narrator: that is, with more rather than less material than the unavailable final version, but also with deletions that are evidently recoverable. By an odd Swiftian coincidence, the first chapter includes another piece of front matter, in the form of a letter from Theodore Carter, a participant and editorial narrator, which resembles Gulliver's 'Letter to his Cousin Sympson' in its extreme gratuitous bad temper (it is rebutted by the primary protagonist, the now presumably assassinated Charles Latimer, in a similarly contemptuous manner, defending the original integrity of his story). It differs from Gulliver's 'Letter' in that its point seems to be not the satirically aggressive one of disturbing the reader's bearings, or disabusing the reader of any placid acquiescence in the story, but, like the other structural elements, of enhancing or intensifying the convoluted mystifications and deceptions of the suspense plot.[50] The 'Letter to Sympson' is perhaps the strongest and most elaborate example of mock-editorial undermining, a destabilizing and alienating prefatory paratext whose relation, or interesting non-relation, to the substantive narrative invites more detailed comment.[51] Ambler's novel, however, has no such charge. It seems no more interested in destroying fictional illusion than in creating it, and these discrepancies come over mainly as the ingenious seasoning of an intricate web of intrigue (e.g. pp. 172–3, 177). They do not contribute substantially to the illusion of reality or (in the Mackenzie manner) to the pathos, but neither do they have much to do with the illusion-dispelling force of

Swift's efforts to derealize *Gulliver's Travels* in the 'Letter to Sympson' and elsewhere.

The role of fragmentary forms in the shaping of novelistic plots is in some ways separate from the satiric or sentimental modes of self-display and their typographical expression, which are the main subject of this chapter, though there is often a live traffic between them, and they contribute meaning and affect to one another. But Mackenzie's lacunae and asterisks do not typically indulge in the tease of withholding information, or pretending to, which we see in Swift, Fielding or Sterne. When Christopher Flint asserts that the asterisks of *A Tale of a Tub* 'had a durable influence on later writers, mostly in the form of prose fiction', his point may be extended to works where a parodic element is absent or recessive.[52] In Mackenzie or even Ossian, I suggest that it is Swift's parodic example, and not a primary 'defective' text edited with asterisked gaps, which acts as the immediate source of underided fictional uses of the device. This is perhaps where satire and the novel merge into one another most visibly, including the novel's more sexualized interests, as in the smutty double entendres castigated in the *Tale* and Pope's *Peri Bathous* on the one hand, and the asterisk-ridden genital non-speak of Uncle Toby and Widow Wadman. Flint shows how the passage from smuttiness to sentiment passes through the printer novelist Richardson's 'ubiquitous dates, internal line breaks, the mesmerizing repetition of adieux (and particulary their symbols for "etcetera"), the signaling of enclosed documents'.[53]

But it is in Sterne that both elements in the combination come over in full force, as expressions of emotional states rather than as mainly satirical or plot-related devices. The asterisks in *Tristram Shandy* often serve the same 'will tell/won't tell' function, usually in sexual double entendres (or more precisely demi rather than double). But they seem to be rare in the early volumes, which rely more on dashes. Their first appearance seems to be in volume III, chapters xiii and xiv, where six asterisks make repeated appearances for a single verbal leer, and then for a line or so in chapter xvii dealing with an obstetrical matter.[54] But it is only in volume V that a few longer blocks of asterisks begin to appear. This pattern corresponds with a more extensive use of grouped dashes (V. ii, vol. I, p. 417; VII. xxxv, vol. II, p. 637), though long individual dashes (V. iii, xxxviii; vol. I, pp. 418, 478) were first introduced in volume I, chapter iv (vol. I, p. 6) on either side of the words 'Shut the door' in the passage initiating Tristram's begetting. The tendency culminates, near the end of volume VI, with the blank page reserved for the Widow Wadman's indescribable attractions, and the two deferred blank chapters of volume IX (xviii and xix), whose text is subsequently inserted after chapter xxv in the service of letting people tell their stories their own way. The blank chapters are followed by the lengthy series of asterisks in chapter xx (vol. II, p. 772), which cause the Widow much blushing. Volumes VII and VIII mark a return to the earlier restraint, if that is what it is, and their typographical high spirits, such as they are, include the set piece on the verbs 'bouger' and 'fouter', with its various dashes (VII. xxv; vol. II, pp. 613–14), and the modestly asterisked doings of Trim and the fair Beguine (VIII. xx; vol. II, p. 700).

In my rough estimation, there are fewer extended asterisk sequences in *Tristram Shandy* than in the *Tale*, in proportion to overall length, although, or perhaps because, Sterne used a wider range of typographical forms of display. The sequences are usually of fewer lines, and there seem to be few of more than one line before volume V, chapter i, in the 'Fragment' on whiskers.[55] They may mimic other *Tale* mannerisms, including the bossy shortcutting, as when a string of asterisks is preceded by 'for this plain reason' (V. xxxi; vol. I, p. 467), or 'for these private reasons' (VI. xxxiv; vol. II, p. 560), as more or less whimsical projections of individual character (Walter Shandy's, or Uncle Toby's, or Tristram's own, for example), as one would expect in a transfer to the mode of novelistic sympathy, rather than in an amalgam of satirized idiocy and satirical hauteur in which the satirist and his character are in a relation of stark antagonism. The mock-editorial lacunae combine mock learning and a lubricious cuteness, whose subject matter ranges from obstetrical arcana to what might or might not have passed between Trim and the Beguine or the location of Uncle Toby's blush-inducing wound (VIII. xx, vol. II, p. 700; IX. xx, vol. II, p. 772).

The most remarkable use of stylistic excitation over a half-revealed mock-scandalous non-event occurs in 'The Case of Delicacy', which is the last chapter of *A Sentimental Journey*, concerning Yorick's treaty with the Piedmontese lady with whom he is to share a room at the inn, while her Lyonnaise maid was to occupy the closet. In the punctilious safeguards agreed upon, there was 'but one point forgot':

> and that was the manner in which the lady and myself should be obliged to undress and get to bed – there was but one way of doing it, and that I leave to the reader to devise; protesting as I do it, that if it is not the most delicate in nature, 'tis the fault of his own imagination – against which this is not my first complaint.[56]

This display of cuteness, including the mock rebuke to the reader's prurience, derives from a narratorial rhetoric much exploited by Fielding, who held back in his own fashion from going into erotic details, of which everyone is aware anyway, for the sake of readers 'whose Devotion to the Fair Sex ... wants to be raised by the Help of Pictures'.[57]

By contrast with Fielding's reticence about an actual event, Sterne nudges and massages the reader into what, in the strict terms of the story, is a leeringly eroticized non-event, a non-consummated sexual encounter whose original plan was ostensibly to remain arousingly unenacted, but whose imaginatively exacerbated non-happening is treated as itself an erotic incident, including the narrator's 'ejaculation' ('O my God! said I – '), which, in a characteristic punning giggle, doubles as a questionably orgasmic accident. The 'complaint' about readers' lubricity, which Fielding treats with urbane reticence, becomes the occasion for a lingering particularity of erotic intimation. The *Sentimental Journey's* closing 'Case of Delicacy' is not, any more than the novel as a whole, given to the same typographical theatricality as *Tristram Shandy*. Its ultimate ostentation in the sphere of sexually fraught asterisks and punctuation is that of a typographical effacement, as when the novel closes, poised on the edge of the hero's never-to-be-completed reaching out to the Fille de Chambre, who had inserted herself 'betwixt her mistress and me'. This incident ends, as has been pointed out, most recently by Madeleine Descargues-Grant, without a terminal full stop, perhaps more visible in its invisibility than the plethora of asterisks at the end of Swift's 'Battel' or the continuing verbalized Nothing of the *Tale* itself, 'one point' decidedly not 'forgot' in its pointed absence.[58]

The lubricious cuteness is not Swiftian, but it is something Swift or Pope would have stigmatized as peculiarly 'modern'. Pope had written in *Peri-Bathous* (published in the Pope–Swift *Miscellanies, The Last Volume*, 1727/8) of that 'principal branch of the *Alamode*', namely 'the PRURIENT, a Stile ... every where known by the *same Marks*, the images of the Genital Parts of Men or Women':

> It consists
> wholly of Metaphors drawn from two
> most fruitful Sources or Springs, the very
> *Bathos* of the human Body, that is to
> say * * * and * * * * * * * * * * * * * *
> *Hiatus Magnus lachrymabilis.*   *   *
> *   *   *   *   *   *   *   *   *   *   *
> *   *   *   *   *   *   *   *   *   *. And
> *selling of Bargains*, and *double En-*
> *tendre.*[59]

The 'very *Bathos* of the human Body' in Pope's inversion of Longinus's *Peri Hypsous* is a throwback to the *Tale's* 'very *bottom* of all the *Sublime*' ('Preface', *CWJS*, vol. I, p. 27) (see above p. 238–9). Swift had written more tartly, in the 'Digression in Praise of Digressions', of 'that highly celebrated Talent among the *Modern* Wits, of deducing Similitudes, Allusions, and Applications, very Surprizing, Agreeable, and Apposite, from the *Pudenda* of either Sex, together with *their proper Uses*' (section VII, *CWJS*, vol. I, p. 97). Tristram's chapter in praise of his own digressions (I. xxii) would alone ensure that this passage cannot have gone unnoticed.

There is of course nothing 'modern' about this, as Swift and Pope knew perfectly well, and neither was above the occasional witty obscenity himself. It is Pope, for once, who offers asterisks, while Swift supplies marginal scholia from Ctesias and Herodotus, illustrating the ancient origins of the modern mind in yet another form of typographic self-exhibition. It is quite likely that neither Swift nor Pope had many examples in their minds that we might identify as proto-Shandean, combining double entendre, buttonholing cuteness and the particular form of typographical sexual tease developed on an egomanic scale in *Tristram Shandy*, though the element of pre-parody speaks eloquently of their acuteness as cultural analysts. What even they perhaps might not have foreseen is the conscious determination with which Sterne would outparody the pre-parody, unparodying it in full awareness of their jeering down to the mock-sanctimonious disquisition, in the 'Fragment on Whiskers', on how 'Noses ran the same fate some centuries ago ... which Whiskers have now done ... Are not trouse, and placket-holes, and pump-handles – and spigots and faucets, in danger still, from the same association?' (V. I; vol. I, p. 414).

Norman Mailer is a conspicuous example of ways of achieving self-advertisement, including advertisement of self-advertisement, through a combination of text, typography and layout, beginning with the title *Advertisements for Myself* (1959), a book that blundered into the world with a clattering appropriateness in the bicentenary year of the first volume of *Tristram Shandy*.[60] The book is divided into sections preceded by a sequence of over thirty individual 'Advertisements for myself', from a First to a Sixth, including also (among a lot of other advertisements with various titles) an 'Advertisement for "Sixty-Nine Questions and Answers"' (preceding a newspaper interview designed with numerological care) and concluding (or more or less concluding) with a 'Last Advertisement for myself Before the Way Out', which is not strictly 'Last', and a final section entitled 'ADVERTISEMENTS FOR MYSELF ON THE WAY OUT', which is not called the last but is. These 'Advertisements', as Mailer points out in

'A Note to the Reader' (p. 7), itself in italics, are *'printed in italics'*, much as Shamela speaks in the present tense, often running to several pages, and intended to be *'more readable than the rest of his pages'*. Unlike Shamela, Mailer speaks in the third person, and likes to call himself a *'literary fraud'*, also in italics. There are two tables of contents, also explained in the 'Note to the Reader', the first listing the items in sequence, the second divided into categories, 'Fiction', 'Essays and Articles', 'Journalism', 'Interviews', 'Poetry', 'Plays'. This second list concludes by grouping together all the self-advertisements except the last, which is mentioned only in the first list, as a genre in their own right under the title 'Biography of a Style', containing some thirty-four items, nearly all called advertisements. It is a feature of both tables of contents that most of the key words, including non-substantives (e.g. Before, Way, Out), are given initial capitals. A salient exception is 'myself', perhaps the most frequently recurring word after 'Advertisements', almost always given in lower case. This has a curious effect of inverse ostentation, which might be read as a typographical way of saying 'little me', a kind of post-Shandean simper.

Advertisements for Myself enacts in whole text the project sketched out in the advertisement of 'Treatises wrote by the same Author' prefixed to *A Tale of a Tub* and intermittently referred to in the body of the book as forthcoming or omitted. Mailer's book consists entirely of such matter, bits of past and future works, drafts and discarded versions, correspondence with publishers, extracts from reviews and responses to reviews. A twenty-page 'Fourth Advertisement' is an account of the tribulations of his recent novel, *The Deer Park*, and its rejection at proof stage by its intended publisher, followed by some twenty pages describing his subsequent departures from the discarded proof version and including a 'Postscript to the Fourth Advertisement', which retails the failure of famous writers who were sent copies of the novel (among them a phantasmagoric Hemingway) to acknowledge receipt (pp. 265–7).

The significant feature is that this material comes over not primarily as a documentary archive, but as a mock archive expressedly projected as a self-promotional gesture. As the title advertises, it does for 'advertisements' what Swift's 'Digression in Praise of Digressions' did for digressions, but at book length and, of course, much more upfront. Even the neutral activity of dating his pieces, since Mailer announces it in his italicized *'Note to the Reader'* (p. 8), assumes something of the self-inflation Swift was mocking when he spoke of composing his work in a penurious garret, in 'this present Month of *August*, 1697'. The whiff of at least generic resemblance is not diminished by Mailer's fantasy of himself at the end of the 'Fourth

Advertisement', and again in italics, as a *'starved revolutionary in a garret'* (p. 247), though after announcing on the same page that his unsuccessful novel *'sold over fifty thousand copies after returns'*, he was not indulging that cute Swiftian fiction too literally.

The 'Fourth Advertisement', like the rest, shows an intense interest in the advertising process in the narrow literal sense, chronicling, for example, the totally inert information that a full-page ad for the aborted edition of *The Deer Park* appeared in *'the first run of* Publisher's Weekly', since it *'was already on its way to England'* before publication was stopped (p. 229). Mailer also announces that in November 1955, after the novel had appeared, he bought an ad in the *Village Voice*, including real or invented extracts from unfavourable reviews (p. 248). This is reproduced as a full-page graphic on page 249 (Figure 2).

Notwithstanding this example, *Advertisements for Myself* is not exceptionally flamboyant typographically, by (for example) L'Estrange's standards. It does not use black letter or Shandean marbled pages, though the text makes up for this in its style of bumptious self-display. The pushy self-regard differs from the Shandean version mainly through a brash machismo replacing Tristram's simpering lubricity. I am not sure to what extent Mailer had charge of his typography or the mise en page of his volume, but this is only marginal to the real issue, which is that the publisher caught the spirit of the book, and that the relationship between authorial display and the resources of bookmaking are precisely the ones Swift identified and Sterne made lavish use of. Even if Mailer was not directly involved in the production process, his text, which expressly indicates the use of italics in the 'Note to the Reader' and supplies the ad from the *Village Voice*, makes clear his interest in typography, including typographical parody and self-parody, as a means of self-promotion.

The 'Fourth Advertisement' contains an interesting discussion of his early practice of *'writing novels in the first person ... even though the third person was more to my taste'* (p. 237). Some of the difficulties involved creating a hero *'who was braver and stronger than me'*, and the anxiety that *'the more my new style succeeded, the more was I writing an implicit portrait of myself as well. There is a shame about advertising yourself that way, a shame which became so strong that it was a psychological violation to go on'* (p. 238). This is all said in italics in 'The Fourth Advertisement for myself'.

The archly old-fashioned way in which the *'Note to the Reader'* refers to himself as 'the author' is a prelude to the use of third-person narrative in Mailer's non-fiction autobiographical books of the 1960s and 1970s (an example is *The Armies of the Night. History as a Novel: the Novel as History,*

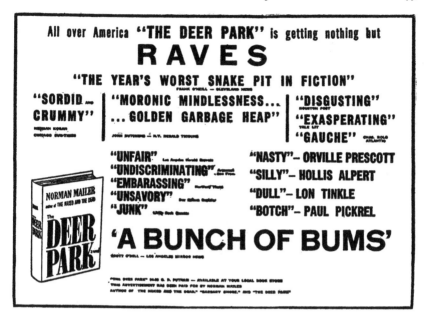

Figure 2 Advertisement for *The Deer Park* from ADVERTISEMENTS FOR MYSELF by Norman Mailer. Copyright © 1959 by Norman Mailer, copyright renewed © 1987 by Norman Mailer, used by permission of the Wylie Agency LLC.

1968). This use of the third person singular of himself (as well as of his reader) was once said by Brigid Brophy to be an insurance against the possibility that the reader might not otherwise guess 'that Mr. Mailer is a he', and also 'against the dread day when the world turns out to contain a Mr. Norman Mailest'.[61] Mailer's fixation on Hemingway in this book (e.g. pp. 19 ff.) is part of an overtly emulative he-manship. The use of the third person instead of the first in order to bring out a full sense of the author as Number One has perhaps not been as fully investigated as it might, a somewhat more modest, or less immodest, case being that of Dylan Thomas's *Portrait of the Artist as a Young Dog* (1940), similarly an example of inverse ostentation.

The 'Advertisements' (which are usually in italics, often running to several pages) engage in the form of reader-grabbing I have drawn attention to as a familiar manner of both the *Tale* and *Tristram Shandy*: '*Any reader who will let me circle back later, in my own way, via the whorls and ellipses of my knotted mind, to earlier remarks, will be entertained en route ...*' (p. 19). The language recalls, expressly or not, Tristram Shandy's exhortation to the reader to 'let me go on, and tell my story my own way,' even 'if I should seem now and then to trifle upon the road' (I. vi; vol. I, p. 9). Mailer's remarks are the prelude to a series of reflections on Hemingway, around whom Mailer weaves a tortuous and ambivalent self-image, which will not detain us here. The sentence also reads like a prose version of Tristram Shandy's pictorial diagrams of the convolutions of his non-linear narrative (VI. xl; vol. II, pp. 570–1), or the curling lines of Trim's argument for celibacy, more telling than 'a thousand' of Walter Shandy's 'most subtle syllogisms' (IX. iv; vol. II, p. 743).

Sterne clearly makes a greater pictorial display of it than Mailer, and one might think it unusual that Mailer should be trumped by a predecessor in this regard, but his is, in some ways, a reversion to a more verbal than pictorial form of chutzpah. I will pause instead over the opening passage of this 'First Advertisement', where Mailer announces bouncily that he will '*settle for nothing less than making a revolution in the consciousness of our time*', the '*true interest*' of his book being '*to present myself as more modest than I am*' (p. 17). It is perhaps a coincidence that this Mailer, who, as has been noted, projects himself as '*a starved revolutionary in a garret*' (p. 247), resembles the *Tale*'s author, also hungry in a similar habitation, praising the feats of self-importance in the Modern era that have generated 'those mighty Revolutions, that have happened in *Empire*, in *Philosophy*, and in *Religion*' (section IX, *CWJS*, vol. I, p. 110). 'Revolutions', meaning both political upheavals and gyrations of mind, figure prominently in the vocabulary of the *Tale*'s speaker, though apparently without Mailer's heroics of intellectual guerilla warfare.

On the following page is a small example of the relationship between typography and ego-trip that the author of Swift's *Tale* presciently embodied, and in a manner of speaking preprogrammed for later writers. In the 'First Advertisement' Mailer writes:

> To write about myself is to send my style through a circus of variations and postures, a fireworks of virtuosity designed to achieve ... [original punctuation] *I do not even know what. Leave it that I become an actor, a quick-change artist, as if I believe I can trap the Prince of Truth in the act of switching a style.* (p. 18)

The idea of the writer as actor or quick-change artist has taken exalted forms in Yeats and Thomas Mann, but the heightened self-derision with which Mailer promotes without disowning it may seem a throwback to the *Tale*-teller's affinity with the mountebanks of the Stage Itinerant. The jaunty conferring of a royal title on his Prince of Truth may also seem preprogrammed in Swift's speaker's 'Dedication to Prince Posterity', which as we have seen is full of proto-Mailerian matter.

The three dots of the non-functional ellipsis typographically prefigure a self-revelation that is not provided but withheld: 'designed to achieve … I do not even know what'. This is another version of the 'will tell/won't tell' routine, similar to Tristram's mystifications about what he did with his 'dear, dear Jenny' (*TS*, I. xviii; vol. I, pp. 56–7), but, on this occasion, apparently minus ostentatious lubricity. It is not necessary to suppose that Mailer had read the *Tale* or *Tristram Shandy*, or anything other than his own writings, in order to see in the outright mockery of the *Tale* the origin of a long series of writings whose mockery, if it exists, is not outright, but becomes itself a mode of self-affirmation, and that both the mockery and the self-affirmation exploit the typographical resources of bookmaking in a way that unparodies parody.

In the 'Note to the Reader' explaining the two tables of contents, Mailer explains:

> *The author, taken with an admirable desire to please his readers, has also added a set of advertisements, printed in italics, which surround all of these writings with his present tastes, preferences, apologies, prides, and occasional confessions. Like many another literary fraud, the writer has been known on occasion to read the Preface of a book instead of a book, and bearing this vice in mind, he tried to make the advertisements more readable than the rest of his pages …*
>
> *For those who care to skim nothing but the cream of each author, and so miss the pleasure of liking him at his worst, I will take the dangerous step of listing what I beileve [sic] are the best pieces in this book.* (p. 7)

The '*admirable desire to please his readers*', the jab at those who read prefaces rather than the book itself, even the image of skimming '*nothing but the cream of each author*', seem exact evocations of the *Tale*, including the cream (section IX, *CWJS*, vol. I, pp. 112, 'Battel', 'Preface', p.142), with friendliness to self and reader (especially self) superimposed on Swift's rejection of these things, and adopted (wittingly or otherwise) in the teeth of Swift's rejection.

It is a conjunction of great interest that the withholding of matter that occurs, on a grander scale, in the 'will tell/won't tell' asterisked paragraph of the 'Digression on Madness' has a small but revealing counterpart on the following page of the 'First Advertisement'. The bossy dismissiveness of the 'clear Solution of the Matter' in the Digression is, as we have seen, a comment on the speaker. It is rejected by the real author, though it is the idiot shadow of a stylistic arrogance that plays no small part in Swift's own satiric manner. But it is the vulnerable and parodied part that has taken root, adopted openly by later authorial selves. The teasing gap in the Shandean manuscript, or the Mailerian sentence, becomes in its own right a cuteness, a coy self-projection, a cop-out from self-disclosure playing at self-disclosure. Mailer's promise of confessional outpourings of *'to achieve ... I do not even know what'* are a mystification in which the typographical void is empty even of a fictive or putative content. Beside Swift's, Fielding's or Sterne's imposing array of asterisks, dashes and blank pages, Mailer's ellipsis is modest indeed, a mini-gap, three mere microdots, but it makes vast claims of a personality in awe of its own being. The ellipsis itself suggests not lost or missing words, merely an absence of words, a pause preceding non-disclosure. That this non-disclosure hints at mysteries would have suited a Swiftian scenario. It is also a modernist scenario, that of Prufrock's 'overwhelming question...', also followed by a three-dot ellipsis:

> To lead you to an overwhelming question...
> Oh, do not ask, 'What is it?'
> Let us go and make our visit.[62]

This example may dignify Mailer unduly, but Eliot plays a part in the story I am telling, which cannot be opened up here, except to say that by 1923 Eliot had become scathing of 'This particular type of fragmentary conversation', which he said 'was invented by Jules Laforgue and done to death by Aldous Huxley'. He added: 'I have been a sinner myself in the use of broken conversations punctuated by three dots.'[63] The dismissal of the early affectation does not, of course, diminish the importance of Laforgue in shaping Eliot's poetry, or the broader role of the fragment form in the whole conception of *The Waste Land*, published the year before this letter.

If the editorial routine of the gap in the manuscript may be seen to have not just informative or mock-informative content, but character-revealing affect, it is open also to larger structuring purposes in epistolary or other novels that purport to be editions of primary manuscripts of characters or character-narrators. Swift would have scorned their pretensions of writing 'to the *Moment*', not an activity he would normally think proper for publication, and whose Richardsonian intimacies he would doubtless have found as abhorrent as Fielding did.[64] But he foresaw and pre-parodied the forms, which we are not committed to repudiating in the way he would have.

It is at this point that the mock edition might appear to part company with an emerging pre-Romantic cult of the fragment. The elevation of the uncompleted work to a value which exceeds that of the classical ordered whole takes many forms, however, and the shadow of the mock edition hangs over some of them, beginning with *Tristram Shandy* itself, and culminating in the great modernist monument of Eliot's *Waste Land*, with its heap of broken images, its shored fragments and (if I may pause for three microdots of my own) … its learned apparatus of notes.

Notes

1 Alain Bony, *Discours et vérité dans Les Voyages de Gulliver de Jonathan Swift* (Lyon: Presses Universitaires de Lyon, 2002); *Leonora, Lydia et les autres: Etude sur le (nouveau) roman anglais du XVIIIE siècle* (Lyon: Presses Universitaires de Lyon, 2004); Baudouin Millet, 'Ceci n'est pas un roman': *L'evolution du statut de la fiction en Angleterre de 1652 à 1754* (Louvain: Peeters, 2007).

2 *A Tale of a Tub*, ed. Marcus Walsh (Cambridge University Press, 2010), 'Preface', *CWJS*, vol. I, p. 29. Future page references given parenthetically in the text are to this edition, except that quotations with special typographical features are taken from the fifth edition (1710), with a reference to the Cambridge edition supplied in the notes.

3 *Epistle to a Lady* (1728?), line 178, Williams, *Poems*, vol. II, p. 635.

4 'Mechanical Operation', *CWJS*, vol. I, p. 179.

5 See Elizabeth Wanning Harries, *The Unfinished Manner: Essays on the Fragment in the Later Eighteenth Century* (Charlottesville: University Press of Virginia, 1994), pp. 21–8.

6 Harries, *Unfinished Manner*, pp. 22–5.

7 E.g. Rabelais, *Oeuvres complètes*, ed. Mireille Huchon (Paris: Gallimard, 1994), Book I, Ch. ii, pp. 1–5, pp. 11, 1069 n. 3: 'Donne l'illusion du manuscrit rongé par les rats.' Subsequent page references given parenthetically in the text are to this edition, following the numbers of book and chapter.

8 E.g. Rabelais, I. xxii, pp. 58–63; III. xxvi–xxvii, pp. 432–41; IV. lix–lx, pp. 676–81, though early editions are not entirely consistent as to this typographical arrangement.

9 *Gulliver's Travels*, Part IV, Ch. xii, Davis, *PW*, vol. XI, p. 296. Subsequent page references given parenthetically in the text are to this edition, following the numbers of part and chapter.

10 'Anima Rabelaisii habitans in sicco', in Coleridge, *Table Talk*, ed. Carl Woodring, Bollingen Series, 2 vols. (London, Routledge, 1990), 15 June 1830, vol. I, p. 167 n. 6, and 11 August 1832, p. 323 and n. 10. The phrase goes back to Rabelais, I. v, and to Augustine, who is said to have said it was not possible for a soul to live in a dry place (*Oeuvres complètes*, pp. 18, 1075 n. 15). See Claude Rawson, *Gulliver and the Gentle Reader* (London: Routledge, 1973), pp. 104, 174 n. 19.

11 Samuel Johnson, 'Swift', in *The Lives of the Most Eminent English Poets*, ed. Roger Lonsdale, 4 vols. (Oxford, Clarendon Press, 2006), vol. III, p. 208 (§III).

12 *TS* vol. IX, ch. viii; vol. II. p. 754. Subsequent page references given parenthetically in the text are to this edition, following the numbers of book and chapter.

13 See Roger L'Estrange, *A Brief History of the Times, &c.* (1687), pp. 1 and 1 (consecutive paginations); see Harold Love, 'L'Estrange, Joyce and the Dictates of Typography', in Anne Dunan-Page and Beth Lynch (eds.), *Roger L'Estrange and the Making of Restoration Culture* (Aldershot: Ashgate, 2008), 167–80, p. 178.

14 Dryden's *Works of Virgil* is complicated by the fact that it not only has front and back matter (dedications, biographical introduction, commendatory poems, an errata list, two subscribers' lists, a postscript and a section of 'Notes and Observations'), but lengthy introductory essays by Dryden and others inside the volume, accounting for almost a quarter of the whole.

15 Claude Rawson, *Gulliver and the Gentle Reader*, pp. 1–5; 'Behind the Tub,' *TLS*, 10 September 2004, pp. 3–4.

16 See Rawson, 'Swift, Satire and the Novel', in Thomas Keymer (ed.), *Prose Fiction from the Origins of Print to 1750*, Oxford History of the Novel in English, Vol. 1 (Oxford University Press, forthcoming).

17 On the date, see *The Works of John Dryden*, ed. H.T. Swedenberg, Jr. *et al.*, 20 vols. (Berkeley and Los Angeles: University Of California Press, 1956–2000), vol. VI, p. 846.

18 *An Essay on Man*, book I, line 14, *TE*, vol. III.i, p. 14.

19 Keats to Richard Woodhouse, 27 October 1818, *The Letters of John Keats, 1814–1821*, ed. Hyder Edward Rollins, 2 vols. (Cambridge, MA: Harvard University Press, 1958), vol. I, p. 387.

20 'Battel', *CWJS*, vol. I, p. 152; Keats to J. H. Reynolds, 19 February 1818, *Letters*, vol. I, pp. 231–2; Pope, *Essay on Man*, book I, line 217, p. 42.

21 Pope, *Dunciad, in Four Books*, ed. Valerie Rumbold (Harlow: Longman, 1999), book I, line 77, p. 108. Subsequent page references given parenthetically in the text are to this edition.

22 Hugh Kenner, *The Stoic Comedians* (Berkeley: University of California Press, 1962, repr. 1974), p. 37; see pp. 37–50 (pp. 48–9 on Sterne); Denis Donoghue, *Jonathan Swift: A Critical Introduction* (Cambridge University Press, 1969), pp. 8–11; Marcus Walsh's 'Text, "Text", and Swift's *A Tale of a Tub*,' *Modern Language Review*, 85 (1990), 290–303, which cites neither Kenner nor Donoghue, informatively discusses the debate over oral and printed authority as part of the contemporaneous argument as to the respective claims of tradition and scripture in matters of faith and doctrine.

23 Love, 'L'Estrange, Joyce and the Dictates of Typography', pp. 168, 167–79. I am indebted to Thomas Keymer, 'Novel Designs: Manipulating the Page in English Fiction, 1660–1800', the John Coffin Memorial Lecture in the History of the Book, London, 20 July 2009.

24 Love, 'L'Estrange, Joyce and the Dictates of Typography', p. 167; also 178 *et passim*.

25 Love, 'L'Estrange, Joyce and the Dictates of Typography', pp. 168–9, 175–7, 179.

26 Love, 'L'Estrange, Joyce and the Dictates of Typography', p. 172.
27 L'Estrange does not rate an entry in the (admittedly somewhat minimalist) index to the Florida Edition of *TS*.
28 Florida note to the marriage settlement in I. xv (vol. III, p. 81) cites Steele, *The Funeral* (1701), for various parallels including a character called Trim, though there is no black letter in the published text.
29 *Dunciad, in Four Books*, book 1, line 162, p. 122. The suggestion of a fool's cap for the King was made by James Sutherland in his edition of *The Dunciad, TE*, vol. V, p. 282.
30 Swift, *Epistle to a Lady*, line 219, Williams, *Poems*, vol. II, p. 637.
31 *Tale*, 'Introduction', *CWJS*, vol. I, p. 40.
32 *Tale*, section IX, *CWJS*, vol. I, p. 110.
33 *The Life of Mr. Jonathan Wild the Great*, book IV, ch. xiv, Fielding, *Miscellanies*, 3 vols. (1743), vol. III, pp. 388–9, corresponding to *Miscellanies by Henry Fielding, Esq; Volume III*, ed. Bartrand A. Goldgar and Hugh Amory, Wesleyan Edition (Oxford: Clarendon Press, 1997), pp. 179–80.
34 Fielding, *Miscellanies* (1743), vol. III, p. 385 (book IV, ch. xiii),
35 Fielding, *Miscellanies* (1743), vol. III, p. 390 (book IV, ch. xiv).
36 James Joyce, *Ulysses* (London: Bodley Head, 1955), p. 30.
37 Jane Austen, *Emma*, ed. Richard Cronin and Dorothy McMillan (Cambridge University Press, 2005), vol. III, ch. vi, pp. 389–90.
38 For interesting insights into Swiftian antecedents of Austen's style, see Jenny Davidson, 'Austen's Voices', in Nicholas Hudson and Aaron Santesso (eds.), *Swift's Travels: Eighteenth-Century British Satire and its Legacy* (Cambridge University Press, 2008), pp. 233–50.
39 On Austen's debt to Fielding, see Claude Rawson, *Satire and Sentiment 1660–1830* (Cambridge University Press, 1994), pp. 267–98 (originally an introduction to *Persuasion*), and 'Showing, Telling, and Money in *Emma*', *Essays in Criticism*, 61 (2012), 338–64; for Wild's place in the development of the novel, see 'Avatars of Alexander', in Claude Rawson (ed.), *Henry Fielding (1707–1754), Novelist, Playwright, Journalist, Magistrate: A Double Anniversary Tribute* (Newark: University of Delaware Press, 2008), pp. 91–114.
40 Fielding, *Joseph Andrews*, ed. Martin C. Battestin (Oxford: Clarendon Press, 1967), book I, ch. xiii, pp. 59–60.
41 Fielding, *Miscellanies* (1743), vol. III, p. 399 (book IV, ch. xiv).
42 *The Life of Mr. Jonathan Wild the Great. A New Edition With Considerable Corrections and Additions* (London, 1754), book IV, ch. xiii, p. 250.
43 *Miscellanies* (1743), vol. III, p. 385 (book IV, ch. xiii); *Life of Mr. Jonathan* Wild (1754), book IV, ch. xii, p. 240.
44 Fielding, *Journal of A Voyage to Lisbon*, ed. Tom Keymer (London: Penguin, 1996), Preface, ad fin., p. 11.
45 Samuel Richardson, *Sir Charles Grandison* (1753), ed. Jocelyn Harris, 3 vols. (London: Oxford University Press, 1972), Preface, vol. I, p. 4.
46 Fielding, *Jonathan Wild*, ed. David Nokes (Harmondsworth: Penguin, 1982), pp. 206–7.

47 Madeleine Descargues-Grant, 'Sterne and the Miracle of the Fragment,' in W.B. Gerard, E. Derek Taylor and Robert G. Walker (eds.), *Swiftly Sterneward: Essays on Laurence Sterne and His Times in Honor of Melvyn New* (Newark: University of Delaware Press, 2011), p. 237.

48 Johnson, 'Smith,' *Lives of the Poets*, vol. II, p. 171 (§19); Harries, *Unfinished Manner*, p. 58.

49 Henry Mackenzie, *The Man of Feeling*, 2nd edn (1771), 'Introduction', p. vii.

50 Eric Ambler, *The Intercom Conspiracy* (1970) (London: Fontana, 1971), Foreword, p. II; part I, pp. 15–19.

51 See Claude Rawson, 'Swift's "I" Narrators' (1998), in Claude Rawson and Ian Higgins (eds.), *Essential Writings of Jonathan Swift: A Norton Critical Edition* (New York: Norton, 2010), pp. 874–89, esp. pp. 874–82, and, for a comparison with Montaigne, Claude Rawson, *God, Gulliver and Genocide: Barbarism and the European Imagination, 1492–1945* (Oxford University Press, 2001), pp. 43–4; Bony, *Discours et vérité*, pp. 46–8; Millet, '*Ceci n'est pas un roman*', pp. 205–14 (esp. p. 207 ff., 'Le torpillage de la fiction éditoriale').

52 Christopher Flint, *The Appearance of Print in Eighteenth-Century Fiction* (Cambridge University Press, 2011), p. 123.

53 Flint, *Appearance of Print*, p. 126; on Swift's satire as advance parody of later fictional forms, including Gothic and sentimental fragment novels, see Bony, *Discours et vérité*, pp. 40–1, and *Leonora, Lydia et les autres*, pp. 53–7.

54 Not glossed in Florida edition, or in the editions by Graham Petrie, introd. Christopher Ricks (Harmondsworth: Penguin, 1969) and Ian Campbell Ross (Oxford University Press, 1983).

55 The Florida commentary offers a list of 'lacunae' from volume V onwards (vol. III, p. 372 n. 460.1–2).

56 Sterne, *A Sentimental Journey through France and Italy. By Mr. Yorick* (1768), ed. Gardner D. Stout Jr (Berkeley: University of California Press, 1967), pp. 285–91; ed. Melvyn New and W. G. Day (Gainesville: University Press of Florida, 2002), pp. 160–5.

57 *The History of Tom Jones, a Foundling*, ed. Martin C. Battestin and Fredson Bowers, 2 vols. (Oxford: Clarendon Press, 1974), book XIII, ch. ix; vol. II, p. 722.

58 Descargues-Grant, 'Sterne and the Miracle of the Fragment', pp. 229, 232.

59 Pope, 'Peri Bathous: Of the Art of Sinking in Poetry', in *Miscellanies. The Last Volume* (1727/8), ch. xii, p. 67; also in *Prose Works of Alexander Pope. Vol. II: The Major Works, 1725–1744*, ed. Rosemary Cowler (Hamden, CT: Archon, 1986), p. 221.

60 Citations of *Advertisements for Myself* are from the first edition (New York: G. P. Putnam's Sons, 1959).

61 *Sunday Times Magazine*, 12 September 1971, p. 53.

62 T. S. Eliot, 'The Love Song of J. Alfred Prufrock', lines 10–12, *Complete Poems and Plays* (London: Faber, 1969), p. 13.

63 T. S. Eliot to John Collier, 4 October 1923, *Letters of T. S. Eliot*, ed. Valerie Eliot and Hugh Haughton, 2 vols. (London: Faber, 2009), vol. II, p. 241. I am indebted to Mr Jim McCue for this reference.

64 There is no mention of Richardson in any of Swift's works or correspondence. For a full, nuanced account, see Peter Sabor, '"A Large Portion of our Etherial Fire": Swift and Samuel Richardson', in *Münster* (2003), pp. 388, 387–401. Richardson's view of Swift, as expressed in his works and correspondence, was almost invariably disparaging (Sabor, pp. 391–401). Richardson printed several of Swift's works, including an abridgement of *Gulliver's Travels*, of which he may have been the editor; *Polite Conversation*, 1738; and a volume of the Swift–Pope *Miscellanies*, 1733 (Sabor, pp. 388–90). He also printed and abridged L'Estrange's *Aesop's Fables* in 1739 (Sabor, pp. 388–9).

Select bibliography

PRIMARY SOURCES

Ambler, Eric, *The Intercom Conspiracy* (1970; London: Fontana, 1971).

Austen, Jane, *Emma*, ed. Richard Cronin and Dorothy McMillan (Cambridge University Press, 2005).

Beard, Thomas, *A Retractive from the Romish Religion* (1616).

Bell, Thomas, *The Catholique Triumph: ...Wherein is euidently prooued, that Poperie and the Doctrine now professed in the Romish Church, is the New Religion; And that the Fayth which the Church of England now myntaineth, is the ancient romane Religion* (1610).

Bentley, Richard, *A Dissertation upon the Epistles of Phalaris with an Answer to the Objections of the Honourable Charles Boyle* (London, 1699).

Blackwood's Magazine

Boult, Henry, *A Supplement to the Abridgement of all the Statutes of King William and Queen Mary, and of King William III. and Queen Anne* (London, 1708).

Boyle, John, 5th Earl of Cork and Orrery, *Remarks on the Life and Writings of Dr. Jonathan Swift*, ed. João Fróes (Newark: University of Delaware Press; London: Associated University Presses, 2000).

Burnet, Gilbert, *History of His Own Times*, 2 vols. (London, 1724–34).

Coleridge, Samuel Taylor, *Table Talk*, ed. Carl Woodring, Bollingen Series, 2 vols. (London, Routledge, 1990).

[Collop, John], *Charity Commended, or, A Catholick Christian Soberly Instructed* (1667).

Critical Review

[Crockat, Gilbert, and John Monroe], *The Scotch Presbyterian Eloquence; Or, The Foolishness of Their Teaching Discovered From Their Books, Sermons, and Prayers; And Some Remarks on Mr. Rule's Late Vindication of the Kirk* (London, 1692).

Delany, Mary, *The Autobiography and Correspondence of Mary Granville, Mrs. Delany*, ed. Right Honourable Lady Llanover, 3 vols. (London: Bentley, 1861).

Dodsley, Robert, *The Correspondence of Robert Dodsley*, ed. James Tierney (Cambridge University Press, 1988).

D'Urfey, Thomas, *An Essay towards the Theory of the Intelligible World. ... The Archetypally Second Edition* (London, [1705?]).

Dunton, John, *The Life and Errors of John Dunton late Citizen of London; Written by Himself in Solitude* (1705).

[Earbery, Matthias], *An Historical Account of the Advantages that have Accrued to England by the Succession in the Illustrious House of Hanover, Part II* (London, 1722).

The Earl of Wharton's Speech to the House of Lords [London, 1711].

Edinburgh Magazine

Eliot, T. S., *Complete Poems and Plays* (London: Faber, 1969).

 Letters of T. S. Eliot, ed. Valerie Eliot and Hugh Haughton, 2 vols. (London: Faber, 2009).

L'Estrange, Roger, *A Brief History of the Times, &c.* (1687).

Ewing, George and Alexander, *An Attempt to Answer Mr. Faulkner's Extraordinary Appeal to the Public* (Dublin, 1758).

Fielding, Henry, *The History of Tom Jones, a Foundling*, ed. Martin Battestin and Fredson Bowers, 2 vols. (Oxford: Clarendon Press, 1974).

 Joseph Andrews, ed. Martin Battestin (Oxford: Clarendon Press, 1967).

 Journal of A Voyage to Lisbon, ed. Tom Keymer (London: Penguin, 1996).

 The Life of Mr. Jonathan Wild the Great. A New Edition With Considerable Corrections and Additions (London, 1754).

 Miscellanies by Henry Fielding, Esq; Volume III, ed. Bartrand A. Goldgar and Hugh Amory, Wesleyan Edition (Oxford: Clarendon Press, 1997).

Flatman, Thomas, *Naps upon Parnassus. … Such Voluntary and Jovial Copies of Verses, as were lately receiv'd from some of the WITS of the Universities* (London, 1658).

Gentleman's Magazine

The Grub-street Journal, ed. Bertrand A. Goldgar, 4 vols. (London: Pickering & Chatto, 2002).

Heath, Robert, *Clarastella* (1650).

Hubert, Francis, *The Deplorable Life and Death of Edward the Second … Storied in an Excellent Poem* (1628).

Jackson's Oxford Journal

Johnson, Samuel, *The Lives of the Most Eminent English Poets*, ed. Roger Lonsdale, 4 vols. (Oxford: Clarendon Press, 2006).

 The Works of the English Poets. With Prefaces, Biographical and Critical, 68 vols. (London, 1779–81).

Joyce, James, *Ulysses* (London: Bodley Head, 1955).

Keats, John, *The Letters of John Keats, 1814–1821*, ed. Hyder Edward Rollins, 2 vols. (Cambridge, MA: Harvard University Press, 1958).

[Lawton, Charlwood], *A Short State of our Condition, with Relation to the present Parliament* (n.p.: n.p., n.d.).

Livy, *The Romane Historie*, tr. Philemon Holland (London, 1600).

'Longinus', *periupsu[Peri Hypsous], or Dionysius Longinus of the Height of Eloquence, Rendered out of the Originall. By J. H. Esq;* (London, 1652).

Lucretius, *Lucretius his Six Books of Epicurean Philosophy: and Manilius his Five Books*, tr. Thomas Creech (London, 1700).

Mackenzie, Henry, *The Man of Feeling*, 2nd edn (1771).

Mailer, Norman, *Advertisements for Myself* (New York: G. P. Putnam's Sons, 1959).

Milton, John, *Areopagitica* (1644), in *Complete Prose Works, Volume II, 1643–1648*, ed. Ernest Sirluck (New Haven: Yale University Press, 1959), pp. 480–570.

Monthly Review

Naudé, Gabriel, *Instructions Concerning Erecting of a Library*, tr. John Evelyn (1661).

[Nethersole, Francis], *Problemes Necessary to be Determined by All that Have, or Have Not Taken Part ... in the Late Unnatural Warre* (1648).

A Strong Motive to a General Pardon (1648).

Nichols, John, *Illustrations of the Literary History of the Eighteenth Century*, 8 vols. (London, 1817–58).

Literary Anecdotes of the Eighteenth Century; Comprising Biographical Memoirs of William Bowyer, 9 vols. (London, 1812–15).

Nichols, John (ed.), *A Select Collection of Poems*, 8 vols. (London, 1780–2).

Perkins, William, *Problema de Romanae Fidei Ementitio Catholicismo* (Cambridge, 1604).

Petowe, Henry, 'Epistle Dedicatorie', *The Second Part of Hero and Leander Conteyning Their Further Fortunes* (1598).

Philips, Katherine, *Poems. By the Incomparable, Mrs. K.P.* (London, 1664).

Pilkington, Laetitia, *Memoirs of Laetitia Pilkington*, ed. A. C. Elias Jr, 2 vols. (Athens: University of Georgia Press, 1997).

Plutarch, *The Philosophie, Commonlie Called, The Morals*, tr. Philemon Holland (London, 1603).

Poem to the Whole People of Ireland (Dublin, 1726).

Pomey, François, *The Pantheon, Representing the Fabulous Histories of the Heathen Gods*, 7th edn, trans. Andrew Tooke (1717).

Pope, Alexander, *The Correspondence of Alexander Pope*, ed. George Sherburn, 5 vols. (Oxford: Clarendon Press, 1956).

Dunciad, in Four Books, ed. Valerie Rumbold (Harlow: Longman, 1999).

The Poems of Alexander Pope, Volume III, The Dunciad (1728) & The Dunciad Variorum (1729), ed. Valerie Rumbold (Harlow: Longman, 2007).

Prose Works of Alexander Pope. Vol. II: The Major Works, 1725–1744, ed. Rosemary Cowler (Hamden, CT: Archon, 1986).

The Twickenham Edition of the Poems of Alexander Pope, ed. John Butt *et al.*, 11 vols. (London: Methuen, 1939–69).

Rabelais, François, *Gargantua and Pantagruel*, bk 2, ch. 7, tr. Sir Thomas Urquhart and Pierre Le Motteux (New York, London and Toronto: Everyman's Library, 1994).

Oeuvres complètes, ed. Mireille Huchon (Paris: Gallimard, 1994).

Richardson, Samuel, *Sir Charles Grandison* (1753), ed. Jocelyn Harris, 3 vols. (London: Oxford University Press, 1972).

Scott, Walter, *The Letters of Sir Walter Scott*, ed. H. J. C. Grierson, 12 vols. (London: Constable, 1932–7).

The Second and Last English Advice, To the Freehoulders of Englan[d] (London, 1722).

Sheridan, Thomas, *Ars pun-ica, sive flos linguarum: the art of punning: or, the flower of languages. In seventy-nine rules. For the farther improvement of conversation and help of memory. By the labour and industry of Tom Pun-Sibi* (Dublin, 1719).

Simon, Richard, *A Critical History of the Old Testament* (London, 1682).

A Critical History of the Text of the New Testament (London, 1689).

Stanley, Thomas, *The History of Philosophy in Eight Parts* (London, 1656).

Steele, Richard, *et al.*, *The Tatler*, ed. Donald F. Bond, 3 vols. (Oxford: Clarendon Press, 1987).

Sterne, Laurence, *The Life and Opinions of Tristram Shandy, Gentleman*, ed. Melvyn and Joan New, 3 vols. (Gainesville: University of Florida Press, 1978–84).

A Sentimental Journey through France and Italy. By Mr. Yorick (1768), ed. Gardner D. Stout Jr (Berkeley: University of California Press, 1967).

Swift, Jonathan, *The Account Books of Jonathan Swift*, ed. Paul V. Thompson and Dorothy J. Thompson (Newark: University of Delaware Press, 1984).

The Correspondence of Jonathan Swift, ed. Harold Williams, 5 vols. (Oxford: Clarendon Press, 1963–5).

The Correspondence of Jonathan Swift, D.D., ed. David Woolley, 5 vols. (Frankfurt am Main: Peter Lang, 1999-).

A Discourse of the Contests and Dissentions between the Nobles and the Commons in Athens and Rome, ed. Frank H. Ellis (Oxford: Clarendon Press, 1967).

Journal to Stella, ed. Harold Williams, 2 vols. (Oxford: Clarendon Press, 1948).

Miscellanies, the Tenth Volume. By Dr. Swift (London, 1745).

The Poems of Jonathan Swift, ed. Harold Williams, 2nd edn, 3 vols. (Oxford: Clarendon Press, 1958).

A Supplement to Dr. Swift's Works, 3 vols. (London, 1779).

Swift vs. Mainwaring: 'The Examiner' and 'The Medley', ed. Frank H. Ellis (Oxford: Clarendon Press, 1985).

A Tale of a Tub: To which is added The Battle of the Books and The Mechanical Operation of the Spirit, ed. A. C. Guthkelch and D. Nichol Smith, 2nd edn (Oxford: Clarendon Press, 1958).

On Wisdom's Defeat in a Learned Debate (1725).

The Works of Jonathan Swift DD, DSPD, Volume VIII of the Author's Works, Containing Directions to Servants; and Other Pieces in Prose and Verse (Dublin 1746).

The Works of Jonathan Swift, D.D., 25 vols. (London 1755–79).

The Works of Jonathan Swift, ed. Walter Scott, 2nd edn, 19 vols. (Edinburgh, 1824).

The Works of the Reverend Dr. J. Swift, D.S.P.D., 11 vols. (Dublin, 1763).

The Works of the Rev. Jonathan Swift, D.D., 19 vols. (London, 1801).

The Works of the Rev. Jonathan Swift, D.D., 24 vols. (London, 1803).

The Works of the Rev. Jonathan Swift, D.D., 19 vols. (London, 1808).

Swift, Jonathan, and Thomas Sheridan, *The Intelligencer*, ed. James Woolley (Oxford: Clarendon Press, 1992).

Temple, Sir William, 'An Essay upon the Ancient and Modern Learning', *Works*, 2 vols. (1720), vol. I, pp. 151–69.

Velleius Paterculus his Romane Historie, tr. Robert Le Grys (London, 1632).

Wanley, Humphrey, *The Diary of Humfrey Wanley, 1715–1726*, C. E. Wright and Ruth C. Wright, eds., 2 vols. (London: The Bibliographical Society, 1966).

Weever, John, *Epigrammes in the Oldest Cut and Newest Fashion* (1599).

Wharton, Philip, Duke of, *Select and Authentick Pieces Written by the Late Duke of Wharton* (Boulogne, 1731).

Whyte, Laurence, *Poems on Various Subjects, Serious and Diverting* (Dublin, 1740).

Wodrow, Robert, *The History of the Sufferings of the Church of Scotland, From The Restauration To The Revolution: Collected From the Publick Records, Original Papers, and Manuscripts of that Time, and other well attested Narratives*, 2 vols. (Edinburgh, 1721–2).

Wotton, William, *Reflections upon Ancient and Modern Learning ... With a Dissertation upon the Epistles of Phalaris, by Dr. Bentley*, 2nd edn with large additions (1697).

SECONDARY SOURCES

Abbott, John Lawrence, *John Hawkesworth: Eighteenth-Century Man of Letters* (Madison: University of Wisconsin Press, 1982).

Adams, Thomas R., and Nicolas Barker, 'A New Model for the Study of the Book', in Nicolas Barker (ed.), *A Potencie of Life: Books in Society* (London: British Library, 1993), pp. 5–43.

Aikins, Janet E., 'Reading "with Conviction": Trial by Satire', in Frederik N. Smith (ed.), *The Genres of* Gulliver's Travels (Newark: University of Delaware Press, 1990), pp. 203–29.

Baines, Paul, and Pat Rogers, *Edmund Curll, Bookseller* (Oxford University Press, 2007).

Barchas, Janine, *Graphic Design, Print Culture, and the Eighteenth-Century Novel* (Cambridge University Press, 2003).

Barnard, John, 'Creating an English Literary Canon, 1679–1720: Jacob Tonson, Dryden and Congreve', in Simon Eliot, Andrew Nash and Ian Willison (eds.), *Literary Cultures and the Material Book* (London: British Library, 2007), pp. 307–21.

Barnard, Toby, 'Bishop Stearne's Collection of Books and Manuscripts', in McCarthy and Simmons (eds.), *Marsh's Library*, pp. 185–202.

Baron, Dennis, *A Better Pencil: Readers, Writers and the Digital Revolution* (Oxford University Press, 2009).

Belanger, Terry, 'Tonson, Wellington and the Shakespeare Copyrights', in R. W. Hunt, I. G. Philip and R. J. Roberts (eds.), *Studies in the Book Trade:*

In Honour of Graham Pollard (Oxford Bibliographical Society, 1975), pp. 195–209.

Bellamy, Alastair, '"Raylinge Rymes and Vaunting Verse": Libellous Politics in Early Stuart England, 1603–1628', in Kevin Sharpe and Peter Lake (eds.), *Culture and Politics in Early Stuart England* (Basingstoke and London: Macmillan, 1994), pp. 285–310.

Benedict, Barbara M., *Making the Modern Reader: Cultural Mediation in Early Modern Literary Anthologies* (Princeton University Press, 1996).

Blagden, Cyprian, *The Stationers' Company: A History 1403–1959* (London: George Allen & Unwin Ltd, 1960).

Bony, Alain, *Discours et vérité dans Les Voyages de Gulliver de Jonathan Swift* (Presses Universitaires de Lyon, 2002).

   Leonora, Lydia et les autres: Etude sur le (nouveau) roman anglais du XVIIIe siècle (Presses Universitaires de Lyon, 2004).

Bracher, Frederick, 'The Maps in *Gulliver's Travels*', *Huntington Library Quarterly*, 8 (1944), 59–74.

Brant, Clare, *Eighteenth-Century Letters and British Culture* (Basingstoke: Palgrave Macmillan, 2006).

Briscoe Eyre, G. E. (ed.), *A Transcript of the Registers of the Company of Stationers from 1640–1708 A.D.* 3 vols. (London, 1913–14).

Bullard, Paddy, 'Digital Editing and the Eighteenth-Century Text: Works, Archives, and Miscellanies', *Eighteenth-Century Life*, 36.3 (2012), 57–80.

   'Pride, Pulpit Eloquence, and the Rhetoric of Jonathan Swift', *Rhetorica*, 30 (2012), 232–55.

Burt, Stephen, 'Empson and the Censor', *Modern Philology*, 107 (2010), 447–74.

Carey, Daniel, *Locke, Shaftesbury, and Hutcheson: Contesting Diversity in the Enlightenment and Beyond* (Cambridge University Press, 2006).

Case, Arthur E., *A Bibliography of English Poetical Miscellanies 1521–1750* (Oxford: The Bibliographical Society, 1935).

Champion, Justin, *Republican Learning: John Toland and the Crisis of Christian Culture, 1696–1722* (Manchester University Press, 2003).

Chartier, Roger, *The Cultural Uses of Print in Early Modern France* (Princeton University Press, 1987).

Colvin, H. M., *A Catalogue of Architectural Drawings at Worcester College, Oxford* (Oxford: Clarendon Press, 1964).

Cook, Daniel, '*Labor ipse voluptas*: John Nichols's Swiftiana', in John Hinks and Matthew Day (eds.), *Authors and the Book Trade* (Delaware and London: Oak Knoll Press and The British Library, 2011), pp. 43–60.

Cornu, Donald, 'Swift, Motte and the Copyright Struggle', *Modern Language Notes*, 54 (1939), 114–24.

Darnton, Robert, *The Devil in the Holy Water or the Art of Slander from Louis XIV to Napolean* (Philadelphia: University of Pennsylvania Press, 2010).

   'What is the History of Books?', *Daedalus*, 3 (1982), 65–83.

   'What is the History of Books: Revisited', *Journal of Modern Intellectual History*, 4 (2007), 495–508.

Davidow, Lawrence Lee, 'Pope's Verse Epistles: Friendship and the Private Sphere of Life', *Huntington Library Quarterly*, 40 (1977), 151–70.

Davidson, Jenny, 'Austen's Voices', in Nicholas Hudson and Aaron Santesso (eds.), *Swift's Travels: Eighteenth-Century British Satire and its Legacy* (Cambridge University Press, 2008), pp. 233–50.

Davies, D. W., *The World of the Elzeviers* (The Hague: Nijoff, 1960).

Dearing, Vinton A., 'New Light on the First Printing of the Letters of Pope and Swift', *The Library*, 4th ser., 24 (1944), 74–80.

Dickinson, H. T., 'The Popularity of "Gulliver's Travels" and "Robinson Crusoe"', *Notes and Queries*, 212 (1967), 172.

Donoghue, Denis, *Jonathan Swift: A Critical Introduction* (Cambridge University Press, 1969).

Downie, J. A., *Robert Harley and the Press: Propaganda and Public Opinion in the Age of Swift and Defoe* (Cambridge University Press, 1979).

'Swift and the Making of the English Novel', *Münster* (1998), pp. 179–87.

Dugas, Don-John, 'The London Book Trade in 1709 (Part One)', *Papers of the Bibliographical Society of America*, 95 (2001), 31–58.

Ehrenpreis, Irvin, *Swift: The Man, His Works, and the Age*, 3 vols. (London: Methuen, 1962–83).

Elias, A. C., Jr, 'The Pope–Swift *Letters* (1740–41): Notes on the First State of the First Impression', *Papers of the Bibliographical Society of America*, 69 (1975), 323–43.

'Richard Helsham, Jonathan Swift and Library of John Putland', in McCarthy and Simmons (eds.), *Marsh's Library*, pp. 251–78.

'*Senatus Consultum*: Revising Verse in Swift's Dublin Circle, 1729–1735', in *Münster* (1998), pp. 249–67.

'Swift and the Middling Reader: Additions to the Faulkner Reprints of Pope's Satires, 1733–1735', *Swift Studies*, 15 (2000), 61–75.

Swift at Moor Park: Problems in Biography and Criticism (Philadelphia: University of Pennsylvania Press, 1982).

Empson, William, *Seven Types of Ambiguity* (New York: New Directions, 1947).

Falle, George, 'Sir Walter Scott as Editor of Dryden and Swift', *University of Toronto Quarterly*, 36 (1966–7), 161–80.

Feather, John, 'The Book Trade in Politics: The Making of the Copyright Act of 1710', *Publishing History*, 8 (1980), 19–44.

'The English Book Trade and the Law, 1695–1799', *Publishing History*, 12 (1982), 51–75.

Ferguson, Oliver W., *Jonathan Swift and Ireland* (Urbana: University of Illinois Press, 1962).

'"Nature and Friendship": The Personal Letters of Jonathan Swift', in Howard Anderson, Philip B. Daghlian and Irvin Ehrenpreis (eds.), *The Familiar Letter in the Eighteenth Century* (Lawrence, KA: University of Kansas Press, 1966), pp. 14–33.

Fischer, John Irwin, 'The Government's Response to Swift's *An Epistle to a Lady*', *Philological Quarterly*, 65 (1986), 39–59.

'Swift's Early Odes, Dan Jackson's Nose, and "The Character of Sir Robert Walpole": Some Documentary Problems', in *Münster* (1993), pp. 225–43.

'Swift's *Miscellanies, in Prose and Verse, Volume the Fifth*: Some Facts and Puzzles', *Swift Studies*, 15 (2000), 76–87.

'Swift Writing Poetry: The Example of "The Grand Question Debated"', in Rudolf Freiburg *et al.* (eds.), *Swift, The Enigmatic Dean* (Tubingen: Stauffenburg, 1998), pp. 41–6.

Flint, Christopher, *The Appearance of Print in Eighteenth-Century Fiction* (Cambridge University Press, 2011).

Frantz, R. W., 'Swift and Voyagers', *Modern Philology*, 29 (1931), 49–57.

Forster, John, *The Life of Jonathan Swift* (London, 1875).

Fox, Christopher, 'Swift's Scotophobia', *Bullán*, 6 (2002), 43–65.

Foxon, David F., *English Verse, 1701–1750: A Catalogue of Separately Printed Poems with Notes on Contemporary Collected Editions*, 2 vols. (London: Cambridge University Press, 1975).

Pope and the Early Eighteenth-Century Book Trade (Oxford: Clarendon Press, 1991).

Gardiner, Anne Barbeau, 'Licking the Dust in Luggnagg: Swift's Reflections on the Legacy of King William's Conquest of Ireland', *Swift Studies*, 8 (1993), 35–44.

Genette, Gerard, *Paratexts: Thresholds of Interpretation*, tr. Jane E. Lewin (Cambridge University Press, 1997).

Gillespie, Raymond, and Andrew Hadfield (eds.), *The Irish Book in English, 1550–1800*, The Oxford History of the Book in English, vol. III (Oxford University Press, 2006).

Goldgar, Bertrand A., '*Gulliver's Travels* and the Opposition to Walpole', in Henry Knight Miller, Eric Rothstein and G. S. Rousseau (eds.), *The Augustan Milieu: Essays Presented to Louis A. Landa* (Oxford: Clarendon Press, 1970), pp. 155–73.

Goldie, Mark, and Clare Jackson, 'Williamite Tyranny and the Whig Jacobites', in Esther Mijers and David Onnekink (eds.), *Redefining William III: The Impact of the King-Stadholder in International Context* (Aldershot: Ashgate, 2007), pp. 177–99.

Goulden, R. J., '*Vox Populi, Vox Dei*: Charles Delafaye's Paperchase', *The Book Collector*, 28 (1979), 368–90.

Gove, Philip Babcock, *The Imaginary Voyage in Prose Fiction: A History of Its Criticism and a Guide for Its Study, with an Annotated Check List of 215 Imaginary Voyages from 1700 to 1800* (London: The Holland Press, 1961).

Grafton, Anthony, *The Footnote: A Curious History* (London: Faber and Faber, 1997).

Griffin, Dustin, *Swift and Pope: Satirists in Dialogue* (Cambridge University Press, 2010).

Guskin, Phyllis J., '"A very remarkable Book": Abel Boyer's View of *Gulliver's Travels*', *Studies in Philology*, 72 (1975), 439–53.

Hamburger, Philip, 'The Development of the Law of Seditious Libel and the Control of the Press', *Stanford Law Review*, vol. 37, no. 3, Historical Perspectives on the Free Press (February 1985), 661–765.

Hammond, Brean S., 'Swift's Reading', in *The Cambridge Companion to Jonathan Swift* (Cambridge University Press, 2003), pp. 73–86.

'Swift's Reading', in *Münster* (2003), pp. 133–64.

Hammond, Brean S., and Nicholas Seager, 'Jonathan Swift's Historical Novel, *The Memoirs of Capt. John Creichton*', *Swift Studies*, 24 (2009), 70–87.

Harries, Elizabeth Wanning, *The Unfinished Manner: Essays on the Fragment in the Later Eighteenth Century* (Charlottesville: University Press of Virginia, 1994).

Harth, Phillip, 'Friendship and Politics: Swift's Relations with Pope in the Early 1730s', in *Münster* (1998), pp. 239–48.

Haugen, Kristine Louise, *Richard Bentley: Poetry and Enlightenment* (Cambridge, MA: Harvard University Press, 2011).

Higgins, Ian, 'Jonathan Swift and the Jacobite Diaspora', in *Münster* (2003), pp. 87–103.

Hill, Christopher, 'Censorship and English Literature', in *The Collected Essays of Christopher Hill*, 3 vols. (Brighton: Harvester Press, 1985), vol. II, pp. 32–71.

Hodges, John C., *The Library of William Congreve* (New York Public Library, 1955).

Hume, Robert D., 'Editing a Nebulous Author: The Case of the Duke of Buckingham', *The Library*, 7th ser., 4 (2003), 249–77.

Irwin, Raymond, *The Origins of the English Library* (London: George Allen & Unwin, 1958).

Jackson, H. J., *Marginalia: Readers Writing in Books* (New Haven: Yale University Press, 2001).

Jaffe, Nora Crow, *The Poet Swift* (Hanover, NH: The University Press of New England, 1977).

Jardine, Lisa, and Anthony Grafton, '"Studied for Action": How Gabriel Harvey Read his Livy', *Past and Present*, 129 (1990), 30–78.

Johns, Adrian, *The Nature of the Book: Print and Knowledge in the Making* (University of Chicago Press, 1998).

Piracy: The Intellectual Property Wars from Gutenberg to Gates (University of Chicago Press, 2010).

Kaplan, M. Lindsay, *The Culture of Slander in Early Modern England* (Cambridge University Press, 1997).

Karian, Stephen, 'Edmund Curll and the Circulation of Swift's Writings', in *Münster* (2008), pp. 99–129.

Jonathan Swift in Print and Manuscript (Cambridge University Press, 2010).

'The Limitations and Possibilities of the *ESTC*', *Age of Johnson*, 21 (2011), 283–97.

'Who Was Swift's "Corinna"?', in Hermann J. Real, Kirsten Juhas and Sandra Simon (eds.), *Reading Swift: Papers from The Sixth Münster Symposium on Jonathan Swift* (Munich: Wilhelm Fink, forthcoming).

Kelly, Ann Cline, *Jonathan Swift and Popular Culture: Myth, Media and the Man* (New York and Basingstoke: Palgrave, 2002).

Kelly, James, 'Regulating Print: The State and the Control of Print in Eighteenth-Century Ireland', *Eighteenth-Century Ireland*, 23 (2008), 142–74.

Kemp, Geoffrey and Jason McElligott (gen. eds.), *Censorship and the Press, 1580–1720*, 4 vols. (London: Pickering & Chatto, 2009).

Kennedy, Máire, 'Reading Print, 1700–1800', in Raymond Gillespie and Andrew Hadfield (eds.), *The Oxford History of the Irish Book: Volume III, The Irish Book in English 1550–1800* (Oxford University Press, 2006), pp. 146–66.

Kenner, Hugh, *The Stoic Comedians* (Berkeley: University of California Press, 1962, repr. 1974).

Keymer, Thomas, 'Novel Designs: Manipulating the Page in English Fiction, 1660–1800', the John Coffin Memorial Lecture in the History of the Book, London, 20 July 2009.

Kilburn, Matthew, 'History, Languages, Literature, and Music', in *The History of Oxford University Press: Volume I, 1478–1780*, ed. Ian Gadd (Oxford University Press, forthcoming).

Kropf, C. R., 'Libel and Satire in the Eighteenth Century', *Eighteenth-Century Studies*, 8, no. 2 (Winter 1974–5), 153–68.

Lalor, Stephen, *Matthew Tindal, Freethinker* (London and New York: Continuum, 2006).

Lipking, Lawrence, 'The Marginal Gloss', *Critical Inquiry*, 3 (1976–7), 609–55.

Lock, F. P., *The Politics of Gulliver's Travels* (Oxford: Clarendon Press, 1980).

Love, Harold, 'L'Estrange, Joyce and the Dictates of Typography', in Anne Dunan-Page and Beth Lynch (eds.), *Roger L'Estrange and the Making of Restoration Culture* (Aldershot: Ashgate, 2008), pp. 167–80.

  Scribal Publication in Seventeenth-Century England (Oxford: Clarendon Press, 1993).

  Swift and His Publishers (Melbourne: Monash University, 1969).

Macaree, David, 'Truth and Fiction in *Memoirs of Captain John Creichton*', *Transactions of the Samuel Johnson Society of the Northwest*, 6 (1973), 11–26.

McCarthy, Muriel, and Ann Simmons (eds.), *The Making of Marsh's Library: Learning, Politics and Religion in Ireland, 1650–1750* (Dublin: Four Courts Press, 2004).

McDayter, Mark, 'The Haunting of St. James's Library: Librarians, Literature and "The Battle of the Books"', *HLQ*, 66 (2003), 1–26.

McDowell, Paula, *The Women of Grub Street: Press, Politics, and Gender in the London Literary Marketplace, 1678–1730* (Oxford: Clarendon Press, 1993).

McGovern, Barbara, *Anne Finch and Her Poetry: A Critical Biography* (Athens and London: University of Georgia Press, 1992).

Mack, Maynard, *"Collected in Himself": Essays Critical, Biographical, and Bibliographical on Pope and Some of his Contemporaries* (Delaware University Press, 1982).

  The First Printing of the Letters of Pope and Swift', *The Library*, 4th ser., 19 (1939), pp. 465–85.

McKenzie, D. F., 'The London Book Trade in the Later Seventeenth Century', unpublished Sandars Lectures, Cambridge 1976.

'Typography and Meaning: The Case of William Congreve', in his *Making Meaning: Printers of the Mind*, ed. Peter D. McDonald and Michael F. Suarez, SJ (Amherst: University of Massachusetts Press, 2002).

McKenzie, D. F. (ed.), *Stationers' Company Apprentices 1701–1800* (Oxford Bibliographical Society, 1978).

McLaverty, James, *Pope, Print and Meaning* (Oxford University Press, 2001)..

'The Failure of the Swift–Pope *Miscellanies* (1727–32) and *The Life and Genuine Character of Doctor Swift* (1733)', in *Münster* (2008), pp. 131–48.

'Naming and Shaming in the Poetry of Pope and Swift, 1726–1745', in Nicholas Hudson and Aaron Santesso (eds.), *Swift's Travels: Eighteenth-Century Satire and its Legacy* (Cambridge University Press, 2008), pp. 160–75.

'The Revision of the First Edition of *Gulliver's Travels*: Book-Trade Context, Interleaving, Two Cancels, and a Failure to Catch', *PBSA*, 106 (2012), 5–35.

Madan, Falconer, and W. A. Speck, *A Critical Bibliography of Dr. Henry Sacheverell* (Lawrence, KA: University of Kansas Libraries, 1978).

Mahony, Robert, *Jonathan Swift: The Irish Identity* (New Haven: Yale University Press, 1995).

Main, C. F., 'Defoe, Swift, and Captain Tom', *Harvard Library Bulletin*, 11 (1957), 71–9.

Maner, Martin, 'An Eighteenth-Century Editor at Work: John Nichols and Jonathan Swift', *Papers of the Bibliographical Society of America*, 70 (1976), 481–99.

'"The Last of the Learned Printers": John Nichols and the Bowyer-Nichols Press', *English Studies*, 65 (1984), 11–22.

Manning, David Stephen, 'Blasphemy in England, *c.* 1660–1730', unpub. PhD thesis (University of Cambridge, 2008).

Marshall, Ashley, 'Epistolary Swift', *Swift Studies*, 26 (2011), 61–107.

'The State of Swift Studies 2010', *Eighteenth-Century Life*, 34 (2010), 83–105.

'The "1735" Faulkner Edition of Swift's *Works*: An Analysis of Its Contents and Textual Authority', *The Library*, forthcoming.

Marshik, Celia, *British Modernism and Censorship* (Cambridge University Press, 2006).

Maslen, Keith, 'George Faulkner and William Bowyer: the London Connection', *The Long Room*, 38 (1993), 20–30, reprinted in *An Early London Printing House at Work: Studies in the Bowyer Ledgers* (New York: Bibliographical Society of America, 1993), pp. 223–33.

'Shared Printing and the Bibliographer: New Evidence from the Bowyer Press', *An Early London Printing House at Work: Studies in the Bowyer Ledgers* (New York: Bibliographical Society of America, 1993), pp. 153–64.

Maslen, Keith, and John Lancaster (eds.), *The Bowyer Ledgers* (London: The Bibliographical Society; New York: The Bibliographical Society of America, 1991).

Matteson, Robert S., *A Large Private Park: The Collection of Archbishop William King, 1650–1729*, 2 vols. (Cambridge: LP Publications, 2003).

Mayhew, George, *Rage or Raillery* (San Marino: Huntington Library, 1967).

'Swift's Political "Conversion" and His "Lost" Ballad on the Westminster Election of 1710', *Bulletin of the John Rylands Library*, 53 (1971), 397–427.

Millet, Baudouin, '*Ceci n'est pas un roman*': *L'evolution du statut de la fiction en Angleterre de 1652 à 1754* (Louvain: Peeters, 2007).

Monod, Paul, 'The Jacobite Press and English Censorship', in Eveline Cruickshanks and Edward Corp (eds.), *The Stuart Court in Exile and the Jacobites* (London and Rio Grande: The Hambledon Press, 1995), pp. 125–42.

Moore, Sean D., *Swift, the Book, and the Irish Financial Revolution* (Baltimore: The Johns Hopkins University Press, 2010).

Myers, Robin, 'John Nichols (1745–1826), Chronicler of the Book Trade', in Robin Myers and Michael Harris (eds.), *Development of the English Book Trade, 1700–1899* (Oxford Polytechnic Press, 1981), pp. 1–35.

Newman, John, 'Library Buildings and Fittings', in Giles Mandelbrote and K. A. Manley (eds.), *The Cambridge History of Libraries in Britain and Ireland, Vol. II: 1640–1850* (Cambridge University Press, 2006), pp. 190–211.

Orwell, George, 'Politics vs. Literature: An Examination of *Gulliver's Travels*' (first published in *Polemic* in 1946), in *The Essential Writings of Jonathan Swift: A Norton Critical Edition* ed. Claude Rawson and Ian Higgins (New York: Norton, 2010), pp. 835–48.

Palmeri, Frank, 'The Satiric Footnotes of Swift and Gibbon', *The Eighteenth Century*, 31 (1990), 245–62.

Passmann, Dirk Friedrich, Appendix E, '*Full of improbable lies*': Gulliver's Travels *und die Reiseliteratur vor 1726*, Aspekte der Englischen Geistes- und Kulturgeschichte 10 (Frankfurt am Main: P. Lang, 1987).

Passmann, Dirk F., and Heinz J. Vienken, *The Library and Reading of Jonathan Swift: A Bio-Bibliographical Handbook, Part 1: Swift's Library in Four Volumes* (Frankfurt am Main: Peter Lang, 2003).

Patterson, Annabel, *Censorship and Interpretation: The Conditions of Writing and Reading in Early Modern England* (Madison: University of Wisconsin Press, 1984).

Reading Between the Lines (London: Routledge, 1993).

Paxman, David B., '"Adam in a Strange Country": Locke's Language Theory and Travel Literature', *Modern Philology*, 92 (1995), 460–81.

Pearson, David, 'Patterns of Book Ownership in Late Seventeenth-Century England', *The Library*, 7th ser., 11 (2010), 139–67.

Pittock, Murray, 'Treacherous Objects: Towards a Theory of Jacobite Material Culture', *Journal for Eighteenth-Century Studies*, 34, no. 1 (March 2011), 39–63.

Pollard, Mary, *A Dictionary of Members of the Dublin Book Trade, 1550–1800* (London: Bibliographical Society, 2000).

Dublin's Trade in Books, 1550–1800 (Oxford: Clarendon Press, 1989).

'George Faulkner', *Swift Studies*, 7 (1992), 79–96.

'Who's For Prison? Publishing Swift in Dublin', *Swift Studies*, 14 (1999), 37–49.

Pooley, Julian, 'The Papers of the Nichols Family and Business: New Discoveries and the Work of the Nichols Archive Project', *The Library*, 7th ser., 2:1 (2001), 10–52.

Potter, Lee H., 'The Text of Scott's Edition of Swift', *Studies in Bibliography*, 22 (1969), 240–55.

Raven, James, 'The Book Trades', in Isabel Rivers (ed.), *Books and their Readers in Eighteenth-Century England: New Essays* (London: Leicester University Press, 2001), pp. 1–36.

The Business of Books: Booksellers and the English Book Trade (New Haven: Yale University Press, 2007).

Rawson, Claude, 'Avatars of Alexander', in Claude Rawson (ed.), *Henry Fielding (1707–1754), Novelist, Playwright, Journalist, Magistrate: A Double Anniversary Tribute* (Newark: University of Delaware Press, 2008), pp. 91–114.

'Behind the Tub,' *TLS*, 10 September 2004, 3–4.

God, Gulliver, and Genocide (Oxford University Press, 2001).

Gulliver and the Gentle Reader (London: Routledge, 1973).

Satire and Sentiment 1660–1830 (Cambridge University Press, 1994).

'Savage Indignation Revisited: Swift, Yeats, and the "Cry" of Liberty', in Claude Rawson (ed.), *Politics and Literature in the Age of Swift: English and Irish Perspectives* (Cambridge University Press, 2010), pp. 185–220.

'Showing, Telling, and Money in *Emma*', *Essays in Criticism*, 61 (2012), 338–64.

'Swift', in Michael O'Neill (ed.), *The Cambridge History of English Poetry* (Cambridge University Press, 2010), pp. 318–32.

'Swift, Satire and the Novel', in Thomas Keymer (ed.), *Prose Fiction from the Origins of Print to 1750*, Oxford History of the Novel in English, Vol. I (Oxford University Press, forthcoming).

'Swift's "I" Narrators' (1998), in Claude Rawson and Ian Higgins (eds.), *Essential Writings of Jonathan Swift: A Norton Critical Edition* (New York: Norton, 2010), pp. 874–89.

Real, Hermann J. (ed.), *Reading Swift: Papers from the Fifth Münster Symposium on Jonathan Swift* (Munich: Wilhelm Fink, 2008).

Real, Hermann J., and Richard H. Rodino, with Helgard Stöver-Leidig (eds.), *Reading Swift: Papers from the Second Münster Symposium on Jonathan Swift* (Munich: Wilhelm Fink, 1993).

Real, Hermann J., and Helgard Stöver-Leidig (eds.), *Reading Swift: Papers from the Third Münster Symposium on Jonathan Swift* (Munich: Wilhelm Fink, 1998).

Real, Hermann J., and Helgard Stöver-Leidig, *Reading Swift: Papers from the Fourth Münster Symposium on Jonathan Swift* (Munich: Wilhelm Fink, 2003).

Real, Hermann J., and Heinz J. Vienken, 'Books from Stella's Library', *Swift Studies*, 1 (1986), 68–72.

Real, Hermann J., and Heinz J. Vienken (eds.), *Proceedings of the First Münster Symposium on Jonathan Swift* (Munich: Wilhelm Fink, 1985).

Rivington, Charles A., *'Tyrant': The Story of John Barber* (York: William Sessions, 1989).

Robertson, Randy, 'The British Index, 1641–1700' (http://susqu.academia.edu/RandyRobertson/Papers/1665622/The_British_Index).

Censorship and Conflict in Seventeenth-Century England: The Subtle Art of Division (University Park: The Pennsylvania State University Press, 2009).

Rogers, Pat, 'The Case of Pope v. Curll', *The Library*, 5th ser., 27 (1972), 326–31.

'Gulliver's Glasses', in Clive T. Probyn (ed.), *The Art of Jonathan Swift* (New York: Barnes and Noble, 1978), pp. 179–88.

'Nathaniel Mist, Daniel Defoe, and the Perils of Publishing', *The Library*, 7th ser., 10 (2009), 298–313.

Rogers, Robert W., *The Major Satires of Alexander Pope* (Urbana: University of Illinois Press, 1955).

Rogers, Shef, 'An Extra Echo to Swift's Epigraph for *Gulliver's Travels*', *Notes and Queries*, 235 (2008), 326.

Rose, Mark, 'Copyright, Authors and Censorship', in *The Cambridge History of the Book in Britain: Volume V 1695–1830*, pp. 118–31.

Ross, J. C., 'The Framing and Printing of the Motte Editions of *Gulliver's Travels*', *BSANZ Bulletin*, 20 (1996), 5–19.

Rudy, Seth, 'Pope, Swift, and the Poetics of Posterity', *Eighteenth-Century Life*, 35 (2011), 1–29.

Rumbold, Valerie, 'Merlinus Verax, T. N. Philomath, and the Merlin Tradition: Print Context for Swift's *A Famous Prediction of Merlin* (1709)', *The Library*, 7th ser., 12 (2011), 400–12.

Sabor, Peter, '"A Large Portion of our Etherial Fire": Swift and Samuel Richardson', in *Münster* (2003), pp. 387–401.

Schakel, Peter J., '"Friends Side by Side": Theme, Structure, and Influence in the Swift–Pope *Miscellanies* of 1727', in *Münster* (1993), pp. 103–12.

'Swift's Voices: Innovation and Complication in the Poems Written at Market Hill', in Howard D. Weinbrot, Peter J. Schakel and Stephen E. Karian (eds.), *Eighteenth-Century Contexts: Historical Inquiries in Honor of Phillip Harth* (Madison: University of Wisconsin Press, 2001), pp. 114–32.

Scouten, Arthur H., 'Jonathan Swift's Progress from Prose to Poetry', in *The Poetry of Jonathan Swift: Papers Read at a Clark Library Seminar 20 January 1979* (Los Angeles: William Andrews Clark Memorial Library, 1981), pp. 27–51.

Sherbo, Arthur, 'Swift and Travel Literature', *Modern Language Studies*, 9 (1979), 114–27.

Sherman, W. H., *John Dee: The Politics of Reading and Writing in the English Renaissance* (Amherst: University of Massachusetts Press, 1995).

Shuger, Debora, *Censorship and Cultural Sensibility: The Regulation of Language in Tudor-Stuart England* (Philadelphia: University of Pennsylvania Press, 2006).

Smiles, Samuel (ed.), *John Murray: A Publisher and His Friends* (The Echo Press, 2006; first published in 1911).

Smith, A. H., 'John Nichols, Printer and Publisher', *The Library*, 5th ser., 18 (1963), 169–90.

Smith, Frederik N., 'Swift's Correspondence: The "Dramatic" Style and the Assumption of Roles', *Studies in English Literature*, 14 (1974), 357–71.

Sobel, Dava, *Longitude* (Harmondsworth: Penguin, 1996).

Stewart, Ralph, 'Swift and the Authorship of Creichton's *Memoirs*', *The Scottish Historical Review*, 72 (1993), 80–9.

Taylor, Aline Mackenzie, 'Sights and Monsters and Gulliver's *Voyage to Brobdingnag*', *Tulane Studies in English*, 7 (1957), 29–82.

Teerink, H., *A Bibliography of the Writings of Jonathan Swift*, 2nd edn revised and corrected by the author, ed. Arthur H. Scouten (Philadelphia: University of Pennsylvania Press, 1963).

Thomas, Donald, *A Long Time Burning: The History of Literary Censorship in England* (London: Routledge & Kegan Paul, 1969).

Thornton, Richard H., 'English Authors, Placed on the Roman "Index" (1600 To 1750)', *Notes and Queries*, 11th ser., 12 (1915), 333.

Tinkler, John F., 'The Splitting of Humanism: Bentley, Swift, and the English Battle of the Books', *Journal of the History of Ideas*, 49 (1988), 453–72.

Tinniswood, Adrian, *His Invention So Fertile: A Life of Christopher Wren* (London: Jonathan Cape, 2001).

Todd, Dennis, 'The Hairy Maid at the Harpsichord: Some Speculations on the Meaning of *Gulliver's Travels*', *Texas Studies in Literature and Language*, 34 (1992), 239–83.

Treadwell, Michael, 'Benjamin Motte, Andrew Tooke and *Gulliver's Travels*', in *Münster* (1985), pp. 287–304.

'Benjamin Motte, Jr', in James K. Bracken and Joel Silver (eds.), *The British Literary Book Trade, 1700–1820, Dictionary of Literary Biography*, vol. CLIV (Detroit: Gale Research, 1995), pp. 198–202.

'Lists of Master Printers: The Size of the London Printing Trade, 1637–1723', in Robin Myers and Michael Harris (eds.), *Aspects of Printing from 1600* (Oxford Polytechnic Press, 1987), pp. 141–70.

'London Printers and Printing Houses in 1705', *Publishing History*, 7 (1980), 5–44.

'London Trade Publishers, 1675–1750', *The Library*, 6th ser., 4 (1982), 99–134.

'Observations on the Printing of Motte's Octavo Edition of *Gulliver's Travels*', in *Münster* (1998), pp. 157–77.

'On False and Misleading Imprints in the London Book Trade, 1660–1750', in Robin Myers and Michael Harris (eds.), *Fakes and Frauds: Varieties of Deception in Print and Manuscript* (Winchester: St Paul's Bibliographies, 1989), pp. 29–46.

'The Stationers and the Printing Acts at the End of the Seventeenth Century', in John Barnard, D. F. McKenzie and Maureen Bell (eds.), *The Cambridge History of the Book in Britain: Volume IV 1557–1695* (Cambridge University Press, 2002), pp. 755–76.

'Swift's Relations with the London Book Trade to 1714', in Robin Myers and Michael Harris (eds.), *Author/Publisher Relations During the Eighteenth and Nineteenth Centuries* (Oxford Polytechnic Press, 1983), pp. 1–36.

Treadwell, Michael, and Michael Turner, 'The Stationers' Company: Members of the Court, 1600–1830', unpublished printout, 1998.

Turner, Michael L., 'Personnel within the London Book Trades: Evidence from the Stationers' Company', in Michael F. Suarez SJ and Michael L. Turner (eds.), *The Cambridge History of the Book in Britain: Volume V 1695–1830* (Cambridge University Press, 2009), pp. 309–34.

Wagner, Peter, 'Swift's Great Palimpsest: Intertextuality and Travel Literature in *Gulliver's Travels*', in *Crossing the Atlantic: Travel Literature and the Perception of the Other* (Ann Arbor: University of Michigan Press, 1992), pp. 107–35.

Walsh, Marcus, 'Text, "Text", and Swift's *Tale of a Tub*', *Modern Language Review*, 85 (1990), 290–303.

Ward, Robert E., *Prince of Dublin Printers: The Letters of George Faulkner* (Lexington: University of Kentucky Press, 1972).

Weedon, Margaret, 'An Uncancelled Copy of the First Collected Edition of Swift's Poems', *The Library*, 5th ser., 22 (1967), 44–56.

Weeks, James, 'The Architects of Christ Church Library', *Architectural History*, 48 (2005), 107–38.

Wiles, R. M., *Serial Publication in England before 1750* (Cambridge University Press, 1957).

Williams, Abigail, 'The Difficulties of Swift's *Journal to Stella*', *RES*, n.s., 62 (2011), 758–76.

Williams, Harold, 'Deane Swift, Hawkesworth, and *The Journal to Stella*', in *Essays on the Eighteenth Century: presented to David Nichol Smith in honour of his seventieth birthday* (Oxford: Clarendon Press, 1945), pp. 33–48.

   Dean Swift's Library (Cambridge University Press, 1932).

Williams, Kathleen (ed.), *Swift: The Critical Heritage* (London: Routledge & Kegan Paul, 1970).

Woolley, David, 'A Dialogue Upon Dunkirk (1712) and Swift's "7 Penny Papers"', in *Münster* (1993), pp. 215–23.

Woolley, James, 'The Canon of Swift's Poems: The Case of "An Apology to the Lady Carteret"', in *Münster* (1993), pp. 245–64.

   'The Market Hill Parody of Richard Daniel's *The Royal Penitent*', paper read at the East-Central American Society for Eighteenth-Century Studies conference at Bethlehem, Pennsylvania on 10 October 2009.

   'Sarah Harding as Swift's Printer', in Christopher Fox and Brenda Tooley (eds.), *Walking Naboth's Vineyard: New Studies of Swift* (University of Notre Dame Press, 1995), pp. 164–77.

   'Stella's Manuscript of Swift's Poems', in John Irwin Fischer, Hermann J. Real, and James Woolley (eds.), *Swift and His Contexts* (New York: AMS Press, 1989), pp. 115–32.

   'Swift's First Published Poem: *Ode. To the King*', in *Münster* (2003), pp. 265–83.

   Swift's Later Poems: Studies in Circumstances and Texts (New York: Garland, 1988).

   'Swift's "Skinnibonia": A New Poem from Lady Acheson's Manuscript', in *Münster* (2008), pp. 309–42.

   'Thomas Sheridan and Swift', *Studies in Eighteenth-Century Culture*, 9 (1979), 93–114.

'Writing Libels on the Germans: Swift's "Wicked Treasonable Libel"', in *Swift: The Enigmatic Dean: Festschrift for Hermann Josef Real*, Rudolf Freiburg, Arno Löffler and Wolfgang Zach (eds.) (Tübingen: Stauffenburg Verlag, 1998), pp. 303–16.

Index

Maittaire library catalogue (1749)
'Stella's Books', Swift Studies, 11 (1996)
J. Jackson, Marginalia (2001)
Toby Barnard, 'Bishop Stearnes...', Marsh's Library (2004)